I0761341

PREACHING AND TEACHING

PREACHING & TEACHING

The Collected Writings of Paul G. Wassenich

Edited by Linda Pilcher Wassenich
from original manuscripts by
Paul G. Wassenich

Photo Editor, Mark Wassenich

Fort Worth, Texas

Library of Congress Control Number: 2022934821

TCU Box 298300
Fort Worth, Texas 76129
To order books: 1.800.826.8911

Design by David Timmons

This book is dedicated to

Paul's Students

The fundamental questions in life for all of us are why am I here, what is my purpose in life, what is the nature of God, and where are we heading. It is hoped that this book will be of interest to those who were students in Paul's classes, heard his sermons, attended his seminars, or simply are wrestling with the above questions, as we are all students of life. Because Paul focused on Contemporary Theology, this book may be helpful to people who want an introduction to Contemporary Theology.

CONTENTS

FOREWORD

Paul G. Wassenich was an exemplary preacher and teacher of the Christian Church (Disciples of Christ). Having served pastorates in Hicksville, Ohio, and Detroit, Michigan, he accepted the call in 1946 to serve as director of the Texas Bible Chair at the University of Texas. During the years that he taught at the University of Texas as director of the Texas Bible Chair, he also helped to organize University Christian Church in Austin and, later, served as part-time minister of the Johnson City Christian Church. He joined the Religion Department of Texas Christian University (TCU) in 1957. In addition to teaching generations of TCU students, many of whom followed him in ministry and teaching, he was the founder of the TCU Honors Program. Upon his retirement in 1976, University President James M. Moudy described him as the "moral conscience" of Texas Christian University.

In 2013, TCU celebrated the fiftieth anniversary of the Honors Program, which had been elevated to the status of a College in the University. As part of the fiftieth anniversary celebration of Honors, TCU set out to capture memories of the program from TCU Honors students, faculty, directors, and deans. Dr. Dan Williams, director of TCU Press, led a committee composed of Dr. Peggy Watson, the first dean of the John V. Roach Honors College; Sarah-Marie Horning, a PhD graduate student in English; and Paul Wassenich's oldest son, Mark Wassenich, to write the history. Several Honors colloquia classes gathered material that resulted in a book, published in 2019.

During this endeavor, Dan asked Mark and his wife, Linda Pilcher Wassenich, if he could read some of Paul's papers, which Paul's wife, Ruth, had meticulously organized into files. When Dan returned the files to Mark and Linda, he commented that he thought there was enough material for a book if Mark or Linda would work on editing the papers.

Since Mark was busy with the Honors history, Linda volunteered to be the editor.

While working on Paul's autobiography, Linda discovered files that contained lecture notes, position papers, outlines for seminars and sermons. Some of the papers were for discussion with other faculty. Some were sermons at state conferences, area churches, even at Trinity Terrace in downtown Fort Worth, where Paul and Ruth lived their last years. The seminar notes and some sermons were in outline form, which Linda converted to narrative and edited lightly for clarity and style.

This memoir includes the entire collection of Paul's available papers, sermons, and seminar notes.

Part I: The Life of Paul Green Wassenich

The Life of Paul Green Wassenich is Paul's autobiography, which he began writing in 1978. He added to it over the next fifteen years and sometimes wrote on the same subject more than once. Linda organized his material and wrote the chapter on the founding of the Honor's Program. Mark added information regarding his father's tour of the Holy Lands in 1954 and his commitment to civil rights.

Paul's autobiography begins with references to his ancestry and memories from his childhood and teenage years in Texas and Louisiana. Those were difficult times for the Wassenich family; nevertheless, Paul had relationships during those years that pointed him toward his future endeavors. In 1930, he enrolled at Texas Christian University and met people who would influence the rest of his life. He also made the Fort Worth news as a bold and outspoken young pacifist! From TCU, he went to Austin, Texas, where he worked for two years at the YMCA while completing a master's degree from the University of Texas in sociology with a minor in philosophy. From Austin, he went to the Disciples Divinity House at the University of Chicago, where he earned another master's degree. In 1933, he met Oberlin College student Ruth Siegfried, whom he married in 1938 and with whom he shared the rest of his life. That life included both Paul and Ruth receiving advanced degrees in 1939: hers, a master's degree from Chicago Theological Seminary, and his, a second degree from the Divinity School of the University of Chicago, the Bachelor of Divinity, later named the Master of Divinity. Their life together embraced meaningful commitments and a growing family. In the early years of their retirement, Paul and Ruth engaged in agricultural pursuits—in particular, growing peaches. They also traveled.

Part II: Sermons and Seminars

Disciples of Christ leaders early recognized Paul's gifts as a teacher and preacher. Key to both his teaching and preaching was his ability to address Biblical, historical, religious, social, and political issues in an accessible and engaging manner. This is evident in his correspondence with progressive editor of the *Texas Observer* Ronnie Dugger. As a result, he had numerous speaking engagements in addition to his teaching of university students at the Texas Bible Chair and later Texas Christian University. Included in this section, along with Paul's exchange with Ronnie Dugger, are the texts of three lectures on the Bible delivered at a State Convention of the Disciples of Christ; a lecture on the Nature of Christ to a Youth Conference at TCU; lectures on the Church's Teaching Ministry; lectures on Healthy Sexuality; and one address celebrating an anniversary of the Texas Bible Chair at a time when Bible Chairs offering courses for credit at public universities were being challenged as violating separation of Church and State.

Part III: Sermons at Churches

Paul also preached at churches. Included in this section are sermons that could have been preached in many contexts, such as the sermon titled "Joyful Living," and others that spoke to a specific event, such as the death of Robert Kennedy and the abrupt resignation of the minister of Paul and Ruth's congregation. Other sermons address cultural movements, such as the "New Morality" of the 1960s. Several of the sermons were preached to students at TCU chapel services. There is great variety in this collection of sermons in terms of the length of the written text and the style of address. Several of the sermons could have as easily been identified as lectures. Indeed, one of the sermons is titled as a lecture. The final series of sermons in this section was delivered at Trinity Terrace in Fort Worth, the retirement community in which Paul and Ruth resided in their latter years. A consistent theme in Paul's preaching is a call to promote the social good. In a sermon preached in 1970, Paul argues that human beings are called to commit themselves "to emerging forms of intelligent new goodness: women's rights, civil rights for minorities, international cooperation, overcoming poverty, balancing the ecological factors in the total ecosystem, unifying the churches, and many other such areas of concern."

PART IV: CONTEMPORARY THEOLOGY

Paul believed that theology was not just for theologians or college students, but for everyone. He offered lectures, and even multiple session courses on the contemporary theology of the twentieth century to churches and other organizations, including the Women's Club of Fort Worth. The earliest date on one of these lectures is 1970. Several of the lectures do not include a date, suggesting they may have been presented to more than one audience. The two final chapters were written especially for his family. The first of these two chapters titled, "My Retrospective Twentieth-Century Theology," was addressed to his three sons. If you read only one chapter in this section, this is the one you should read! The last chapter, "My Essential Self: Examples of Moral Courage," was written at Ruth's request.

Finally, a personal note. I met Paul Wassenich in the fall of 1978. Paul had retired two years earlier, but was still actively involved in the life of the university. I was a twenty-eight-year-old newly appointed assistant dean and assistant professor of church history at Brite Divinity School, the separately incorporated graduate theological school of Texas Christian University. Paul and Ruth invited me to dinner at their home, located on a lot that is now part of Leibrock Village, Brite's graduate student housing complex. Ruth, who had taken courses in library science at the University of Texas, had recently retired after twenty years of service in the Catalog Department of TCU's Mary Couts Burnett Library, having served for several of those years as chair of the department. Though I still remember the warmth of their hospitality, I was just beginning to discover the depth and significance of the preaching and teaching of Paul G. Wassenich. May you discover the same!

DR. D. NEWELL WILLIAMS
Professor of Modern and American Church History
and President of Brite Divinity School

INTRODUCTION

I met Paul Wassenich in 1961 at the beginning of my freshman year at Texas Christian University. He was assigned to be my academic adviser. Little did we know that four years later, I would marry his oldest son, Mark, and he would become my father-in-law.

At the end of my freshman year, I was frustrated, as I didn't think I was being challenged enough at TCU. However, I heard about the Honors Program that was to start in the fall of 1962, so I decided to stay and give it a chance.

Participating in the Honors Program was a peak experience for me. Years later, after Dan Williams, director of TCU Press, asked to read Paul's papers, he returned them to us with the comment that he thought those papers could constitute a book, if someone would edit them. So I volunteered.

Starting in 1978, Paul wrote his memoirs over the next fifteen years, and sometimes wrote on the same subject more than once. I organized this material chronologically, merged his writings that were on the same subject, retained the first-person narrative voice, and edited lightly for consistency and style.

Then Mark and I realized that there were some areas that were not adequately covered in Paul's writings. Mark added to the chapter about his father's trip to the Holy Lands in 1954 (Chapter 8) to augment Paul's description of his travels in Turkey. I wrote the chapter (Chapter 10) about Paul founding the Honors Program, and Mark wrote about Paul's work in civil rights while he taught at the University of Texas at Austin in the Texas Bible Chair and at TCU (Chapter 11). As the photo editor, Mark found, labeled, and got reprint permissions for the fifty-plus photos in this book.

While working on Paul's autobiography, we discovered some files that contained lecture notes, position papers, outlines for seminars, and sermons. Some of the papers were used for discussion purposes with other faculty. Some were sermons at state conferences, area churches, even at Trinity Terrace in downtown Fort Worth, where Paul and his wife, Ruth, lived their final years. The seminar notes and some sermons were written in outline form, which I converted to narrative and edited lightly for clarity and style.

The entire collection of his available sermons, papers, and seminar notes is presented basically in chronological order in order to see the evolution of his thinking, although some documents on the same or similar subjects are grouped together. With this orientation, the reader can gain a sense of Paul's personal growth, although he was always regarded as having an uncommon maturity. It also serves as a historical background for the burning issues of the day: racism, the Cold War, the link among the three Abrahamic religions—Judaism, Christianity, and Islam—and the variations in prejudice. This book can also be read selectively if one is interested in a particular theologian. There is some repetition in a few parts of the book for the benefit of those readers who are reading selectively. Readers will also want to be aware of Appendix II, which gives information on the many names cited.

As this book came together, I was struck once again by what remarkable people Paul Wassenich and his equally wonderful wife, Ruth Siegfried Wassenich, were. Paul had a traumatic childhood. His father went to prison for a few years and then, a couple of years after his release, died in the 1918 flu epidemic when Paul was seven years old. His mother, who struggled financially for several years, suffered a nervous breakdown. He assumed adult responsibilities at an incredibly young age and committed to a life of Christian service while he was in high school.

Paul was morally committed to certain values, such as pacifism, until he could not intellectually defend that stance in the face of Hitler's Nazism. Despite being raised in the segregated South, he was a strong believer in interracial experiences and often held church and youth events that were integrated.

From his writings we gain a glimpse of a child who, despite his difficult early years, was regarded as exceptional by his teachers and youth leaders. He matured into a man with strong principles who was willing to act courageously and speak out volubly on issues. Well into his ministry, he recognized that his true calling was to be a teacher. He touched the lives of thousands of students, and they loved him.

—LPW

Part I

THE LIFE OF PAUL GREEN WASSENICH

Chapter 1

PAUL GREEN WASSENICH'S CHILDHOOD

Researching our ancestors, my wife, Ruth, and I went to Seguin, Texas, several times over a period of fifteen years when we visited our son Tom in nearby San Marcos, where he owned a restaurant called Grins, adjacent to the Texas State University campus. On January 10, 1978, we spent about three hours visiting two cemeteries and checking birth records and the deed of trust records, as part of our genealogical research. The birth records were of no help, as the earliest records began in 1909.

Seguin is the location of the graves of my great-grandparents, Joseph and Josephine Zorn Wassenich, who were both born in Germany and emigrated in 1842 to Seguin, which was then part of the Republic of Texas. Their son was Louis Joseph Wassenich, my grandfather, and his son was Louis Adolph Wassenich, my father. On our January 30, 1978, visit, we found Josephine Zorn Wassenich's grave. When we were back there on November 11, 1981, we also found the grave of Joseph and took pictures of both graves. Joseph's stone has been knocked over.[1]

My father and mother were very young, nineteen and seventeen years old, respectively, when they married on January 25, 1910, in Houston, Texas. My father, Louis Adolph Wassenich, was born April 5, 1890, in New Orleans to Louis Joseph Wassenich, who had been born in Seguin, Texas, in 1854, and his wife, Amelia Schwaner Wassenich. My mother, Idessa Madge Green, was born in Salida, Colorado, September 4, 1892. Her father, Grant C. Green, was a dispatcher for the Denver & Rio Grande Railroad. She was reared mostly in St. Louis, Missouri, where she graduated from high school.

According to my mother, my father was imprisoned at Huntsville,

[1] Paul had the headstones repaired, and Tom and his wife, Dianne, have worked to preserve this old cemetery.

Madge Green, Paul's mother at lower right; her parents Grant and Mae are seated right. Center seated are Richard and Adeline Streeter, her grandparents and successful farmers in Licking County, Ohio. Standing and holding baby is Dr.Warner Stockberger, who became assistant secretary of agriculture and developed the US Civil Service pay and benefits system. Photo ca. 1898. Wassenich family collection.

Texas, for theft of money from a bank in Houston. She said he was not guilty but was "the fall guy" for an officer of the bank who actually stole the money. Dad was only a cashier.

My Childhood

I was born in Houston, Texas, September 20, 1911. My first memories of life are from Terrell, Texas, where Grant C. Green and his wife, Mae Streeter Green, my maternal grandparents, lived in 1913–14. Mother apparently took me to live with them while Dad was in prison. I always had a special fondness for Grandpa Grant Green. Mother was his only child, so I guess he took a special delight in having a boy grandchild. He once

Grant Colfax Green, 1868–1941, Paul's grandfather, riding in Terrell, Texas, parade 1914. Auto is probably a 1911 Auburn Model N. Wassenich family collection.

lifted me up to look down in a well on the back porch of this house. It was my first remembered experience of fright. He reassured me.

Being very close to her mother, my mother was devastated when Mae died in a Dallas hospital on February 23, 1915. I remember being in a hospital room in Dallas to visit "Mama Mae," apparently shortly before her death. I would have been three years old.

My maternal grandmother, Addie Mae Streeter Green, was born December 13, 1869, presumably in Croton, now Hartford Township, Ohio, to Dick Streeter and his wife, Adeline E. Cook. At the time of her death in February 1915, she was forty-five years old. Her husband, Grant C. Green, was born and reared in nearby Johnstown, Ohio, the son of Corwin C. Green and Ann Bever Green.

I recall riding a tricycle and falling off it on a "steep" hill when I was coming back from a small grocery store near the house. Years later, about 1931 or 1932, I was in Terrell, Texas, with my TCU roommate, Herschel Gipson (later manager of the Brown Schools in San Marcos, Texas, 1947–75), and his sister and her husband, who taught at Terrell Military Academy. I told them of my memory of the house, the grocer, the hill. They

Paul's transportation in Terrell, Texas, 1914. Wassenich family collection.

took me to the place. The "hill," to my amazement, was a ridiculously small incline!

On that Easter weekend, we also went out and looked for my grandma Mae's grave. We couldn't find it, but it is there. At Madge's death I used part of her small estate to pay for the perpetual care of Mae's grave.

Gaining and Losing a Father

When Dad was released from prison, he and Mom moved to Shreveport, Louisiana, where my brother, Louis, whom we called Lou in his childhood, was born. I remember three things about Shreveport: a cedar tree in the front yard of an old house in which we had "rooms," a cotton warehouse and railroad a block or so away, and a walk downtown at night with Father and Mother when we saw an empty store with a noose and butcher knife ominously displayed in the window. I didn't understand what Mother and Father were saying, but it had fearful overtones. My impression was that it was a Ku Klux Klan symbol.

Between Shreveport and DeRidder, we lived in Creighton and Lake Charles. In Creighton, I remember Dad drove a laundry truck. I wanted to go with him one day. He wouldn't allow it and drove off down a dusty road with meadows on each side and a railroad track off to the left. I cried as I ran after him while my mother was at the door, shouting for me to come back.

We must have moved in a month or two to a house in town. It was painted green and had a multicolored window, something like a small church window; that fascinated me. We never went to church as far as I can remember until we moved to DeRidder. However, my mother said she was greatly helped by a Disciple minister of the Christian Church (Disciples of Christ) denomination in Terrell during those difficult days when my father was in prison. She joined the Christian Church (Disciples of Christ) in Terrell. My father and his people were Roman Catholics. My parents were married by a priest, and I was christened in the Catholic Church.

My real conscious memory of life events began in 1917 in DeRidder, Louisiana. I started public school kindergarten there under a delightful teacher, Miss Henry. The next year I was put in the second grade; skipping the first grade was a mistake, I think. I remember being George Washington in a school play and wearing a costume (my first of any kind). It must have been February 20, 1917. I also remember pervasive fear of the crowd and forgetting my lines.

We went to Sunday school at a white frame church next to the courthouse. Our house was on the edge of town. I had good feelings about home and family at this time. We didn't have a bathroom in the house. We took baths in a tin tub. When it was warm, we put the tub out in the garage. I remember Dad and Mother romping around in connection with bathing. They were very happy and doing well for the first time. Dad was a bookkeeper for a furniture store and was invited to join the Elks or some lodge. As part of a neophyte hazing, he had to hold a tethered goat out in the main street near his workplace. He seemed to enjoy this hazing, which I couldn't understand. I suppose it showed his acceptance by leaders in DeRidder and that meant the end of his long "exile" since Houston.

Paul's father Louis Adolph Wassenich 1890–1918. Wassenich family collection.

I recall trainloads of soldiers going off to war, particularly when we lived briefly on Front Street, which paralleled the railroad. At our home on the edge of town, we could see the pine forest only a block away. When we experienced a particularly severe storm, the house shook, and looking out the front window, I could see tall pine trees being blown over by the wind. Thunder roared and lightning flashed. I was so frightened I hid under my bed.

Dad was prospering. He bought a phonograph! One nice day we were enjoying being on the front porch and listening to the phonograph. When the music ended, Dad told me to go quickly and turn the machine off. I ran in, slipped on a throw rug, slid under the phonograph, and, of course, cried. Dad and Mom came in to comfort me and turned off the phonograph.

My sister, Marguerite Elizabeth Wassenich, was born on March 20, 1918.

In the fall of 1918, probably September, we bought or rented a large house up the street a block or so, cater-cornered from the Bass home. Mr. Bass was Dad's boss. Dad sent me to get a box he had seen in the backyard of the new house so we could pack it with utensils for the move. I took my little red wagon, went to the backyard, turned over the box, and was attacked by bees! I fled to the gate, had trouble getting out because my wagon was parked there, and got lots of bee stings. I was six years old, or perhaps just turned seven.

My father died in that house, of flu and pneumonia, on October 25, 1918. At the time, Mother was so ill with the same disease that she could not go to Beaumont for the funeral. My grandmother, Louis's mother, Amelia Schwaner Wassenich, came from Beaumont to stay with us during this terrible crisis. She took me to Beaumont for the funeral. While still in DeRidder, I recall her having me kneel at her knee as she taught me to say the Lord's Prayer. She was a devout Catholic.

My Mother's Struggle

Mother survived, thank goodness. I don't know what life would have been like for the three of us children, ages seven years, two years, and six months, if Mother had died too. At age twenty-six, she was left with three young children. She took the $5,000 insurance money, paid for the funeral, moved to Beaumont, Texas, and contacted Corwin C. Green, her grandfather, who had recently retired from the MKT Railroad. She opened a small "cash and carry" grocery store, called the Sabine Cash Grocery, at 1010 Sabine Pass Avenue in a building she rented from an Italian named Giardano. It had living quarters behind it, a kitchen, bath, and two bedrooms but no yard.

The store did not make an adequate living for us, so Mom got a stenographic job at the wholesale Jefferson Drug Co. She worked from 8:00 a.m. to 5:00 p.m. every day, got home around 6:00 p.m., and usually had to fix supper. If I hadn't washed the breakfast dishes, I got a spanking.

The work at Jefferson Drug was difficult. When she quit, they hired three women to replace her. Mr. Doak Proctor, for whom she worked, remained a fine, lifelong friend. He took me with his three sons to the YMCA swimming pool in the early mornings one summer when I was eleven and taught me to swim.

In addition to the work at Jefferson Drug, when Mom got home, already exhausted, she had to get supper, keep books for the store, tell Grandpa Green, who ran the store during the day, what to order from the wholesale grocers, and wash clothes for us children before going to bed. After two or three years, she had a nervous breakdown.

She tried many things. She took me with her to an orphanage in South Park where she was going to put me, I guess, and try to take care of the two little ones. She looked the place over and went with the lady to the front door. I can remember looking up at her. She stuck her chin out and said to the lady, "Well, no thank you. We'll make it somehow."

I really admired Mother for this and the way she stayed by us kids, never remarrying. Every offer of marriage she had, she would confide in me and conclude, "No, I don't think he would be a good father for you kids."

Nevertheless, Mom came home at night exhausted and was sometimes easily angered. One evening I got up from the supper table and went out in front of the store to watch the cars go by. I played a game of seeing how far off I could recognize the make of the car. She called me back and without explaining why, she whipped me with a whip we had gotten at the circus recently. It cut my leg so badly that it bled from a rather deep cut. I asked why she whipped me. She said she had told me, as I left the table, to close the store and put the milk bottles out by the box in front of the store. I hadn't heard her. This was the first sign of my deafness. There were many others before the three armed services turned me down for the chaplaincy in World War II. I wore hearing aids from 1944 on.

One time, Gerald Wilson, a neighbor boy, took my brother, Lou, into a hole in a vacant lot across the street. Mom, who had just arrived home from work, went berserk and screamed at Gerald. I tried to help by throwing stones at him, but that threatened Lou too. Neighbors gathered because of the noise. Mama fainted. That was the critical point. I didn't know how such friends as Elizabeth Sperling and others found out about it, but they arranged for Mother to change jobs, sell the store, send me off for the summer, and send Lou and Marguerite to Mother's good friend from high school, Elizabeth Rose, whose husband was a banker in St. Louis. She kept them for an entire year. These friends at First Christian Church helped Mother through the next year. She and I lived in a little white house on Pennsylvania Avenue in Beaumont. I was ten years old.

The friends got Mom a job with E. L. Nall, an attorney, a job she kept until she retired. She was twenty-eight or twenty-nine at the time she took this job. Within that year, the "Judge," as we called him, helped Mother buy a house about two blocks from the store at 1205 Pennsylvania Avenue and remodel it into a duplex. We lived in the larger side and rented out the other side, which covered the mortgage payments for the entire house. Mother and Marguerite slept in the downstairs bedroom. Louis and I slept in the upstairs bedroom, which had been added on to the house in the remodeling. There was a servant's house over the garage. Edie, a Negro servant, lived there, cooked our meals, cleaned house, and did the washing.

I'm not sure what Corwin did during this year. I was still ten years old in the summer of 1921 when he took me on the train, through New Orleans and Cincinnati to Columbus, Ohio. I stayed there with his son, my grandfather, Grant Green, and his third wife, for three months. They lived at 28 W. Lane Avenue, near the Ohio State University campus. In 1991, when I checked on that house and others on that street, they had all been destroyed.

On this train trip to Ohio, I was intrigued by the mountains of Tennessee and Kentucky. We went through twenty-one tunnels! My grandfather, Grant, and his wife, Irene, took me in his Model T Ford coupe to visit his brothers, Uncle Earl in Danville, and Uncle Clyde in Lorain. Uncle Earl, who was probably much younger than Grant or Clyde, had three boys and one girl. The boy nearest my age took me on a hike across the hills. His mother had prepared a delicious basket lunch that included my first roasting ears of corn. This boy was mischievous. He put some bolts on the railroad track near the house. The trainmen came over and bawled him out. He lied. His father did not discipline him. He also urinated on me in the bed we shared, and I bawled him out about it. The other kids who had been hiding in the hall laughed out loud. Their mother came, gave us dry linens, and scolded the boy. I was embarrassed. We didn't do things like that at our house.

Mother, who demanded obedience, was very strict with us about

Madge, Paul, Marguerite, Louis, Christmas 1935. Wassenich family collection.

cursing, lying, etc. When she once overheard me say "damn," she took me into the bathroom and washed my mouth out with soap and water. I think she was so afraid that Dad's imprisonment would somehow lead us to foul deeds that she was extremely conscientious with us.

As the summer of 1921 ended, my grandfather put me on a train for St. Louis, where I was met by my mother and Aunt Betty (Elizabeth Rose). I was glad to see Lou and Marguerite, who were about five and three by then. Uncle Rose, who real name was H. B. Rose, took us on a canoe trip on the Merrimac River in his beautiful wooden canoe. I paddled in front and he in the rear with seven of us in the canoe for five miles upstream. I'll bet he had a rough time, but he didn't complain. He and Aunt Betty had no children. Aunt Betty was certainly kind and helpful to Mother. Although she was not a biological relative, she and Mother were close high school friends.

I had my eleventh birthday (September 20) on the train from Columbus, Ohio, to St. Louis, Missouri, so I was about a week late starting school. I attended Pennsylvania School, where Mrs. Greer was the principal, and teachers I remember were Mrs. Fowler, Miss Alford, and Miss Menefee. I was a B student.

I rarely had fights at school, but I do remember one. In a physical education drill, they lined us up according to height and marched us around campus. I was in front with Walter. We were the smallest. As we marched, the boy behind me, a rich kid, kept tripping me. Recess followed. I beat him up, much to the delight of the other boys and the teachers who stood far off pretending not to see. But in the end, they took both of us to the principal. We had to stand in the hall near the principal's office as the kids marched in to class. They all razzed us.

My First Job

Probably the most important new activity in that eleventh year of my life was getting a paper route. The route started at Railroad Avenue and Doucette Street and went down Doucette and Madison to the gates of the Magnolia Refinery Company. It paid about $5 per month. This amounted to about fifteen cents a day. Terrible! At first I had twelve or thirteen extra papers which I sold for 5¢ each to workers coming out of the refinery at 5:00 p.m. That gave me an extra 60¢ per day! However, the *Beaumont Journal* soon put a stop to that. They gave me only one extra, for my own family.

I had to get up at 4:00 a.m. and walk three miles through all kinds of weather in the Negro section between Sabine Pass Boulevard and the Magnolia Refinery. Several experiences from this period are worth recording. I cut my thumb with a saw, not badly, but it got infected. The doctor took the nail off on my right hand, and every time I threw a paper, the blood rushed into that thumb and it hurt!

One very dark, cold morning, I threw a paper on a porch and two huge dogs literally jumped on my back. One bit my hand. Luckily, I had a hand-me-down Mackinaw coat (from the Duttons of Houston, for whom Grandma Wassenich did sewing). Since it was so cold, I had let the sleeves down to cover my fingers, which had to be bare to fold the newspapers. The sleeve protected that left hand. The people inside called off the dogs.

Another morning it was warmer, but foggy. I arrived at a family grocery run by a black man. He had not opened yet. I was tired and hungry, so I lay down on his porch to rest and await his opening. As he opened the door, I rose up with my dirty white paper bags over my shoulders and opened the screen door. He drew back in fear. He couldn't talk. It was not until he had gotten me the candy I had asked for and paid him that he found his voice and said: "Lawd, I thought you all was a ghost!" I chuckled and went on my way, refreshed.

Yet another morning I started out in the rain, threw about half of my route, and came to a wide-open field near the refinery where I usually walked on an ungraded dirt road. The road was a foot under water. When it came up over the leather boots I was wearing, I turned around and walked home. When mother woke up about 7:00 a.m., I told my story. She drove me downtown where we purchased some rubber boots. I went back and completed my route. I was late to school that morning, but Mrs. Fowler, who admired my courage and tenacity (and wished her son had some of the same qualities), understood and did not embarrass me in front of the class. I kept that paper route for two years, when I was twelve and thirteen years old.

On Sunday mornings we had to pick up our huge bundles at 4:00 a.m. I could hardly carry the 100 papers for my route. One morning they were late arriving, and several boys got to playing and making noise. The noise awakened a crochety old one-legged man who lived across the street from the filling station where we picked up our papers. He called the police to arrest us for disturbing the peace. The police came out in a Model T Ford touring car. They took all fourteen of us boys to the police station, where we were booked and told to come to court Monday morning.

Of course, the judge simply lectured us, but I was scared, as were all the boys. We were naturally late to school. When I walked in, Miss Menefee insisted on knowing why I was late; so I had to tell the entire class the story. It was very embarrassing. There was one other fellow, X. L. Granthum, who was a friend in the same class, who was also involved. The last time I saw him was about 1932 when he was working in the Greyhound bus station in Houston and I transferred buses going from Fort Worth to Beaumont.

The next year I turned twelve and became a Boy Scout. Judge Nall gave me one dollar for each year of my age. I used it to buy my Scout uniform. He also got a 2x4 board cut to a point and put a pulley and rope on it so I could have a flagpole in the side yard.

My Teenage Years

I was allowed to quit my paper route for the summer of the second year so I could attend YMCA Camp Ross Sterling on Trinity Bay near Goose Creek. I enjoyed it immensely. Eddie Jones, a young YMCA Secretary, became a role model for me. First, he rode a bicycle to my home to administer a test over Biblical material we had studied at the Y, since I had the measles. (He had already had them so was immune.) Eddie was also assistant director of the Summer Camp at Ross Sterling. He was planning to be a Baptist minister and to attend Baylor University in the fall. One moonlight night, he and I went out on the pier (800 feet long) and talked about things, including religion and college. Later he shifted from the ministry to medicine. He practiced for many years but died in his 50s.

I developed my first friendship during this period. Frank Hopkins lived near me, was in the same grade, and had three brothers. He was musical and played the piano. He was also athletic; he and I were the best hurdlers in our school. In practicing for a meet, I overdid it and was too sore to participate in the event, which he won. He represented a Houston school and won the pole vault. I ran the mile in a field of forty and came in thirteenth. That night, at a party, Frank entertained everyone by playing the piano. He was quite a guy.

Another less talented friend in the neighborhood was Ben Pipkin. He was slow, but sweet spirited and patient. He had to milk the family cow every morning and stake it out in the field where we played baseball. We also dug a cave out there and often talked far into the evening, which for us was maybe to 9:30 p.m. The baseball field was near our house at 1205 Pennsylvania. In one baseball game I hit the hardball so far that it broke a window in our house. Trouble! One day a boy named Howard, a big fellow, was catching. He had no mask. I tipped the ball. It hit Howard on his nose and broke it!

There was a very tall sycamore tree in Howard's yard. I remember climbing it and surveying the world from that perspective. That gave this fourteen-year-old a sense of power.

When I was fifteen, I threw papers along Park Street, picking them up at Pearl and Railroad Avenue. But I began to go to parties and dances. Furthermore, I was a high school junior, and it was increasingly hard to get up at 4:00 a.m. One morning the delivery of papers was a bit late. I lay down on the cement and fell sound asleep. When the delivery wagon came, they threw the bundle of papers so it landed right by my face. I woke up all right!

In the spring of 1927, I quit so I could party more comfortably. During this time George Shear and I were close friends. He and his family attended the same church as we did, Washington Boulevard Christian Church, and we were both active in the Christian Endeavor (CE) group. I served as president when I was fifteen years old. I committed myself to full-time Christian service in a CE meeting. I also preached my first sermon at Washington Boulevard Christian Church. Granville Walker[2] was also a member of this church and had preached the previous Sunday. He was about three years older than I and did a much better job!

I often taught a boys' Sunday school class. A year or so later at age sixteen or seventeen, I was elected president of the District CE. We had meetings in Port Arthur, Orange, and Orangefield. My first date was with one of the girls in this CE group, Madge Wyser. She invited me to go to a party in South Park with her. While in the house at the party, a boy I didn't know came up to me and said some boy outside wanted to see me. I learned that he was jealous of me because of Madge Wyser. Outside, there were three boys around a fire. I thought I was going to have a fight on my hands, but he backed down without a fight. Going home Madge broke a heel on her high heeled shoes. I offered to carry her, but she declined . . . thank goodness! She limped home, a distance of about two miles.

In the summer of 1927, when I was still fifteen, George Shear's father gave me a job tending an ice platform on Sabine Pass Avenue, catercornered across from our old grocery store. I developed muscle. People drove up and ordered twenty-five or thirty pounds of ice, which I would cut from a three-hundred-pound block, put on their front fender, and collect the money. One day the manager of the root beer stand, which was across the street in that lot where Gerald Wilson held Lou and terrified Mother such that she had a nervous breakdown, wanted me to give him some ice and accept some coupons I was not authorized to accept. I turned him down. My boss, Mr. Powell (husband of my math teacher) bawled me out for this but didn't fire me.

---

[2] Granville Walker was a revered minister in the Christian Church (Disciples of Christ). He was the senior minister of University Christian Church in Fort Worth, Texas, from 1940–1973.

When there were no customers, I went into the freezer and practiced lifting and lowering three-hundred-pound blocks of ice. I delighted in the bulging muscles in my arms and shoulders. That same summer, I had my first real girlfriend. Maude Page Walker was a beautiful girl, intelligent, well dressed, and well mannered. She made it apparent that she would like to date me. I asked her to go to the junior-senior prom with me. She said yes. That was the beginning of a two-year romance that involved many dances, swim parties, beach parties, and visits with my family. Her father was a dentist. She had a brother about a year younger than I. When I broke up with her the summer before I went away to TCU, she was devastated. I had assumed there were plenty of guys who would date her immediately.

My reasons for breaking up with her were complex. She did not care for sports, like tennis, etc. I did. She was not going to college; I was. I could not see how we could carry forward the relationship for four years with me in Fort Worth and her in Beaumont. If she had gone to SMU in Dallas, we could have continued the relationship, but her father thought he could not finance her education and her brother's too. Her brother became a dentist like their father. The separation was hard on both of us.

In the first months at TCU, I was so lonely that I wrote her asking if she would give me a date at Thanksgiving. No answer. I had to go out to Lubbock to speak to an Older Boys Conference. My roommate, Herschel Gipson, knew I wanted that letter with a positive answer. It came, and he forwarded it to me in Lubbock. I was buoyed up for my speech to 1,000 boys.

When Thanksgiving came, we had the date, but it wasn't the same. When I returned to Fort Worth, I didn't write her. I didn't date her at Christmas vacation. In the spring, I was asked to speak to a Boys Conference in Beaumont. Her brother called me and said that Maude Page was ill and wanted to see me. I dashed out to her house. In the sick room I found not only her, but her mother, an aunt, and her former boyfriend standing beside the head of the bed. I said, "I'm sorry you are ill. Hello, Hampton." I greeted the ladies and left. That was the end of that, I thought!

However, in 1946, when Ruth and I, Mark, and little baby Tommy (aged five months) were visiting Mama Madge prior to our move to Austin, the newspaper carried a story of Maude Page trying to commit suicide by taking an overdose of sleeping pills. At that point she was still alive in the hospital; so I called her brother, the dentist, and asked if there was anything I could do. Should I go to visit her in the hospital? He said No! Later I learned that she had married Hampton Mabry, the fellow who was standing beside the bed when I last saw her. He had been unfaithful to her, which prompted her suicide. They had one son.

One time our band was to meet a Houston band at the railroad and parade downtown and later to the ballpark. Our drum major was ill; so the band elected me to take his place! At the station, the bandleader gave me the signal to start. I whistled, twirled my baton, and started. A while later I didn't hear the band behind me. I looked around and found that I had walked half a block while they were still stationary. The bandleader had changed his mind, and I didn't hear him. It was another early sign of deafness.

Also, in that senior year, I was president of a Hi-Y Club of fifty members. Ben Pipkin was sergeant-at-arms. We met on school time, whereas previously we had met in the evening at the Y. I was also vice president of the State Hi-Y Conference that met in Temple, Texas. We took a railroad carload of boys to Temple. Many of them stole some silverware from cafes. Ivan Singleton, the Y Boys Secretary, asked me to talk to the boys about returning the silver. I stood on a seat while the train rumbled along on its way to Beaumont and spoke effectively enough that all the silverware was turned in to Ike, and he sent it back to the merchants of Temple. That year, I was also president of a social organization called "The Overall and Apron Club," which had been developed by the teachers to cut down on expensive dressing.

I went out for track in the spring when the band was relatively inactive. I could not beat the fastest men in the hundred-yard dash, or the 440, so I tried out for the mile. There was one other miler, a tall, skinny Indian named Walter Clasby. He usually beat me, but I was not far behind. When the team went to Nacogdoches in Coach Dimmitt's old Ford sedan, I was not invited. So I went up by train. In a field of forty runners in the mile, I almost beat Clasby. Our men in the stadium were yelling for me. That did my soul good. Coach made room for me in the Ford going home.

My first radio, which I paid for myself ($25), was a one-tube set, made by an electrician in Beaumont. It had a base board and a Bakelite front with one dial and an on/off switch. I used headphones. It was thrilling; I could get Cincinnati, Des Moines, and Chicago. I thought it was great. I put a copper aerial on top on the house from the chimney out to Edie's servant house.

The Y rather than Boy Scouts was my main activity. Gym, swimming, tennis, boxing, wrestling, weightlifting, tumbling, basketball, softball, and handball were some of my sports. Most important of all was Hi-Y, for which I was vice president in my junior year and president in my senior year. That year the meetings were at school during a period when everyone had to choose some club. It was much more difficult to discipline fifty boys in the club than when it was a group of fifteen or twenty meeting at the Y in the evening. I went to statewide conferences at Texas A&M, Temple, and Waco. I was a speaker and elected vice president.

Grover C. Good, state secretary for Hi-Y Clubs, became a very important father figure for me, encouraging me in every way. I spoke at his funeral in Irving, Texas, in 1982. His daughter and I dated some during our college years. She attended what is now Texas Woman's University in Denton and later taught in San Antonio and at the University of Texas in Austin. Her field was physical education.

Mother had insisted that I take shorthand and typing in high school rather than a college prep course. I did well in the courses and worked in Judge Nall's office one summer. It must have been in 1925 after my freshman year in high school, when I was fourteen years old. In those days school went through the eleventh grade, so I graduated at age sixteen.

Mother got a vacation and took Lou and Marguerite to California, where she visited some relatives and did some sightseeing. I stayed home and took care of myself, with Edie's help in the food department and clothes washing. Judge Nall had promised Mom he would get rid of my female rat-terrier, "Tex," who had too many puppies. We drove down to a town near High Island and let Tex out on a road with no people in sight. I looked back longingly at her as long as I could see her.

Mother taught me to drive at age fifteen. You didn't have to get a driver's license in those days. I was ticketed for running a red light on Orleans Street at the railroad crossing. I was petrified when I appeared in court. I paid a fine, but the judge did not ask my age. I was lucky to get off so lightly because the law said you must be sixteen to drive.

When I was almost sixteen in the summer of 1927, I drove our Model T sedan to Arkansas and back. Some of the driving in those hills was very dangerous, especially in the rain on clay roads! There were "Sound Klaxon" signs at corners (square corners with ditches on both sides). Aunt

Betty had come from St. Louis to be with us. As a devout Catholic, she sat in the back seat with Mom and Sis and "prayed" I wouldn't lose my nerve. Once when I drove in the rain from Bentonville to Eureka Springs, Arkansas, on a muddy road in the mountains, we made 100 miles in ten hours.

After Aunt Betty had left to go back to St. Louis and we were on our way back to Texas, we came to a hill so steep that the old four-cylinder Ford wouldn't pull us and our luggage (on the running board) up that hill. I had heard that the reverse gear was stronger than low gear. So Mom, Sis, and Lou got out and walked while I backed the Ford up to the top of the hill.

Chapter 2

TCU STUDENT

The Great Depression started in October 1929 and wreaked havoc across the nation. It had a devastating impact on TCU. Paul's memories of this time reveal how the university struggled to help its students stay in school by hiring them for jobs on campus. Regrettably, TCU had to reduce faculty by layoffs in 1933.

I had saved $500 from various jobs, including the two years I worked at the Y in Beaumont, as Secretary to Hastings Harrison, the General Secretary, and then for Ivan Singleton, the Boys Work Secretary, while I attended South Park Junior College for one year, 1929–30. I earned twenty-four hours credit from this junior college which I transferred to TCU with me.

In Beaumont, when I worked for Hastings Harrison at the Y as his secretary, I made $100 a month. During that year, Reggie Newton, who was Harrison's bookkeeper, and I were given the job of classifying all the bids on all the items to finish the new Y building on Calder Avenue in Beaumont. On several nights we worked very late into the night. Then we aided Harrison as he met with the Building Committee to make decisions on each item. When some of these smaller items arrived at the freight station, I went over in Harrison's Dodge and picked them up. Some I took to the old Y, some to the new Y on Calder Avenue.

When this work was finished, probably August, Mr. Harrison gave Reggie and me $25 each and told us to take a weekend off. We did. We went to Galveston and stayed at the Buccaneer Hotel on the waterfront. Now it is a fine home for the elderly.

In the summer of 1930, when I had made up my mind to choose TCU, Mother took all three of us kids on a trip around Texas in her little green Chrysler roadster. We saw a good bit of Texas: Kerrville, Austin, Fort

Worth, Dallas, and points in between, including Houston. Going into Houston on the way home, I was driving the Chrysler "50" at about 55 or 60 miles per hour. A cop on a motorcycle drove up beside me, scaring me, and told me to slow down. He noted that I was going too fast in that little car loaded the way it was. I loved that little green Chrysler with the stick shift and the rumble seat.

In Fort Worth we visited with Mr. Tucker, the registrar, at his home on University Drive, about a block south of the campus. His wife was there. She later taught me introductory psychology, which changed my mind about majoring in psychology. When I came to teach at TCU in 1957 (twenty-nine years later), she was nearing retirement. Her husband had died several years earlier.

Going off to college at TCU in Fort Worth was life's greatest adventure at that point in my life. Grover Good got C.G. Fairchild, Boys Work Secretary, and a wonderful man, to hire me to work with Junior Hi-Y clubs. (Incidentally, I presided at and gave the burial address at the funeral of his wife, in Austin, years later, after we had moved to Fort Worth, probably 1960.) Later I handled all Hi-Y Clubs in Fort Worth. That's the main way I financed my college education. TCU gave me reduced costs on tuition, room, and board.

The Y paid me $60 per month for thirty hours of work per week the first year. Of course, the stock market crash of 1929 had started the Great Depression of the thirties. So, in 1931–32, my salary was cut to $50 a month, and I had to buy a car. I paid $200 for a two-year-old Model A Ford roadster. In my junior year, 1932–33, the Y had to let me go for financial reasons. Fortunately, TCU saw me through. Mother loaned me $200 for incidentals like dry cleaning, etc. This loan was one reason I accepted the job in Austin in 1934 instead of going directly to Disciples House in Chicago.

I met Dr. Edwin A. Elliott, who had recently received his doctorate from the University of California, at a Hi-Y Officers Retreat at a camp near Glen Rose. From then on, he was my favorite professor. Though I tried psychology and sociology as majors, I finally majored in economics because of my fondness for Dr. Elliott. He stimulated me to read authors like Upton Sinclair's *The Jungle*, Sinclair Lewis's *Arrowsmith*, and others in addition to studying the economics texts and the lecture notes. He was a wonderful lecturer. He asked me to be his assistant during my senior year, but this didn't materialize.

Instead, he went to Washington, DC, and the Roosevelt "New Deal" in 1933. There he got into labor mediation and spent the rest of his life with the National Labor Relations Board in the Southwest. I attended the huge retirement dinner for him at the Texas Hotel (later called the Sheraton and then the Hyatt Regency) in the mid-60s.

The other professor who was very influential in my life was H. L. Pickerill. He was the University of Chicago graduate who had been National Director of Religious Education for the Disciples. He used dynamic discussion as a teaching method. His classes met around a large table, which was really about six tables put together in the center of a room so about twenty-five people could sit around them. The walls were lined with books. We kept a record of the pages of the books we read, and this was one basis for our grade.

When my job at the Y played out because of the Depression, TCU hired me as a stenographer to "Pick" Pickerill and other members of the Brite Faculty, who also comprised the Religion Department: Dr. Morro, Dr. Lockhart, Mr. Hutton, "Pick," and Dean Colby Hall. The next spring the financial situation was so tight that "Pick" and twenty-four other faculty members were dismissed. I helped mimeograph a protest, running forty pages, which was submitted to the young American Association of University Professors. However, they were unable to do anything because TCU was in serious financial straits. "Pick" was later responsible for my move from First Christian Church in Hicksville, Ohio, to East Grand Boulevard Christian Church in Detroit, Michigan, in 1941. We saw each other often while we were in Michigan from 1941 to 1945. The University of Michigan Trustees named a new cooperative dormitory Pickerill Hall in his honor when he retired.

Herschel Gipson was my roommate for two years in Clark Hall and at a home near Weatherford St. and the railroad (near where the parking lot for the busses to DFW is now located). Gordon Voight was my roommate during my junior year while I worked on campus in Goode Hall, located where the present Clark Hall stands. The present Sadler Hall stands where the Clark Hall of the 1930s stood. During my senior year I was back in Clark Hall, and my roommate was Hubert Stem, who became a lifelong friend.

Hubert attended Chicago Theological Seminary (CTS) while I was in the University of Chicago Divinity School (1936–39). Ruth was in CTS some of that time. Hubert consented to be the best man at our wedding.

He paid his own expenses to come from Chicago to Columbus where we picked him up. People in Croton loved him, as did we. He is shown in pictures of the reception line with us after the wedding. The year was 1938. Hubert married a beautiful and intelligent girl who had been born to missionary parents in China. Jean won "Outstanding Teacher" in Ohio in 1990. Hubert had been reared in Fort Worth and was a member of Hemphill Presbyterian Church. When that church celebrated their 100th anniversary, they invited Hubert to come preach. He and Jean came and stayed with us at Trinity Terrace. We took them to the Stock Show and other places in Fort Worth. We had been at their house in Akron in 1987 and admired his paintings (a retirement hobby). We bought one from him in 1991 which hung over our bed.

TCU was not a great university when I was a student there. Its enrollment ranged from 1,800 down to 850. By the 1990s, it was among the top 100 universities in the country and had an enrollment of more than 6,000 students. It offered forty masters degrees and six PhD degrees, in addition to the D.Min. from Brite Divinity School. About 1,200 degrees were granted each year in the 1990s.

The Pacifist Incident/Problem

Of all my contacts at TCU, I admired Dr. Edwin A. Elliott so much, more than any other faculty member. I also admired Dr. Jack Hammond, professor of history, and Professor H. L. Pickerill, professor of religion. Another adult whom I admired and who thought very highly of me was the State Boys Work Secretary of the Texas YMCA, Grover C. Good. He thought I was the outstanding boy among the thousands he knew. Of course, that caused me to "purr."

Dr. Hammond sponsored the International Relations Club at TCU, assisted by Dr. Elliott. Franklin Roosevelt was elected in 1932, and these two men were enthusiastic about Roosevelt's new programs. Dr. Elliott left TCU during my senior year to go to Washington to head up the National Recovery Administration's "Grocery Code." His father owned a grocery store, and Dr. Elliott had worked in it and even managed it before World War I. He went off to France and was decorated with the French Croix de Guerre or Legion of Honor. He wore it in his suit lapel all the time.

Our International Relations Club was invited to speak at Older Boys Conferences and at churches in the area where TCU ministerial students, like Gene Cox and others, preached. Freddie Miller, Johnny LeBus,

Nat Wells, Hubert Stem, and I were among the favorite speakers.

In my senior year at TCU, while working for the Y again, I helped with an Older Boys Conference in Fort Worth. I arranged for our International Relations Club to give an evening program on "Issues of War and Peace." Hubert Stem, Dean Harrison, Johnny LeBus, and I were the speakers. Dr. W. J. Hammond, of history, was the sponsor of the club. In my speech I made an impassioned plea for pacifism as the Christian answer to war. I made an extreme statement with reference to munitions makers and other profiteers on war, saying, "We young fools fight their wars for them." A *Star-Telegram* reporter chose that statement as his only quote from all that was said in those four speeches and wrote a short article on an inside page of the morning edition about the occasion. This is the type of journalism I have always despised.

The next weekend, I took off for Galveston to speak to an Older Boys Conference at Ball High School. Grover Good had a speaker back out on him; so he asked me if I would call Dr. Elliott who was in Houston by that time working for the National Labor Relations Board to see if he would come over on the interurban and speak to the conference on Saturday evening. I called, and he accepted. I introduced him! He asked me how I was going back to Fort Worth and when. He met me in Houston at 1:00 p.m. on Sunday and took me to his apartment. We both lay down and took a nap. Then he took me to the railroad station where I caught the train to Fort Worth.

While I was gone, all hell broke loose in Fort Worth. The American Legion Post, of which both Elliott and Hammond were members, took umbrage at what I had said and wrote me a letter, which I kept. They called the press and said they were going to have J. Edgar Hoover (yes, he was heading the FBI as early as 1934) investigate me for "sedition." My roommate, Hubert Stem, wrote me a letter and enclosed clippings. Grady Spruce, the great Boys Secretary of the Dallas Y, handed me the letter while I was on a gunboat of the US Navy out in the Gulf of Mexico. When I got off the train at the Santa Fe station in Fort Worth (yes, the same one that still stands and where the Amtrack train meets passengers), a red cap was calling my name and pronouncing it correctly. When I responded, he whispered to me, "Your roommate says 'Don't say nothin' to nobody.'" Bless his heart: I was so flustered that I didn't even remember to tip him.

Well, there was acrimonious debate in the papers and elsewhere for two weeks over my statement.

Dr. Hammond offered to go with me to bait these lions (the American Legionnaires) in their own den, but I said, "Thanks, but no thanks. I don't think they are sensitive enough to understand where I'm coming from." Incidentally, the next year, 1935, Dr. Hammond ran for mayor of Fort Worth as a Socialist and won!

Nat Wells, son of the great East Dallas Christian Church preacher, L. N. D. Wells, and H. L. Trimble were invited to speak over the radio station of the controversial Frank Norris, pastor of the fundamentalist First Baptist Church. I accompanied them to the radio station. Frank Norris introduced the program and likened us Christian young people to a lighthouse and those who attacked us as gnats and other bugs who would beat themselves to death against the Christian truth of peace on earth and good will to men. I was amazed that he would take such an adamant stand in our favor.

Here is the American Legion statement of March 1, 1934, as mailed to Paul.

> The members of Blackstone Post No. 482, American Legion, note with amazement a report of a meeting of young men sponsored by the Young Men's Christian Association, and held on the Texas Christian University campus. Appearing in the star-Telegram [sic] of February 15th, 1934, this report reads as follows:
>
> "The 'crazy economic situation' that calls upon young men to fight in the name of 'so-called patriotism' was condemned by Paul Wassenich, student leader at Texas Christian University, before the Older Boys' Conference of Central and North Texas last night at the university auditorium.
>
> "Wassenich called upon the boys to join the International Relations Club, which is rapidly spreading in the colleges. Members of the club oppose fighting for their country.
>
> . . . "He said that leaders in the economic life of nations call upon youth to fight their wars.
>
> "'You and I and the other fools,' Wassenich said, 'fight their wars for them. But it is better to face the situation of being called yellow or a coward than to go to war. It is better for your friends, your girl, even your parents to think you are a coward than to be loyal to the rotten kind of leadership that gets us into wars.'

"Wassenich called upon the boys to pledge: 'I'll not go to war. It's wrong. It's unchristian [sic].'

"He said 50 students at the university belong to the club and that meetings have been held at churches and elsewhere in this section in the interest of the movement.

"Preceding Wassenich, Hubert Stem said the main causes of war are nationalism, militarism, and the economic system. Following him, Dean Harrison summed up the material and spiritual cost of war. Both are students at the university.

"Johnny Lebus presided. Officers were elected but will not be announced until 9:30 o'clock this morning at the same place. Glenn Rothell, Fort Worth, president of the Young Men's Conference of the YMCA, gave an inspirational talk and Otis Hilliard led a devotional program.

"A quartet from the negro YMCA sang.

"The three-day conference will close at a meeting at 11 o'clock this morning. Rev. Perry Gresham, pastor of the University Place [sic] Christian Church, will speak. George D. Levell, Waco, will talk at the 9:30 session."

Investigation reveals that the story of this meeting as reported is substantially correct.

The members of the Blackstone Post No. 482 are astonished to learn that there is an organization in Texas Christian University called the International Relations Club, whose membership includes fifty students, one of who is student leader... which organization adheres to the principle that "it is better to face the situation of being called yellow, or a coward, than to go to war. It is better for your friends, your girl, even your parents, to think you are a coward than to be loyal to the rotten kind of leadership that gets us into war."

Mr. Wassenich, Mr. Stem, Mr. Harrison, would you stand supilely [sic] aside, and without protest, witness the ravishment of your mother, your sister or your sweetheart by an invader of your home who does not even speak your language? We do not believe you would. We do not believe that Texas breeds that kind of man, and yet...you would witness the ravishment of your country by a foreign invader without lifting your hand in restraint.

Young gentlemen, you and the other members of the International Relations Club are not to be condemned. It is the earnest belief of Blackstone Post No. 488 that you are victims of insidious propaganda, originating beyond the borders of the United States of America. We cannot believe that you regard George Washington as a "rotten" leader…Bunker Hill...those whose bloody feet turned red the snows of Valley Forge, as "fools"….Were they but "fools" who died at the Alamo and at San Jacinto that you might, under the Stars and Stripes, enjoy the advantages of Texas Christian University…

…be it RESOLVED BY Blackstone Post 482, American Legion…

1. That the above statement is, and shall be, recorded in the permanent records of this post as an integral part of these resolutions;

2. That the trustees and faculty of Texas Christian University be unreservedly condemned for fostering within the walls of the university a student organization which is wholly unpatriotic, if not actually treasonable;

3. That the leadership of the Young Men's Christian Association be unreservedly condemned for the organization of, and participation in, Young Men's conferences where speakers whose thoughts are wholly unpatriotic, if not actually treasonable, are invited and encouraged;

4. That Texas Christian University be urgently requested to cease encouragement of wholly unpatriotic, if not actually treasonable, organizations among the students, and substitute therefore organizations which will inculcate the ideals of patriotism of our fathers.

5. That the Young Men's Christian Association be urgently requested to desist from further participation in programs which are wholly unpatriotic, if not actually treasonable, and that patriotic programs be encouraged;

6. That the Blackstone Post No. 482 reiterate its often publicly stated conviction that the American Legion is unalterably opposed to wars of aggression, and to war itself, as an institution,

but that we are not opposed to war when, and if, necessary to defend our homes, our institutions, and our nation;

7. That copies of these resolutions be forwarded to Mr. Paul Wassenich; Mr. Hubert Stem; Mr. Dean Harrison; Mr. Van Zandt Jarvis, Chairman of the Board of Trustees of Texas Christian University; Dr. E. M. Waits, President of Texas Christian University; Judge Hal Lattimore, President of the Board of Directors of the Young Mens Christian Association; Mr. C.G. Fairchild, General Secretary of the Young Mens Christian Association; Department of Texas of the American Legion; National Commander of American Legion; and the Daily Newspapers of Fort Worth, Texas.

This statement was also reported in the Fort Worth Star-Telegram *on February 18, 1934. A flurry of articles appeared in March:* "Legion Flays T.C.U. and 'Y' Peace Clubs, Post Calls International Relations Movement 'Unpatriotic'" (*Fort Worth Press*, March 2, 1934).

"Hint of Sedition In Peace Talk, Legion Reports Wassenich Remarks to Hoover, Head of U.S. Investigators" (*Fort Worth Press*, March 8, 1934).

Then support for the student groups quickly emerged: "Demand Legion Prove Charge or Recant" (*Fort Worth Star-Telegram*, March 8). "Peace Champion Declines Legion Bid, Explanation, Wassenich Has No Apologies to Make, Will Not Attend Legion Meeting, But Open for Session on 'Neutral Ground'" (*Press*, March 8). "Students Rally to T.C.U. Club, Dean Hall Says That He is 'Astounded' at Legion's 'Peace Row' Attitude" (*Star-Telegram*, March 10).

The controversy continued on the airways with Mineral Wells Legionnaire Edward Hayes supporting the Fort Worth Post *on WBAP. Other Legion support came from Granbury. However, a Great War veteran and Legion member also from Mineral Wells wrote a carefully crafted four-page letter supporting Paul.*

March 11, 1934, Mr. Paul Wassenich

Dear young American:

I was much interested [in] Buddy Edward A Hayes illogical attempt to brand free speech, opinion and conscience as treason,

> unpatriotism [sic] and disrespect for those Buddies of mine who have given their lives in wars of aggression. [*He continues for three pages on rights of free speech and religion and concludes*] With all honor and respect to my Buddies who sleep in Flanders fields and those—who like myself lie with battle shattered bodies, and minds in beds of living death—while a brutal government takes our pitiful pensions away from us—I can only say our sacrifice failed—And our honest burning patriotic sacrifices were burned on the altar of insatiate greed—in vain! . . .
>
> Jack Carmichell, a battle front disabled veteran and Legionnaire, Mineral Wells, Texas.

When I came to the TCU faculty in 1957, Hammond was still on the faculty, and Elliott had retired but was living near the campus. I was asked by my friend Louis Saunders to chair a committee for the Fort Worth Council of Churches on integration. I asked Hammond and Elliott to be members of the committee. Both accepted, but they warned me to be moderate and careful in the first meeting. Both had been singed badly by the McCarthyite atmosphere.

By 1995, all four of the men I have mentioned who meant so much to me in my formative years were deceased. Pickerill, like myself, had never gotten his PhD. After he was let go in the depths of the Depression, he went to head Disciples student work at the University of Michigan. He distinguished himself, and a cooperative dormitory was built and named for him. When he retired, I was asked to sponsor a move before the TCU Faculty Senate to honor him with a doctorate. It passed unanimously. The doctorate was a great satisfaction to him, as he never felt good about being dismissed in the depths of the Depression.

Grover Good had asked that I be the minister at his funeral. When he died, his daughter, Aileen, called from El Paso and reached me while we were at our farm near Mineral Wells, Texas. As I was on top of the house helping Mark with a reroofing job after a hailstorm, Ruth took the call. The funeral would be in Irving. Yes, I would be there. The only car Ruth and I had was a white Ford truck (1976) which we had bought for the farm and used as our only means of transportation. Consequently, I asked to ride with the mortician to the cemetery. At the funeral I was impressed with the service of the Masons, which followed my sermon.

I have added to this list the names of some other men who influenced me. Some of them were "father figures," replacing my dead father. They were, in addition to those mentioned above, Hastings Harrison, C.G. Fairchild, Block Smith, Frank Jewett, and friends closer to my age, Perry Gresham and Granville Walker.

Chapter 3

MEETING RUTH

In August 1933, I was in Carl and Alice Streeter Hoover's living room in a little yellow house on the west side of the Croton town square. (Croton was the railroad name for a switch and water tank. After the railroad was abandoned, the name reverted to Hartsford Township, Licking County, Ohio.) I had met Sylvia Siegfried through my work in the YMCA in Fort Worth a year or so earlier. She was a Disciples missionary in the Philippines and, following her retirement, had been in Fort Worth to speak to the Ladies Missionary Society of First Christian Church as a representative of the United Christian Missionary Society of the Christian Church (Disciples of Christ). She and my mother participated in a "Round Robin" newsletter among relatives and friends.

The crowd in the small parlor opened, and across the room I saw this beautiful brunette (see picture) whom I had never seen before and didn't even know existed. "Aunt" Sylvia was standing nearby; so I said to her, "Aunt Sylvia, who is the beautiful girl?" She said, "Oh, don't you know Ruth?" I said, "Ruth who?" "Ruth Siegfried. She is my niece. Would you like an introduction?" "Sure!" Aunt Sylvia arranged the introduction.

Shortly thereafter we all walked across the square to the Christian Church for lunch in the basement. I asked Ruth if she and I could sit together. She said, "No, I have to sit with the Hoovers (the husband) and you with the Streeters (the wife)." So I could only get an occasional glimpse of her in the crowded basement during the apparently dull program. I can't tell you one thing that transpired. I don't even remember eating.

When the lunch was over, I asked my mother if I could borrow the Buick. She said, "Yes." I asked Ruth if she would like to go for a ride with me. She said, "OK, if I can bring my cousin Elnora along."

Ruth Siegfried, West High School, Cleveland, Ohio, senior photo 1932. Wassenich family collection.

Paul mailed this portrait to Ruth after their meeting. Wassenich family collection.

I didn't know where to drive; so I asked Ruth and Elnora. They suggested a small lake, north of Croton a few miles. It was a beautiful afternoon. We enjoyed desultory conversation. I learned that she attended Oberlin College and Elnora attended the famous Ohio State University in Columbus. I learned that the mother of Elnora was a sister of the mother of Ruth. They were named Dess and Alice. Their family name had been Dixon; now they were Dess Innis and Alice Siegfried.

Sometime that afternoon I managed to work out a date with Ruth for that evening. We drove west along country roads seeking the site of a light beacon. Then we drove back to Ruth's summer home in Croton. We sat under a big, beautiful maple tree that we became quite attached to. After much conversation and sharing of experiences, we exchanged a few kisses. Around 11:00 p.m. I said, "Well, goodnight. This has been wonderful, but I guess it has no future, with you in Ohio and me in Texas." I got up and started to the car. She was quiet for a minute. Then she came running after me and said, "Now don't say so lightly that this affair has no future. We can at least write."

And, write we did! A letter per week and often more.

The next day as Mother, Sis, Louis, and I drove north, I happily sang a number of the popular songs of the day. One was "When It's Springtime in the Rockies, I'll Be Coming Back to You!" Mother said, "What happened to you last night?" I couldn't find words to explain, so I said "Oh, nothing." (But next June she gave me $50 so I could ride the bus three days and nights to visit Ruth.)

Remember it was the depths of the Depression, and I was earning my way through college. I had lost my job at the Fort Worth Y the previous year but got a job as stenographer for Brite College of the Bible at TCU. When we reached Chicago, I had a telegram waiting for me saying the YMCA could rehire me as Hi-Y Secretary. I left Mom, Lou, and Sis in Chicago so they could visit the World's Fair, and I went to Fort Worth on the Greyhound bus. I had seen the World's Fair earlier that summer, as a counselor for a YMCA trip with about fifty boys.

After five years of writing letters and occasionally getting together in Cleveland, Indianapolis, Austin, Beaumont, Mexico, and Chicago, we were married in that same little Croton Christian Church on June 16, 1938. Elnora was Maid of Honor; her fiancé, Ralph Shilling, was an usher and photographer. The best man was Hubert Stem, my roommate from my senior year at TCU. The minister was Neil Crawford, who had been

Ruth Siegfried Wassenich's ancestral home on Bennington Chapel Road, Hartford Township, Licking County, Ohio. The lower right portion is a dugout built just after the War of 1812 when Ohio opened for settlement. It was a family home until the 1950s and remains an occupied, well-maintained home today. This photo is from about 1940. On the same road is the Hartford Cemetery where Paul and Ruth and other members of the family are buried. Both Paul's and Ruth's families are from this township. The families maintain records back to seventeenth-century colonists in America and include a number of ministers, teachers, newspaper publisher/editors, fresco painters, congressmen, and military and civil officers. Many were basically farmers, along with the other pursuits. Historically known family names include Hopkins of Jamestown and the Mayflower; Cook of Massachusetts; Lee of Virginia; Mitchel of Maryland; Putnam of Massachusetts and founder of Ohio; Poppleton of Vermont's Green Mountain Boys; Pomeroy of Massachusetts; and Siegfried of Siegfriedale, Pennsylvania. (The Wassenichs are "recent immigrants" having arrived in the Republic of Texas in 1842.) Wassenich family collection.

Ruth's pastor in Cleveland and was now pastor of the Christian Church in Athens, where the University of Ohio was. I paid him $10. He looked shocked! But that was all that I could afford, and I thought he should have done it for free. In fact, the $10 merely paid for the gas he used in his trip to Croton and back to Athens.

Ruth and I spent the first night of our honeymoon in a lovely hotel, Granville Inn, in Granville, Ohio, where Dennison University is located. Ruth's dad had attended one year of college at Dennison.

We took the train from Columbus to Chicago and stayed at the Morrison Hotel. I spoke to the Chicago Disciples Ministers the next day about my MA thesis, just completed a couple of weeks earlier. Two days later we shepherded eighty kids on the Burlington Zephyr to Denver and on to the Cheley Camps at Estes Park, Colorado, where we both worked. Three months later, we brought them back and took the train on to Beaumont where I officiated at the wedding of Marguerite and her handsome husband, Jimmy Ezell, in Mother's home at 2520 North St.

Then Ruth and I took a Pullman back to Chicago and a tough year in which we finished our formal education. She graduated summa cum laude with a master's degree from Chicago Theological Seminary. I graduated—no cum laude—from the University of Chicago Divinity School. We left for Hicksville, Ohio, and our first ministry.

Throughout my life, my wife, Ruth, has been the light of my life. Her profound love and loyalty have made my life secure and happy.

Chapter 4

GRADUATE SCHOOL

In the spring of 1934, Granville Walker and Perry Gresham, the new pastor of University Christian Church, took me to the coffee shop across from Brite College and asked what I planned to do next year. I said I was going to try to get a YMCA job as Boys Work Secretary. They said, "Why not consider the ministry? Would you consider asking Dean Ames of Disciples House, Chicago, for a scholarship?"

My reply was that I didn't think my grades were good enough for that. They asked if I would allow them to write Ames on my behalf. Well, I thought that would be okay. They wrote and were persuasive enough that Ames invited me to accept a scholarship at Disciples House, University of Chicago. That did my ego good! I have always been indebted to Perry and Granville for their concern and action on this matter.

Before word from Ames reached me, I had a letter from Block Smith of the University YMCA in Austin. I had met him in some of the Hi-Y conferences I had addressed, including a recent one in Austin. He offered me a job as secretary, bookkeeper, and supervisor of the dormitory, total salary $100 per month, plus free room. I could take one class a day and work on a master's degree in the university. I sure needed the money, but I couldn't see turning down Dean Ames's offer. So I wrote him to that effect. He wrote back that Dr. Jewett (Texas Bible Chair) had called Ames and gotten his agreement to extend that scholarship two years. So-o-o-o, I accepted Block's offer. Ruth didn't like it because it delayed our wedding two years. But in retrospect, it proved a valuable two years.

I counseled at Cheley Camps in the summer of 1934 where I directed Ski-Hi, one of eight sections of Cheley Camps, and climbed Flattop, Twin Sister, Chapin, and Long's Peak. In the fall, I showed up in Austin to work at the University YMCA for "Block" Smith.

I learned to keep a set of books and served as secretary to "Block" and as head resident of the dormitory. With my pay of $100 a month, I was able to pay Mother the $200 I borrowed from her my last year in TCU, pay the Beaumont Rotary Club $50 they had loaned me, and repay a loan on my $1,000 insurance policy. I was also able to buy engagement and wedding rings for Ruth. I went to Croton in the summer 1935 and asked her father for her hand. He seemed satisfied to have me as a potential son-in-law. He and Mom Siegfried were always wonderful to us. They loved the grandchildren we presented them.

While in Austin those two years, I finished a master's degree in sociology with a minor in philosophy. In the middle of this time, Dean Colby D. Hall, Dean of Brite College of the Bible at TCU, wrote to ask if I would like to be ordained in University Christian Church with several other men whom I knew, including Oliver Harrison, Fred Vasquez, and Chester Crow. I accepted. Perry Gresham, the pastor of University Christian Church, was the main one I remember who laid his hands on my head. Oliver Harrison and Chester Crow were lifelong friends.

The two years in Austin were years of maturation for me. They prepared me for the vicissitudes of Chicago. I worked in the office answering the phone, taking dictation, typing letters, keeping books, collecting the rent on rooms, handling any problems in the dorm, and keeping track of Charlie Washington's finances. Charlie was the Negro janitor.

While I worked for the YMCA, I was released one day a week to attend class. In my second year, I researched, wrote, and defended a thesis entitled: *Some Effects of the Depression on the Negro Population of Austin*. I became a member of the sociology honors fraternity, Alpha Kappa Delta. Years later, the TCU sociology chair asked me, considering that membership, to address that group at a dinner. I minored in philosophy. My classes with Miller, Brogan, Tsanoff, and Gentry were helpful to me when I went to Chicago.

The University Y in those days was important as a moral and intellectual center of the university. It had a good building at University and 22nd, which was subsequently sold, as the Y's significance on campus declined after the death of "Block" Smith. But in 1934–36, "Woody" Woodbury, the program man, did a wonderful job, especially with freshmen. His group numbered 100 to 150 attending a meeting once a week. They had many related activities.

Some of the interesting students I remember from those days are Jack Lewis, Bud Elkins, Gus Levy, and Jenkins Garrett, president of the student body. I had known Jenkins in Fort Worth as one of my Hi-Y boys. Other people I became close friends with were Beverly Sheffield, "Sug" Mueller, "Onnie" Hollander, Tom Currie, "Dulce" Landry, Art Cunningham, Alvin Scaff, and Joe Brown. Joe loaned me his Ford roadster to take Ruth to Monterrey, Mexico, when she visited me at Christmas 1935.

Sociology professors were Gettys and Rosenquist. Dr. Rosenquist was so thorough in supervising my MA thesis that when I wrote two theses at Chicago, I had no trouble with the lady whom all other graduate students feared because she had final say over form and grammar in theses. I even typed my own papers. I stayed up to 3:00 a.m. many nights that summer of 1936 and ate very little to get that thesis finished. When I met Mom and Marguerite in Dallas for the trip to Croton, prior to entering the University of Chicago, I was thin as a rail and exhausted.

Following my ordination, Frank L. Jewett of the Texas Bible Chair asked me to preach at the chapel service he held on Sundays. When I left Austin, Dr. Jewett told me he wanted me to do well at Chicago and to succeed him in the Bible Chair. I thought he was just being nice, but he meant it. I did succeed him ten years later, in 1946.

First Pastorate

There was one other event from that period of my life I should record. Rev. Klingman was pastor in Taylor at First Christian Church. He came to my office at the University Y, introduced himself, and, noting that I had been ordained recently, asked if I would consider serving the Elgin Church on a two-Sundays per month basis. Thus, I undertook my first pastorate; I went there on the bus.

One Sunday, I asked the youth in our church to invite youth from other churches to our church. They were mostly Baptist and Presbyterians and comprised an interdenominational group of about 100. When June rolled around, the graduating class wanted me to do the baccalaureate sermon. I agreed. On the appointed Sunday, it was raining and very wet. I caught the bus and got to the town of Manor all right. But south of Manor, a flood of considerable proportions stopped the bus. The driver turned around and decided to go to Houston by a different route, which completely missed Elgin. I got off the bus when it got back to Manor and telephoned Mr. Bradshaw, a member of the Elgin church who worked for the railroad, to ask if he could come get me on a railroad work/repair car. He said he worked for the other railroad and didn't have a railroad work/repair car.

However, he told me to come back to my side of the river, and he would drive to the other side, which was about five miles in each case. He said he would get me there somehow because people were already arriving for the baccalaureate service. Believe it or not, I found a taxi in Manor and got back to the flooded creek. The water was about 300 yards wide. Many people were stranded there, watching it. To their amazement, I took off my pants, rolled them and my Bible and sermon notes in my raincoat, leaving my shoes on. I waded into the stream and soon the water was up to my waist. I moved one foot along beside the other, fearing that I would be swept off my feet and get tangled in that barbed wire downstream. Finally, I got across safely.

Bradshaw and someone else took me to Mrs. Connally's house where I had often eaten Sunday dinner. She had a hot bath ready. I handed my shoes and socks out to her. She put them in the oven and dried the tail of my shirt while I bathed. I dressed again and got to the Church just as the processional began. Needless to say, I had the undivided attention of the audience because they had been told what I had endured to get there.

I was saddened to discover that the man who followed me in ministry at that church was a "hell-fire and brimstone" type. I went there just before going to Chicago and heard him preach in a revival. He had signs on the front wall of the church such as "Where will you spend eternity?" However, he won more converts during his ministry than I did during mine. They enlarged and improved the church building. Later (probably 1948), I had a youth, Clyde Lane, from Elgin in my class at the Texas Bible Chair. He went on to TCU and became a Christian Church minister.

Chicago 1936–39

The stately gothic architecture of the University of Chicago, including the Disciples House, did not surprise me because I had been on campus in 1933–34 when we took a train car load of Fort Worth boys to the World's Fair. C. G. Fairchild was in charge. I was an assistant. We stayed at the YMCA not far from the University of Chicago. But the quiet streets and the cool late afternoon of a September day as Jones, Boren, and I walked to a nearby restaurant for my first meal in Chicago all seemed strange and lonely. Later I became very fond of the area.

"The Wranglers" horse riding divinity students from Texas at U. of Chicago, 1936. Bob Sulanke, Oliver Harrison, Paul, Bill Jones. Wassenich family collection.

I was much impressed with everything at the Disciples House and the University of Chicago, especially Dean Ames. Dean Harrison and Fred Miller, two of my TCU friends, had just left Disciples House. Oliver Harrison had been there one year.

Barney Blakemore, later dean of the Disciples House, was there. Irvin Lunger, later pastor of University Church and at the time president of Transylvania College, Lexington, Kentucky, was there and left soon for a year of study in Edinburg. Rolland Sheaffor, later director of Church Extension of the Disciples, was in my class, having just graduated from Phillips University in Enid, Oklahoma. I also met W. C. Bower, J. H. Garrison, Sam Kincheloe, and H. L. Willett.

There were only four men in each of the three classes. There were a few non-Disciples living in the house like Jacobson, a Congregational seminarian, and Steve Reynolds, a law student. Mrs. Gary Sutcliffe, daughter of Judge Gary of U.S. Steel, was an "angel" who gave large donations to the House and entertained us in her lovely home on 50th Street.

Of course, Dean E. S. Ames was the centerpiece. He had just retired from chairing the University of Chicago Philosophy Department, where he had achieved world renown as author of a book entitled *Religion* and another entitled *Psychology of Religion.* He was tall, handsome, silver-haired, dignified, yet friendly. His smile had an enigmatic quality. You felt he was thinking two or three thoughts ahead of the discussion.

One of my most memorable encounters with him was at our weekly luncheon. He started a discussion about the nature of God. Finally, it was an argument between him and me. I stymied him by forcing him to admit that his view of God was merely symbolic; there was no reality behind the symbol. He had said in his book *Religion* that God is like "Uncle Sam." I took Wieman's point of view that God was Creativity in the very depth of the natural processes. He gave me that quizzical smile, pulled out his pocket watch, looked at it for a while, and said, "It's time to adjourn." All the men laughed loudly.

I had some of the greatest scholars in the world as professors at Chicago: Shirley Jackson Case, Edgar Goodspeed, H. N. Wieman, W. C. Bower, E. C. Colwell, William A. Irwin, W. E. Garrison, E. E. Aubrey, Charles Hartshorne, Paul Douglas (Types of Economic Reform). Douglas was later a senator from Illinois and was touted for president, but he would not run. I wrote an MA thesis with E. J. Chave and a BD thesis with Charles Gilkey, dean of the Rockefeller Chapel, who taught homiletics.

At Chicago I did an MA thesis under Chave. The title of that thesis was *The Disciple Laymen's Concept of the Function of the Disciples Minister.* It involved developing a research instrument and treating the results statistically. I had taken statistics at Texas, and Chave taught statistics in the Divinity School. I thought my thesis was great. The boys at the House were in awe of me because several of them had had a rough time pleasing Chave.

I was invited into a secret society of theologians that had been established about 1912 because it was unpopular to be liberal. The next year I was elected president, following Oliver Harrison. I spent my year convincing the membership we should write "finis" to this organization. It was no longer needed. A few diehards among the faculty who had been early members were upset, but we killed it. (Years later, 1959, I tried to kill the weak "Dad's Club" at Bruce Shulkey School in Fort Worth's Wedgwood area while president of it, to strengthen the PTA, but failed.)

A particularly important event occurred that summer while I was directing Ski-Hi section of Cheley Camps in Colorado. Ruth, unbeknownst to me, applied for and got a scholarship to Chicago Theological Seminary, just a block south of Disciples House. She was a Congregationalist, having been baptized by the minister of the First Congregational Church at Oberlin during Religious Emphasis Week. I remember being so pleased and proud of her when she stepped off the train in Chicago that fall. We could finally be together.

Ruth was a marvelous student. She took an MA in two years and graduated summa cum laude. Her major work was with Eastman in Religion and the Arts. She also found what would be her ultimate career in a part-time job in the library of CTS. Years later that proved very helpful and meaningful.

Following our marriage on June 16, 1938, and a brief honeymoon, Ruth and I went to Chicago, where I had to report on my thesis to the Disciple ministers in the Chicago area. It was not received with much enthusiasm. They had a more sentimental concept of ministry. I remember that Irv Lunger and Davison, later of South Bend, were there. I've forgotten the others.

The next day, Ruth and I supervised the departure of eighty youngsters for Cheley Camps. I learned that "Chief" Cheley, owner of the camps, had put Ruth and me on the Union Pacific train with eight Jewish campers. They didn't like being segregated like that, and I didn't blame them. It was done without my permission or even awareness. We took the big red busses of the Estes Park Bus Co. to Estes Park from Denver. I directed the Intermediate Boys Camp (Ski-Hi) for the third time (1934, 1937, 1938), and Ruth worked in the arts and crafts area and in the camp store.

At the end of camp, in late August, we brought the Chicago gang back on the Zephyr with no segregation this time. After spending the night in Kimbark House of CTS, where we were to live starting about October 1, we took a train for Beaumont, where I performed the marriage rites for Marguerite and Jimmy at Mother's home, 2520 North St. It was a rainy afternoon. We waited for the rain to stop so Judge Nall could come over for the wedding.

Ruth and I then went to Croton for a couple of weeks before the opening of school. We settled into our newly refurbished apartment in Kimbark House. We and the Channels, for whom I had performed the marriage that fall, challenged Dean Ames on the "no marriage" rule. (Dean Ames did not allow married students to continue their scholarship while a Disciples scholar.) He capitulated.

We ate at the Kimbark Cooperative next door. We paid $3 per week and worked six hours per week for ten meals. Meals were served on Sunday, but I was away at my church in Hollywood, Illinois. Occasionally, Ruth went with me.

I served as minister to Hollywood Community Church, west of Chicago near the Brookfield Zoo during 1938–39, which had previously been served by Fred Miller and then Oliver Harrison. The people were genuinely nice to us when we got married. I remember especially the Bishops, the Hoffs, Robert and Helen Goss. The Sessions clock that sat for years above the fireplace in our house on W. Lowden, Fort Worth, was a gift from the Bishop family. We were able to stay in touch with some of these families for many years.

We thoroughly enjoyed this year of study and life together. Ruth really found herself and made a straight A record. She has a keen, retentive mind. Dr. Wilhem Pauck, who taught theology, and whom Ruth studiously avoided, said to me, after she graduated summa cum laude, "In my family, the men have the brains." Ruth had passed the theology section of the comprehensives by reading one book by Brown on the history of Christian thought. Pauck had graded that section. I had studied under Pauck and made Bs and As. Ruth enjoyed Eastman and Spinka, who taught Church History, with special emphasis on Eastern Orthodoxy. Years later we attended Eastern Orthodox services of the Russian variety in Helsinki and in Kiev.

I took a second master's degree at Ames's insistence in 1938 and earned a Bachelor of Divinity in 1939. The Disciples House and the scholarship meant so much to me. I was happy to be able to make a gift that more than repaid the scholarship money that I received many years ago. It has been deeply satisfying to be a Chicago Disciples House graduate.

Chapter 5

PASTORATES

As my academic career ended, or so I thought, I applied to the State secretaries of the Christian Church (Disciples of Christ) in Texas, Indiana, and Ohio. No response from Pat Henry of Texas or Guy Hoover of Indiana. Ohio Secretary Gaines Cook enthusiastically invited us to look at the Hicksville Christian Church. Harold Munroe, Yale BD, had just spent five years there in a uniquely successful ministry. After going over on the train for a trial sermon, I was invited to become the minister of First Christian Church, Hicksville, Ohio. My BD thesis, under Gilkey, had been in preaching values in contemporary drama. I don't think I used one stitch of that material in sermons the twenty months I was there.

However, it was a constructive ministry. Munroe had left a fine heritage. We followed as best we could with camps, youth conferences, and weekday Bible School in cooperation with the public school, which was just a block away. There were some fine people there: Don Evans, Doctor and Mrs. Hofmeister (Osteopath), Mary Jane Carr, Max Carr, Gordon Rowe, and many others. We continued to hear from some of them for many years. In 1980 we met the Evans boy and his wife and the Hofmeisters in Defiance on our trip to Canada and New England with Dan Dipert Tours.

The most memorable event at the Hicksville Church was the Christmas play in 1940, our second year. A thirty-five-year-old man, decorator-artist, son of a local osteopath, had had an affair which the community knew about. He felt guilty and wanted to do an act of penance for the entire community. He got my support. We went forward with our Christmas pageant, much as in previous years, but he created three beautiful angels out of plaster of paris which were hung from the highest point of the roof, with the help of Karl Fox and some others. Karl was a carpenter.

Bolts and a pulley were put through the roof; a dark blue denim curtain covered the organ pipes, and these angels hung in front of the denim. The effect was magnificent. I took a picture using time exposure with a camera I had given Ruth. In the pageant Ruth and Farrell Evans arranged a light dimmer with buckets of salt water. The pageant was highly effective. Most of the people in Hicksville came and filled the sanctuary for both services we offered. I was the reader. All of our eighty youth participated.

Just before Christmas, three strange men appeared in the congregation. H. L. Pickerill, my old TCU professor now at the University of Michigan, had called me about East Grand Boulevard Church in Detroit and said that I might be visited. These men were Sam Ball, Ken Siler, and Floyd Jarnagin. They heard the sermon and, after church, came to the parsonage and invited us to come to Detroit to meet with the Board of Elders. We made this journey in our little green Chevy that Dad Siegfried had given us. We ate and spent the night with the Ken Silers, visited with folks the next day, met elders that night, and drove home through a blinding snowstorm because we had to be back for the Bible classes at the school the next morning. When I closed my eyes about three a.m., I could see snowflakes coming at us through the car headlights. The invitation came, and we accepted. Thus began a very interesting, significant, and enjoyable four and one-half years in Detroit.

However, the Hicksville folks were quite mad at us for leaving after a year and a half as their minister. There was no farewell party. Gaines Cook, the state secretary, came to help them choose a successor. He confirmed that they were mad at us for leaving so soon. The salary there was $100 per month and parsonage. We paid utilities and all auto expenses out of that salary. There were no "perks." At the Detroit Church we started at $2700 per year, but we paid our own rent for a four-room apartment. It cost $50.00 per month. It had a western exposure on the second floor at 978 East Grand Boulevard. Ruth and I felt a great sigh of relief. Hicksville had rather smothered us. Detroit was more like Cleveland, Chicago, Columbus, Fort Worth—our heritage.

East Grand Boulevard Christian Church

We moved to Detroit about February 1, 1941. We had avoided a pregnancy in Hicksville. Now, in Detroit we conceived, and Mark was born July 7, 1942. When I announced his birth to the congregation, they broke into applause. Dr. Edgar DeWitt Jones, pastor of Woodward Avenue Christian

Paul as pastor in Detroit 1941. Wassenich family collection.

Church and former president of the National Council of Churches, sent a congratulatory telegram, saying, among other things, "Why didn't you begin with Matthew?" I wrote him a note saying: "Didn't you know that Mark was written earlier than Matthew; in fact, it is the first Gospel."

The Detroit folk were delightful. They liked us, and we liked them. They were high school graduates, not college people, with a few exceptions. They were laboring people and members of labor unions, working in the auto industry and related businesses such as steel and rubber. They were genuinely Christian and, as "Pick" had said in urging me to accept their invitation to be their pastor, "If they're convinced something is Christian, they will try to do it." I found this to be true.

I'll never forget Sunday, December 7th, 1941—Pearl Harbor Day! (Ruth and I visited Pearl Harbor thirty-seven years later, December 10, 1978, and saw those sunken ships and visited the shrine erected above them.) On December 7, 1941, I preached morning and evening sermons. I changed my evening sermon topic to try to minister to our need for calm and courage in the face of this attack and our entry into World War II.

That summer of 1941 Ruth and I had driven through Ohio, West Virginia, Pennsylvania to New York City, Cape Cod, New Haven, Connecticut (Yale University), Boston (Harvard), and Salem, Massachusetts. It was our last trip for fun for the duration of the war, because of gasoline rationing.

Detroit geared up for war. It was known as "the arsenal of democracy." People came to church and insisted on continuing the evening service, but many of them fell asleep in the evening service despite my stimulating sermons.

I was a pacifist. When I registered for the draft in Hicksville, I signed as a Conscientious Objector. I had been razzed and jeered about it by "the village idiot," but not by responsible people in my Hicksville Church or my Detroit Church. In Detroit I told my Elders about my pacifist convictions and preached a sermon about it. When the Civil Defense asked preachers to sell war bonds, I said: "No, I cannot conscientiously do this." I called the Elders together and told them about it. They discussed the matter and said, "Don't worry about it. If you get any undue pressure, refer that person to us." I did think I could conscientiously serve as an air raid warden. I took the training and went to block meetings where I was treated as some odd character because of my CO position and my not drinking beer.

Walking the streets during an air raid practice session was scary. All lights were off. Everyone except wardens, fire, ambulance, and police stayed indoors until the "all clear siren."

At the height of the war, the church had fifty-five people in the military services, including one woman. I sent them a monthly newsletter. I had baptized about twenty-five of them. We had a very active young marrieds class.

One of those I baptized was Charles "Chuck" Bare. He had gone to one year of college and had pronounced himself an atheist. Our youth group had invited him to explain why he was an atheist. This had happened about a month before I arrived on the scene. His wife taught Sunday School. One day she arranged for me to meet Chuck when he came in the car to pick her up after Church. Then she arranged for Ruth and me to come to supper, after which she left Chuck and me alone in the parlor while she and Ruth washed the dishes.

Chuck and I hit it off very well. The next New Year's Eve, they suggested we stay up all night to welcome the new year. We did that. About 3:00 a.m., he said, "That lady sponsoring the youth group isn't really up to the job. I could do a much better job." I said, "Well, sure, Chuck, but the Board wouldn't stand for a non-member to sponsor the youth group." He said, "Well, I think we can take care of that very soon." So we talked about confession, baptism, and church membership. The next Sunday morning, he came forward and made the good confession.

When I baptized him that evening, the church was full. Leon Jett, a bachelor of about thirty-eight years, stood in the balcony as close as he could get to the baptistry. After the baptism, Leon came into the robing room all aflutter, saying, "Preacher, preacher, you didn't get one hank of his hair under the water." At first, I couldn't imagine what he meant. I asked, "What did you say?" He repeated it. It dawned on me what was bothering him. He thought the devil might lay hold of that hank of hair and snatch Chuck away from Jesus and God. I said, "Leon, let's just let the devil have that hank of hair."

Amazingly, Chuck declared for the ministry, but he did not want to have an exemption from the war. He went off to war in Europe as a private and fought in the Battle of the Bulge. His wife, Mae, and their son, Phil, born about the same time as Mark, came to Chicago the next year when we were there and found a job. Her idea was to have things set up so that Chuck could attend the University of Chicago. When he got there, he took a battery of tests that would give him his BA degree if he passed three of the four sections. He passed two. So he went to Lexington and enrolled in Transylvania, got a BA in three years, and then enrolled at Transylvania Theological Seminary and got the BD. He served several pastorates. His wife died at about age fifty. He remarried and sold insurance while he ministered to churches in Florida on Sundays. We exchanged Christmas greetings, and he came to see us once in Austin and once in Fort Worth at Trinity Terrace.

In the middle of the war, about 1943, I changed my mind about pacifism. I had followed very closely the famous argument published each week in the journal *Christian Century.* I felt Niebuhr's arguments were more reasonable than Charles Clayton Morrison's. Niebuhr said that although war is profoundly evil, pacifism is not always the Christian answer. Hitler, and all he meant for the future of Europe and the world, was worse than war. Hitler must be defeated or Christian values would have no chance of survival.

Having worked out this new orientation, I thought I should volunteer. I went to Navy, then Air Force, then Army; but none would take me because I was hard of hearing. I bought my first hearing aid, a Zenith, for $25.00. I carried batteries in my hip pocket and in the case in my chest pocket. It wasn't a particularly good aid. In 1978 I paid $900 for aids in both ears.

After living with this idea for about three months, which changed my basic orientation of the past ten years, I preached a sermon expressing my changed position before my congregation in Detroit. The people of East Grand were wonderful. No one said "Aha, I told you so." All had been exceedingly kind and understanding of my pacifist position.

Floyd Jarnagin, an Elder who was a University of Michigan engineering graduate and then with Chrysler-Plymouth, suggested that I mimeograph the sermon and send it in my next letter to our fifty-five service men and women. I did so.

Answers came back from all over the world. Among the replies I got were two of special significance. One was from Kenneth Springer. He had gone into the service as a CO to work as a Red Cross orderly. He told me what happened to him. He went into the jungles of New Guinea daily to rescue wounded men. The lines were so unclear that he often ended up behind enemy lines. Several of the hospital corpsmen had been killed by the Japanese, who had no respect for the Red Cross they wore on their uniform. His commander had asked him to wear a side-arm for self-defense. He just hoped he would never have to shoot anyone, and he didn't.

Another response was from a married man with one child who was a pilot flying supplies over the Burma hump. He said he was sorry to read of my changed position because when he was discouraged about why he was there, he told himself he was fighting for my right to be a conscientious objector.

Many people from Kentucky and Tennessee came to Detroit to work in the defense plants. They brought their prejudices with them. In July 1943 there was a terrible race riot in Detroit. Thirty-three people were killed (thirty blacks and three whites). Just before this riot, Rosa Page Welch, a black Disciple from Chicago who had a beautiful voice and a very pleasing personality, had been to our church as part of a "Preaching Mission." The preacher was Watterworth of Lansing. I had preached for him the previous year. Rosa Page stayed in the home of Mr. and Mrs. Paul Bunch. The people loved her. I wrote a report of the race riot and sent it to the *Christian Evangelist*, as I was the Michigan correspondent for that journal. I received widespread favorable comment on it from all over the US.

Russell H. Koppin was the outstanding layman in that church. He was chief executive officer of Koppin and Chrysler, a firm that made special refrigeration units for industry. On the first Labor Day of my ministry there, I preached a sermon from a Christian perspective about laboring people and their rights. Russ Koppin, seated in the front row, squirmed noticeably during the sermon. I began to realize he disagreed almost totally with what I was saying. After church, I invited him to dinner. We didn't talk much about the sermon, although he did say that it was very difficult for him to agree with me from a manager's point of view. But he continued to be supportive of my ministry. I baptized his son a year later.

In 1944 we decided that after the war we would move the church five miles east to Cadieux Road and change the name to Bethany Christian Church. We bought six lots and dedicated them with the help of Dr. Edgar DeWitt Jones. The church did build there under the pastors who followed me. We bought a parsonage nearby, 6184 Oldtown Street, so Ruth, Mark, and I moved out of the apartment on East Grand Boulevard. We lived in the parsonage about two years.

When we left, at the last board meeting, Russ Koppin stood up and said they would remember Paul Wassenich for many things, but especially for what he taught them about race relations. Russ told me privately that he thought I wasn't dry behind the ears when I preached that Labor Day sermon in 1941, but as I continued to emphasize Christian, humane labor relations, he said to himself that if he was a Christian, he would have to try it out. He added, "Darned if it didn't work. We have a much better spirit in our work for now. So, thanks for that, too. I couldn't bring myself to say that before the board because some of my employees are on that board."

Following is a letter written by Paul on D-day to his church's servicemen. A copy of it was found by Evelyn Speak and her husband of Stockport, England, when they were cleaning out his father's house after his death in 2016. Mr. T. B. Speak of Scarborough, England, served with the Fleet Air Army during World War II and was in the Pacific flying Hell Cats from the British aircraft carrier Indomitable, which was attached to the US Pacific fleet. Evelyn and her husband were moved by the sentiment and faith that Paul showed. They researched Paul on the internet, found Mark's name in the obituary, looked up his address, and sent a copy of the letter to him. Following her generous and thoughtful act, Mark and Linda have enjoyed a correspondence with Evelyn and hope to meet her someday.

Detroit, Michigan
"D" Day
June 6th,
1944

Dear Friends in the Service:
It is 7:15 a.m. on "D" day and I am at the office. At 4:50 this morning Mr. Herbert Cundiff called (he works nights at Packard) and informed me that "The invasion is on." I could not sleep after that, thinking of the horror and the crucial importance of it. I dressed, came to the Church, and at 6:30 put a sign on the outdoor bulletin board reading: "Today is "D" Day—Come in and pray—Church open all day." Then I fixed the interior of the Church as beautifully as possible, turning on the indirect lights in the chancel and the one over the baptistry which lights the cross. As yet no one has come in to pray. Then I took the Service Men's Roll and the pulpit Bible into the pulpit with me. I read Psalm 140 and verses 38–48 of the fifth chapter of Matthew. I prayed a long prayer audibly, as though there were an audience and you and your parents, particularly, were in it. I prayed for justice, righteousness, for our enemies—that they might be chastened in spirit and that we might be too—so that our minds

and souls may meet on a common, redemptive, spiritual ground after the fighting is over. I prayed for each of you by name, reading your name off the Service Roll and praying for your spiritual and physical needs and safety as best I could understand them. I prayed for your parents and your loved ones, wives, children, friends. I prayed particularly for those of you whom I knew to be in the invasion area and possibly at that very moment being wounded. My very soul goes out to you. I prayed both for you and for enemy youth that out of this dreadful experience, which somehow coordinates and brings to focus all our corporate sin for generations, you may gain an insight by which you may be able to point mankind to a spiritual as well as a political solution to the world's ills. Your words will be listened to with tremendous interest when you return. Give much thought and prayer to what you will say about the enemy, about war, about anything when you come back. Undoubtedly before you arrive home, you will have a furlough or at least considerable time on deck a steamer returning home. Think about what you will say and what you will leave unsaid.

And think about it in God's presence—conversing with Him about it.

May God in his infinite wisdom minister to your needs.

Yours in Christ, Amen
Paul G. Wassenich, Your Pastor

P.S. Now, on the Communion table are the Service Men's Roll, the open Bible, a global map of the world, and a lighted candle. Whether or not anyone comes in to pray, these symbols of the Church's concern are here in God's house where you loved to worship when you were at home. Our people are not in the habit of coming to the Church at off hours for prayer. They doubtless are praying at home and will be all during the day and the terrible weeks ahead.

PGW

Chapter 6

CHICAGO, PREPARING FOR TEXAS

It was too bad that the call to the Texas Bible Chair came at this time. I would have liked being at East Grand to welcome our fifty-five service people home from the war.

Bob Hopkins of the United Christian Missionary Society came to worship with us and to talk to me about succeeding Frank L. Jewett at the Texas Bible Chair. Oh! What a difficult decision! Ruth and I thought our Detroit work was very significant, and we hated to leave at this time. However, Dr. Jewett was seventy years old and needed to retire. Teaching did appeal to me. I had recently taught a theology course at Great Lakes College in Detroit, having been recommended for that job by the executive of the Detroit Council of Churches.

So, after turning it down once and having Bob Hopkins come back to me to insist that I undertake it, I made a deal with him that Dr. Jewett would stay on another year while I took refresher courses at the University of Chicago Divinity School and possibly worked on a PhD. We agreed to go; the salary was $3,000 plus parsonage and utilities.

The move was hard on us emotionally and hard on the members of the church. As I said the benediction, the choir and congregation surprised me by singing "God be with you 'til we meet again." I was overwhelmed and broke into tears. I had managed the final sermon very well, but the united singing of that hymn undid me.

Ruth cried all night the night we made the decision to leave. We loved those Detroit people. Thirty-five years later, on our way to Canada in September–October, 1980, we were surprised by thirty-three of them at a dinner given by Russ Koppin at the Detroit Athletic Club.

When we returned to the University of Chicago Divinity School, I had hoped to get most of the work on a doctorate completed that year, but could not. I learned a lot that year that was useful to me in my thirty years of teaching, but it would have been better if I could have completed the class work and prelims for a doctorate.

Mark was three years old during this year. He had an old tricycle given to us by the Wilbur Hoff family of Hollywood, Illinois. He rode around the block on nice days.

I remember clearly that when the news came out that the US had dropped the atomic bomb on Hiroshima, I took Mark in my lap and, looking out at the university from our front window, I tried to explain to him what had happened. I tried to instill in his mind the ideal of peace on earth so that such devastation would not be repeated. I doubt that he could understand much of what was happening.

When V-J Day came, Carter Boren and I went down to the loop and watched the wild celebration of the end of the war. Irvin Lunger, Pastor of University Church, asked me to address the Sunday Luncheon about the atomic age. He didn't agree with what I said. I said as terrible as the bomb was, it wasn't any worse than the millions of bombs that Germans and Americans had used to annihilate European cities. I didn't think it would stop wars. I didn't think we could stop nations from developing it.

It now appears I was essentially right. But, as of this writing, there has been something like a nuclear stalemate. It has become more clear to me that an allout nuclear war would be the end of civilization. Today's nuclear bombs are a hundred times more destructive than those first two bombs dropped on Hiroshima and Nagasaki.

Years later (probably 1959) in Fort Worth, the bombardier who dropped the Hiroshima bomb was speaking in Fort Worth, and Irv Lunger's brother, Harold, and his wife had him to lunch at their house. They asked me to join them. He was overwhelmed with guilt, and we tried to help him recover his self-esteem.

The best thing that happened was that Ruth and I conceived Tommy. He was born at Chicago Lying-in Hospital, right across Maryland Street from our apartment, on March 30, 1946.

We spent June and July of 1946 with Mom and Dad Siegfried in Croton. We had sold our car to a dealer in Detroit, from whom we had bought it. He promised to sell us a car, which we needed to go to Texas, but reneged on his promise. So we headed south on the train. Mom and the judge met us in Houston and took us to Beaumont, where we spent about four days. Then Mom rented a house at McFaddin's beach, or perhaps High Island, and Marguerite and Jimmy and their kids joined us for a few days. Louis and Mickey came down for a couple of days. Louis had a craft shop business in Beaumont. He was back from his stint in the Air Force during the war.

Chapter 7

TEXAS BIBLE CHAIR

The remainder of our lives were spent in Texas, primarily Austin (eleven years) and Fort Worth (from 1957 on). I went to Austin about the third week of August 1946 and got the furniture into the huge Bible Chair parsonage at 2007 University Avenue, right across the street from the impressive main entrance to the university with its fountain and prancing horses and the walk leading up to the skyscraper library, the centerpiece of the university.

Someone, probably Bill Hilgers, took me to Lockhart to meet Mrs. Blanks, Bill's great-grandmother, who had given the funds to start the Bible Chair in 1905. The property for the Bible Chair, across from the fountain, was an unbelievably valuable asset. When we arrived in August, we were amazed at the size of the house.

The war had ended, and the campus was inundated with GIs, many of them seeking religious understanding that covered the unusual experiences they had in the war. Housing was in truly short supply with the campus overflowing with ex-service men who were taking advantage of the GI Bill of Rights, which provided significant help for a college education and boosted the enrollment by about 20,000. When I took my MA there ten years earlier, the enrollment was 7,000. By 1991, some forty-five years later, it was 50,000!

As we were moving into the Bible Chair parsonage, a delivery man said to me, "How in the world did you get housing like this?" I told him some of the history of Texas Bible Chair and that we were really living a very public life in that we were housing six people in this place in addition to the student classes and an infant church. He was mollified!

Because housing was scarce, men, particularly veterans, were begging for rooms. We ended up with six men, all veterans, living on the place. Two men, Sam Lauderdale and Frank Smith, ran a water line and gas line

Texas Bible Chair and Parsonage, 2007 University Blvd. Austin, TX, 1950. Courtesy of Texas Bible Chair.

from the residence to what had been servant quarters behind the house and lived there for a year. Two ex-Marines lived in one of the bedrooms on the second floor of the residence. Two other GIs, Clyde Isaachs and Conrad White, lived in the western room on the second floor of the Bible Chair Building.

Four of them, Lauderdale, Smith, Isaachs, and Charles Sansom, were immensely helpful in starting the church and the Disciples Student Fellowship (DSF). The two buildings were yellow brick with a lovely garden patio between them where the DSF often met. Forty-five years later, it had a million-dollar building, but it had not flourished in terms of membership.

After I started the DSF, we often had fifty students there on the patio or in the building on Sunday nights. Some of those students became lifelong friends. I also started a state DSF. We held our first meeting at a Lutheran Camp near Round Rock.

My main work was teaching. UT gave course credit for Bible classes taught by seven Bible chairs. The Texas Bible Chair was the first established in 1905 by Frank Jewett. I preached at University Christian Church, Austin, in 1985 at the celebration of the eightieth anniversary of the founding of Texas Bible Chair. Charles Cox, who succeeded me in 1957, taught there for nearly thirty-five years. Bible Chairs were thrown out of all state colleges and universities in Texas in 1987.

Some people (Frank Jewett, Chester Crow, Judge Beauchamp) pressed me to start University Christian Church. Chester Crow at Hyde Park Christian Church even sent several students over to help us. They included Sam Lauderdale, Frank Smith, and several girls, one of whom was a pianist who helped us considerably. John Barclay, pastor of Central Christian Church, and others pressured me not to start University Christian Church. Pat Henry, Sr., the State Secretary, would not lend his support. It seemed to me that since we were the only major denomination that did not have a church at the campus, we should start such a church.

Starting in the fall of 1946, I continued the courses that Dr. Jewett had found most popular: Life and Teachings of Jesus and the Life and Letters of Paul. Enrollment in the four courses totaled about fifty per semester. After I failed a GI (who threatened to beat me up for flunking him), the attendance dropped to about thirty. I thought I was going to have to give up.

University Christian Church began in September 1946. We met in the chapel where we had pews but no cushions. There were twelve original charter members. (Ruth said eight of them were librarians.) We grew rapidly, but they were mostly students, about eighty. Judge Beauchamp had insisted that there be a category of associate members; so many people belonged to Central Christian Church and were associate members of University Christian Church.

When Lawrence Bash came as the minister in the fall of 1949, there was 76¢ in the treasury. One of his first demands was that all associate members become full members. At that point, this church really took off.

Charley Sansom was the church's first paid employee. She not only did the bulletin and a thousand other things on a part-time basis, but she also helped Ruth raise the kids. One day Tommy was crawling around on the porch while Charley watched him. She got busy in the office; and when she looked for him, he was gone. She found him next door in the Alpha Phi house.

Our first Christmas the DSF wanted a big banquet. We cleared the pews out of the chapel and set up tables and chairs. Mary Jane Horton led a group who cooked in the Wassenich kitchen for fifty or more. It was a terrific turkey dinner. Clyde Isaachs presided and introduced the speaker, a biologist who had just published a significant book. He said, "We have all enjoyed this turkey filled with sage; now we are going to hear from a sage filled with turkey."

Another memory from that evening was the piece of mistletoe hanging under the stairway. Sam Lauderdale backed Mary Jane Horton under the mistletoe and gave her a very significant kiss. They later married and established a bakery, Mary of Puddin' Hill, in Greenville, Texas.

During our first year, we filled the chapel, opened the office, and set up folding chairs. All space was utilized. At the end of the first year of University Christian Church, we were having 100 to 125 in church each Sunday. They were mostly students, but we had about thirty adults and graduate students who were either members or associate members. I had hoped the board (Tom Beauchamp was Chairman) would invite me to be the minister of the church. But, No! I had invited Negroes over to speak to DSF, and Beauchamp wanted none of that. The rest of the board followed him.

They looked at Harold Glen Brown (assistant at East Dallas Christian Church) and turned him down as too young. Actually, he was too liberal. He became an extraordinarily successful minister at Memorial Christian Church in Midland; First Christian Church in Portland, Oregon; and Community Christian Church in Kansas City. When he retired, he was invited to teach ministerial practice at Brite Divinity School, which he did for five years. A professorship in ministerial practice was established in his name.

The board chose an Australian, T. W. Sisterson of Bonham, to be pastor of the one-year-old University Christian Church. He was a fine man but didn't have the personality to attract students. He left after two years.

Next, the board, led by F. W. Savage, chose Lawrence Bash from St. Joseph, Missouri, to be the pastor of University Christian Church. He led the church in building the present million-dollar structure. At age forty-five, in 1958, he accepted the call to Country Club Christian Church, Kansas City, Missouri. In Fort Worth he told me that he really felt guilty going off and leaving the congregation of University Church with a heavy debt, but this was about as late in life as he would get such a call; so he thought he must go. I concurred. However, no pastor since has been able to galvanize the people at UCC, Austin, to action the way Bash did.

This is the way the Wassenichs read the Christmas story together on the night before Christmas. As Daddy reads, Mark, left, and Tom, right, move the figures of the crèche in keeping with the story. Jim will soon be old enough to help.

Helping Families Read Together

By Paul G. Wassenich

"DADDY, why was Daniel put in the lions' den?"

"Why, because he prayed to God, instead of King Darius, Mark. Why do you ask?"

"Well, the teacher at school read us a part of the Book of Daniel during the story hour today and I didn't understand it at all. Could you read the Book of Daniel to me?"

"Yes, I could, Son, but it is rather long and we couldn't read all of it tonight. But we could read a couple of chapters each evening until we complete the book."

That is just what we did. And with it we had some real discussions about miracles. We read the Book of Daniel from the American translation so that it was more easily understood. It is not exactly a book one would select to read to a third grader, yet since he was interested and puzzled we decided to go ahead.

Last Christmas we had a delightful time reading the birth stories as given in Luke and Matthew. We have a set of figures—the infant Jesus, Mary, Joseph, manger, stable, camels, wise men, shepherds, angels, sheep, donkey. As Daddy read the story of the shepherds coming to the manger as given in Luke, and then of the wise men coming and the flight into Egypt as in Matthew, our two boys, eight and four years old, manipulated the figures on the coffee table, before the fireplace. It was our most satisfying "Night before Christmas."

Psalm Serves as Grace

Church school helped us a lot with grace at meals by having our oldest child read scriptures. He gradually learned Psalm 100, from the Authorized Version of the Bible. He told us one evening that he had recited this psalm in a worship program. We have always wanted him to have a happy experience in saying grace at meals. But, usually it was quite forced and so we have resorted to singing "For health and strength and daily food we praise thy name, O Lord." This particular evening we asked him to say Psalm 100 while we bowed our heads.

Mother noted after the "Amen" that the last two verses provided a lovely grace at meals: "Enter into his gates with thanksgiving, and into his courts with

Paul G. Wassenich is director of the Texas Bible Chair, serving students of the University of Texas, Austin, Texas.

28

Courtesy of *The Bethany Guide.*

The new church building was built around the old Bible Chair to maintain a continuity of teaching and church services. Then the old building was demolished and the bricks sold one at a time as a building fund-raiser. The state capitol is in background, 1954. Courtesy of University Christian Church brochure.

As part of the Bible Chair, I introduced a course in 1950–51 called "The Great Ideas of the Bible" and used Harry Emerson Fosdick's text. I had a section formerly called "Christian Teachings about Courtship, Marriage and Family," or "Marriage and Morals," as the students called it. The enrollment took off, and soon my annual enrollment figures in all four courses totaled 399. I publicized this news among the Christian Churches and reported annually to the Texas State Convention.

While this good news was helping the Bible Chair, Lawrence Bash was developing the church rapidly. University Christian built a nice parsonage for the Bible Chair at 810 East 32nd Street. They took over the old parsonage to use it for Sunday School rooms, tore down the Bible Chair Building, and included classrooms, library, and an office for the Bible Chair in the new University Christian Church building.

We loved the house they built for us. There were five huge oak trees on the lot. We moved in January 1950. Our third son, James Paul, was born

1954

An Invitation to You . . .

This is an invitation to the Christian people of Texas to attend the dedication of the new University Christian Church in Austin on Sunday, May 23rd. The picture above (taken April 1st) shows the building as it appears from the University of Texas campus. It was taken before the windows were placed. At the left is the four-story Robert E. Lee dormitory and at the right is the Texas Bible Chair building.

We are suggesting that every church in Texas appoint an "official representative" to the Dedication Service. Morning Worship will be at 10:50 a.m. and the Dedication Service at 3 p.m. The services are open to everyone, of course, but we want those attending the State Convention to feel they have a special invitation in recognition of support and encouragement the convention has given in recent years to the building of this church.

Primarily to serve students from all over the state at the University of Texas, this sanctuary is the first of two units planned. An educational plant is to be added as soon as funds are available.

Speakers for the Dedication Service will include Dr. Cleveland Kleihauer, Hollywood, president of the International Convention; Dr. George Oliver Taylor, Indianapolis; Dr. M. E. Sadler and Rev. Chester Crow.

Rev. Lawrence W. Bash, minister, will preach at the morning service.

UNIVERSITY CHRISTIAN CHURCH

University Ave. at 21st — *"Across from Littlefield Fountain"* — Austin, Texas

Building University Christian Church, Austin, 1954. Courtesy of University Christian Church brochure.

MEXICO BOUND are these four students who spent two weeks in Aguascalientes on a goodwill mission sponsored by the University Christian Church. They are shown above with the Rev. Paul G. Wassenich, director of the Texas Bible Chair, who conducted the trip. Five other students went. Front row, kneeling: Dane Bowen and Mr. Wassenich. Standing center: Joyce Yocum. Seated in car: Dick Crews and Evelyn Cheatham.

Paul led student groups on service trips to Disciples missions in Mexico. Courtesy of *Daily Texan*, University of Texas.

June 6, 1950. With three little ones, we were happy. The boys had friends and loved the neighborhood. The Swensons, Hailes, and Foxes were good neighbors.

Dr. Emmett Redford, chairman of the Government Department, invited me to consider a half-time ministry at Johnson City. University Christian Church called Clarence Doss, a friend from Chicago days, to do the student work, so I could accept a pastorate. Lyndon Johnson was a nominal member of the Johnson City church. He and Emmett Redford were good lifelong friends. After we moved to Fort Worth, Emmett's mother died. I was asked to handle the funeral. The church was packed, so when Lyndon Johnson showed up, late as usual, there was no more room. He stood during the service. He was a senator at that time.

While in Austin, I served as vice president of the Austin Ministerial Alliance (1947–48) and as president of the Campus Religious Workers' Association (1951–52). In 1956–57, I served as vice president of the State Convention of Christian Churches.

April 25, 1956

Dear Dr. Wassenich:

When I first came into your class nine months ago, I came as one who felt himself being shoved into the ministry. Because of your insight into the practical and real values of service, because of your devotion to a living Christianity, I feel as if I have truly met a man whose cup runneth over. Now I know I am being led.

Believe me, there is far more behind these two words, "Thank you."

Sincerely yours,

Bill

Bill Moyers

Dr. Paul Wassenich
Texas Bible Chair
University of Texas
Austin, Texas

Thank-you letter from student Bill Moyers. Wassenich family collection.

When we started DSF in 1946, we had fifty to sixty students who were active. At the end of that first year, I was given a tennis racket for my work with the DSF and the fifty sermons I had preached for the infant church that consisted of mostly students.

When I retired in 1976, Harold Dowler, who was pastor then of University Christian Church, called me and asked, "Wasn't this church your last pastorate?" I told him it was, except for a few interims that I had done. He invited me to come to Austin on a certain date as they wanted to give me the Honored Minister's Pin. They also gave me a check for $3600 from 360 former students and friends in the present University Christian Church. This surprise event was organized by Charles Sansom. Coincidentally, Ruth and I happened to be in Tyler a few years later to present a series of lectures and were able to be with Charley when Charles died.

In the late 1990s, a whole new role for the Bible Chair opened. Three people deserve recognition: Charles Cox, a thirty-plus year professor in Texas Bible Chair and a member of the board; David Green, director of the Texas Bible Chair and of student work for University Christian Church; and Dr. Michael White, chairman of the Classical Studies and Department of Religious Studies at the university. I also praise Bill Hilgers and his son, Paul, for the great work they did in this transition and the development of a new and significant way to teach religion at UT Austin.

I taught at many summer conferences in Athens, Brownwood, the Valley, and Center Point and spoke in many churches and at Religious Emphasis Weeks at Texas State University, Texas A&M, Texas Tech, Southern Methodist University, and at interdenominational conferences in Oklahoma, Colorado, New Mexico, Minnesota, Wisconsin, and Indiana.

Paul gave speeches and delivered sermons all over Texas throughout his life. Here is a sample from the 1940s and 50s:

- Five talks plus visits to dorms for discussion during Religious Emphasis Week, March 8–12, 1948, Southwest Texas State College, San Marcos.
- Baccalaureate address to West Texas State College, May 20, 1948, Canyon.
- Religious Emphasis Week addresses in Chapel and Fondren Auditorium, Southern Methodist University, Dallas, February 16, 1949.
- Sermon "Through Waterless Places," First Christian Church, Corpus Christi, December 3, 1950.
- Convocation address to "a packed gymnasium . . . his topic 'Theos or Chaos'" Religious Emphasis Week, Texas Technological College, Lubbock, November 6, 1951.
- Commencement Sermon, Huntsville High School, Huntsville, May 18, 1952.
- Bible study: "A Man Who Made a Comeback," and a seminar on "Choosing a College," Texas Youth Convention of the Christian Churches, TCU, Fort Worth, July 23–25, 1952.
- Sermon "On Loving Yourself," First Christian Church, Beaumont, August 9, 1953.
- Address "Religion at State University," Rotary Club of Beaumont, September 23, 1953.
- "Teachers are needed by parents to help raise children," address to Austin Teachers Workshop. Sharing in the workshops were Governor

Allan Shivers and Dr. M. S. Savage, president of Huston-Tilletson College, 1954.

- Chapel address, Religious Emphasis Week, Southern Methodist University, Dallas, February 17, 1955.
- General Session addresses and workshop leader, Texas Convention of Christian Churches, Galveston, April 16–20, 1955.
- "Pilgrimage to Palestine: A Word Picture from Actual Observations," Exchange Club, Driskill Hotel, Austin, December 15, 1954.
- "Paul the Apostle," slide show and talk on his 1954 summer sabbatical trip following in the steps of Paul and taking 600 slide photographs of the Holy Lands from Egypt through Palestine, Syria, Turkey, Greece, and Rome, Central Christian Church, Dallas, January 27, 1956. Paul gave this lecture almost one hundred times including at the Annual Preaching Mission, First Methodist Church, Eagle Pass.
- Conference leader American Christian Ashrams, Mt. Wesley Encampment, Kerrville, August 21–28, 1956. (This is an example of many summer camp teaching opportunities.)
- Dedication sermon of new building, "We Build with Thee," Memorial Christian Church, Midland, April 15, 1956.
- Bloys Camp Meeting, Alpine, Texas, five days in August, 1958. The family stayed in the Brite family cabins.

Ruth's father, Simeon Siegfried, died in Croton in May 1952. Ruth took the boys and went to be with her mother. I had to stay to cover my classes for the first summer six-week term.

Following Dad Siegfried's death, Mom Siegfried bought a house in Austin on Waller Creek, a block from us, and moved there in 1953. We all loved to go to her house. Among the attractions was a TV set, since we didn't have one. We loved our house and having Grandma near us.

After ten years as the Bible Chair, my salary as a homeland missionary had gone up only $900. I realized that I needed to begin planning for the boys' college years. I told Oliver Harrison that I was looking for a pulpit because this job couldn't pay enough for us to move into the teenage and college years. He said that his young people who were at UT reported that I was such an excellent teacher, and my work in weekend retreats with the Corpus Christi men confirmed that opinion, so he thought I should stay in teaching. He asked if it would be all right if he looked around TCU. (He was a member of the Board of Trustees.) I said that would be fine.

Paul teaching at Texas Bible Chair, 1946–1957. Courtesy of Texas Bible Chair.

In 1954, TCU gave me an honorary LLD degree. I also took a three-month sabbatical for travel and study in the Middle East.

Dean Jerome Moore went to work on Oliver's proposal. First, I was offered the Dean of Men position. I knew enough about myself to know that I didn't like administrative work. I had turned down two jobs in Indianapolis in the last decade: National Director of Student Work and Associate in Barton Hunter's Social Action Department, so I also turned down the Dean of Men job at TCU. Then I was asked to give an address to the faculty at TCU. Several of my former professors were still on the faculty. I was well received, and Noel Keith, with Dean Moore's urging, invited me to join the religion faculty.

Two honors arose from my time at the Texas Bible Chair. One was the naming of the Wassenich Classroom at University Christian Church and the Texas Bible Chair in Austin in 1958. This honor was related to my student work in the church as well as my first year as the founding pastor of UCC. There is a picture of me in the classroom which is used by both the Bible Chair and the Church.

PAUL

"Always carries a sword and a book. He was a fighter for Christianity, and he is shown as that kind of man in a very forthright pose." John Hutton.

Paul was born a Roman in Tarsus. Saul, which was his name in Hebrew, was a great persecutor of the Church, evidence of which was his approval of Stephen's death (Acts 7:58-8:1), but Stephen's victorious death made its impression on him. Later, he was converted on the road to Damascus after being struck blind (Acts 9:1-19; 22:5-16; 26:12-18). He recovered his sight when the Holy Spirit filled him. Shortly after, he went to Arabia (Galatians 1:17). He was the great world missionary of the New Testament, and in Gentile territory he used his Roman name Paul.

Paul's three missionary journeys are recorded in Acts. He is the author of most of the New Testament Epistles. Paul has been called the most powerful human personality of the New Testament.

This window was given in honor of Dr. and Mrs. Paul Wassenich of Ft. Worth.

Apostle Paul window in Tyler First Christian Church, commissioned by Tony and Gladys Howard to honor Paul G. Wassenich. Courtesy of Tyler First Christian Church.

The second honor came from a couple who met in my "Marriage and Morals" class. I performed their marriage ceremony in Bethany Christian Church, Houston. Tony and Gladys Howard moved to Tyler, Texas, where Tony was a petroleum engineer and developed a successful business cleaning up oil wells that had been abandoned before they were depleted. They gave five etched glass windows to First Christian Church in Tyler, where they were members, when the church moved from its downtown location to the south side of Tyler. The windows were dedicated to the writers of the four Gospels and the Apostle Paul. Each window was also to honor a living Christian. The Apostle Paul window was established in my honor.

In 1956, after ten years of serving in the Texas Bible Chair, Paul was honored with an event at University Christian Church. Below is a letter of appreciation from a UT Bible Chair student.

Corpus Christi, Texas
22 April 1956
Dear Dr. Wassenich,

I was delighted to learn of the appreciation luncheon being planned in your behalf and would not lose the opportunity of adding a brief word. Though I can't attend in person as I'd like, I'll certainly be present in spirit, in a big way!

It's hard to realize ten years have passed since I took up residence in the unused room of the then uncrowded Bible Chair. As conditions were at that time, I could not have returned to the University, except for the generosity and cooperation of you and Mrs. Wassenich.

It is impossible to realize to what extent I was benefitted personally by you, Mrs. Wassenich, "Squeak," and Frank, and others with whom I made daily contact on the Bible Chair premises. (How could I omit the Sansoms—even for a moment?)

I think back now to your organization of the University Church—how little I realized the future magnitude of our small-scale beginning. As I remember, not a member of the entire staff and student congregation possessed a car until Ray Peeler's coming along later in the year.

In addition to the work and fellowship in the organization of the church, I have personal memories more numerous than other students:

- The many meals eaten at your table
- Babysitting with Tommy (or was it Mark?)
- Times you and I have motor-boated together
- The summer I spent in your house as its custodian, while you were on a vacation.

The one brief semester that Conrad White and I audited your class in the study of Paul stands as one of the unique experiences in my University academic work. I wish I could have gotten half so much from other courses.

I would not be so ungrateful as to omit thinking of Mrs. Wassenich. She was as good as a second mother to me. I realize her importance not only in your work and achievements but also as a wonderful Christian influence and inspiration for us all. I honor her especially along with you.

In closing, I send my best regards to all who are gathered with you for such a wonderful occasion, and I join them in wishing you every pleasure and achievement in the year to come.

Sincerely, and with much love,
Clyde Isaachs

Chapter 8

HOLY LANDS PILGRIMAGE, 1954

Paul had a wonderful opportunity to take a sabbatical for the summer of 1954. He had the time but not the money to go to the Holy Lands to study on-site the development of Judaism and Christianity. Friends from the churches raised funds for much of the trip, and a second fund purchased large quantities of Kodachrome slide film so he could report his travels and observations to the churches upon his return. At that time there was virtually no tourism, and flying to Cairo to begin with was an expensive, four-flight affair.

To understand this trip, one needs to keep in mind what travel and the Middle East were like in the 1950s. Airplanes were much slower; local transportation in the Arab world was primitive; Israel had just been founded seven years earlier and was very small, and tour agencies did not operate in that part of the world. Arab students from Egypt, Transjordan, and other Arab countries were flocking to the University of Texas and other schools with petroleum engineering programs as the oil boom was on. Several thousand Arab students, almost all male, organized the "Arab League," the largest student organization on campus, to help themselves adapt to the strange American culture.

No employee of the university would agree to be faculty sponsor, a requirement of any campus organization. Paul volunteered to be faculty sponsor, as he felt the students really needed a social support group. That proved to be a challenging position. Some of these students had money, bought a car, drank alcohol for the first time, and partook of freedoms unavailable to them at home. They did not know about such things as driver's licenses, traffic rules, etc. Paul was called by students or sheriffs throughout central Texas on Saturday nights to negotiate the post-arrest outcome for a student. When these students heard Paul was planning a trip to the Middle East, they volunteered to help, among other things teaching him some Arabic phrases and telling him about the local customs. They offered Paul the opportunity to stay with their families in Egypt and Transjordan.

Paul toured Egypt for about two weeks and took wonderful photos of ancient temples and other ruins from Cairo to Aswan. He traveled by taxi through Sinai, more or less following the route of Moses and the tribes of Israel. Before the trip he made arrangements to study at the American School of Oriental Research (ASOR) in Jerusalem and for the staff to assist him in seeing the most significant sites and finding good guides. Jerusalem was a divided city with most of the important sites, including the Dome of the Rock, in the Jordanian sector. One could not cross the border as a shooting conflict was on.

One morning Paul was walking down a street near the ASOR when Israeli artillery shells started dropping on that street, with each hit getting closer to him. He hid in a recessed doorway of a home. The Arab family within sensed someone at the door and let him in, where he hid with the whole family in a sunken room designed for such emergencies. Through the ASOR, he gained access to the first modern, scientific dig at Jericho, where archeologists discovered six distinct layers of previous cultures, including a layer probably from the time of Joshua, ca. 1400 BC. The city is believed to be ten thousand years old. His photos of this are instructive and amazing.

Paul's visit to the birth site of Christ in Bethlehem was emotional. Days after dodging the artillery, he was briefed by clerics who maintain the Basilica of the Nativity, first built by Crusaders, on how they attempted to repair the property with five different religious groups controlling parts of the Church. They could not agree on repairs, and much of the huge facility was in deplorable condition. When he and his guide crawled through the tiny door into the nativity, which was kept small to protect from vandals and horses getting in, he broke down and sobbed uncontrollably. His Arab guide comforted him and said that many pilgrims experience such emotion. In describing this experience later, Paul said the many and violent conflicts around the holy sites and even within the birthplace of Christ clashed in his mind with the love of Christ he felt.

After a month in and around Jerusalem, Paul traveled to Beirut, Lebanon, which was at that time the most advanced city east of Athens, beautiful and peaceful. He visited Baalbek and continued to Damascus, Syria, and other sites from Biblical times. The border crossing from Aleppo, Syria, into Turkey was difficult. He and three other men traveling together in a taxi arrived at the border at night. The Turkish guards said the border was closed due to some political fracas. The cab driver negotiated, convincing the guard to call the officer who drove up later, and after negotiations, considerable paperwork, and some money changing hands, allowed the four to walk across the border around midnight, where the previously ordered Turkish taxi had been waiting for hours.

In Paul's trip across Turkey he was able to visit most of the cities where Paul, the Apostle, started churches and to which he wrote the letters. He was also able to find a retired missionary who took him to the then-forgotten site of Troy, which is now a major tourist destination.

—*Mark Wassenich*

PAUL'S WRITINGS ABOUT TURKEY

After spending about two months (June and July) in Egypt and Jordan, I decided to try to follow in the steps of St. Paul. This decision meant cancelling that part of my round-trip air ticket on which I would have flown from Beirut to Istanbul. I flew from Beirut to Aleppo, Syria, spent the night, and the next morning joined three other men plus the driver and took off for Adana, a city of 100,000 about twenty miles from ancient Tarsus.

I went to Tarsus and had a fine tour of St. Paul's hometown, courtesy of a black man from Tennessee who was the only missionary on duty at the Congregational mission school, which was located near the mound of ancient Tarsus.

Upon returning to Adana, I contacted the hotel manager, whose mother had shown me the ruin of the ancient church in Antioch where the disciples were first called Christians. He exchanged (illegally) some American traveler's checks into Turkish money for me. The next morning, about 6:00 a.m., he took me to the railroad station in a horse and buggy. At noon, the train arrived!

There were hundreds of Turkish soldiers hanging out the windows and doors. An old man with whom I had made friends picked up my two bags and ran into the nine soldiers on the end platform of the nearest car. I got on and sat on my suitcase surrounded by these nine Turkish privates. Soon a captain and a sergeant came on. The sergeant apparently said to the privates, "What's he doing here?" They indicated that they didn't know. He ordered one of them to bring me and my bags and follow him. He took me to his compartment where five or six of us could sit.

Just before the train pulled out, someone handed the sergeant a basket and a clay water jug through the window. The train pulled out. Thus, began a fifty-hour adventure which was also something of an ordeal.

The Taurus mountains were ahead of us. We started up them about 5:00 p.m. We got into a tunnel, but the single engine was too heavily loaded. We stopped inside the tunnel, and the smoke started suffocating us. The train backed down. The engineer tried three times to make it. I suggested we get out and walk, but the other men all laughed at me. Finally, just after dark, another engine arrived, and we cleared the top of the Taurus mountain pass.

Through the night we had to try to sleep sitting up. We finished all the food that the sergeant, Turan Akyol, had in his basket. Morning came, but we were nowhere near our destination of Izmic.

About midday we arrived at ancient Lystra. I really wanted to get off, but I had no way of knowing when I would get another train. I took a good look at Lystra knowing I would never get a look at the ruins of ancient Lystra nearby.

In mid-afternoon we stopped at a station where young boys were selling boiled eggs at the station. We tried to buy some, but the hundreds of Turkish soldier privates bought all of them before we could get off the train. At one station our window stopped beside a well. Of course, all the privates got drinks. The sergeant, Turan Akyol, ordered one of the privates to fill his empty clay jar. He did, so we had water!

A funny thing then happened. Turan offered me some water to fill my empty canteen. I gladly accepted. He and the others drank thirstily out of the clay jar. I put a halazone tablet in my canteen of water and waited the prescribed thirty minutes for the tablet to cleanse the water of germs. All the men looked at me as if I were crazy. They indicated that I should drink the water now while it was cool. I was unable to explain to them why I had to wait thirty minutes to drink the water in my canteen.

During this long afternoon as we sped across Turkey at about thirty miles an hour, I used a Turkish-American paperback dictionary that the black missionary at Taurus had loaned me. Turan and I were able to communicate fairly well using it.

At one stop, which we were told would last about thirty minutes, Turan and I walked back about half a mile to a store to buy food. The only thing we could find that we could use were some raw peanuts. We bought them and ate them and had some to share with the men in our "stateroom."

As night came, Turan explained to the conductor that I had a first-class ticket. He asked if I wanted to move to the first-class car. I said "No, I want to stay with my friends." The conductor then told us that there were many empty compartments in the first-class car and that if we wanted to sleep in there that night, it would be all right. We did get a good night's sleep.

The next morning, about 8:00 a.m., we arrived at the station in Izmir. Instead of the promised twenty-four hours, the trip had taken fifty hours!

Over the following years, we sent Turan Akyol and his family a Christmas letter every year. He learned some English and sent us an Islamic greeting early in the following year. When I led a tour over the same territory in 1964, I wrote Turan telling him when we would be in Istanbul. Even though our hotel reservations were changed to a different hotel, he found us! He and his wife had driven over two hundred miles to greet us, a four-hundred-mile round-trip. We met in the dining room and offered them dinner. They declined, saying they were staying with relatives and would eat with them. A waiter spent half an hour translating for us, and I forgot to tip that truly kind, intelligent man.

Corinth and Athens, Greece, were other Pauline sites chronicled in the New Testament. On Mars Hill, below the Acropolis, where Paul, the Apostle, addressed the philosophers of Athens (Acts 17: 22–34), Paul was again moved emotionally. He was traveling alone, but there were other tourists wandering about the hill. He told them how meaningful the site was to him. They knew not the Biblical event there, so he held an impromptu short seminar, for which the tourists were grateful. Today a plaque with the scripture is located at this site. In Rome, the Biblical pilgrimage concluded at the site of the jail cell near the Roman Senate, where Paul, the Apostle, was held, wrote his last letters, and was executed.

Back home in Austin for the fall semester, Paul found that people from many walks of life were greatly interested in his travels. The wonderful slides were projected while he lectured on his trip. His lectures emphasized the development of religious thought over several thousand years, starting with classical Egyptian religion, through early and later Jewish thought, and on to Greek classical and Christian thought. His pictures illustrated each era and ideas of that particular time.

Paul also brought a collection of ancient oil lamps from Jordan. These were from 4000 BC to the Roman era and showed the evolution in the art of lamp making. He used several Biblical light metaphors in his lectures. Churches, civic groups, and university organizations requested his presentations such that he was usually doing one or two every weekend for over a year. Son Mark, age twelve, was usually the projectionist. Mark learned the slides so well that on two occasions when Paul had scheduling conflicts, Mark gave the lecture to children's groups.

In the 1960s and 70s, Paul and Ruth led two TCU student groups on trips to the Holy Lands. They followed much the same routes but on an abbreviated schedule.

—MW

In 1964, Paul led a tour to the Holy Land. This photo overlooks the Dome of the Rock and ancient Jerusalem. (From top left) Frank Webb, Paul W., Elnora Shilling, Sallye Sheppeard, Harry Robinson, Anita Hillman, Mary Cleo Smith, Diane Daccis, Mary Catherine Inglefield (behind), Ruth S. W. (kneeling), James P. W., Nancy Sheppeard. Wassenich family collection.

Chapter 9

FORT WORTH AND TCU

I was happy to be invited to the faculty at TCU with the rank of Associate Professor. The Texas Bible Chair situation was so unclear with reference to the university that we had no ranking. Generally, we were considered instructors.

At TCU, all faculty taught five courses, instead of the four at UT. Furthermore, some of our classes totaled seventy students. That first year at TCU I taught over 550 students, probably a record for one professor—pardon me, associate professor. In addition, I had to rewrite my course notes for the Bible courses because TCU has syllabi that I had to follow. It was a rough year.

To my amazement, I was selected by the students for the award of "Outstanding Professor." That did a lot to restore my confidence in myself. There was some jealousy among other faculty members, but most were friendly.

When we came to Fort Worth in 1957, we bought a house in Wedgwood at 5721 Walla. It was in a new subdivision about five miles from our work at TCU. The move to Fort Worth did not include Grandma Siegfried, who had bought a house near us in Austin which she enjoyed. However, it wasn't more than three months until neighbors, the Hailes and the Swensons, called us and said we had better come get Alice, which we did. She paid for building an additional room and bath on the house at 5721 Walla.

Ruth, having taken courses in library science in the brand-new Library School at UT, was given a half-time job in the TCU Library Catalog Department. She could be home when the kids came home from school. The boys made a rather good adjustment to the change. Mark entered high school. Tom entered junior high. Jim was in the second grade. All had to be transported long distances to three different schools. Also,

TCU Religion Dept. faculty, 1958, (standing) Drs. Leggett, Wassenich, Fowler, (seated) Jarmon, Keith (chairman), Edens. Courtesy of TCU.

since we joined University Christian Church and the kids were in youth groups there, they had to be driven back and forth to church as well as school. Altogether, we had three or four round trips a day to the TCU/Paschal/University Christian Church area; and Ruth, who never liked to drive, had to do most of the driving. We had two cars at that time.

In the summer of 1960, we found a house with five bedrooms, three baths, a living-dining room, a kitchen, breakfast nook, den, and double garage just five blocks from campus. We bought it for $17,500 and sold it for $75,000 in 1983. That was one of the best investments we ever made. We sold our house in Wedgwood for about what we had paid for it, after having rented it for four years plus putting in an air conditioner and painting it twice. We didn't make any money on the Wedgwood house, but we sold it just in time to finance Ruth and Jim's trip with me to the Middle East in 1964 on a TCU tour. The students got credit for writing papers on their findings. We went to Lebanon, Egypt, Syria, Jordan, Israel, Turkey, Greece, Italy, Switzerland, Germany, France, and England.

The family on the Appalachian Trail backpacking trip, 1956. Wassenich family collection.

We were much happier in the new home at 2501 W. Lowden. All three boys attended Paschal High School, just a block away. Ruth and I could walk to our work at TCU, just four blocks in the other direction. Grandma Siegfried had a large room with a small kitchen and a bath. Mark even lived at home while attending TCU. He had a room off the garage and shared the bath with Grandma. There were pecan and other trees on the place.

Ruth could now work full time at the TCU Library, and she soon became chair of the catalog department. She held that position for ten of her twenty years there. She led her staff in recataloging the entire holdings, which numbered nearly one million books, from the Dewey Decimal system to the Library of Congress system. They also began the move into computerization, joining the national network that had its main office at Ohio State University. They no longer had to make cards for each new acquisition, since the cards were printed in Ohio and distributed. They catalogued rare book and other acquisitions of old books.

When I retired in 1976, the head librarian, Paul Parham, urged Ruth to stay another year, which she did. I was offered the Interim Deanship of Disciples House in Chicago, but I turned it down and instead

This book was made possible by the loving, lifelong collection of documents, articles, and photographs kept and organized by Ruth Siegfried Wassenich. Photo at her catalog desk in Mary Couts Burnett Library, TCU. Courtesy of TCU.

taught seminars at various churches around Texas: Tyler, Center, Lufkin, Wichita Falls, Lubbock, Austin, San Antonio, and numerous Fort Worth churches. I also worked many days alone at Mark's farm near Mineral Wells, which he had bought in 1972.

When we moved to Fort Worth and TCU, I not only began teaching large classes as indicated above, but I also taught several courses that I had never taught before: Christian Ethics and Current Trends in Christian Thought (theology).

In 1961, Dean Moudy called me in and requested that I develop an Honors Program for TCU undergraduates. Well, not having been an honors student myself, I was overwhelmed. He quieted my fears by saying I would have an associate director, Dr. Manning, a psychology professor, and an Honors Council to assist me. Both the council and Dr. Manning were very helpful, indeed, as I felt my way into establishing the Honors Program. It has succeeded very well.

I stayed with that job for six years. The program was well established by that time, but I did not enjoy administration, especially because it took me away from two of my classes. By that time, the normal load had

Wassenich family collection.

been reduced to four classes. I knew what I liked was teaching. I didn't like administration, although I could do it. (*Chapter 10 covers this subject further, as does Chapter One "Building the Honors Program," pages 21–39, in* Honors at TCU: Celebrating Fifty Years of Achievement *[TCU Press, 2019]).*

When TCU observed the twenty-fifth anniversary of the Honors Program's founding, I was recognized at the Honors Day Assembly as the founding director. Also, seven years into retirement, I was asked back to teach the Values Colloquium again. In 1996 the Wassenich Founder's Medal was established. We gave $70,000 to endow a prize to the annual winner of the medal. The Honors Program had six directors in its first twenty years.

Some other administrative jobs I was forced to take either by the administration or by fellow faculty members were these: chairman of the committee to write a constitution for the newly formed Faculty Senate (I declined chairmanship of the Faculty Senate on two occasions in the next ten years, mainly because of my impaired hearing); next, president of the TCU chapter of the American Association of University Professors (we had a big fight with Chancellor Moudy over faculty salaries); vice president (1970) and president (1971) of the Southwest Section of the American Academy of Religion (I did not do a very good job; but thanks to the help of the secretary, things went fairly smoothly).

Then in 1972–73, Chancellor Moudy handed me a tough assignment:

chairman of the Priorities Committee. Higher education was generally in a bind. We started by reading the Princeton Report. They had a $2 million deficit per annum, so they were cutting faculty and programs. TCU was solvent, but Moudy feared such deficits. We heard reports from all deans, schools, and many department chairmen. However, the administration would not release sufficient information to enable us to make sound decisions about what should be cut. I made quite a scene when two members of the committee did a very poor job of investigating our budgetary situation. When I went to Dr. Moudy, he said that the university kept this information close to the chest. I replied that I was not willing to make a report for the Priorities Committee declaring that the university was in good financial condition unless I knew more than I did right then about TCU's finances.

So Dr. Moudy set up a meeting that included Cecil White, vice chancellor for Fiscal Affairs; C. Leigh Secrest, vice chancellor for Advanced Studies and Research; himself; and me. They were able to convince me that there was no major financial problem, other than the faculty dissatisfaction with salary scales. I pressed the issue. They said there was nothing they could do until basic financial conditions changed. So I wrote the final report with that reassurance. Copies were printed and distributed to administrators and faculty. One sociology class used the report as a corollary reading regarding institutional self-evaluation. I was not actually pleased with our work, but it was a factor in the 1973 celebration of the Centennial of TCU.

In 1963, the students in the Honors Program selected me to be the Honors Professor of the Year based on the contribution that the Honors Program made to "the intellectual life of the University."

Also in 1963, there was a more vigorous desegregation emphasis in Fort Worth and all the South. Working with Louis Saunders, executive director of the Fort Worth Council of Churches, I served as chairman of the Social Concerns Committee. When Little Rock and many other school systems had such a bad time with integration, we feared what might happen in Fort Worth as we approached the opening of school that fall. We had conferences with ministers, lawyers, doctors, politicians, and finally a big meeting at First National Bank with thirty to thirty-five leading citizens. We worked out several supportive things to do so that the public schools would not have to bear the total weight of integration. Among other things, we had pictures in the *Star-Telegram* of citizens en-

Ruth hugs Paul, named Honors Professor of the Year, and son Mark is elected student body president, March 28, 1963. Courtesy of *Fort Worth Star-Telegram.*

—Star-Telegram Photo

BIG DAY FOR THE WASSENICHS—Mrs. Paul Wassenich jubilantly hugs her husband, who was named professor of the year at TCU Thursday, the same day her son, Mark Wassenich, was elected president of the TCU Student Congress.

Prof, Student Son Win TCU Honors

A father and son won all the honors Thursday at Texas Christian University.

Dr. Paul G. Wassenich, associate professor of religion, was named professor of the year at TCU's first Honors Day, and his son, Mark, a junior, was elected president of the university's Student Congress.

The professor was selected by Alpha Chi, national scholastic honor society, for his outstanding contributions to the "intellectual growth of Texas Christian University during the 1962-1963 school year." He also received the title for 1957-1958.

Dr. Wassenich, director of the honors program, came to TCU in 1957. He frequently lectures or preaches at leadership training schools, church conventions and Religious Emphasis Week observances.

Dr. Logan Wilson spoke at the Honors Day banquet Thursday night in Brown-Lupton Student Center.

Pointing out that in 1930 a high school diploma was considered evidence of sufficient education for the average young man or woman, Dr. Wilson said, "Today a college education stands about where a high school education stood a generation ago."

Mark Wassenich will head a slate of officers, also chosen in the all-school election Thursday, which will include Don Holt of Denton, vice president; Nancy Savage of Midland, secretary; Mike Watters of Fort Worth, treasurer, and Palmer McCarter of Burbank, Wash., director of the activities council.

TCU's sweetheart and six cheerleaders will be elected Friday in a run-off election.

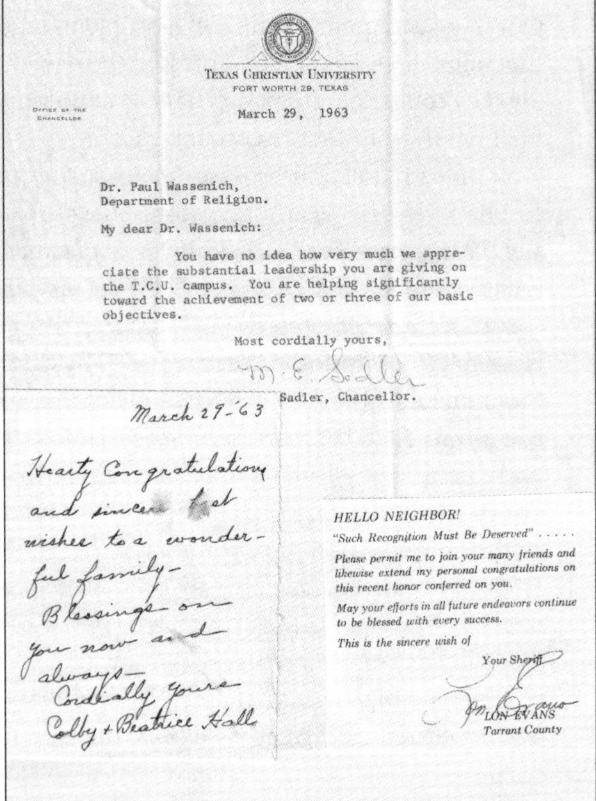

Texas Christian University
Fort Worth 29, Texas

Office of the Chancellor

March 29, 1963

Dr. Paul Wassenich,
Department of Religion.

My dear Dr. Wassenich:

You have no idea how very much we appreciate the substantial leadership you are giving on the T.C.U. campus. You are helping significantly toward the achievement of two or three of our basic objectives.

Most cordially yours,

M. E. Sadler

Sadler, Chancellor.

March 29-'63

Hearty Congratulations and sincere best wishes to a wonderful family—
Blessings on you now and always—
Cordially yours
Colby + Beatrice Hall

HELLO NEIGHBOR!

"Such Recognition Must Be Deserved" . . . . .

Please permit me to join your many friends and likewise extend my personal congratulations on this recent honor conferred on you.

May your efforts in all future endeavors continue to be blessed with every success.

This is the sincere wish of

Your Sheriff

Lon Evans

LON EVANS
Tarrant County

Letters from Chancellor M. E. Sadler, retired University Dean Colby D. and Beatrice Hall, and Sheriff Lon Evans in response to Professor of the Year and article. Wassenich family collection.

couraging people to calmly support the desegregation process. The first picture, with accompanying article, appeared July 29, 1963, showing Harold Odum, a Negro member of our committee; Forrest Markward, an attorney; and myself. Our efforts were part of the reason Fort Worth had no violence in connection with desegregating the schools. *(Chapter 11 covers this subject further.)*

Around 1968, I thought I might be getting an ulcer. The doctor confirmed it and put me on a strict diet. He told me to cut down on my work load. I resigned from nineteen boards and committees. I retained five such obligations. It worked, and in a year I was healed.

I kept the chairmanship of the Building Plans and Erection Committee at South Hills Christian Church. Led by our able Dallas architect, Kent Broyhill, we built the beautiful, functional sanctuary, courtyard, parlor, and offices used by South Hills until 1991, when they remodeled and enlarged the building at a cost of $600,000. We had a budget of $200,000 twenty years earlier.

Al Smith was the able contractor. He lost money on this and several other building projects, including the Sid Richardson Science Building. It was too much for him. He died soon after this project. We paid off our debt in ten years.

The church grew extremely fast under the able leadership of Bryan Feille. We had had fine pastors, but none were able to attract new members and hold ones as Bryan did. He came through the TCU Religion Department, was a grader for Ambrose Edens, and took an Honors Colloquium with me. He attended Brite and earned a Doctor of Ministry degree. In 1991, he joined the faculty of Brite Divinity School.

Our dear friends Stella Mae and Quentin Barber, longtime members and leaders at South Hills Christian Church, endowed a scholarship at TCU in honor of Ruth and me. It is known as the Paul and Ruth Wassenich Disciples Scholarship and supports a student who is a member of the Christian Church (Disciples of Christ). Quentin was our family's dentist.

In 1968, I did an interim ministry at Midway Hills Christian Church in Dallas, just before they called Frank Mabee. In 1981, my son Mark was chairman of the Pulpit Committee when Frank left to be the regional minister for the Houston Area Christian Churches. Mark later became Chairman of the Board in 1991–92. Their next minister was Tom Plumbley, one of my former students and a participant in the Honors Program.

I did two interim ministries at First Congregational Church in Fort Worth about 1970–71 and 1974–75. Ruth had been baptized in the Congregational Church by Professor Wicks of Harvard at a Religious Emphasis Week at Oberlin in her sophomore year, 1934. She really preferred the Congregational Church to the Disciples, although her parents belonged to the Disciples Church and her aunt Sylvia went as a Disciple missionary to the Philippines. We had a great experience at First Congregational and often went back to visit. Conversations have been held between the Disciples and the Congregationalists about working toward various levels of unity and cooperation.

As I have grown older, I have given up on my early dreams of "One Church." The best we can hope for is cooperation in various ways among similar denominations. The basic reason is twofold: (1) the vested interests of bureaucracies such as publishing companies, mission board groups, denominational headquarters groups, etc. and (2) the conservative, self-centered attitude of most people who often say, "If it ain't broke, don't fix it."

I recalled those in whose light I had stood. I thought of the best of "best teachers I ever had," and recognized what Julie (an Honors student) *was saying. I recalled, especially, a Dr. Paul Wassenich who, smack in the middle of his lecture on comparative religions, stopped*

Paul teaching 1970. Courtesy of *This is TCU Fall 1984.*

and exclaimed, "Oh, it's a wonderful time to be alive and to be able to think!" I remember the light that flashed out with that statement over his young listeners, and I remember wanting to stand and shout as the anthropologist-essayist Loren Eisely did when caught up in the moment of throwing stranded, dying starfish back into the life-giving sea, "Yes! That's it, that's it!"

—*Joan Hewatt Swain '56,* TCU Magazine, *December 1991, p.46*

Religion professor Paul Wassenich '34 walked into the classroom with a warm smile, alert eyes, keen mind, and loving heart. A committed Christian, he was open and inclusive as he energetically and wisely challenged his students to grow in their understanding of God, God's good creation, their own lives, and the lives of others. As a person and a dynamic professor, he made faith compatible with reason. Paul and Ruth Wassenich have graced TCU with a wonderful legacy of love and excellence.

—*Max K. Jones, '60,* TCU Magazine, *Fall 2003, p. 34*

Chapter 10

THE EARLY HISTORY OF THE TCU HONORS PROGRAM

When Paul carpooled with James Moudy, dean of the Graduate School, to the TCU campus from 1959 to 1961, their conversation often focused on matters of interest to these two TCU stalwarts. Paul's oldest son, Mark, was a backseat observer to the making of history as he hitched a ride to Paschal High School.

Both Paul and Dean Moudy were concerned that TCU was not doing enough to meet the needs of its best and brightest students. Dr. Moudy appointed a committee consisting of himself; Dr. Calvin Cumbie, registrar; and Dean Lawrence Smith, dean of students, to conduct a special self-study of the needs for and advisability of starting a program that would bring about early identification of superior students and assist them in more nearly achieving their potential. This report, with its specific recommendations for setting up such a program, was presented to and adopted by the University Council on October 11, 1961.

Dr. Moudy appointed Paul to research and design an Honors Program. Paul felt he needed help in designing the program, so Moudy appointed an Honors Council with Paul as the director and Dr. Winton Manning, psychology, as the co-director. The others on the Honors Council were Dr. Richard Douthet, speech; Dr. Arthur Ehlmann, geology; Mrs. Lucy Mae Jennings, office administration; Dean Lawrence Smith, dean of students; Dr. Sandy Wall, dean of Graduate Education; Katherine Bratton, nursing, acting secretary; Dr. Calvin Cumbie, registrar; Dr. Troy Crenshaw, English; and Dr. Marguerite Potter, history. Student members included Patsy Barry from Alpha Chi National College Honors Society, Joan Bennett from Student Congress, and Lewis Mondy, a psychology student who was working with Drs. Manning and Dial on testing and criteria. Student Congress also passed a resolution supporting the establishment of an Honors Program,

—LPW

According to the minutes of the Honors Council, TCU, like many universities, served a wide span of students. Attention was being placed on students who were admitted but needed special remedial work because they had been low achievers; but up to this point, no special attention had been directed to the superior student.

At its first meeting on December 19, 1961, the Honors Council reviewed the recommendations of the Self-Study Committee, which were as follows:

1. That TCU improve its effectiveness in serving superior students.
2. That TCU soon participate in advanced placement programs.
3. That AddRan College of Arts and Sciences introduce an honors program, with the proviso that:
   a. The program would be voluntary to the student.
   b. Only the top 15% would be eligible.
   c. To participate, a student would have at least one seminar per semester, or directed private study, and would be expected to do additional research in his regular courses.
   d. A student should enter the program as a junior, or by special permission of his department, as a second semester sophomore.
   e. A senior should take a comprehensive examination in his discipline.
   f. Each department may have the right of instituting or waiving the program.
   g. Institute an Honors Day Program.

The recommendations of the Self-Study Committee that needed immediate attention of the Honors Council were as follows:

1. Clarification of the goals of such a program.
2. Definition of relationships between such a program and existing organizations and functions such as Alpha Chi and other honor groups, undergraduate scholarship decisions, graduate fellowship promotion and advisement, etc.

The Honors Council projected the following objectives at its meeting on January 5, 1962:

1. To identify, attract, encourage, and counsel undergraduates who show unusual promise of becoming outstanding students.

2. To encourage each department to challenge superior students. Some of the ways suggested were: to give invitational sections of required courses, or in some instances to allow the student to bypass a required course on the basis of achievement on an exam covering that area of knowledge; secondly, to develop interdisciplinary courses; and thirdly, to develop advanced seminars for superior students.
3. To develop new and expanded means of suitably recognizing superior achievement.
4. To counsel and encourage students to pursue graduate study and assist them in getting graduate fellowships.
5 To encourage the faculty to articulate and integrate more carefully the junior and senior years of study with plans for graduate school.

As it developed, the program had three main parts. First year and sophomore students could take special sections of required courses designated for pre-Honors. Departmental Honors required a junior seminar and a senior research paper. The third component was University Honors. Four colloquia were developed on the Nature of Man, the Nature of the Universe, the Nature of Society, and the Nature of Values. University Honors required students to step outside their specialization to correlate the essential ideas of all major disciplines.

One of the early areas of disagreement about Honors was the element of elitism in determining who would be invited to participate. As the reliability of test scores was debated, the criteria for being part of the Honors Program was under attack. A composite SAT of 1200 was still required to be invited into the program, but if students were willing to accept the extra work, and after consultation with the Honors director, they could try the pre-Honors classes and then be reevaluated on an equal basis along with other Honors Students at the end of the sophomore year.

A considerable amount of time was spent discussing the courses in the department's first year and sophomore students in pre-Honors could take. Some council members wanted these pre-Honors courses to be clearly identified with the Honors Program. The concern was with no additional faculty, it would be difficult to develop new sections of these courses just for the pre-Honors students.

Paul's personal goals for Honors were, first, to ensure that a quality program was designed and implemented to meet the needs of the high academ-

ic achieving students. He felt that study in small settings where ideas and thinking could be richer and deeper than the normal classroom was the goal. Second, he felt that interdisciplinary learning was important to create the richness and to challenge thinking beyond normal disciplines. Out of this, the colloquia concept developed and became the centerpiece of TCU Honors.

"Richer and deeper" was preferable to "more work" for Honors students. Interdisciplinary colloquia often required two professors to lead. As faculty were in short supply, this required professors to take on additional teaching load with no extra compensation. Many cheerfully took on this load in the interest of furthering interdisciplinary inquiry. Paul and a science professor would often teach the "Science and Religion" colloquium.

Tim Weaver, TCU Honors Graduate '72, recounted an orientation session that was designed to give an overview of the Honors Program. Dr. Wassenich commended the group for being good students and encouraged them to be open-minded and avail themselves of the opportunity to broaden their thinking during their time at TCU. He cited an example that Tim paraphrased.

"I expect that most of you have grown up with the teaching that God never changes, that He, as the great hymn says, is 'from age to age the same.' That concept of God is fine and good, but today I'd like to challenge you to at least consider the possibility that God, being all powerful, is Himself capable of change over time."

Tim then said, "I was startled by Dr. Wassenich's words. In fact, they made my head spin. Yet, I realized that the concept he'd expressed was profound and one deserving of continuing deep thought. In fact, fifty years later, I still think about that statement from time to time. The Honors Program orientation session led by Dr. Wassenich was a memorable and transformative moment for me."

Beyond academics, Paul strongly felt that to be truly effective for the students and for the university, Honors students should be recognized for their achievements. He was even heard to say, "Perhaps someday Honors students will be admired at the level that student athletes are today." He was so quoted in the Skiff. *He supported organizations and awards for student intellectual achievements. Upon his retirement, Paul and Ruth established an endowed award called the Wassenich Founders Medal, an annual competition of student papers which explore value-centered and interdisciplinary subjects and ideas.*

To further on-campus recognition, Paul started Honors Day almost as soon as the program started. A convocation with a scholarly address is given by a guest speaker, the Honors Professor of the Year is named, and various honor societies inductees are announced. This was the first visible activity on campus for the students and the program. It grew to be Honors Week in April each year with the presentation of senior student papers and creative projects and a festive dinner on Friday night. By 2018, with more than 1,200 students from all colleges involved in Honors, the name was changed to Academic Convocation.

Fellowship among Honors students was another of Paul's goals. As a former YMCA youth leader and pastoral minister, he had deep experience with camps and retreats. He started Honors with a weekend retreat at a local YWCA camp. Later and for many years, YMCA's Camp Carter, which had a good swimming pool, became the gathering place. Picnics were also held. All this predated the era of Frog Camp, which is now a TCU standard gathering program to help new students transition to college.

Communication among students and faculty were also enhanced by "fireside" gatherings in faculty and staff homes on the weekend. Following the example set by Paul and Ruth and the Moudys, most professors who volunteered to lead an Honors colloquium invited that class or a larger group to their homes for an evening or Saturday afternoon. As many of these sessions happened in the winter and the students sat on the living room floor by a fire, the name took hold.

There was vigorous discussion among the faculty on the Honors Council about what type of criteria should be used to measure achievement in the Honors Program. Paul felt strongly that the goal of the Honors Program was not to require more work but rather to help students probe and think more deeply on a particular subject.

Paul felt that Honors needed student involvement in designing the program and that the program needed feedback from students to be effective. The Honors Cabinet, consisting of twelve students, with three from each class, met monthly to discuss activities, next programs, or any problems that had come up. The Honors Cabinet developed an Honors Evaluation and Selection Committee so students could have some influence on which professors were selected to teach certain sections.

***

Michael Wiseman
Research Professor of Public Policy,
Public Administration, and Economics
George Washington Institute of Public Policy
805 21st Street NW, Washington, DC 20052
Phone: 202 994 8625 • Fax: 202 994 8913
Email: wisemanm@gwu.edu
July 7, 2018 Web: www.MichaelWiseman.com

Memories of Paul Wassenich

Paul Wassenich was the first Texas Christian University faculty member I met as a student, and he endures in my memory as the face and heart of TCU. I arrived in Fort Worth in August 1962. I was part of the first group of freshmen (some were distaff) recruited for the honors program that Paul (then always Doctor Wassenich) had assembled. He and sidekick Jan Stone held a picnic at Lake Benbrook for us before classes began as a sort of kick-off. At the time Paul was fifty years old; ten years older than my father. That seemed very old. To me he looked every bit the wise scholar he was then and that we honor now.

I learned later that Paul had faced considerable opposition in setting up the honors program. Long subsequent personal experience as a faculty member makes me now far more appreciative of the challenge of academic innovation than I was at that first encounter. Regardless of conflict, it was clear Paul was very excited about the program of study that he and his supporting colleagues were building for us. In Paul's mind the honors program was not about establishing an elite, as some had sneered. It was about making TCU attractive to and productive for the young people he loved.

"Dr. P" and I had many subsequent interactions. I chaired the first "Honors Council," a sort of governing body for participating students. He consoled me when I screwed up. He led me to Paul Tillich, Pierre Teilhard de Chardin, Viktor Frankl, Martin Buber—heady stuff for a Campbellite kid. But Paul also created doors: Without the honors program, I doubt I would ever have met Betsy Colquitt and so many other interesting scholars outside my economics/ history major.

Fueled by hamburger and coleslaw, on that first day at Benbrook I began to think about becoming a teacher myself. By my fourth year, I was in the fellowship competition and looking to graduate school. My interview for the Woodrow Wilson fellowship was a disaster, reflecting both my cranial deficiencies and the weakness of economics training at TCU at the time. Paul went to bat (to telephone, actually) for me, and I got the prize in a mysterious second round of announcements. That fellowship was a first step on a long path to tenure in economics (so there!) at Berkeley and beyond. While I still don't know how Paul pulled the Wilson thing off, I do know he walked such extra miles for many, many of his students. We're all better because of it.

And we all owe the kind of debt that great teachers create among their students. It's a debt we work off in teaching and caring for the next generation, just as Dr. P did for us. I'll never forget him, and I am pleased to honor him in this way.

MICHAEL WISEMAN

***

The Honors Program has maintained its basic structure since it was first implemented in 1962. A *This Is TCU* article in the summer of 1972, written by Janis Butler and Steve Urban, Student Honors Cabinet Co-Chairs, concludes with this statement:

> The strength of involvement, the sense of spirit, commitment, and personal growth is, perhaps, the most outstanding quality of the Honors Program. Those who participate are constantly aware of the vitality of other participants—the sparks of intellect seeking and meeting challenges previously unknown. Those outside the program recognize and applaud the active dedication that makes involvement not a refuge for intellectualism or elitism but a catalyst for both better teaching and better learning at TCU.

ANNOUNCEMENT OF THE PAUL WASSENICH AWARD

By Dr. Bob Frye
Award first given April 1997

It is my pleasure this evening to announce a new award for which

Honors Students can compete. It is "The Founder's Medal," otherwise known as "The Paul Wassenich Award," named after the founder of the TCU Honors Program. This award was conceived of by Dr. McDorman, and initial planning was done by a committee consisting of Drs. Sharon Reynolds, School of Education; Roger Pfaffenberger, School of Business; David Grant, Department of Religion; Bob Frye, Department of English; and convened by me. To compete for the medal, one must submit a substantial scholarly achievement. Such achievements may be in the form of research papers or essays, collections of original poetry, artistic or musical creations accompanied by interpretative commentary. Such works must reflect some of the dimensions of the person for whom the award is named. What are those dimensions?

To give you some idea about Paul Wassenich, I have excerpted some passages from the citation approved by the Board of Trustees, signed by Chairman of the Board William C. Conner and Chancellor James M. Moudy, and read at his retirement from his position as Professor of Religion. (It is serendipitous that the award is announced this year, for it is the twentieth anniversary of his retirement from TCU.)

> Paul Wassenich has been the moral center of TCU. We hold him dear. He did what needed to be done for us, and he helped us to inquire what was right. Surely we may be forgiven if we ask, "What shall we do without Paul Wassenich?" . . .Twice cited by students as professor of the year, he has been known for his exciting lecture and for his open, searching dialogues. Students call him up to memory when they wish to name the university at its best. He was a guiding spirit in the formation of the Honors Program, and its first director. . . . He has served us again and again in major and in menial ways, and he was glad of both. He has offered his colleagues quiet advice or vigorous urging, contending with us, prodding us, helping us change, teaching us to become what we might be. Remembering this, we know what we shall do without Paul Wassenich. . . .We shall miss him and await his visits. And we'll do what he has taught us

> to do. We'll do the work that must be done, we'll prod each other into great expectations, and we'll teach each other, as he taught us, to face the future with open gladness and great joy.

In that light, a scholarly work or creative activity in competition for The Founder's Medal must examine or reflect questions of value, the problems and possibilities in culture, and must be interdisciplinary in nature. Furthermore, the work should have a "first person" quality in that it must reflect one's own values about the subject presented. An information sheet about the criteria and specifications for competing for the award will be available in the Honors Program office before the end of this semester. In addition to the medal itself, the Wassenich Award will carry a substantial monetary prize. Furthermore, the names of the annual winners will be inscribed on a permanent plaque in the Honors Office.

What have we done without Paul Wassenich? We have been true to his vision in maintaining an excellent Honors Program which has challenged two generations of students since he began it. It is now entirely fitting to announce this award in his name. This time next year The Founder's Medal will be awarded, and so in perpetuity, in recognition of the academic excellence of future generations of students and in honor of a man of vision, creativity, integrity, great faith, and dedication to education of the highest quality, Dr. Paul Wassenich.

The following is an address that Paul gave to the Texas Association of College Registrars and Admissions Officers on the advantages of setting up an Honors Program and a little bit about the structure of the Honors Program at TCU.

THE SUPERIOR STUDENT: CHALLENGE AND OPPORTUNITY

Conserving and Developing a Major Source of Power

Texas Association of College Registrars and Admissions Officers, November 7, 1963

In education, we've long given special attention to the marginal students.

It is time to give more attention to the superior student. They comprise fewer special groups, which will make the university's work easier. We recognize high-achieving students with graduation honors, Dean's list, and Honor societies, which have been part of universities for years, but more is needed. One might ask, "Why is so much special attention paid to athletes?" I don't know the answer either.

Honors Programs have been the major development of the last decade. There are now 200 programs in colleges and universities. The first Honors Program was at the University of Colorado, Boulder, and was led by J. W. Cohen and his successor, Philip Mitterling. *The Superior Student*, published in a magazine, was sent to 11,000 educators. There were innumerable other articles in journals of education and popular magazines. Out of 700 institutions, about one-fourth of colleges have an Honors Program; about three-fourths evince some interest.

Sputnik was a background factor in the growing interest in an Honors Program. Any adequate Honors Program will upgrade all offerings, not just science. There will always be some who drag their feet, but there are many reasons why it should be university wide.

The purpose of an Honors Program is to stimulate the top 10 percent to appropriate levels of achievement. Few universities are at the honors level campus-wide; examples include Harvard and Rice Universities. Students at the 2.5 grade-point average need to be welcomed by universities like the University of Texas, Southern Methodist, Baylor, Texas Tech, North Texas State University as well as TCU. These students can make a fine contribution to society. But these universities also need to provide the best possible education for the top 10 percent, who usually go East for graduate work and are often shocked at the contrast.

The Honors Program should be designed for depth and breadth, not acceleration or more work. It would be absurd to give the extremely bright student ten problems and the average student five; these numbers should be reversed.

Identification and selection of students to be in an Honors Program would be easy if only the grade point average (GPA) were used, but even then the variations in high schools pose a problem. SAT scores are very helpful and can be used with the GPA and an assessment of the quality of the high school. Personal interviews and the assessment of high school counselors are helpful. Including the SAT scores when considering a student for the Honors Program is especially helpful for the underachiever who may have an SAT score of 1400 but a high school GPA of 2.5. It is also important to give consideration to the occasional student who is an overachiever.

I believe that it is most important that a program have a freshman-sophomore level and be offered university wide. TCU has the Pre-Honors program for underclassmen. A curriculum that has three dimensions is desirable: Pre-Honors, Departmental Honors, and University Honors.

These three dimensions accomplish certain purposes. The Pre-Honors program helps the student's self-concept to begin to see himself at Honors material. Some 20 percent to 30 percent of students invited into the Honors Program do not accept. Pre-Honors offers small sections of core curriculum and more opportunity for discussion, deeper and broader treatment of the subject, more writing and recitation with fewer quizzes, some acceleration in courses like biology and chemistry, and in some cases, bypassing courses, possibly in foreign languages, to use the student's time to better advantage.

Departmental Honors offers the added value of seminars with superior students, special writing and recitation opportunities, tutorial and research opportunities, and a three-year master's plan. University Honors provides breadth through interdisciplinary studies that feature reading and discussion.

The rewards of an Honors Program are tremendous. It is absurd to expect this quality of hard work out of many students without proper motivation, which means rewards. We don't expect football players to play just for the fun of it. Scholarship aid should be closely related to the Honors Program, although it should also be available to students who do not participate in Honors, such as married students and working students.

There is also the subtle aspect of having an Honors Program that creates an atmosphere in the university that "Honors" education is admired and appreciated. Some of the tools to achieving this atmosphere are holding an Honors Day, inviting students to faculty homes, recognizing students at graduation, and key faculty giving personal attention and encouragement to students, especially when things are difficult. Honors can also offer specialized psychological services for serious underachievers.

In conclusion, I quote Thomas Jefferson in his Notes on the University of Virginia, "By that part of our plan which prescribes the selection of the youths of genius from among the classes of the poor, we hope to avail the State of those talents which nature has sown as liberally among the poor as the rich, but which perish without use, if not sought for and cultivated."

The Registrar and the Admissions Officer are of inestimable value to a university in setting up and maintaining an Honors Program. Using the same SAT cut-off point for enrollment of high-aptitude students at TCU in the Honors Program, their numbers doubled in one year after the Honors Program was inaugurated. I don't know just how much credit to give Mrs. Anna Wallace, our admissions officer, but I do know she was most cooperative in presenting the program to promising candidates for the Honors Program. And Calvin Cumbie has been a member of the original planning committee, then of the Honors Council, and helpful all the way. That university is fortunate that has that kind of cooperation.

Professor Ron Klein succeeds Paul as Honors Director, 1968. Courtesy of TCU.

Chapter 11

PAUL WASSENICH'S INVOLVEMENT IN CIVIL RIGHTS AND RACIAL INTEGRATION

The civil rights movement following World War II led to the integration of some aspects of community life, but schools remained segregated. The Supreme Court, in Brown vs. Board of Education *in Topeka, ruled in 1954 that separate but equal schools were unconstitutional. Over the next twenty years, people struggled with how to achieve integration in a safe and sane way.*

In 1956, the University of Texas was desegregated for the first time. There was some anxiety around Austin that the segregationist forces which had been somewhat boisterous might cause trouble for the incoming Black students. The Disciples Student Fellowship (DSF) at University Christian Church was a strong group of some one hundred students. They met in the Nordan Lounge, the well-appointed basement of the church which was designed and built for them with their own separate entrance. The church could be closed, at night for instance, but the Nordan Lounge remained open. The students used this facility all week for meetings, socials, and study hall. Paul was the adult leader of DSF and helped the students design and prepare programs and weekly Sunday vespers.

Upon the arrival of the first Black students, some fifty or so to the university, the DSF invited them to attend Sunday vespers and wanted them to know that they were welcome on campus. A dozen or so came. Some other organizations acted similarly. There was no overt difficulty on campus or in Austin that year over the integration. However, some members of University Christian Church Board objected to inviting the Black students to DSF. They raised their objections with Paul, who said it was the students' business, not theirs. If they wanted a segregation policy, it should be taken up by the Church Board, but he would argue against it. On the Sunday prior to the next board meeting, that group of men formed a line in front of the doors to the church and told Paul that he could not enter until he got the students to stop the Blacks from coming. Paul told them he was going up the stairs and into the sanctuary and that they would have to throw him down the stairs to stop him. He went up and they parted. They lost the vote at the next board meeting, and most then left the church with their families. While there were prominent people—doctors, lawyers, and business leaders—who left, they were a small minority of the church congregation.

A year later Paul and his family arrived at TCU, which was still segregated. This seemed like a step back in time. Small quiet groups of students, faculty, alumni, and community leaders were meeting informally to move integration forward at TCU. At that time all the comparable private schools in Texas remained segregated. At TCU, Brite Divinity, the nursing program, and off-campus courses for defense contractors and Federal employees admitted Black students. By 1959, a small group of students was writing letters to the administration and to the trustees urging integration and associating themselves with similar community groups who were working on desegregating the public schools, lunch counters downtown, and other public accommodations. Paul occasionally met with these groups or acted as unofficial or official faculty adviser.

As an example, in the summer of 1960, Valerie Brown (later Ford), a student from Dallas and a member of one group, wrote Paul to say she was a delegate to the Human Relations Seminar of the National Council of Churches of Christ, to be held in Minnesota, and had been asked by the associate director of the National Council to deliver a report on the status of racial integration in Dallas and at TCU. She requested that Paul send "profound words of wisdom . . . plus practical knowledge . . . of what has been done and what is now being done at TCU to further our cause." Paul responded two days later:

Dear Valerie:
July 12, 1960

It was good to hear from you. Both your present and your projected activities sound wonderful.

I hasten to send you some report on the situation here at TCU. But I urge you not to get yourself quoted in the national press on this matter if you can avoid it. If you do have to make a statement that might get quoted in the press, choose your words wisely, thinking of TCU's public here in Texas.

1. Brite College is integrated. There are usually three or four Negro students in the 150 in Brite. This took place in about 1955, as I recall, possibly earlier.
2. By special arrangement TCU has been educating Negro teachers in Fort Worth off campus. Dr. Sadler said there were 30 of these.
3. Classes TCU offers at Carswell Air Force Base are integrated.
4. A student committee (Ken Nunnelly, Danny Owens, Chas. Johnson, Brenda Towles) supported by thirty to fifty students, interviewed Dr. Sadler this Spring. He set them to work interviewing the trustees on the integration issue. Then he said and did three things of great significance in indicating the direction TCU will move.
   (A) He told this committee and Frank Mabee *(Southwest Regional Minister, Disciples of Christ)*: "TCU will never be another Vanderbilt as long as I have any influence here." [James M. Lawson, Jr. was expelled from Vanderbilt's School of Divinity for his involvement in the organization of Nashville's Sit-ins.]
   (B) He worked through with these students, Frank Mabee, and the Board of Trustees an arrangement for Negro Delegates to the State Youth Convention this August to be housed in TCU dormitories just like all other delegates. Frank had been working on this for four years.
   (C) He indicated a plan that calls for integration of the graduate school next, and finally the undergraduate school, and, as I understand it, presented this to the Board of Trustees. He is taking a clear position and leading the Board of Trustees. I'm proud of our President, I mean, Chancellor.
5. Another development of significance: over the past two years Negroes have gradually been given eating privileges at the TCU Cafeteria, until now it is an established norm.
6. Negroes on campus use the library freely.
7. Of course, Negroes are served in Weatherly Hall.
8. Negroes attend Carr Chapel and various functions in Ed Landreth Auditorium.
9. Of course, there are students from many nations here—forty-four different students last year. I do not know how many

different nations were represented. Dr. Fowler is not here or I would ask him.

10. You might tell about the Jarvis Scholarship that Chi Delta Mu *(religious honors society)* sponsors each year, and bringing the speakers up here.
11. Also you might tell about Danny Owens and Chas. Johnson going over to Marshall, just after that difficult sit-in demonstration there, to a Y conference on integration.
12. A group called "The Public Affairs Forum" is being formed this summer, to meet regularly next year, to stimulate concerns in this area among all on campus. Dr. Jack Hammond and I will be the sponsors.

Best wishes. Have a great time at the Minnesota conference.

Kindest regards to all,
Paul G. Wassenich

By 1961 Paul was chairing the Committee on Social Concerns of the Fort Worth Council of Churches. This committee and similar ones of the Fort Worth Bar Association, the Chamber of Commerce, and Fort Worth Mayor's Human Rights Committee also met and encouraged peaceful integration. Paul and the chairmen of these groups met to coordinate the public message.

Paul met with Amon G. Carter, owner of the Fort Worth Star-Telegram, *to coordinate the message of peaceful integration and to see that as many groups as possible were communicating a consistent message. In 1960 Paul wrote a letter to the editor of the* Star-Telegram:

> I genuinely appreciated your editorial . . . on the religious basis of our democratic culture. . . .
>
> In keeping with the religious principles you affirmed in that editorial it does seem to me that one policy of the *Star-Telegram* needs rethinking. I notice that you always put the word Negro after the name of a person of that race when he is arrested or acts in some anti-social way. But rarely is he identified when he does something creative, such as giving money to the Goodfellow's Fund or the United Fund. It gives the impression that only white people do good things. Furthermore, I never see a record of births and deaths of Negroes. Are these not printed? I have read

records of Negroes being murdered. Surely some Negroes die natural deaths.

Undoubtedly the single greatest contribution of the Judeo-Christian faith to our democracy is its insistence that all men are children of God and that we shall be judged by God both here and hereafter in terms of whether we treated our fellow men as children of God.

Thank you for your many contributions to the public welfare.

Cordially yours,
Paul G. Wassenich

Efforts to integrate public schools moved slowly. The primary method of integration was bussing. The public universities had been integrated, but in 1963 TCU had only made a few steps to integrate. African Americans were admitted to Brite Divinity School, Harris College of Nursing, and some night classes. The majority of the university, i.e. the undergraduate daytime classes, were still segregated. The Student Congress, led by President Mark

LARGEST COMBINED DAILY CIRCULATION IN TEXAS
30 PAGES IN 2 SECTIONS

FORT WORTH STAR-TE

FORT WORTH, TEXAS – WHERE THE WEST BEGINS •• A FORT WORTH-OWNED NEWSPAPER ••

RESPONSIBLE TRANSITION – I

Peaceful Integration Eyed

BY GENE ORMSBY

One of the most important stories of Fort Worth's transition to desegregated public schools has never been told.

It's the story of how community leaders in the last major city in Texas to desegregate public schools have been working behind the scenes to insure that the big change in September will be made peacefully, with civic responsibility.

Groups which have been working toward a peaceful transition include the Council of Churches, General Ministers Association, Chamber of Commerce, the Mayor's Human Relations Committee, Fort Worth-Tarrant County Bar Association, Fort Worth Board of Education and Fort Worth police department.

Individuals involved in the effort include ministers, school officials, business men, city officials and Negro leaders.

There are perhaps other organizations and individuals, too, working quietly but diligently toward the goal.

An organization active in work toward a smooth transition is the Council of Churches' committee on social concerns.

The main concern of the committee, explains its chairman, Dr. Paul G. Wassenich, is that there be law-abiding, peaceful change this fall.

Dr. Wassenich is associate professor of religion and director of the honors program at Texas Christian University.

He has been chairman of the committee for two years, most of which time he has worked on the problem of desegregation.

"We have talked with many public officials, trying to decide what would be the most creative and reasonable thing to do," says Dr. Wassenich.

"In the process, we feel that we have helped to create a calm, intelligent concern on the part of some community leaders to influence public opinion for peaceful behavior during the period of desegregation and to achieve calm co-operation in the forces of law and order as this change is made.

"We've worked with Catholics, Jews and Protestants, and some independent churches whose pastors are not members of the Council of Churches, and have encouraged them to think about this question also.

"This summer, the committee is calling together representatives of the co-operating churches to discuss how we might hold talks in our various church organizations, parents and children included.

"The churches will in this way try to prepare their people for sane and calm co-operation with the law."

Dr. Wassenich also pointed out that the committee has set up a speakers bureau to tell about desegregation, urging law-abiding, peaceful behavior when schools open.

They speak on an invitational basis only.

Another church organization which has thrown its weight behind the effort is the General Ministers Association.

At its February meeting, the association adopted a resolution expressing "appreciation to the officers and members of the Fort

Turn to City Leaders on Page 2

Amon Carter, owner of the *Star-Telegram*; Marian Hicks, manager of General Dynamics; and other community leaders wanted peaceful integration of Fort Worth. Courtesy of *Fort Worth Star-Telegram*.

TELEGRAM EVENING
MONDAY
JULY 29, 1963
EIGHTY-THIRD YEAR, NO. 179—PRICE FIVE CENTS

—Star-Telegram Photo

THREE FOR PEACE — Three leaders in the community who are working toward a smooth transition to school desegregation are, from left, Forrest Markward, immediate past president of the Fort Worth-Tarrant County Bar Association; Dr. Paul Wassenich, chairman of the Council of Churches' committee on social concerns, and Harold Odom of the mayor's Human Relations Committee.

In spite of leadership support, it took personal courage to have one's photo on page 1 supporting integration. All who did so received criticism and some threats. Courtesy of *Fort Worth Star-Telegram.*

Wassenich passed a resolution in support of integrating the entire university, which was to be discussed at the Board of Trustees meeting on November 22, 1963. The assassination of President John F. Kennedy delayed that meeting, but the decision to integrate completely was made in the Spring of 1964.

On a personal level Paul and Harold Odom developed a strong friendship. Odom, a local businessman, had two sons near the same age as Paul's oldest son, Mark. They both observed that their high school-age sons had never met a student of the other race. So the five had a good long visit together, the main subject of conversation being: where are you planning to go to college? The Odom boys went to fine Eastern schools.

Paul's motivations to improve race relations were inspired by both his religious beliefs expressed in the Star-Telegram *letter and his practical, economics-trained view of society. He also used his studies in economics and sociology to focus on race relations. Neighborhood transition and "block busting" were major issues in Fort Worth in the late 1950s and throughout the 1960s.*

The following is a short address or essay to an unidentified audience. Some of these thoughts derive from the statistical research and conclusions of his master's degree thesis at the University of Texas in 1936.

THE COST OF PREJUDICE October 26, 1960

We pay a high price for keeping any segment of the population in subjugation. For instance, if we deny them healthy living conditions because they are poorly educated, "the last hired and the first fired," receive unequal pay for equal skills, then they are likely to contract diseases of various sorts. These disease germs know no color barrier. If one part of the corporate body is denied health, we all suffer.

One of the expressions of this in the economic sphere is that when an oppressed minority need housing and are able only to afford slum housing, their living quarters may tend to blight all adjacent housing.

But a number of instances, both in public housing and in private housing, mostly in the North, indicate that this need not be the case. I have seen whole sections of Detroit, for example, where Negroes have moved into the area on both sides of Famous Woodward Avenue and they continue to keep the property in particularly good condition. Some of it is rental property. Some of it is owned by the occupants.

As the economic and cultural level of the Negro is elevated and he can gladly identify with a culture that gives him this opportunity, he tends to imitate the high standards of the culture—in caring for property, owning property, keeping healthy, etc.

A friend in Kansas City told me recently that when public swimming pools in the heart of the city were integrated, whites quit coming and began going to clubs and private swimming pools. But the pools owned by the city are just as nice as the private pools. Prejudiced whites, for the most part, were simply denying themselves the use of these pools.

Property values do often drop when Negroes buy into a fringe area. But this is the result of prejudice, as a lot of people in the area take an economic loss to protect their threatened personal feelings and move out. But often if the demand among Negroes is great for said property, the price rises on a competitive basis. The true value of the property might remain stable were it not for the panic caused by fear and prejudice in the early stages of this ecological shift.

A person working for human rights for oppressed minorities will not be happy over the economic loss that may be sustained by persons in the early stages of such an ecological shift, but basically, he must stand for human rights and endeavor to overcome prejudice, establish economic rights of all, and thus gradually adjust in the eradication of that condition which deprives both the Negro purchaser and the white seller of property of their appropriate rights.

Prejudice is costly. Christian commitment and education are the only ultimate answers to the problem of economic losses sustained by those involved in the changing character of neighborhoods.

Chapter 12

OUR FAMILY

Grandma Siegfried lived with us in Fort Worth, first in Wedgwood and then at 2501 W. Lowden, until her death in October 1969. She died one week after a fall which occurred after Tom's marriage to Elizabeth Aston. After she died, Ruth and I flew to Columbus and Croton with the body. We had a graveside service in Croton with a few old friends present. When Ruth and I were in Croton in 1987, we arranged with the same tombstone company in Newark who had done the Siegfried stone to match it with a Wassenich stone to mark the site where Ruth's and my ashes would be buried. We had become aware of how important tombstones are in tracing genealogical lines.

Grandma Madge Wassenich came to live in an apartment just two doors south of us in 1968. During the three years she lived there, I went over daily to give her an insulin shot. She had enough money, with Social Security and interest on savings of about $7,000, to live modestly. Her wants were few, except for sweets, which were forbidden.

She had a stroke in 1970 and became less able to care for herself; so we convinced her to go to a nursing home where they could supervise her food and insulin intake. She improved at Arlington Villa. Ruth and I went out to see her each weekend. She was aware that her great-grandson, Paul Mason Wassenich, was born on September 22, 1973, to Mark and Linda. On October 1, 1973, one week after his birth, Madge died in her sleep.

Harry Robinson presided at the funeral. He had been on the trip to the Holy Land with us in 1964 and was now associate minister at First Christian Church, Beaumont, where I was baptized at age eleven. Harry died about ten years later from Huntington's Chorea. Madge was buried beside her husband, Louis Adolph Wassenich, in the Magnolia Cemetery in Beaumont.

While we were living at 2501 W. Lowden, Mark graduated in 1964, having been president of the TCU student body. There is a news clipping in the files showing Ruth smiling proudly as her son was elected president of the student body at the same time that her husband was named Honors Professor in 1963. Following graduation, Mark had a four-year commitment to the Air Force, having been in the TCU ROTC. He spent a year in Denver training for Air Force Intelligence and then was assigned to the Air Base in Bitburg, Germany.

Before departing for Germany, he and Linda Pilcher were married on May 14, 1965, in the sanctuary of University Christian Church by Granville Walker, senior minister of University Christian Church, and Ralph Stone, minister to students in the Disciples Student Fellowship. Their wedding was a huge social event with hundreds of students, TCU staff and faculty, friends, and family filling University Christian Church. It was beautiful, as was the bride.

Our home was the place to receive friends and gifts. We had the house redecorated by Jim Haygood and new, full house air-conditioning installed. Linda and Mark had a brief honeymoon in Galveston, after which Linda came back to take final exams and Mark flew to New York to take a cargo plane to Germany. Linda followed about six weeks later, after graduating with the first cohort of students to go through the new TCU Honors Program.

In 1968, Mark and Linda came home after three years in Bitburg. Mark was very tense and anxious from his nerve-wracking work. He gradually relaxed as he worked on his master's degree in city and regional planning at the University of North Carolina at Chapel Hill. Linda got a master's degree in social work. After graduation, Mark got a job with the City Planning Department in Dallas, and Linda was employed as a social worker with the family courts, advising the judge what to do about children in divorce cases. Difficult work.

As mentioned before, Paul Mason (named for both grandfathers) was born on September 22, 1973, just a week before Madge died. Madge never saw him but knew about his birth. David Mark was born to Linda and Mark on June 15, 1976, the same month I retired from TCU and gas was discovered at Mark and Linda's farm. They had bought 143 acres just west of Mineral Wells on the Brazos River from Mrs. Reedy in November 1972. It was paid for by November 1982. The ranch/farm was good for Ruth and me, since we spent a lot of time caring for and selling peaches from the orchard there.

After fifteen years with the City of Dallas, Mark tried the real estate development business with a friend and former director of the regional HUD office. They focused on HUD grants for housing for the disabled but decided after three years that this period of recession was not the time to start out in the real estate development business. Mark then took a very responsible job with the newly created Resolution Trust Corporation as the director of the affordable housing program. His work was complex, but basically he evaluated, advertised, and sold properties that had reverted back to the failed savings and loan operations.

Linda had some very responsible jobs, too. After working as a counselor with the family courts, she stayed home with the boys. She went back to work in 1980 with the Visiting Nurse Association as the director of Government Relations and then as director of the VNA Hospice Program. Next she was executive director of the newly established Incest Recovery Association, followed by a position as associate executive director of Camp Fire USA. She returned to the VNA in 1989 to head up the VNA Foundation.

In 1988 she was honored as the Social Worker of the Year by her fellow social workers in Dallas County and in 1999 was named Outstanding Fundraising Executive by the Dallas Chapter of the Association of Fundraising Professionals. She was also named the Field Instructor of the Year by the University of Texas at Arlington School of Social Work. In 2003 she received the Lifetime Achievement in Social Work award from the Dallas branch of the National Association of Social Workers. Most important of all, she is the mother of two delightful, bright, well-behaved sons, Paul Mason and David Mark.

Paul and David went to Lake Highlands High School. They excelled in school and played in the band. On my 80th birthday, September 20, 1991, Ruth and I, along with Linda's father, Mason Pilcher, attended a Lake Highlands High School football game. We watched not only the game but also the performance of the band, which included our beloved grandsons. Paul and David were also active in their church, Midway Hills Christian Church (MHCC). In fact, they gave the sermon on Youth Sunday in 1991. Both Linda and Mark have held leadership positions at MHCC.

Tom, our middle son, graduated from TCU with a major in history in May 1968. He had served as president of his fraternity, Phi Delta Theta. He was, as millions of other young men, opposed to the Vietnam War.

He decided to enlist in the Army Reserve. After one year, they sent him to train in Russian language at Monterrey, California. He hated it but graduated high in his class. He came home to marry his college sweetheart, Elizabeth Aston of Farmersville, Texas, in October 1969. He only had a week-end. He and Lib flew back to Monterrey where she got a job teaching school. They had a humble apartment.

Tom was turned off by basic training. He decided he could not conscientiously kill people, not in Vietnam anyway. He applied for conscientious objector status, was tried in the military court, and granted it. We admired his courage and ethical probity.

However, this experience was very upsetting to him. It changed his goals and purposes for life. He was in limbo for about three years. He studied TV at UT-Austin, tried being a TV cameraman with Channel 11 in Fort Worth, decided that was not for him, quit, and went back to Austin. Lib, bless her heart, followed him through these peregrinations, always finding a teaching job.

In Austin and San Marcos, he worked for and with a friend in a small grocery store and played guitar in a band. Tom had become a good guitarist and began composing country music. Finally, he and this friend bought a hamburger eatery near the Texas State University campus, called Grins. Soon this friend lost interest. Tom managed to borrow money and develop this eatery into a viable restaurant in 1975. It has grown ever since and in 1991 had 75 employees and grossed $1.3 million per year.

However, he and Lib grew further and further apart. They separated in 1977, and both eventually remarried. The financial settlement in the divorce was quite difficult, but Tom finally paid it out while clearing up debt on the business and building a new house in the country on the San Marcos River.

Tom told me the love between himself and Lib was gone several years before they divorced, but Tom would not leave her out of respect for her father, who died after nine years of lingering illness. I participated with two Baptist ministers in Mr. Aston's funeral. Ruth and I maintained a fond relationship with Lib for several years after the divorce. When Lib remarried, we let the contact taper off. She and her husband adopted two children. Interestingly enough, despite the divorce, Lib joined University Christian Church in Austin and was very active, even becoming an Elder.

Naturally, the divorce was upsetting for a sensitive person like Tom. Fortunately, he was extremely busy with his newly acquired restaurant,

Grins, "The World's Greatest Gourmet Hamburger Place." He often worked seventy hours per week. He bought a house in the northwest part of San Marcos. He had a dog or two. A fellow roomed at his place most of the time. He dated several different ladies, some of whom we met when we visited him.

During this period he met Dianne Hannusch at her bakery. Not long after that, Dianne's house burned down. Fortunately, Tom was there to help save some things Dianne valued. However, the fire was quite a shock for Dianne. Soon another shock hit her. The owner of the building she leased for the bakery reneged on the lease. Dianne and her partner sued and finally won, but it was a difficult period.

Tom and Dianne lived together happily for eight years. Both had suffered divorces and were afraid of marital commitment. But, finally, on June 13, 1989, they were married in a civil ceremony in Santa Fe, New Mexico. They built a lovely, functional home on the high ground of their beautiful acreage on the San Marcos River in Martindale, about five miles east of San Marcos. They refurbished the original house on stilts as a guest house, which we enjoyed many times. They also rented it on weekends as an attractive Bed and Breakfast accommodation. *Country Home* magazine published an excellent article about the home and Dianne's tile business in their June 1991 issue.

Dianne had a shop in Austin and kept busy with her tile business. She is now the executive director of the San Marcos River Foundation. She was named to the San Marcos Women's Hall of Fame and received a Lifetime Achievement Award from Keep Texas Beautiful. Tom has been composing songs, playing, and recording country music. He was going to Nashville about once a year trying to break into the "big time." In the meantime, Grins flourished.

Jim, or "Red" as he likes to be called, graduated from Paschal High School in May 1968. The following Monday we took him to Dr. Levy at the Bone and Joint Clinic to ask his opinion regarding an obvious deformity of his spine that had developed recently. It was a shock to hear his diagnosis. Scoliosis! If not surgically treated, he faced death by the age of forty and serious deformity and possible invalidism between now and then. Poor Jim! He was understandably crushed! We decided it must be done, and the date was set for about a week later.

Ruth and I took him on a trip to San Antonio to try to cheer him up, or at least get his mind off it. The surgery and six months recuperation were by far the most excruciating experience our family suffered. However, Jim was courageous and long-suffering.

Ruth was a wonderful mother, spending hours with Jim in his recuperation, besides carrying forward her library job. Also, Jim's friends were loyal and sustained him as he spent three months flat on his back and another three months in a brace, with extremely limited activity, at home. He had to be taught to walk again. He took a course or two at TCU in the latter part of his invalidism, but his heart was set on going to UT-Austin.

We drove him to Austin in September 1969 and installed him in a freshman dorm on San Jacinto Street, not far from both the Bible Chair, University Christian Church, our home on 32nd St., and Grandma's home. Jim had an interesting, "unorthodox" career at UT. He published a humor sheet and even ran for student body president on some silly platform. He, Tom, and others put on a radio show ridiculing politics. He marched with 25,000 UT students from the campus to downtown Austin to protest the Vietnam War. It was like my action in 1935 with Tom Currie, Alvin Scaff, and others, when we had our antiwar float in the Spring parade protesting the profiteering on munitions.

When Jim graduated, he wanted to stay in Austin but could not find a job in TV, his major. He finally got a job as a telephone operator with Bell Telephone Company. He did not like having to be nice to all callers no matter how rude they were, so he quit. He sold plants for a year or so and eked out a living. Then, in 1975, he decided to go to graduate school in library science.

He got an MLS in 1977 and took off for New York City with his girlfriend. He made a go of it there, working at a couple of colleges and especially the Museum of Natural History as a reference librarian. He loved it but was fired under strange conditions neither he nor we ever fully understood. It was basically due to the cancellation of federal funds by the Reagan Administration in June 1981. He had arranged a trip to England and France, so he went ahead with that, even though he was without a job.

When he returned, he got a job with Putnam Publishers as a reader and continued in that position as long as he remained in New York. In January 1984, he and Penny left New York in a rented truck with all their earthly possessions in it. Jim soon had a job as a reference librarian with the Austin Community College and kept that job with promotions until he retired. Penny got a job doing illustrations for one of the UT publications. She and Jim split after a year or so. She still lives in Austin.

On November 5, 1988, we all enjoyed Jim's marriage to Karen Pavelka, whom he had met at a party next door to the house he had recently purchased. Karen was working on a master's in library science at Columbia University and was assigned to do research in the rare book library at UT-Austin. The marriage was held in a public park facility near Barton Springs with a wonderful view of the city and the university across the Colorado River.

Karen is a paper conservationist who has restored manuscripts such as those by Hemingway and James Joyce. She has spoken internationally about document restoration and preservation in Dresden, Barcelona, Prague, Edinburgh, Budapest, London, Paris, Guangzhou, Buenos Aires, and Vilasande Dalt in Spain. Jim was able to go with her to these international meetings. Karen has also received the Texas Excellence in Teaching Award two times.

Our family has given us much delight. We have three wonderful sons and three lovely and intelligent daughters-in-law. As "Grandma" and "Grandpa," we are especially grateful for our two precious grandsons.

MY FAMILY
(September 27, 1992)

I love my family
And my family tree,
Father and mothers,
Aunts and Uncles,
Grandparents, and
Sons and Daughters-in-law.
Genealogy is intriguing
And soon becomes
Very Complex.

When I ponder the complexity
Of the genes that structured me,
I am grateful and amazed
At the ups and downs

The ins and outs of that family tree.
When I look upon my grandsons
And weigh all the hope
Their parents and I have for them,
I tremble for them
So complex that hope.

Whence the individuality
That made me be me,
Rather than that which
My mother hoped for me?
How will the individuality of those
Grandsons emerge and what will it be?
What part of their parents wish
Will they fulfill and
What will they reject
To be true to their essential selves?

And where is God in all of this?
How does he inject his will
In the texture of each life?
How did God bring the
Unique human brain and psyche
Up from the monkeys or other predecessors
Of human beings?
Certainly no person can see
The ultimate shape of the self
In those early years.

He hopes and dreams
He strives and strains.
He backs up and tries again.
He responds to openings
And makes the most
He can of opportunities
And when he is finally shaped
He accepts it with gratitude and amazement.

I am what I am—
Self, environment, genes, and inheritance
Effort and hard work
And the Grace of God.
And so will my grandsons be.

The family at fiftieth wedding anniversary, June 12, 1988. Wassenich family collection.

Chapter 13

PEACHY RETIREMENT SURPRISES

When I retired at the age of sixty-five, I had mixed feelings. I was ready to quit teaching but didn't know what else to do, so I continued to teach under different circumstances and became a farmer! I was given the title of Professor Emeritus, Religion Department, Utopia University. But the reasons I couldn't stop teaching were: (1) a fellow professor and friend asked me to teach that first fall semester in the evening college master's program and, for several reasons, I accepted. It proved to be a remarkably interesting course, mainly because of the mature, interesting students taking the course. One was a student I had taught as an undergraduate years before. She had become a school teacher and was now taking a master's degree, just for fun and enrichment.

When the semester was over, she and her husband, another faculty member, asked Ruth and me to go with them on a trip to Mexico over the Christmas holidays. We did this; it was remarkably interesting to be in Mexico (Guadalajara and Guanajuato) at Christmas time. We attended a midnight mass presided over by the bishop. We visited five churches on Christmas Day, and all were interestingly different, including one that concluded with a marriage. The sanctuary was full! We noted that friends do not do mean things, like tie tin cans to the get-away car. They put flowers on the car and a sign that said "Best wishes."

A real surprise was presented by Landon and Betsy Colquitt, a faculty couple. They invited Ruth and me to Sunday evening dinner. When we got there, we were overwhelmed by about one hundred student and faculty friends. After a delightful meal and a short program given by students, I was asked to say something. For once I was nearly speechless. I really didn't do justice to the occasion. The next day I brought Betsy

Portrait of Paul and Ruth, 1982. Wassenich family collection.

a Norfolk Pine and apologized for my fumbling talk which didn't even thank the Colquitts.

During the next twenty or so years, several different denominations of local and area churches in the state asked me to teach seminars or lecture on certain topics. I accepted, hoping that my continuing to try to communicate biblical and theological ideas would keep my mind from deteriorating. I gave Ruth instructions to tell me when I ceased to make sense. Fortunately, that hasn't been necessary.

Three years before I retired, our oldest son, Mark, and I decided to look for some farm land that he might purchase. I came across a fine piece of land on the Brazos River. Mark had aspired to ten acres; this property was 143 acres with 2,000 feet of river frontage. It was a bargain but also stretched our joint financial strength at that time. However, it was a great investment, as it tripled in value in twenty-five years, and natural gas was discovered on it in 1974, which more than paid for the land purchase.

What to do with the property? We were surprised, when spring and summer came, to find an old orchard that bore fruit, so we decided to plant peach trees on five acres of the property. We got some professional advice from the Texas A&M Extension Service horticulturist at Stephenville, forty miles south of us. We bought all the trees from an excellent nursery in DeLeon, which he recommended. We planted forty-eight trees in 1974, 120 trees in 1975, and sixty-eight trees in 1976. We added about twenty trees in each of the next two years and a few more in subsequent years.

The horticulturist taught us how to plant, harvest, market, and care for fruits and vegetables. Lo, and behold! We were successful at farming for a period of sixteen years! Ruth and I did most of the work while Mark was the boss and entrepreneur. When winter pruning time came around, our three sons and their wives came and helped us prune. When harvest time came, they helped us harvest. We brought the fruit, berries, vegetables, etc. to the farmers market in Dallas and Wichita Falls, about 100 and 50 miles away, respectively. We also got involved in setting up a farmer's market in Fort Worth where there had not been one.

Numerous interesting and sometimes frightening and/or humorous things happened to us during those years. First, we knew peanuts grew nearby; so we bought some peanuts to plant. We found an old plow on the place, hitched it to the back of our sedan automobile, and plowed the ground. We planted the peanuts, but we never harvested any peanuts because they didn't grow! We had better luck with the fruit orchard. Friends gave us a sign, WASSENICH ORCHARD, which we put up by the gate.

When we decided to plant 120 trees the second year, I asked the members of a seminar if they would like to help plant the trees the next Saturday. Bless 'em; about six of them joined six of the family, and we got those trees planted in that one day! Two of those students are now married and have children. One of them was David Odell-Scott, a professor of philosophy in a state university, who named his son for me.

Mark and I decided to irrigate our orchard from a well at the edge of this five-acre tract of land. That meant a lot of work, digging trenches, laying plastic pipe, putting drippers in, etc. Alas, gophers ate the roots of small trees and holes in our buried irrigation pipes. One day I found a leak in the irrigation system, dug a hole two feet deep, found the leak, and was repairing it, lying in the sandy loam on my stomach. When dinner was ready, Ruth came running from the house when she couldn't see me from the window. She found me lying on the ground and thought I was dead!

There are many pests that hamper production in an orchard, including birds, bees, wasps, skunks, squirrels, possums, borers, and many more. One is the cutter ant who, with thousands of helpers, can strip a tree of all its leaves in one night. Then, of course, the fruit wither and die. After going out one evening with a flash light and some poison to kill a bed of cutter ants, I was returning to the house with my hands full of the flashlight and the poison can. Suddenly, I saw a three-foot rattlesnake coming down the hill from the house toward me. I called to Ruth to bring me the gun, a .22 rifle. She hurried out with it and took the things I had in my hands. I got the rifle out of its cover and took a shot at the rattler who had passed me on my left as I moved to the right. He had turned to face me, then coiled, stuck his tail up and rattled, while I kept the flashlight on him. I shot and missed. He leaped at me, but I was too far away. He coiled again. I shot and hit him. He jumped at least a foot in the air, turned and slithered off into the weeds. I decided it was the better part of wisdom to call off the fight. The next morning I couldn't find any sign of him. I never met him again. Maybe he crawled into his hole and died?

Another rather demanding aspect of raising fruit in an orchard is the late freeze ritual. Ruth and I often spent the entire night, especially from midnight to daylight, burning about six or seven fires to save the blossoms or young fruit from the late freezes. Sometimes we succeeded completely, sometimes partially, sometimes not at all.

We each assumed responsibility for three fires. We kept walking back and forth among them, raking the coals into a pile so they would ignite the fresh wood we threw on the pile. One year, we went in and collapsed in bed about 7:00 a.m. We got up about 9:30 a.m., had breakfast and went about our chores around the house and garage. About 1:00 p.m. Ruth yelled, "Look at the orchard." The grass was on fire. There was a fairly strong south wind. We fought the fire with wet tow-sacks but could not control it. We called the fire department; they did not come. We called again; they said they got our call confused with a neighbor's call who said it was a controlled fire to burn grass. "We're coming," they said.

When they got to our farm, the fire had practically burned itself out. I had been able to use a hose to protect the house and barns. However, there was the danger that 100 acres of cedar, elm, mesquite, and oak would be burned down. The firemen managed to put out the fire at that north end of the orchard and save the woods. Our fruit trees had not been seriously damaged; in fact, the fruit trees came on well that year. Ruth and I were really exhausted after fighting that fire for an hour and a half. If I were ever to die of a heart attack, it would have happened then and there.

One of the most demanding chores was spraying the fruit. We sprayed about five times a season. We had bought a tractor which pulled a 100-gallon sprayer. When I drove, I dressed in rain gear, mask, rubber gloves, and rubber boots. In the summer, it was plenty hot. I lost five pounds every time I sprayed in the spring and summer. On windy days it was especially difficult, as the spray would blow back on the driver. You could smell it and feel it on any part of your skin that was uncovered. I knew that was not good for me. However, there was nothing else to do. After spraying, I would always take a shower. I worried about whether those sprays would harm the folks who consumed the fruit, so I read a number of articles on organic farming. Unfortunately, it was impossible for us to grow that fruit without using sprays, but I did cut down on the number of sprays.

Early in the history of our orchard, Tom came up to help Ruth and me harvest fruit. When we had picked all but a bushel of the ripe fruit, we decided to leave the rest on the trees until the next morning when we would pick them so Tom could take them back to San Marcos and share them with his employees. However, when we went out to pick the next morning, they were all gone! Where could they have gone? It wasn't the work of varmints. Finally, we realized that some itinerant workers who had worked for our neighbor rancher had come over after dark and stripped the rest of the peaches. Every last one! Well, we didn't go to the rancher-neighbor to tell on his hired hands. Later, however, we did take him to court on another matter.

This neighbor-rancher hired an aviator and his plane to spray for weeds on a 500-acre pasture next door to our orchard. We happened to be in the orchard thinning that spring day. As the aviator-sprayer made his turn from one end of the acreage to head back to the north end, he, of course, turned off his spigots. However, when our fruit ripened a month later, it was deformed. We took samples of the fruit to an agricultural specialist. Finally, he asked if anyone had been spraying weed-killer nearby. Then we made the connection. The wind caused the 2-4-D that the aviator-sprayer was using on the rancher's weeds to drift over the orchard. This crop, the best we ever had in eighteen years of farming, was completely ruined. We had to pull the peaches off the trees, throw them on the ground, and disk them into the ground, as the horticulturist advised. We didn't dare try to sell them. We had to file a lawsuit against the rancher, the aviator-sprayer, and the provider of the weed-killing spray to recover damages. The horticulturist was the main witness; our case was so strong that all three defendants ended up settling out of court.

Going to market was quite an experience. Ruth and I picked all day, sorting the select, good, medium, and small ripe fruit into boxes on carts that Mark had made. Then we put them in the truck. After supper, we started to market, which was 100 miles away, around 9:30 or 10:00 p.m. We arrived about midnight and got in line. Ruth slept in the front seat of the truck, and I slept on the tailgate. We might have gotten four hours of sleep. Around 4:30 a.m., the managers of the market turned on the lights. Everyone woke up and got the space they had paid for. About 5:00 a.m. others wanting to buy a truckload of fruit showed up. One morning one of those merchants bought our entire load. We left for home at 6:30 a.m. after eating breakfast at a nearby café.

On the farm there were always repairs to be done. The tractor, the truck, the sprayer, the fences, the farm house roof, the interior, the roofs of the barns, all surfaces of house and barns needed to be repaired or painted. We also added to our barn and storage space by building lean-tos against existing barns. Neighbors sometimes came to help. One storm blew the large pieces of tin off barn number one. Two of my sons and I put new tin on in January, when it was cold and windy. That's dangerous and uncomfortable work, to put it mildly!

After a hail storm ruined the roof of the farm house, there were six of us, including me, at one time on the roof tearing off old shingles and putting on new ones when the daughter of Grover C. Good, who had been a mentor to me, called from El Paso. Ruth conducted the conversation to save her the long-distance costs. She wanted to know if I would conduct the funeral of her father, who had just died. The answer was yes; I had agreed many years before that I would do that. He had been like a father to me, since I lost my own father when I was just seven years old.

I am no skilled mechanic. Yet, the tractor and the truck often needed small repairs at the farm. It was too far to take either into town, even if I could get them started. So I took my personal car, drove to Mineral Wells five miles away or to a small town eighteen miles away to get parts, then came back and installed them. If they were the right parts I had only lost an hour or two of work that day, but if they were the wrong parts and I had to go back to the supplier, I lost half a day or more. For one who has no mechanical aptitude, this repair work can try one's patience and vocabulary.

I am no skilled plumber either, but the plumbing was always stopping up or the drainage system was blocked by something like tree roots. Finally, I just called a country plumbing company, and we put a whole new drainage system in and connected it to the toilet at one end and the septic system at the other. What a relief!

Sometimes the drinking water system wouldn't work. One time the old well in front of the little house broke down. I called a well service that was thirty miles away. The excellent service man pulled up the old wooden sump poles that brought water up from 100 feet below. One of the sump poles was broken. He put in a new one; water would still not come up. The well had gone dry! We had another well on the place which we used to irrigate the orchard. It was 1,000 feet away! Unless we wanted to pay several thousand dollars to drill a new well near the house, we had to connect the pipes in the house to that more distant well. We accomplished that at a cost of $1,000, and it worked well thereafter. The only problem was when we irrigated the orchard, the well would run dry. That meant no water at the house; so we turned off the irrigation to get water at the house.

One time a family of skunks got under the house. We could not get them out, and we certainly weren't going to climb under the house to kill them or get them out. The house was too low anyway. So, in the night when the skunks go out to seek food, we blocked all possible passages and saved our habitation. However, wherever they nested, they stayed in the area and when the peaches became edible, they joined the possums, birds, and other native inhabitants in feasting on our fruit. Although I am a peaceable and kindly man, I had to save my crop, so I took my .22 rifle and shot the skunks I could find still about in the early morning. One tree was still being molested; so I set a trap and caught a skunk one night and a possum the next night. I had to shoot them because there was no way to get them out of the trap without considerable discomfort and possibly illness. Skunks, especially, get rabies.

We had lots of gophers who run along underground chewing through the fruit tree roots, the irrigation hose, and anything else they encounter, instead of going around it. We set traps for the gophers. Sometimes we caught them; sometimes we didn't. Like the cutter ants, we kept trying.

One season the deer (we counted twenty-three in one herd) ate $1,000 worth of peaches. I put electric wiring around the top of the barbed wire fence. The deer tried to jump over it, broke it and set the grass afire. This happened one time when we were away, and our neighbors had to deal with the dangerous fire. I hired cedar-cutters to cut fifteen-foot poles. For each one pole they cut for me, they took three eight-foot poles they could use or sell. I didn't check on them, but I noticed their truck going out each night was weighed down so the springs were flat against the axles. Mark and I borrowed a drill, attached it to the tractor, and, after pulling up the old, short posts, drilled holes and put up those fifteen-foot poles. A neighbor said, "What on earth are you doing?" I told him about the depredations of the deer. He said, "Your fence doesn't need to be that high." Later, I had to admit he was right.

It was difficult for two of us to stretch that four-foot goat wire around the lower part of those posts with our somewhat inadequate fence stretchers, but we got it done in that cold winter. Then we stapled four strands of the old barbed wire above that goat wire so that the types of wire reached a good eight or nine feet high. If we found the deer jumping over it, we could have gone up another two feet, but they did not jump the fence. However, some of the smaller ones jumped through the barbed wire and even the goat wire. A mean deer hunter who knew that an old

Selling Wassenich Orchard peaches from back of the farm truck. *This is TCU Fall 1984.*

deer trail went right through our orchard cut the goat wire so deer could squeeze through it, and they did. When we discovered it, we patched it effectively, but they still jumped up through the barbed wire sometimes.

When we were away, hunters and poachers cut the wire where they saw a deer track, and the deer gladly went through it. I patched those places, but the deer continued to try to jump over the fence and would hurt themselves when I chased them with the tractor. Consequently, we continued to lose fruit to the deer, but not as badly as before.

Stink bugs were tough enemies to deal with. They took a bite out of a beautiful peach and went on to the next one. The only defense was to spray pesticides.

Selling fruit in various towns and cities nearby was an interesting new dimension of life for us. When we began, the only market open to us was the Dallas Farmers Market. It was a rough schedule, as previously mentioned: picking all day, driving to Dallas, arriving about midnight, getting four hours of sleep, selling from daylight to noon or 3:00 p.m., going back to the farm, sleeping an hour or two, cleaning up the truck, folding half-bushel boxes for the next trip, taking a bath and getting a good night's sleep, and getting up the next morning to start picking again. As we got older, we had to have a day's rest in between these forays to market. We sold at the Dallas, Fort Worth, and Wichita Falls markets; the Weatherford market would only allow Parker County farmers to sell there.

A humorous experience that is typical country stuff occurred at the Dallas Farmers Market. As we talked with an East Texas farmer and his wife about some of the problems we faced, including hail storms and late freezes which ruined a good crop even more completely than the deer did, I said I had some theological problems with a God who wasn't very helpful, in fact seemed downright mean and inimical to people trying to produce food. The wife said, "Well, maybe you haven't been living right, and He is trying to tell you something." My response was, "Well, maybe so, but do you suppose all the farmers in Palo Pinto and Parker Counties have been so sinful as to deserve a late freeze that kills all the fruit?"

We helped form the Fort Worth Farmers Market. I served as treasurer for three years until my cancer showed up and I had radiation which so weakened me that I declined to serve as treasurer any longer. Finally, after another two or three seasons plus the fire in the orchard which Ruth and I fought so hard that we nearly died of exhaustion, we wrote Mark a formal resignation from the partnership in 1992, eighteen years after we planted the first trees.

Looking back over those eighteen years, we found them to be interesting, difficult, and sometimes delightful. We met people we had never dealt with in our cloistered lives as minister and librarian. We had no regrets, only thanks for the chance to explore another dimension of life in our maturity.

Chapter 14

RETIREMENT AND TRAVEL

I retired from teaching at TCU in May 1976 and was asked to teach a graduate course in the Master of Liberal Arts program that fall, which meant I really finished teaching in December 1976. Then, Ruth and I went to Guadalajara, Mexico, with our good friends, Ralph and Lavon Guenther. He was a professor of music.

We enjoyed our retirement very much. We spent about six months per year on Mark and Linda's farm near Mineral Wells. We grew and sold the peaches. After selling mostly in the Dallas Farmers Market, which was quite demanding physically, in 1986, we helped form the Fort Worth Farmers Market, for which I served three years as treasurer. As of 1991, it was still thriving. We also sold peaches from our house, then from Rothrock's yard (Dr. Rothrock was a professor of French), at Trinity Terrace, our church, TCU, and from Bill and Mary Lu Hall's yard (Bill Hall was a professor of Missions at Brite Divinity School).

Another of my activities in retirement was giving lectures at innumerable places. An appendix lists the churches where I gave lectures and sermons after I retired.

We were especially fortunate to be able to take a nice trip each year. Ruth and I both loved to travel. Besides domestic travel, we went to these places in the years indicated.

1954—Paul alone to the Middle East and Europe.
1964—Paul, Ruth, Jim, Elnora Shilling, and eight others, to the Middle East and Europe.
1969—Mexico City and Acapulco.
1970—Spain and Morocco on a TCU Tour.
1970—Summer in Germany for a Theological Seminar.
1971—Scandinavia, Soviet Union, Eastern Europe, on a TCU Tour.

1973—San Francisco, etc.

1974—Guatemala and Yucatan, etc.

1975—Holland and Eastern Europe.

1976—Western Canada, Vancouver, Banff.

1976—Guadalajara with the Guenthers at Christmas.

1978—To the Orient (Japan, Philippines, Singapore, Central India (Delhi, Agra), Nepal, Bangkok, Hong Kong), Hawaii, Los Angeles area.

1979—Freighter (Lykes Line) from New Orleans, Cartagena, and Baranquilla (Columbia), Panama Canal, Lima (Peru), Cusco, Macchu Pichu, Puno, Lake Titicaca, Arequippa, Iquitos, Amazon River camp (Paul sick), back to Lima. Flew to Miami, then to Atlanta to visit Marguerite in Macon, GA.

1980—Dipert bus tour to Detroit, Eastern Canada, Eastern US (wonderful visit with East Grand Boulevard Christian Church friends arranged by Russ Koppin at Detroit Athletic Club).

1981—Caribbean Cruise. Flew to San Juan, Puerto Rico, took "Sun Prince" to Curacao, Caracas, Martinique, Palm Island and St. Thomas, back to San Juan and home.

1982—Sold the house and planned move to Trinity Terrace, vacation trip to Puerto Vallarta.

1983—February 17, moved to Trinity Terrace.

1983—Trip (August 10–September 7) to Gstaad/Saanen, Switzerland. Side trips to Zermat, Lucerne, Bern, Montreaux, Interlaken, and the Jungfrau, which was the high point. On the way back to Fort Worth, we visited Red in New York, Ellis Island, and Wall St.

1984—University of Chicago tour of "Ancient Civilizations of the Mediterranean," which included a Nile River Cruise from Aswan to Luxor. In Cairo at Port Said, we boarded the Illyria and went to Ashdod, Israel, while some went to Jerusalem for the day, then to Cyprus, Rhodes, Mikonos, Izmir and Ephesus, Istanbul, Athens, and home.

1985—February 26, for Ruth's birthday, we flew to Santa Fe and visited Tom and Dianne.

1986—August 26–September 2, trip to Alaska, inland passage on "Noordam" of Holland-American line.

1987—Oct. 7–30, auto trip of 4,200 miles to Arkansas, Indiana (Pickerill), Michigan, Ohio, Kentucky (Louisville Assembly), Ohio, Tennessee, North Carolina (Ashville), Georgia (Macon), Mississippi, Alabama, Louisiana.

1988—No trip. Spent $5,000 celebrating our 50th wedding anniversary at Worthington Hotel (283 guests).

1989—August 22–September 5, Amtrack train trip of 6200 miles; Chicago (Channels), Glacier National Park, Grand Canyon, Phoenix, and home through El Paso, San Antonio.

1990—August 16, Acapulco on American Airlines.

This is TCU Fall 1984.

1991—June trip to Ohio with Tom and Dianne, met Mark and family in Granville (Buxton House), viewed Croton and Johnstown cemeteries. Mark and Tom renewed memories of early visits to Croton.

1991—July 30–August 7, discovered "Inn of the Mountain Gods" near Ruidoso, rested from peach crop work.

1991—September 13–20, celebrated Paul's 80th birthday in Lake Buchanan, San Marcos, and Dallas.

1995—Jemez Springs to visit Ralph and Jan Stone, Bandolier and Chaco Canyon National Parks in New Mexico, Grand Canyon, Zion, and Bryce National Parks with Mark and Linda.

1996—Siegfriedale, Gettysburg, Valley Forge, Amish Country, and Philadelphia, then to Washington, DC, for Paul Mason's graduation from Georgetown University, with Mark and Linda.

1999—Ohio (Croton), Pennsylvania, Tennessee, North Carolina for David's graduation from Wake Forest University in Winston Salem, North Carolina.

2001—Galveston with Mark and Linda to celebrate my 90th birthday.

Part II

SERMONS AND SEMINARS

Paul studying in the quiet of the Faculty Lounge, Reed Hall, TCU. Courtesy of *This is TCU 1962.*

Chapter 15

THREE LECTURES ON THE BIBLE

I. God of Law
II. God of Conscience
III. God of Love

Given as Texas Bible Chair
At the Sixty-fourth Annual Texas
Convention of Christian Churches
East Dallas Christian Church
April 25–27, 1951

These sermons were delivered in 1951 at a state convention of Christian Churches. It was at the start of the Korean War. The Cold War was at its height, and people were fearful about Russia. Paul's comments about Russia were sometimes aimed at the country but sometimes referenced the people, which was probably not his intent.

I. God of Law

It is my conviction that the most important of many causes of our contemporary chaos is that so few of us have a vital experience of the living God. Few pursuits are more refreshing than to seek knowledge of God. But, the more one discovers, the vaster appears the unknown. One echoes with conviction words of Reinhold Niebuhr: "Man is finite; God is infinite." In these three morning sessions on the Bible, we will attempt to see God through three of the basic revelations of God given in Scripture.

We can keep in mind the transfiguration experience as a key to these three insights. On the Mount of Transfiguration, Peter said: "Master, it is good for us to be here. Let's erect here three tabernacles: one to Moses, one to Elijah, and one to Thee." Why did he choose these three persons? Because they represent these three basic revelations of God with which we will be dealing: Law, Prophecy or Conscience, and Love.

***

The Psalmist has expressed better than we can the feeling of awe at the grandeur and orderliness of creation which overwhelms us in moments of deep appreciation.

> O Lord, Our Lord, how excellent is Thy name in all the earth. . . .
> When I see Thy heavens, the work of thy fingers,
> The moon and the stars which Thou has formed,
> What is man that Thou shouldst think of him,
> And the son of man that Thou shouldst care for him?
>
> Yet Thou has made him but little lower than the angels,
> And dost crown him with glory and honor.
>
> Psalm 8

The earth, the heavens, the entire universe speaks meaningfully when we see and reverence the law and order of the Creator.

> The heavens declare the glory of God,
> And the firmament showeth his handiwork
> Day unto Day uttereth speech,
> And night unto night showeth knowledge.
>
> Psalm 19

The literature of many pagan religions reflects a sense of fear in the face of the vast universe. It is not a friendly universe but full of many strange and terrible demons that cause trouble, sickness, drought, and death. Even the Old Testament and some of the New Testament reflect this attitude. But as Moses, the Prophets, and the Messiah show man the truth about God, fear is displaced by a sense of law and order which is one continuing and creative expression of the divine.

> God is our refuge and strength, a very present help in trouble,
> Therefore, we will not fear though the earth be removed
> And though the mountains be carried in the midst of the sea. . . .

God is in the midst of her. She shall not be moved.
God will help her and that right early.

Psalm 46

I will lift up mine eyes unto the hills, from whence cometh my help.
My help cometh from the Lord, who made heaven and earth.
He will not suffer thy foot to be moved; he that keepeth thee will not slumber nor sleep.

Psalm 121

Thus, God is the benign orderliness which sustains us through chaos. Though the world seems mad, there is One who saves it from chaos, despite chaotic men. Our God is the Source of law and order, cosmic physical order, and human moral order.

God has revealed God's self to us in immeasurable ways. The more appreciative we are of of God and God's orderliness, the more likely we are to achieve order in those realms yet unordered where we have some freedom and therefore some responsibility—that is, our personal lives and our society. God orders nature and animal life; but in creating us with freedom and more in God's image, God expects us to bring order and beauty into our personal and corporate lives. Both are rather chaotic these days. If they are to have "the peace of God which passeth understanding," they must lay hold of the laws of God which lead to understanding. Through Moses, whose roots reach back into Egyptian history and religion and whose shadow reaches forward through the wilderness period of Israel into the Kingdom period, we get the fundamental statement of the ten commandments—the core of the Law. Two almost identical versions of them are given in Exodus 20 and Deuteronomy 5, but in Exodus 35 a priestly version is given which is quite different. We will work with the Jahvistic and Deuteronomic versions.

I think we can get considerable insight into the structure of moral law that these ten commandments define if we reach forward into the New Testament (Matthew 22:37) and Jesus's poignant summary of the whole law in the double commandment: "You must love the Lord your God with your whole heart, your whole soul, and your whole mind." And "You must love your neighbor as yourself."

The first has to do with your relation to God, the second your relation to man. May I apply two ancient Greek terms to designate these two sections of the ten commandments. *Theos,* meaning God, will apply to the first four commandments, which deal with our relation to God. *Ethos*, meaning custom, will apply to the ethical section or final six that deal with man's relation to his fellow man.

Moral law in terms of *theos:*

1. I am the Lord your God, you must have no other Gods before me,
2. You must not carve an image for yourself, nor bow down to images.
3. You must not invoke the name of the Lord your God to evil intent.
4. Remember to keep the Sabbath day holy, a day of rest for you, your family, your servants, and your animals.

Moral law in terms of *ethos:*

5. Honor thy father and mother.
6. You must not commit murder.
7. You must not commit adultery.
8. You must not steal.
9. You must not bring a false charge against your fellow.
10. You must not covet your neighbor's house, wife, animals, or anything that is his!

It is particularly important to observe that man must achieve order in terms of *theos* and in terms of *ethos.* Regarding *theos*, there are admonitions to observe four elements of order, four procedures that save from chaos.

"I, the Lord, am your God, you must have no other Gods before me." Moses did not challenge polytheism. Later Judaism and Christianity did. But even in the Mosaic form, the basic first principle is: I must have a personal experience with God. He must be my God.

Elton Trueblood in *Foundations of Reconstruction* says we must first quit talking about a god, or many gods, or a concept of god, and talk about God period, the only God there is. We must come to terms with God. And we must quit seeking to escape by saying, oh that's just God's conception. We must all be willing to subject ourselves to honest pursuit of objective reality and not cling so tenaciously to concepts simply because we have an emotional attachment to them. Jesus even says, "He who loves father, mother, brother, sister more than me is not worthy of me." So say the commandments. It implies the law of highest value. In the hierarchy of values, God, the very Source of Value comes first...otherwise, CHAOS!

The second law of *Theos* is a subhead of the first. If I forget first things and make a secondary value with my hands and call that a primary value—make it an image—saying essentially this is god—then, CHAOS! That has happened recently in Germany, Japan, and now, apparently, Russia. The end of such idolatry is ruin! And often many innocent people suffer in this life with the guilty. The true God blesses, redeems, exalts. All secondhand gods curse, hurt, destroy. In America there are thin lines that we allow to get blurred between the true God and our own wealth, gadgets, nation, and denominations.

The third Law of *Theos* says you must not misappropriate the name of God! How lightly some people use it. When I lectured on the ten commandments in one of my classes last fall, a girl blushed blood red. Noting it, one of her friends said, "Oh, some people use God's name lightly, but they don't mean it." I tried not to embarrass the girl further but to make it clear that it is precisely the light use of God's name which is devastating. It implies not caring about God, not sensing the majesty of God as seen by Isaiah and recorded in Chapter 6:

"In the year that King Uzziah dies, I saw the Lord sitting upon a throne high and lifted up and his train filled the temple." Ultimately the inevitable effect is felt by Isaiah. "Woe is me! I am a man of unclean lips and I dwell in the midst of a people of unclean lips, for mine eyes have seen the king!"

According to our vision, be it unto us. We desperately need many people in our society who, when they have used God or God's name lightly will feel guilty and say, "Woe is me!"

Also, here we see the relation between *theos* and *ethos* in the ten commandments. Those who take the name of God lightly take God's ethos lightly. If they treat God with disrespect, it almost invariably follows that they treat their fellows irresponsibly. It was true in Japan and Germany. It is true in Russia! The sanctity of the individual person is inalienably related to the sanctity of God!

Remember to keep the Sabbath Day holy! It matters not whether it be the seventh day as with the Jew or the first day as with most Christians, the Lord's day and its recognition cannot be lightly set aside without dire consequences. Recently, in Austin there was a legal quarrel over grocery stores remaining open on Sunday. I was not so pained over the fact of the quarrel as over the many things that had obviously become accepted facts in our public mind. It was really a squabble between chain and independent grocers. Most participants didn't really care whether God's name was honored on Sunday or whether men rested and worshipped. Instead they cared whether they could work the financial angle and keep their customers.

Taking the Sabbath lightly is very closely related to taking God lightly. I do not mean this in a legalistic sense, but in terms of worship. My reasoning runs like this: Do I adore God sufficiently to build a pattern of regular worship into my life? If I do not, this whole pattern of *theos* and *ethos* will not be nurtured in my life. And, only thirdly do I put what the psychologist invariably puts down as the first and usually the only value of worship: everyone needs, for his own mental health, to regularly recognize something higher and "other" than himself. He also needs fellowship with kindred spirits around the highest ideals of mankind.

Just as in Jesus's thinking love of God is inseparable from love of man, so the Mosaic law *ethos* stems from *theos*. A survey of cultures indicates that the presence of these ethical principles strengthens and heightens the security of life and the quality of life in a culture. The absence of same weakens and destroys a person or a culture.

Honor your father and your mother. Duvall and Hill in *When You Marry* say we learn the subtleties of making a happy home by living in a happy home as children. The person gains his basic psycho-spiritual security from his father and mother. His sense of the sanctity of home and family ties, his willingness to sacrifice for them—these are all tied up with this command to revere father and mother. It helps the grown child to become a good father or mother. In our time more democratic conceptions have developed, but they do not deny this basic appreciative attitude toward parents, home, and family. They simply add to it the responsibility, as Paul the Apostle puts it, that the parents also honor and love the children. The Christian democratic home is a fellowship where each is honored by all and mutual love and responsibility is operative.

You must not commit adultery. Contrary to modern state theories in Hitlerite Germany and Stalinite Russia, sexual life is sacred. It is the source of life. One of the loveliest statements of this reverence that I have ever heard or read is Peter Marshall's sermon: "The Keeper of the Spring." I commend it to you for reading. It is in his posthumously published book, *Mr. Jones, Meet the Master.* It would be a lovely, helpful thing to give to young ladies to read. Back of this sixth commandment is the assumption that life is valuable. We must reverence life. Sex is the source of life. We must use its power responsibly. If we treat sex lightly or irresponsibly, we are very likely to think of family irresponsibly and even to treat life irresponsibly.

It is significant that sexual license goes hand in hand with war, where reverence for life breaks down. Jesus added to this command the key idea that our motives must be pure. We must consider lustful feeling evil and begin to correct and control ourselves there, rather than after the act is committed. It is the intent of God that we be loyal to our mates and our children—that we build a sacred wall around man, wife, and children. Within that sacred relation, we practice agape or divine love and teach our children by word and example the meaning of divine love. Thus does Jesus use the family as a parable of the relation of man to God and man to his fellow man. Only through stable family life can we develop stable, Christian individuals who build stability and love into our community life.

You must not kill or commit murder. Hereby Mosaic law says: life is sacred to God. Just as it has said family is sacred, sex is sacred, now it says life is sacred. Albert Schweitzer states it positively when he says the cornerstone of a high ethic is reverence for life. This is the rich background of western culture. It is a life-affirming culture—a progressive culture.

At present there are two expressions of this golden thread running through Judeo-Christian western culture. First, there is the pacifist who takes literally this commandment and the teaching of Jesus, which goes beyond it—"do not even be angry," "love your enemy, turn the other cheek, go the second mile, pray for those who despitefully use you."

Secondly, there is the reconciler. He responds to this basic command of Old and New Testaments by working as a reconciler of differences through the United Nations and other media. But he feels that force is necessary for restraint of criminals. There is an honest difference among Christians here. Each should be appreciative of the other. Arnold J. Toynbee has shown in recent statements published by the *Christian Science Monitor* that he feels that ultimate peace and the preservation of values cannot be attained by literal adherence to "thou shalt not kill," but by working toward a world order that will provide the security and order for all of the world's people. We now have in the US a small part of the world's people. Toynbee considers armies and force a necessary part of this procedure but hopes that they can evolve into a police force, which they are not now.

We must all be prepared, however, to find that when we have girded for war, we brutalize ourselves so that we are blind to spiritual truths which alone can bring eventual peace. There is a grim warning for our day in the words of Jesus: "He who taketh the sword shall die by the sword." The moral law is that every action which detracts from the sense of the divine value in each person brings chaos. Ours is the terrific problem of deciding which action gives both my fellows and me the best opportunity to express the divine in us.

There is much help in the words of Socrates in his *Apology*, written by Plato, to gird a man for deciding what he thinks is right and dying for it—either as a soldier or a pacifist: "Wherefore, O judges, be of good cheer about death, and know this of a truth—that no evil can happen to a good man, either in life or after death. He and his are not neglected by the gods. . . . " (Apology, last page)

Jesus said: "He who loses his life for my sake shall find it." Matthew 10:39.

Thus, the moral law presses the conscientious person to create a better social order in which killing is stopped or brought to a minimum, where men "beat their swords into plowshares and their spears into pruning hooks."

Thou shalt not steal. Thou shat not lie. These seem to me to go together. They say: you must not misappropriate property or ideas. Much stealing and lying, legal and otherwise, goes on in America. Basically, a social order cannot hold together without a large group, probably a majority, whose yea means yea and whose nay means nay, and, in whose hands, property of self or others is safe. Integrity of word, person, and property is ultimately essential to the survival of a culture. That is why many of us are so frightened of Russia—such chaos she creates by tremendous lies—calling war, peace and dictatorship, democracy; saying South Korea was the aggressor in the present war.

Here is a place where we can really work on ourselves! The white lies we tell eat away like a cancerous sore at our basic integrity both as persons, as Church and as nation. Before world order can be achieved, there must be a great upsurge of concern for integrity. There are many good signs of this these days. The fine statement in TIME Magazine for April 6, 1951, by Senator Fulbright is one. In part he said: "Much of the evil of the world is beyond the reach of law. . . . As our study of the RFC progressed, we were confronted more and more with problems of ethical conduct. . . . How do we deal with those who, under the guise of friendship, accept favors which offend the spirit of the law, but do not violate its letter?

"What of the men outside Government who suborn those inside it? They are careful to see that they do not do anything that can be construed as illegal. . . . Many businessmen, ostensibly reputable businessmen, employ knavish lawyers to circumvent the law and enrich themselves at Government expense.

"Who is more at fault, the bribed or the bribers? The bribed are often simple men who weaken before temptation. The bribers are often men who walk the earth, lordly and secure, members of good families, respected figures. . . . Is it too much to ask of them that they behave with simple honesty—with that honesty which looks, not to the letter of the law, but to its spirit? . . . What we see in government is a reflection of many other areas of our national life. . . .

"The vast majority of great civilizations have been destroyed, not as a result of external aggression, but as a consequence of domestic corruption. . . . Democracy is more likely to be destroyed by the perversion of, or abandonment of, its true moral principles than by armed attack from Russia. . . . Too many people in our nation do not believe anything with conviction. They question the concepts of God or man, indiscriminately. The values of life which were clear to the Pilgrims and the Founding Fathers have become dim and fuzzy in outline."

The phrasing of this tenth command interests me because of its specificity as well as its moral insight. Thou shalt not covet thy neighbor's house, ox, or wife! A covetous people start wars. A covetous people have a little green devil inside which eats away at integrity and charity and all the good qualities of life.

Mrs. Wassenich recently noted that even in our ideal neighborhood, where we are real friends, when one family gets a new car, everyone raises his eyebrows and says, "Hmmm! How did they afford that?" Pretty soon, they all have the bug to get a new car. She said it is no wonder that the "have not" nations are jealous of the great plenty of America and hate us for it. I mentioned this to Kagawa on his recent visit to Austin and he said, "Not hate, envy!" Well, envy is close to covetousness, and covetous leads to hate, and hate leads to violence. The moral law here is best stated by Jesus in his Sermon on the Mount, where he pushes each issue back into the human emotions, for examples, "You have heard it said . . . 'do not kill,' but I say to you do not even be angry." Out of the heart are the issues of life, to paraphrase Proverbs 4:23.

Jesus said he came not to destroy the law, but to fulfill it. When the rich young ruler asked, "What must I do to inherit eternal life?" Jesus listed the *ethos* commandments. Jesus's love ethic does not obliterate the moral law, but strengthens and lengthens it.

I am profoundly convinced that if man would spend one-tenth the time, talent, and money in research into the nature of moral order that he has spent in research into physical order, we would soon be on the way to a world of abundance, peace, and goodwill. It is my faith that the same God who created this physical order also created a marvelous moral order. The ten commandments are a minimum beginning description of it. Jesus's Law of Love is an enlargement of our understanding of it. The basic principles are stated. What is needed is much sincere, trustful experimentation with it. One of the most interesting studies of our time is that of Ernest M. Ligon, once of TCU, now of Union college, who has a $100,000 annual grant for "character research." This is only a modest beginning in this direction.

II. God of Conscience

The Bible very often uses the term "heart" to indicate that sensitive feeling-after-righteousness, and deep commitment thereto, that we mean by the modern word, *conscience.* Conscience is highly subjective. Moral law is more objective. We cannot be so certain of the dictates of conscience as we can of the dictates of moral law. Even though some men's consciences may mislead them, God, as in the prophets, has often reached into the life of mankind through persons of sensitive conscience.

The first inkling of the idea of man's sensitive conscience in the canonized scriptures is the story of the fall of man. Adam, having partaken of evil, feels guilty and hides himself from God.

In the sense that Moses argued with God at the burning bush, we might see the dawn of conscience there. A deep and burning pressure to go back and do the dangerous thing in delivering his countrymen from bondage. Certainly that is the kind of pressure we see conscience exerting in the prophets where it is the primary religious motivation. In James Henry Breasted's great study, *The Dawn of Conscience*, he traces the rise of conscience to sensitive Egyptians, particularly Amenothep IV or Ikhnaton, a very humane, deeply religious, and progressive Pharaoh of 1375–1358 BCE. That period is about seventy-five years before Moses if we accept the late dating of the exodus.

The real flowering of the conscience among the Hebrews came with the prophets. The prophets are the men who served essentially as a collective conscience for the people. Their roots go back into men like Moses, who are morally sensitive for the people, as Moses was in the incident of the golden calf and the receiving of the ten commandments. The prophets are preceded by men like Eli and Samuel who were basically judges, or tribal leaders. Yet Samuel, in particular, was morally sensitive, like the prophets. When the people demanded a king, Samuel pointed out that kings will mean autocracy and the loss of the spiritual best in their tribal life.

The prophetic conscience carries through the Kingdom period in Nathan who, when David wantonly takes Uriah's wife and has Uriah killed, accuses David publicly to his face. He tells a clever parable. Once there was a poor man who owned one beautiful little ewe lamb. It was his pride and joy—his all. Next door lives a man with many sheep—a whole flock of them. Yet, the rich man took away the one little ewe lamb of the poor man. David, in righteous indignation, said "Let him be killed." Nathan, acting as national conscience, said: "Thou are the man!" Yet, if Nathan is to be equated with conscience, we can readily see that the conscience is not always reliable, for Nathan later collaborated with Bathsheba to put Solomon on the throne, and Solomon caused the moral collapse of the kingdom and its division into Israel and Judah.

That is always true about conscience. It must be checked and double-checked by reason and all possible means. Scripture and other devotional literature help in checking it. Friends of deep religious insight can help us check our consciences to see whether they are leading us astray. The koinonia, or fellowship of the Church, can help us in checking our conscience. However, the Church will not always stand by a person of sensitive conscience who is really trying to know and do the will of God. One of the loveliest spirits of our age, Albert Schweitzer, relates an experience which may easily happen to any conscientious person. At the age of fifty, with three doctorates and an assured life of creative service as a teacher, preacher, and musician, he felt his conscience was being goaded to help the people of darkest Africa. When he told his Christian friends about his plan to take an M.D. and go to Africa, they all discouraged and ridiculed him. He says much about this in *Out of My life and Thought.* I will quote only this paragraph.

> My relatives and my friends all joined in expostulating with me on the folly of my enterprise. I was a man, they said, who was burying the talent entrusted to him and wanted to trade with false currency. . . . I felt as a real kindness the action of persons who made no attempt to dig their fists into my heart, but regarded me as a precocious young man, not mockery. . . . Anyone who proposes to do good must not expect people to roll stones out of his way, but must accept his lot calmly if they even roll a few more upon it.

In my estimation, the first great figure of the Bible who displays a deep and rather reliable conscience is Elijah. Of course, I don't think his conscience was operating very reliably when he, acting like a Torquemada, killed the 450 Baal priests. Torquemada may have gotten his ideas from Elijah when, in the fifteenth century, he killed over 10,000 Moors, Jews and other "heretics."

But here is the lovely thing about Elijah. After he had so boldly spoken for God, when no one else would, when it was very unpopular to do so, he was threatened by the Queen herself—Queen Jezebel, who had supported the priests of Baal whom Elijah killed. She was a strong-willed woman! Having met a few such, I am entirely sympathetic with Elijah for fleeing. However, when he had fled as far south as he could go—even unto Horeb or Sinai—he hid in a cave. After many days, when he was worn out and had probably seen many nightmares of Jezebel walking into the cave and tearing him limb from limb, he began to be ashamed of himself.

<u>Blessed is the man who can be ashamed of himself.</u> Elijah's conscience began to become sensitive again to the voice of God. One of the most haunting pictures in scripture is I Kings 19:13 wherein is recorded the climax of Elijah's timid reapproach to Jehovah. A storm came up and all the old practices of mankind first appealed to him. He listened for the voice of God in the thunder, and for lights from God in the lightning, and for a word from God in the wind. None came! But after the storm, "a still small voice" came. 'Twas the divine whisper of God, through conscience. It began to taunt him, saying, "Elijah, what are you doing 'way down here?"

Then, it laid hold on the best and deepest in Elijah and said, "Get thee up and return unto Damascus and anoint Hazael to succeed Ahab as King and Elisha to succeed you as prophet."

Once Elijah had gotten up and acted boldly in terms of the instructions given by the "still small voice of God," he gained in boldness and insight all down the line. He denounced Jezebel and Ahab for the infamous murder of Naboth and theft of his vineyard. The Bible always links conscience and moral law inseparably.

Would that some men of deep conscience arise behind the Iron Curtain to denounce the infamous seizure of Czechoslovakia, of North Korea, of Tibet, of Indo-China. And would that a similar prophet of God arise among us to point out, as Amos did to Israel, how we build winter house and summer house, lie on ivory couches and grow sleek and fat like the cows of Bashan, when the rest of the world starves. He would declare that the misery coming upon us is caused by the morally reliable nature of the universe, that in the last analysis we shall not survive whether we win or lose the first engagements militarily unless we are profoundly changed religiously. How can we justify our shallow lives when the world is in such pain? If we can respond creatively to this challenge, then we may survive. But it calls for such profound religious thinking and living as any generation has ever been called upon to do. Alone, we are not equal to it. However, I do believe that through creative faith and by the Grace of God it can be done. If there is anyone here who has not been pressed back upon the grace of God in these difficult days, it means that his lines do not go far enough out into the world.

Elijah's conscience was not as reliable as that of Amos. It may be that Amos was in a better position to be vindicated than Elijah, for he spoke his conscientious piece and disappeared from the scene as suddenly as he entered it. He was like a flaming evangelist who appears in the community briefly and then disappears. He doesn't have to keep the new converts reconstructed like the local pastor does. There are several important things to note about this great voice of conscience, Amos of Tekes.

He came from obscurity, a non-professional country bumpkin, and preached on the street of Bethel without pay or pulpit. He spoke with authority and not like the scribes and Pharisees, as Jesus said 750 years after Amos. He started out diplomatically, saying to Israel that there were moral faults in all the surrounding countries.

Then he delighted the people of Israel, pointing out that the following practices of their neighbors angered God:

- traffic in slaves by Philistia, Phoenicia and Edom;
- unjust war on weak nations by Syrians and Ammonites;
- the burning alive of a captive king by the Edomites (sounds like contemporary society, doesn't it?);
- the Southern Kingdom of Judah, Amos's native land, rejecting the word of God and living a lie, pretending to be holy but really is not. (Is there anything pertinent to modern America here? Do we really model our foreign policy after the Sermon on the Mount? Are we a "Christian" nation in a vital sense?)

Now, Amos dramatically turns to speak of the Israelites, his auditors. Up to this point, they have been boisterously enthusiastic toward his statements about their neighbors and enemies. Now they grow strangely quiet. We do not receive criticism of ourselves so enthusiastically as we receive criticism of others. He tells them:

- They have sold the innocent for silver, and the needy for a pair of shoes. They have enslaved laborers and profiteered off human life.
- They trample on the heads of the poor, even taking a man's sleep garments in mortgage.
- They live in sexual license, the fathers teaching the sons, and in the name of the decadent religion of the Baals, with their sacred prostitutes.
- Wine, taken as an unjust fine, is drunk in the holy places.

All these things you do, said Amos, when you ought to be moral in gratitude to God who has made you so prosperous. And there they called his hand. Look about you at all this prosperous land. How can you say God is displeased with us? Thus spake Amaziah, the pompous priest. You are uttering blasphemy and traitorous remarks against the king! Away with you! What authority have you to speak anyway? Who are you?

Amos replies: It is true I am no professional prophet nor a member of a prophetic order, but God called me away from tending the sheep and trimming the sycamore fruit trees. The Lord told me to go prophesy and now you must hear the word of the Lord. He speaks from conscience. He presents his basic theology.

- God has been close and good to them, leading them out of Egyptian bondage and into the promised land. Yet, they have grown callous and have not kept their moral conscience alert.

- This is a universe of moral order. Two men do not walk together without appointment. A lion does not roar unless he has a prey. A trap does not spring without being stepped on. So, when the lion roars, who will not fear?
- Then, he roars down doom upon Israel. They will be stripped and plundered by their surrounding foes. His basic principle is that because God loves them, God will punish their wrongdoing, using their foes, particularly Assyria, as the rod of his anger.
- Thus punished, perhaps a chastened and wisdom-filled remnant may return unto the Lord. His hope is that something creative may come out of the violence and destruction. These God will exalt into a "peculiar people unto the Lord." It is not a way of glory and majesty, but as Jesus later put it, a way of the cross and a way of purposeful and redemptive suffering.

Isn't it strange that all this tremendous, bold message was born into the conscience of a humble, nonprofessional, uneducated man? Isn't it amazing that he and not Amaziah became the recognized voice of God when, with the perspective of seven or eight hundred years, the Rabbis at the Council of Jamnia in 90 CE chose the books of the canon? Whom do you suppose Christians a thousand years hence will decide spoke for God in the middle of the twentieth century? Whose is the lonely, but creative, voice crying in the wilderness of our worldly obsessions?

Now, let us look at another of the towering figures of the Old Testament period. Unlike Amos, this man came from the ruling classes. Unlike Amos, he saw his vision in the Temple. Unlike Amos, he was educated. As both humble shepherds and dignified wise men worshipped the Babe of Bethlehem, so in the renaissance of conscience both very humble and very wise men heard the voice of God. In between is the mass of humanity with its attention upon wealth, power, position, and worldly security. As on Golgotha we crucify those who are either too good or too bad. We honor those in between. It seems to be a conspiracy toward moral mediocrity.

In his call, Isaiah has recorded a most fundamental description of how the human spirit and conscience is stirred by God in the regular worship in churches and temples of the Judeo-Christian religions.

In the year that King Uzziah died, I saw the Lord,
High and lifted up, and His train filled the temple.

Above him stood the seraphim. Each one had six wings.
With two he covered his face and with twain he covered
His loins, and with twain he did fly.
And one cried to another and said, holy, holy, holy
Is the Lord God of Hosts. The whole earth is full
Of his glory.
And I said: Woe is me, for I am undone.
I am a man of unclean lips
And I dwell in the midst of a people of unclean lips,
For mine eyes have seen the king, the Lord of Hosts,
And then one of the seraphim flew to me with a live
Coal which he had taken with the tongs from off the altar
And he said to me, "Lo, this hath touched thy lips and thine
Iniquity is taken away."
And then I heard the voice of the Lord say,
"Whom shall I send and who will go for us?"
And I said: "Here am I, Lord, send me!"
And he said: "Go and say to this people:
You will listen and listen and never understand
And you will look and look and never really see
Because the heart of this people has grown fat
And their eyes they have shut (to spiritual values)"
And I said, "How long, O Lord?"
And he said, "Until the cities be wasted away without inhabitant,
And the land be left utterly desolate."

In other words, Isaiah's great vision after much intelligent thought upon the complex problems of his time ended in this kind of conclusion. The hope of our time is that men will turn unto the Lord and, at whatever price, will do the will of God toward their fellow man. But they have so long been accustomed to turning a deaf ear and a blind eye to God's deepest demands that there is no chance that any but a remnant will do so. The inevitable result is decay and destruction. The moral law can promise nothing else. Then, all will have to be rebuilt through a spiritually sensitive remnant. No prophet ever made a more precisely correct analysis of the forces at work in his time than that. History certainly vindicated Isaiah. It was a lonely job, saying those unpopular things to the people.

The climactic and most majestic of the prophets is, I think, Jeremiah. He didn't prophesy and disappear. He lived for forty years or more through all the tragedy he saw coming. And we see in him the painful necessities that burden him, almost forcing him to insanity. It involves a deep sense of "Would that I could escape from this heavy hand of divine obligation upon me and be normal like other men, but I cannot."

Unlike either Amos or Isaiah, Jeremiah is the son of a priest. Here is Jeremiah's own record of his call as recorded by the scribe, Baruch:

> The word of the Lord came to me saying,
> "Before I formed you in the womb, I knew you.
> And before you were born, I set you apart,
> I appointed you a prophet to the nations."
> Then said I: "Ah, Lord God! I cannot speak;
> For I am only a youth."
> (Like Moses of old, he tries to escape.)
> But the Lord said to me,
> "Do not say 'I am only a youth';
> For to all to whom I send you shall you go,
> And all that I command you shall you speak.
> Do not be afraid of them;
> For I am with you to deliver you,"
> This is the oracle of the Lord.
> Then the Lord stretched forth his hand and touched my mouth.
> And the Lord said to me,
> "See, I put my words in your mouth;
> This day I give you authority over the nations and kingdoms,
> To root up and to pull down, to wreck and to ruin,
> To build and to plant."

And the majestic figure grew old in the service of the Lord, living in tottering Jerusalem, during the reign of the good King Josiah, who did all that he could do to reform the kingdom to bring it into accord with the will of God, but it was apparently "too little and too late." There is a moving painting of Jeremiah brooding over Jerusalem as the Babylonians despoil it in 586 BCE. It is an unforgettable experience to study that picture if you know the life and thought of Jeremiah.

One of the occasions in the long life of Jeremiah which best gives us the sense of how wretched and yet how blessed can be the experience of living true to the "still small voice of conscience" is the following from Jeremiah 19:14 ff.

> Jeremiah stood in the court of the Temple and prophesied:
>
> Thus says the Lord of hosts, the God of Israel: Behold I am bringing upon this city and upon all its towns the full disaster that I pronounced upon it, because its people have stiffened their necks so as not to listen to my words.

Now when Pashhur (possibly meaning "safety on every side") who was the son of Immer the priest who was a chief overseer in the house of the Lord, heard Jeremiah prophesying these things Pashhur beat Jeremiah and put him in stocks at the upper Benjamin gate where everybody laughed and railed at him as they passed by. He remained in the stocks all night.

The next morning Pashhur released Jeremiah, and Jeremiah said: "The Lord calls you not Pashhur ("safety all around") but "Terror all around." For thus says the Lord, Behold I am making you a center of terror to yourself and to all your friends. You shall see all your friends fall at the hand of the enemy and all of Judah shall fall into the hands of Babylon. And you, Pashhur, and all your house shall go into exile in Babylon. You shall die there, for you have prophesied falsely.

But, poor Jeremiah, after making this bold statement to Pashhur, fled to the privacy of his home, and addressed God thus in his deep embarrassment (Jeremiah 20:7–13).

> Thou hast duped me, O Lord, and I let myself be duped.
> Thou hast been too strong for me, and hast prevailed.
> I have become a laughing-stock all day long.
> Everyone mocks me.
> As often as I speak, I must cry out.
> I must call, "Violence and spoil!"
> A reproach and a derision all day long.
> If I say "I will not think of it,
> Nor speak any more in His name,"
> It is in my heart like a burning fire,
> Shut up in my bones;

> I am worn out with holding it in—
> I cannot endure it!
> For I hear the whispering of many,
> Terror all around.
> "Denounce him, let us denounce him!"
> Say all my intimate friends,
> Who watch for my tripping;
> Perhaps he will be duped, and we shall prevail over him
> And take our revenge upon him.

This is the terrible "valley of despair" which every prophetic spirit must endure. The people do not want to hear the truth, but the honeyed words of the false prophet. This is Jesus upon the cross hearing "Let him come down from the cross if he is the Son of God," and running over the 22nd Psalm in his mind, beginning "My God, My God, why hast Thou forsaken me," yet ending in a paean of triumphant faith.

Nevertheless, every truly committed spirit learns that though he can hardly live with God, he can certainly not live without God. So he turns his spirit Godward again and listens to hear what the still small voice will say. And the voice said to Jeremiah:

> But the Lord is with me, even as a dreaded warrior,
> Therefore, my persecutors shall stumble, and they shall not prevail.
> They shall be put to bitter shame. . . .
> To everlasting confusion, which shall not be forgotten!
> O Lord of hosts, Thou who testest the right,
> WHO SEARCHEST THE HEART AND THE CONSCIENCE,
> Let me see thy vengeance on them.
> For to THEE have I confided my cause,
> Sing to the Lord, praise the Lord
> For he has saved the life of the needy
> From the hand of the wicked.

After that soul-searing experience, typical of any deeply conscientious person who cannot go easily and naïvely along with the surface trends of religion, Jeremiah was more certain of himself and his experience of God.

When he dramatized a later prophecy and was embarrassed by

Hananiah, he immediately recovered. Jeremiah went about with a wooden yoke on his shoulders, saying that Babylon would conquer Judah.

His yoke of wood dramatized this, so even the simple-minded could get his point easily. This angered Hananiah, the priest, so much that he grasped the wooden yoke from Jeremiah's shoulders and broke it on the stones of the street. The people all laughed. "Thus," says Hananiah, "will Yahweh break the yoke of Babylon!" Due to his basic timidity, Jeremiah was at first deeply embarrassed, but going to his home and praying over the matter, he soon went to the smith and had an iron yoke fashioned. He reappeared on the streets of Jerusalem saying the same old thing, "Babylon shall be a yoke on Judah, thus saith the Lord!"

The divine tragedy in it all is that he was right. The people listened and listened and didn't understand because their ears had grown heavy with hearing the din of worldly things and they couldn't hear the "still small voice."

We live in such a potentially creative time! Never before have the potential rewards of creative goodness been so great. Never have the potential punishments of spiritual failure been so terrible! We now see that military might alone is not enough. God is not necessarily on the side of the heaviest artillery or the most atom bombs. God may not be on either side. God's purposes seem to be something beyond the reckoning of either side. The hungry must be fed and the naked clothed. The imprisoned must be freed and the spirit must be unshackled. The rich must share with the poor, but the poor must be humane. Out of the chaos and confusion can come the "New Jerusalem" if we can say with sincerity and depth of conviction "None is righteous, no, not one!" If, with Toynbee, we will seek new depths of religious understanding and keep sensitive to the painful prodding of conscience by the God of Moral Order.

III. God of Love

Does it seem to you that man will never learn to "love his enemies," as God urged us through Jesus to do? As Abner said to Joab, "shall the sword devour forever?" (II Samuel 2:26). In a somewhat similar vein, it must have seemed to sensitive prophets like Hosea and Micah that man would never learn that the old concepts of "I am a jealous God; I am a vengeful God" were not adequate to describe the true God.

Even as we talk about the God of Love and the Love of God, we must also keep in mind the other facet of God's nature that we called Law, or

Justice. Jesus never forgets the Judgment of God while talking about the love of God. I often tell my classes that Jesus says, in effect, God has two hands, the hand of Love and the hand of Justice. Man has sufficient freedom to choose whether he will have God deal with him in terms of love or justice. God must deal with each of us. If we will not respond to God's long-suffering love, then certainly at death, and often in this life, we must face judgment. It behooves us to remember, as Isaiah (64:6) says, that all our righteousness are as filthy rags in the presence of God. Or, as Paul puts it in Romans (3:23), all have sinned and come short of the glory of God. Who can stand in the judgment? "If Thou, O Lord, shouldst mark iniquities, who shall stand?" (Psalms 130:3). We are all, as Paul emphasizes, deeply dependent on the Grace of God. By that he means the creative, merciful love of God (Romans 3:23–24).

Apparently, the peoples of various ages of history are subject to vast moods. Faith seems easier in some ages than in others. This age will probably not be remembered as an age of faith! It is not particularly open to the Love of God. A Schweitzer or a Grenfell seems "out of this world"! This is an age of doubt. Consequently, it is an age of cynicism, cruelty, and despair. Those of us who see the Love of God, albeit as through "a glass darkly" are what the prophets called a "remnant"—let us hope a creative remnant. It is the role of Christianity to be constructively critical of all cultures.

First, let us look at the reasons why so many Russians doubt the love of God or the existence of a God of Love in our time. Though millions among them believe in God and spiritual reality, the mainstream of thought and action, particularly among members of the ruling party, is completely materialistic. Marxism is an utterly materialistic philosophy. Spirit does not matter. Only matter matters! Only the physical is real! That doctrine is accompanied by a fiendishly consistent attitude that individual life doesn't matter. Only the state matters. This is the principle of the greatest good for the greatest number carried to its logical conclusion. Christianity teaches that every single individual is dear to God and ultimately the supreme value. Jesus's parables of the lost sheep, the lost coin, and the lost boy in the fifteenth chapter of Luke is poignant evidence of this. For the moment, the 99 do not matter; here is one in trouble. Ultimately in Christianity we come to what Schweitzer continually emphasizes, as we said once before: "Reverence for life!"—any minute drop of it. We cannot create it. The Lord gives it. Only the Lord, in the last analysis, has the right to take it away. It is for man to bow in reverence before the fact of life in humility and reverence. Woe to that civilization which is irreverent toward life! Love is, in the last analysis, reverence.

Consequently, since Russia worships matter and is irreverent about life, or what we had better call soul, or the divine spirit in man, she is pressed to hate! Instead of appreciation of one another and trust for one another, and honesty with one another, Russians are pressed to hate and distrust one another. A part of the moral law of God is that hate tears down. "Love builds up," Paul says (I Corinthians 8:1). This means, I believe, ultimate destruction for the present Russian regime, just as it has for many other nations down through the centuries.

The frightening thing is that these same forces of evil are at work in America too. There is much blatant materialism. There is much fear. Fear of what? Fear of loss of our material bodies, our precious gadgets, our precious "standard of living." There is also much hatred of one another, much lying to and about one another, much cheap accusation of one another—calling each other "communists," "Reds," "Reactionaries." Already the seeds of hate and dissension that are rife among the Russians are also sprouting among us. Though we are officially religious, we show ourselves to be actually irreligious in many of our actions. We basically believe that victory will go to the side with the greatest battalions, or the most fearful weapons.

In the last analysis, that is not true. Victory in the long run will go to the side with the greatest souls! "That cause can neither be lost nor stayed which takes the course of what God has made!" If the Love of God and its inevitable corollary of Love of Man were obvious and apparent in the lives and behaviors of Americans, there would be less wavering on the part of India and other nations as to which way to turn. It frightens me that a young republic like India has difficulty choosing between America and Russia. We want God on our side, but we are not too concerned to be on God's side. It is perilous to identify the Christian gospel with any particular economic system. We must keep the value of persons in view.

Where there is no basic love between the people within the group (as in a nation), their basic insecurity becomes rampant. From that insecurity springs divorce, delinquency, insanity, crime, and war. They are symptoms of the human structure falling apart for lack of the cement of love.

Furthermore, it isn't that God is off asleep either. God is ever seeking for us. That's when the full tragedy of it breaks in upon you—when you realize how man's behavior must pain God. It seems profoundly true that "Where Love is, there God is." Where no love is, there God is denied. Which is cause, and which is effect? They go hand in hand. God loves. Man must respond. Where Love and God are, there life flourishes, becomes abundant. Where Love and God are denied, there life shrivels and dies.

Now, let's look at some of the rich teachings of our Bible about our God as Love. Hosea, the prophet of the eighth century BC, is the first man to discover that God is loving, forgiving and long-suffering. The fifty-third chapter of Isaiah carries this theme to its height. The cross and the incarnation are greatly illuminated by the reading of Isaiah 53.

These days, *Agape* is the term used by theologians to express this reality of Christian love. It is, of course, Greek and is brought into our vocabulary to distinguish Christian love from *Eros*, or physical, animal, or Hollywood love. When Jesus was asked, as Jews loved to ask their wise men, to distill the cream of Judaism into one command, he replied: "It is not one, but two, you shall love God with all your heart, mind and strength; and love our neighbor as you do yourself." In brief, he is saying that the key to abundant life for all, the key that opens the door to the loveliness and orderliness of the Kingdom of God is *Agape*. We have a threefold obligation to love: God, others, and self. Christianity teaches that there is a legitimate self-love. No man should despise himself. In the last analysis he is not his own, he is God's. He has been created in love and God has paid a great price for his creation, in the suffering of Christ, and in his own suffering.

As man should not hate or despise himself, neither should he love himself too much. Paul says: "I bid every one among you not to think of himself more highly than he ought to think. . . . do not be conceited" (Romans 12:3, 16). Reinhold Niebuhr, in *The Nature and Destiny of Man*, spends about forty pages on the thesis that pride is the cardinal sin of man. It separates him from his fellow man and from God. At the same time, neurotic depression, which is found so often these days, is not Christian either. One needs to think of himself and of others as children of God, humble, yet glorified through divine love and significance. All of life should be sustained in a quality of vast and endless love as the sea sustains the ships that sail upon it. As I John points out, though, this vast love can never be real unless we make love real in the little things of daily life.

Here is the logic of love. It can be approached either *a posteriori* as seen in the life of man, and from thence understanding the nature of God, or *a priori*, stating it as the nature of God and seeing the logical consequences of that assumption. Let's follow the latter, God is Love. God loves you and wants you to love Him. Such a relationship elicits from us our very best. Thus, it leads to abundant life for all that it touches. For Paul, faith and love are very much akin. He says in Romans that we are saved by faith through grace and in Corinthians that Love is greater than faith. Is he not saying that you really cannot separate the two? What is grace but outgoing love of God combined with power? What is faith but a loving, trustful, and grateful relationship to God?

A person of faith would certainly do everything he possibly could to please God. Such a person would be wonderfully good. With few exceptions, if a person isn't good, he must have no faith or love, or too little of these. It is inconceivable to Paul that one who had once entered into this vast power and relationship of love with God and brethren could deliberately be evil. When, through ignorance or weakness, we fall short ("that which I would, I do not . . . "), then God's love is merciful, kind, forgiving—and so should our love be toward one another.

Love is the *summum bonum*, the ultimate. It is creative. Love alone, with a deep sense of security in it, is the only force that can conceivably lure us on to greater efforts at creative goodness, even though we do fail occasionally. Fear certainly cannot. Fear is stifling. Thus, Paul says, "The law killeth, but the spirit (of love) giveth life" (II Corinthians 3:6).

The letter of James falls a wee bit short of this profound insight into divine truth when it says; "Show me your faith without works and I will show you my faith by my works." It is nearer the truth when it says "Faith without works is dead." Because of the factor of differing talents, persons differ in the number and quality of good works they can do, but certain it is that those who feel the love of God flowing through them cannot avoid doing helpful things for their needy neighbors. It is the "magnificent obsession" of the Christian man. But the moment he says "Ah-ha, my works are better than yours, therefore, my faith is greater"—that very moment he has separated himself from the love of God and has become vindictive and legalistic in outlook. He has killed the creative relationship between himself and his neighbor.

Another section of the late writings that presents another facet of this truth is I John 4. There alone appears the lovely phrase: "God is love." The author wraps it all up in a beautifully interrelated principle. "If one goes about saying 'I love God,' he is already on shaky ground. For love is sufficient unto itself. It does not have to artificially call attention to itself. But, if one says, 'I love God' and hates his neighbor, he is a liar! For, if he loves not his neighbor whom he hath seen, how can he love God whom he hath not seen?"

There are terrific implications here. Jesus defined neighbor in the Good Samaritan parable as anyone who has need of you. Now, when we carry this Christian principle that far, we have to deal with "all those unpleasant people, and those dirty, slovenly and foreign people" as some would put it. The stark implication of John's statement is this: if you don't like them, you probably won't like God either. It is at this point that I say to myself: "Oh, God, who can stand in the judgment?" or with Peter: "Who, then, can be saved?" Jesus's reply to Peter shows our ultimate reliance on God: "With man, it is impossible. But with God, all things are possible."

Let's round this out. God is love. All men are God's children. God loves them all. It is our vocation to, likewise, love all God's children. Again, the moral law comes into play. When we refuse to do so, we sow the seeds of chaos. God has two hands: the hand of love and the hand of judgment.

Now comes the most difficult implication of our faith in God as love. "Love your enemy." "If you love only those who love you," says Jesus, "what merit is there in that?" (Luke 6:32). "Even heathen love those who love them. But you must love those who hate you and pray for those who despitefully use you." Why? Well, basically, because it is the most functional of human relationships. It creates effective human relationships. But for the man of faith, a deeper reason for loving one's enemy is that God has often loved that same man of faith when he didn't deserve it. "He maketh his rain to fall on the just and the unjust." He loved me when I wasn't worthy of it, why should I refuse to love my enemy when he isn't worthy of it? As God's continued love of me called me back to his presence, so my continued love of my enemy will heal the breach between us creatively. The only hope of changing your enemy is through love.

So, it is obvious that forgiveness is a part of this moving drama of love with these three great players on the stage: God, self, and neighbor. After giving the Lord's prayer in the Sermon on the Mount, Jesus says: "For if you forgive not your brother's trespasses, neither will your heavenly Father forgive your trespasses." Forgiveness is not possible without love. One has to feel very secure to forgive. Thus, one cannot love his enemy without feeling secure. Loving one's enemy means forgiving him. But, it is far more creative than that sounds. It doesn't simply mean: "Let's forget the past." It means, "Let's build creatively into the future."

Suppose you promised God that you would go to church regularly, tithe your income, and spend fifteen minutes daily in prayer as a minimum standard of commitment and expression of your love. Then, suppose you attended only half the time, gave only five percent of your income, and only prayed once a week. Of course, I know that none of us present would do such a thing, but just suppose. Would God cause your house to fall down? Would God stop your heart from beating? Would God cause your husband or wife to lose his love for you? Would God withhold sun and rain from you? No. God "causes God's rain to fall on the just and the unjust." In other words, God is continually having to forgive us. Love and forgiveness go hand in hand. Those of you who are parents know that. Those of you who have husbands or wives know that. Those of you who are pastors or laymen know that. A human relationship cannot endure without almost daily forgiveness. We do it daily. But, as Paul often said, so let's say today, "Only do it more and more."

When we fail in our love and forgiveness, the creative order intended of God breaks down and chaos ensues.

Let's apply that baldly simple example of Jesus: "If a man smite thee on the one cheek, turn to him also the other." Well, first that is what God does with us all through this life. Why is it too much to ask of us to do this with our fellows? Secondly, after God had turned the other cheek thousands of times and we suffer—then it is that we are overwhelmed with contrition and turn to God so that God's creative love can heal us. Likewise, it is only when we have forgiven an enemy so often ("seventy times seven times—infinitely") that he finally dredges up that best self which he has been repressing and begins to be contrite. It is only then that a creative relationship can be developed between us.

If A strikes B, the animal thing to do would be to claw him back, but good! There would result a downward spiral relationship doing no one any good and permanently injuring one or both. Frequently, death occurs from such trivial incidents. But, if B pauses, thinks—like a human being should—then says something like this: "Well, A, old man, what's ailing you today? That isn't like you. Can I help you?" then creative possibilities emerge. A, not to be outdone, will pause, think (it's always encouraging when people think instead of simply emoting) and perhaps say, "I guess I am acting like a fool, old man, pardon me." He may make known what the real cause of his behavior is and then they can get to work on that cause. In a way it is not untrue to say that *agape* or Christian Love is simply the higher intelligence. It is the highway, the hopeful way, the saving way, the Godly way. For truly, God is Love.

God does not simply wait quietly and patiently for us, either. As Revelation puts it, Jesus, as the incarnation of God, "Stands at the door and knocks" (Revelations 3:20). But, he does not force the door. We must respond and open the door.

Francis Thompson has handled this superbly, through a daring symbol in his unforgettable "Hound of Heaven." Picturing God as a great hound, he has God "follow, follow after." "I fled Him down the nights and down the days. I fled him down the labyrinthine years of my life. Yet, with unhurried chase unperturbed pace, He followed, followed after." 'Til, having tried all the blind alleys of life, man lay prostrate and penitent and God says "Ah, fondest, blindest, weakest, I am He whom thou sleekest. Thou fledest love when thou fledest me."

Is it too extreme to say that modern man has fled God to the very margin of the world and faces the abyss of chaos?—that his only hope lies in turning penitently to the long-suffering God of Love for forgiveness, and laying hold on love and moral order to rebuild?

Chapter 16

THE NATURE OF CHRIST

Youth Conference at TCU, July 15, 1956

Introduction

We have seen that man is a sinner because he is at odds with God. Jesus became the Christ, says Paul Tillich, by becoming completely transparent to the will of God. He could say and mean it: "Not my will, but thine be done," even though that meant death on the cross. In doing so, he acted like God. He acted like God wants man to act. Needy, sinful man can look through the transparent Christ and see God. So we call him the Son of God, the Savior, the Messiah, the Christ.

Jesus Christ is the answer—we can say, God's answer—to man's sin. Jesus Christ has been seen by centuries of Christians as God's triple-barreled answer to man's sin. First, he is a substitutionary sacrifice. That is, he takes the place of animal sacrifices that we made in Judaism. Instead of man suffering as they deserve to suffer for their sins, he takes their sins upon himself and suffers in our stead. Second, this noblest of all human behavior (seldom will a man die for the one he loves, much less those who hate him) shocks man awake to the cost of his sin. Third, Jesus became The Way for man to follow so that he too may become a son of God.

Jesus Christ is God's answer to sin because:

I. Jesus Christ is unseparated from God.

In this temptation experience, Jesus is tempted in all things like we are: to use his powers to feed his own selfish hunger, impress other people by jumping off the temple tower, exalt himself and rule over other people (See Matt. 4:1–11). His basic answer to all three was in his answer to the last temptation: "You shall worship the Lord your God and him alone shall you serve." He was true to this through the difficult years of his ministry; so in Gethsemane he finally said: "Father, if it be thy will, let this cup pass from me. Nevertheless, not my will, but thine be done." This is ultimate commitment. This is what God expects of man. Thus, Jesus becomes the Christ, showing man at the same time the cause and the cure for his sin. The cause is that he is committed to his own selfish will. The cure is commitment to God's will.

The powerful and moving parables of Jesus regarding lostness speak to this point: the lost coin, the lost sheep, and the lost boy (Luke 15). They are all lost or separated from their owners, or the father. This lostness or separation from one's best state of being is the case of man's trouble. But the prodigal son story speaks more deeply to man's condition. Most of our lostness is due to our willful demanding of our portion of the inheritance, our willful going into a far corner of the soul, our gradual deterioration to some shocking condition, where we suddenly awaken to our state of "lostness" and long for the home country and the Father's presence. Many a modern boy seems to go all the way to juvenile court before he sees the implication of what he is doing. A recent article told of 300,000 high school youngsters who run away and must be handled by the police of America each year!

This sense of separation from home, church, friends brings a sense of separation from God and all my past being. I have to become a new being. I have to rediscover God, whether I get back to my parents or not. Here is where one needs to know the possibility of "becoming a new being in Christ." Christ provides man with a bridge back to God when man has gotten separated from God.

Quite often in college when a young person, separated from mother and dad, home, church, and friends, loses faith in God and flounders in the never-never land of agnosticism and atheism, it is Jesus Christ whom they can still call real. Clinging to their love of him, they are able to live through these difficult days when the face of God is veiled, until they can discover a deeper conception of God and learn to love God as they now know God.

"The Son of Man came to seek and to save the lost" (Lk 19:10). He came to reunite with the Father those who are separated from Him. He shows man the way by his own complete unity with the Father, his transparency to the will of God. "He who believes in me believes not in me, but in the one who sent me" (John 12:44).

II. Jesus Christ is the ideal orderly, disciplined self.

I get frightened at the undisciplined, disorderly characters of people today. Of course, man was always pretty much this way. I remember that twenty-five years ago, someone was much more likely to haul off and pop you one if they didn't like you than they are now. There was much more fist fighting. We have made a little progress in that matter. But, still, you are aware of a high proportion of people whose lives are so undisciplined that when things go wrong, they break up the marriage and run home to mother, or the high school kids who run away, or the people who splinter a church, or all kinds of irresponsible statements that are made about someone with whom they disagree.

Jesus Christ becomes our Savior by showing us the way to a disciplined self. He is the very incarnation of perfect goodness. He is so long-suffering and patient. He loves his enemies. He will not let himself hurt his enemies. He even prays "Father, forgive them for they don't know what they are doing" when he is being crucified. It is true that he overturned the tables of the money changers in the temple, and according to one Gospel account (John 2:13–16) he even used a whip in doing so. This seems quite out of character for him. But, even so, he did not harm the people. He acts here as judge of those who willfully do wrong.

Most of his life is given to teaching the way of righteousness and love, and to showing by example, even unto the cross, what this actually means in practical situations. He says: "Be ye perfect as your Father in heaven is perfect" (Matt. 5:48). He says: "If any man would come after me, let him take up his cross and follow me" (Matt. 16:24). When Peter complained about others at the close of Jesus's earthly ministry, Jesus said to him, ". . . what is that to you, you follow me!"

One simply misses the point of Christian faith and life if he does not see it as a disciplined and orderly life of commitment. A recent book by Oldham is entitled *Life is Commitment*! It has been well received by Christian students at the University of Texas. [*Paul was still teaching at the Texas Bible Chair at UT Austin, when he gave this address.*]

We find ourselves, says Jesus, by losing ourselves in disciplined commitment to God's way as revealed in Jesus Christ. In this way, too, he is our savior. He takes our Quixotic parts (you know: Don Quixote!) and assembles them, sets us on great white chargers, and points us in the direction of the world's great need—unified, disciplined, committed!

While one in twelve in America will go to mental hospitals, those with this kind of discipline and commitment under Christ will not be found in mental hospitals. This is a healthy way of life. This is the buoyant, creative, joyous life. This is the life! This is what Paul Tillich calls "Being grasped by the power of Being!"

III. Jesus Christ is Truth Overcoming Falsehood

When the Gospel of John quotes Jesus as saying, "If you continue in my word . . . you will know the Truth and the Truth will make you free" (Jn. 8:31–32). And again, he said "I am the Way, the Truth, and the Life . . . " (Jn. 14:6), which implies that when you know Jesus, you become fearlessly loyal to the Truth. He will show us all truth if we continue to be committed to his way. It is a way of fearless, loyal questing after the pattern of Jesus Christ.

We live in a day when there is little respect for the truth in mass communications. The things claimed in some advertising for beer, liquor, automobiles, and most any other product are known by the poor, captive TV audiences to be gross stretching of the truth. The cynical creed of Hitler won the day all over the world. What you say doesn't have to be true. Just say it over and over and over to all people and finally enough of them will believe it.

I can remember when the cigarette ads back in 1930 first had a woman appear, she said to the man "Blow some my way!" Not long thereafter, the woman was shown taking a cigarette out of the pack, then she was smoking. Similarly, since the war, women have been shown in groups where people are drinking beer and liquor. Next, the whole family was shown, and now women are drinking in the ads. They are also beginning to show young people at the summer cottage, off in the distance swimming and being told to "come and get it." These ads will, unless some great mass media like the church does something about it, soon have all the young people drinking. The laws will be changed so they can. They will demand it, and it will be done—just as the prohibition laws were broken by public demand.

It matters not that between 50 to 75 percent of all traffic accidents involve liquor. It matters not that in nearly all stabbings, rapes, shootings, kidnappings, there has been drinking. These things do not take place where Jesus Christ holds sway in a life, because he is Truth. These things feed upon untruth.

Jesus Christ is like the sun which moves into a swampy, mosquito breeding area and dries it all up so it can become creative and productive. Jesus Christ, as the Truth, demands sincerity, honesty, integrity in a person. Where this spirit pervades a person, the swamplands of his soul are cleared of the debris so frequent in our time. He becomes a better friend, a better husband, a better student, a better athlete, a better sweetheart, a better employee. No significant human relationship can develop on lies and untruth.

IV. Jesus Christ Is Love Overcoming Hate

The thesis of the entire Bible is that God's love is overcoming man's hate. It is stated in John 3:16 that God so loved the world (this sinful world) that he gave his only begotten son, that whosoever (any sinner) believes in Him might not perish but have everlasting life."

When Jesus taught his disciples in the Sermon on the Mount to "love your enemies," he meant it. He meant it so much and so deeply in his inner, real-being that he didn't forget to do it in the extreme pain of crucifixion. His prayer from the cross for his enemies, "Father, forgive them for they don't know what they are doing" has been called by Overstreet the maturest statement ever uttered by a suffering human being about those causing his suffering.

Instead of being obsessed with self, Christians have a "magnificent obsession" with others. In the parables of lostness, it is apparent that God's love goes out most to those who need it most. He leaves the 99 sheep safe in the fold to seek the one that is lost. Both God and the 99 should rejoice when the one is found. Sometimes the 99 do not rejoice, but are resentful, which shows that they do not have Christlike love either.

Christian love really wills the good, the redemption, the well-being of others. It does this at its own expense if necessary. This is the ultimate, amazing grace revealed in Christianity. This is not apparent in other religions, except the suffering servant strand of Judaism, which Jesus chose to fulfill.

But this, which is called Agape love in theology today, is the way to man's hope. When the Apostle Paul said "Now abide faith, hope and love, these three, but the greatest of these is love" (I Cor.13), he meant that love was greater than faith in spite of the fact that he tells the Romans and the Galatians that we are saved by faith. The point is that it takes a loving person to have faith. Faith grows in a loving relationship.

This we must learn in our time. We must first love God before we can have faith in God. We must first love Christ before our faith can grow very large. We must first love our enemy before we can have any faith in him. Hate is the opposite of love, and fear is the opposite of faith. Hate and fear are destructive, damning. Love and faith are constructive, creative, saving.

We live in a world filled with prejudices, fears, and hates. We Christians have our work clearly cut out for us. It is to go into all the situations of life and sow love where there is hate, faith where there is fear. In this way Christ will indeed overcome the world. "This is the victory that overcomes the world—even our faith" (I John 5:4).

This enables YOU to say: "Not my will, but thine be done." This keeps one unseparated from God, disciplined and orderly, truthful, and loving. This is a description of a person living in the Kingdom, being saved, and "grasped by the Holy Spirit or the power of being." Verily, it is a fearful and wonderful thing to fall into the hands of the living God!

Chapter 17

CORRESPONDENCE WITH RONNIE DUGGER, *TEXAS OBSERVER*

December 7, 1960
Dear Ronnie:
It was indeed delightful to have you on our campus, to hear your speech to the forum and especially to converse with you about the meaning of life. I was especially happy to hear from you and would have answered the letter last week had I not been going to Denison each evening last week. That, in addition to my regular work, left me exhausted. Now, today, I have this additional letter, and I have some leisure to respond.

I can certainly see why you think my position essentially agnostic. For me to claim that I <u>know</u> ultimate truth completely would be for me to play god. What I know, I know in terms of experience with nature and reasoning about such experience. But, though much of my life is lived at this rather simple level, the meaning of these experiences, especially experiences with other individuals and groups where love and emotional involvement develop, presses me to make generalizations about the meaning of life. In this leap of faith, I must make an affirmation of the Ultimate Nature of Reality. It is in such an affirmation that I find the many selves drawn together in a person. My essential self is shaped by this central affirmation. The picture of Ultimate Reality that I affirm is the core around which my many selves are drawn into some consistency and given the will and purpose to grasp and shape reality, but it comes to be meaningful, as Tillich puts it, as "being grasped and shaped by an ultimate concern."

That which concerns you ultimately is your picture of the ultimate possibilities of life. This is "all the very much" one can know of God, or Ultimate Reality, as you prefer. This makes sense out of and gives meaning to all the little projects and tentative purposes of life. Is this deviant, or is this on the main line of meaningful activity? We must constantly ask

The Texas Observer

RONNIE DUGGER
Editor & General Manager
WILLIE MORRIS
Associate Editor
SARAH PAYNE
Office Manager

An Independent-Liberal Weekly Newspaper
504 W. 24th St.
Austin, Texas
Phone GR 7-0746

HOUSTON OFFICE:
MRS. R. D. RANDOLPH
MRS. KITTY PEACOCK
419½ Lovett Blvd.
Houston, Texas

Nov. 28, 1960

Dear Professor Wassenich:

I have thought some more about our conversation, which was, for me, an event. I believe I made a point late in our talk that I was "one-up" on you logically in that my position, quite apart from my suspicions, was, "I don't know." I must withdraw that point now. This is your position, too. I sought to find some better ground in the difference between your faith, and my suspicion. I do still think that there is a good deal of difference between them; the one has somehow much more to do with the Christian tradition than the other. And action which follows after faith ("affirmation") is perhaps believed by the person faithful to have some source of validity from the affirmation, which suspicion could never give me as a strength for action. In fact, I find the complex of what I reasonably know (putting aside the ontological questions about "know") adequate to action, and the area to which I must address "suspicion" about the truth is outside my acknowledged sources of action; if I cannot make sense without the assistance of an attitude toward that which I cannot reasonably know, then, I must conclude, I am not sense. As I began to say, though, your position is also agnostic, logically. You are, in fact, the first agnostic Christian I have met, and recognized. For you, as I heard you, "I have faith" does not mean, "I believe," but does mean, "I affirm, because it helps me make sense out of the universe." Well, this is a lot stronger than I could ever go, you do see the emotional difference between a leaning-forward affirmation and a shoulder-shrugging suspicion, but I was somewhat surprised later that I had not given before serious thought to the logical possibility of agnostic Christianity, a possibility you brought to personal life for me.

I shall read the books you mentioned some time in the future. I am glad to know you.

Ronnie

Professor P. G. Wassenich
5721 Walla
Fort Worth 15, Texas

cc Valerie Drew

Letter from Ronnie Dugger, founding editor of the *Texas Observer*, after his presentation to TCU students. Wassenich family collection.

ourselves. We constantly judge by some such standard whether our time is well spent struggling with this particular project.

Reiterating that I cannot know completely the nature of Ultimate Reality, I affirm that it makes sense that life is not purposeless, and as I quest for my purpose, I look for purpose in other lives. I find the core meaning and purpose in life in the Judeo-Christian tradition. The moral law is a meaningful minimal structuring of the relations among men and to the Ultimate. Yet, the legalistic and puritanical behavior that sometimes develops out of this affirmation, as in the Pharisees and the Puritans, I think is deviant. But the prophetic orientation that develops out of this, especially as this comes to fruition in Jesus, does give me a sense of direction; and I affirm that here was a man really committed to being and doing all the truth he understood. He was very receptive toward others who were not Pharisaic in orientation (and pretty harsh on the Pharisees). Though Paul and the other early Christians formed and shaped a tradition about Jesus which often becomes Pharisaic, this is not his fault. This is what he fought.

So, as Tillich puts it, Jesus became absolutely transparent to the will of God as he understood it and called upon other men to do the same. He never defines the details of this will of God because he was trying to keep it from becoming another law (a "heteronomy" as Tillich calls it). In this commitment, he remained open and creative and committed. This is the stance that is creative. It trusts God, even though it does not fully know God. It trusts what it does not know of God, or Ultimate Reality, based on what it does know and can reasonably affirm as being possible and loving and creative. It involves self with all men as children of God. It works through the various forms and structures of life knowing that none of these is ultimate, but that forms are necessary.

In this position, I am not any better "armored" than you. It has a tragic quality. After all, the cross is at the heart of it. But, it also has the resurrection, which is the symbol of ultimate victory. (Don't get embroiled in literalism regarding this doctrine, or you misunderstand me. The resurrection is the eternal "new being" that emerges with infinite possibilities of new goodness.) There is an overall sense of well-being because one is involved in this finite way with the purposes of Infinite Reality.

You say you would not advocate any one act on your "suspicions," but you do this in your speaking and your writing constantly. You try to show people answers on which they will act. You are a reformer at heart, by your own definition.

It occurs to me that the reason you are suspicious of my position is that it is so alien to dogmatism which has characterized much orthodox religion. But you know too, don't you, that liberals for a century or so have been developing religious thought on an undogmatic basis. You have much in common with liberal Christians of several varieties. They do not try to live "autonomously" as though they could live alone and uninvolved. Nor do they try to call any "heteronomy" the ultimate will of God, but they live under God as individuals who endeavor to be men of integrity in their various involvements with fellow man. This is their orientation, their purpose, that which gives coherence to their lives. They fall short and think of themselves as unacceptable to God, yet loved and accepted by him anyway, and go at it again, endeavoring to be worthy in this complex situation.

Well, sorry I couldn't handle it more briefly. When I'm in Austin, I hope to visit with you and would welcome your visits whenever you are here or our paths cross elsewhere.

I greatly respect and appreciate you. Very best wishes in your efforts to keep *The Observer* alive. I am talking it up to friends. Wish I were able to underwrite more of it.

Cordially,
Paul

Chapter 18

WHAT THE CHURCH MAY TEACH

A 1964 Lecture at the Regional Christian Education Conference, Oklahoma City

What the church teaches will depend on how the church views itself. I am assuming that the Church is the fellowship of the ones who feel themselves called out of the world into a unique fellowship for the blessing of the world. They are the people who are genuinely endeavoring to be the "Body of Christ" because they profoundly feel that Christ is the revelation of God as he is relevant to human life.

This is not an irrational or unexamined "feeling." It is a faith venture that makes sense at many levels. Viewing the many philosophic and theological pictures of what man is and ought to be, these Christians have decided that the picture of Jesus as the Christ is the best picture of what is noble, good, and possible by the grace of God. They have decided with Christianity and against Buddhism that they want a life-affirming, not a life-denying religion. They are not seeking Nirvana. They seek to participate with God who is the Way, the Truth, the Life in the establishment of a Kingdom on earth that is of God. God, they believe, has shown God's self to be for man, by the character of the creation and its development, by the development of the people of God through the law, the prophets, and particularly the revelation in Jesus the Christ. Jesus as the Christ has given us an insight into last or final things, too. We have decided that the pictures in the eschatological passages of the New Testament which say essentially that in the end a Christ-like God will pass judgment on all God's works makes sense. It is of one piece, logical with the conception of God as the Creator and Sustainer of the Universe.

We see the Bible, therefore, as revelatory of the character of God and

God's requirements for man. These requirements are expressions of love, not antagonism. God is ultimately revealed, particularly in the cross and resurrection, as God-with-us or God-for-us.

We acknowledge that even the revelation of God in Christ would not be accessible to us without the Bible. We recognize that our Bible is a product of reverent interpretation of historic events by Jews and Christians. The Christian era began with Jesus and his disciples in dynamic fellowship, wherein he taught them for perhaps a year or possibly a year and a half, as indicated in the synoptic gospels. Then came the crucifixion, the shaking of the foundations. It was the ugly fact of evil made poignantly clear. Even the priests of the people of God can be blind to God's word and oppose his will, as the New Testament and the Old Testament clearly show. But the pivotal event is the resurrection. The facts are that hopeless disciples became adamant apostles, the twelve and the hundred and twenty became three thousand, then five thousand, and ultimately millions, believing that through the resurrected Christ they saw the sovereign God who had made the crucified one both Lord and Christ. Our New Testament developed as believers sought to communicate this saving word in written form. In the first 150 years, so many written documents emerged and such a variety of traditions that leading Christians and finally councils had to define the canon. Our students must be clearly informed about this process of development of the Bible and come to love it and appreciate it as a product of the faith of the early church.

We must teach responsible pictures of the resurrection faith. As in the gospels themselves, there is room for difference of opinion about details, but the main thrust is basic: God, not man, is ultimate. Good, not evil, is sovereign. Resurrection, not crucifixion, is final. It is God who has made Jesus both Lord and Christ. The main thing we must teach about Jesus as the Christ is that he is revelatory of the character of God as it is relevant to man. God is the loving, redemptive Father. God constantly struggles with evil as God did in the crucifixion. God ultimately brings a creative new reality into being. This God is the Sovereign Lord of history—personal history and corporate history. Not only is each one of us to meet God in daily life as well as at death, but each civilization must answer to God's love, power, and justice. Hitler will not have the last word.

This is God, the only God there is. God is not simply the God of church members. God is the God of everybody, whether they know it or not. The Church, when it is really the fellowship of the called-out ones, knows this. It, like God, loves especially the lost ones, the dumb ones, the prodigals. Like God, the vocation of the Church is not to prosper in magnificent isolation, but to move out into the so-called secular world and help it understand itself. It is God's world. Men who think they are sovereign instead of God must be told that God is sovereign before they end up in some hog-pen of life, taking many others with them. The sheep-like people who have not sufficient self-sense to affirm themselves must be protected from the wolves. The only way these things can be done is for Christians to be involved in politics. Read Paul Lehmann, *Ethics in a Christian Contest.* The hungry must be fed, the naked clothed, the imprisoned visited with a redemptive message of a new vision of self. Unless the church changes radically, it is in no position to feed the hungry, heal the sick, clothe the naked, and visit the imprisoned. But, in a democratic society like ours, the koinonia or fellowship of the called-out ones have a vocation—to make human life human—not just for themselves, but for those voiceless millions who cannot speak for themselves. "To whom much is given, of him must shall be required." The churches today are filled with well-to-do and middle-class people. Rarely are the poor found among them. The millions of school drop-outs dropped out of Sunday School and church long ago. These are the lost sheep. These are the fields ripe unto the harvest. These cannot be reached by a personal evangelism that is hit or miss, dependent on the mood of an individual Christian and a happenstance meeting in the supermarket. The Church must imitate big business or big government or big labor in being realistic about where and how you get your message across to the people. Business, labor, and the representatives of government act from selfish motives. But we Christians must become "wise as serpents and as harmless as doves." We must use the sociological skills and the psychological insights to save the lost, not to manipulate them. We must help them discover where their own depth fulfillment is available—in the fellowship of Christ, being a part of the answer instead of the problem of modern society.

Therefore, the Christian education program of the church must be much more profound, thorough, realistic and practical. By the time a child is in junior high school, he should be thoroughly conversant with the Bible and able to make distinctions between unimaginative literalism and responsible interpretations. He should then begin to see his city as a field in which he and his Christian friends are to act as a task force for God to bless the hurt ones, the weary ones, the blind ones.

He should begin to see that unless the Christian call for peace on earth and good will among men is sounded and heard, mankind could blast himself off the face of God's good earth. He needs to be enlisted with a sense of urgency in establishing intelligent good will in every facet of life he touches. But he can't do it alone. To say these "idealistic" things in church and never think them again 'til next Sunday is futile. There must be a continuing koinonia—a fellowship of the redeemed in the midst of the so-called "secular" activities of life, thinking, plotting, planning redemptive work. Precisely what they do or say cannot be laid down as a law. It must be imaginative, lovingly responsive to what the other person says. A dialog of redemption must develop. It may speak mostly of penultimate things, but as Bonhoeffer points out, these point beyond, inevitably to the ultimate things. Our involvement in the world must be such that it draws all men unto God who is our light and our life.

By the time this youngster is out of high school, he will be ready to utilize new dimensions of power that accrue to him as an adult to express love and achieve new norms of justice in life which will draw those blest by this justice to the source of that power and love—namely Jesus Christ, whom this man names as Lord and Savior.

Now, there is much more that must be taught adults if Christianity is to appropriately redeem society, or be used of God for the redemption of men. In its theological depth and its ethical relevance, the Bible is very profound. There are areas of Christian education which have been completely neglected by the Church, as least the Disciples of Christ. They have to do with church history, theology, ethics, the history of world missions, the history and development of the ecumenical movement, the history of the denominations, and the beliefs of the various denominations that are distinctive. Also, there are numerous practical courses that need to be taught concerning the operation of the state and local council of churches and the denominational structure and restructure. Courses need to be offered in social ethical areas such as alcoholism and its cure, means of helping minorities gain equality of opportunity, how the United Nations operates, is financed, and what it has accomplished.

If we keep in mind the primary task of the educational ministry of the church, the content possibilities are multitudinous. The task of Christian education is to equip the saints for redemptive life in the world. It must help the Christian deepen his own faith-understanding, to lead in the solution of moral and religious problems in society, to develop an exemplary family life, and to be a resource person to the needy, pointing them to Christ and the Church as the inexhaustible fount of help.

The Challenge to the Church's Teaching Ministry
A 1964 Lecture

Paul Douglas, speaking at Disciples House, Chicago, in 1939, said he had read the debate between Alexander Campbell and Robert Owen, the agnostic. He characterized it as two trains of thought passing in the night without even touching, much less colliding. I often sense that what the minister is saying is not really relevant to life as it is lived by the businessman, the mother, the teacher, the city planner. The challenge to the church school teacher is the same as the challenge to the minister. It is the challenge to communicate, to be relevant.

First, the teacher needs to know the gospel, to be in Christ, to be ontologically involved with the Gospel. Second, he is challenged to communicate the Gospel by the essential character of his own being, as well as by clear words and illustrations that come out of the life of the hearers. Just as a preacher cannot preach well if he is not a good pastor who listens well, so a teacher cannot teach well unless she can listen well and hear not only the words the pupils are saying but the depth meanings of the words.

That means that teaching the Gospel is different from imparting facts, even though they may be scriptural facts.

I suppose I have as liberal a view of the Bible as anyone here, but I have often been puzzled when people whom I consider quite conservative have expressed warm appreciation for Biblical teaching that I have given. It finally dawned on me that their appreciation arose because I try to give something more than facts. I try to make the facts relevant in terms of meaning. This is possible by living with Paul and then translating Paul's experiences to contemporary man's experience, avoiding so far as possible the peril of modernizing Jesus or Paul, but not being rigid with fear and therefore dull. This is even essential for effective communication to adults. It is even more necessary for communicating with children and young people.

Third, another challenge to the teaching ministry and to the entire membership of the church is the challenge to avoid mediocrity. We live in a world of specialists. We see good football, hear good musicians, see good swimmers, ski-jumpers, skaters. Our best brains collaborate to put rockets and Telstars together to achieve fabulous results. The church is not going to attract people long if its work is shabbily prepared and presented. People must do their vocational work first. They can only give leisure hours to the church. If the church insists on working the layman as a teacher, an elder, a functional committee chairman, representative on the council of churches, program committee chairman for the men's fellowship, and a few other things, he can't possibly be a good and thorough teacher.

There is needed in the church a philosophy of socialization. I told my minister and board chairman of our church that the time I had available was just so much. I thought the best use of my time would be in teaching. I requested to be left off the board and committees. It worked for a while, and then I weakened and accepted board membership and then membership on the education committee and then a place on the Council of Churches board. Recently, they hit one of my vulnerable spots and made me chairman of the social action committee. This is not wise, either on their part or mine. It is I who should say no. Yet, Christian educators should protect their teachers and foster such a sense of specialization. I greatly admire the specialists in Christian education of children at various age levels whom I know. This is wise expenditure of time, talent, and energy. Christian educators need to contend for a philosophy of specialization in lay Christian service.

Fourth, the obvious next challenge is to use well the time and talent the layman thus lays on the altar. This involves good chalk, board, maps, scissors, crayons, possibly visual aids, recorders, etc. Above all, it involves adequate teacher training opportunities. I was thoroughly in sympathy with the education committee of my home church when they said recently let's drop this monthly workers' conference where we just rehash problems discussed many times and not call a meeting unless we have a relevant agenda on which we can really see the possibility of some meaningful action. They also decided that they would have divisional workers' conferences, where there was a universe of discourse about materials and methods.

I know a church which met another challenge with ingenuity and imagination. They had a good Bible teacher who attracted a large number of adults. When adults were asked to teach children's or youth classes, they honestly said, "I'm learning so much in this class that I don't want to leave it and I think I am not entirely selfish in this. I need to know the things I am learning to be an effective Christian." The Education Committee came up with a compromise solution. They offered to get a recorder and tape the Sunday School lessons, then have the church secretary type them up to get some adults to teach children's classes. Several adult members dropped out of their Sunday School class to do that.

This church also set up a five-year adult curriculum that is primarily content-oriented while carrying on two other adult classes that are different in character. It is agreed that the adults who take this five-year course will then put their knowledge and skills to work. They take examinations, receive letters of credit and commendation, and are recognized in the worship service in church.

Another challenge to the teaching ministry is to be less sheep-like regarding materials and methods. Materials and methods become stereotypes, or styles. They have their day and all the "hip" people scorn the other people if they don't do it in just the "right" way. One thing that is right about the conservative political position in our time, in my opinion, is the emphasis on the individual. In many ways, we are in danger of becoming a nation of sheep who follow blindly and unthinkingly certain styles that emerge. In my opinion, the truly creative teacher is the one who can bring out of his treasure things both new and old which communicate the Gospel. He is neither unduly resistant to the new, nor unduly scornful of the old.

A subtle, complex challenge which is difficult to meet is to properly relate past, present, and future. Relevant teaching must start with the present, reach intelligently into the heritage of the faith for appropriate ideas about and incarnations of the faith, make the application to the present, and challenge those he teaches to make the transformation of behavior and human relations that will shape the future for God. It is a challenge to teach so that the pupils sense that their teacher is a colaborer with God, the Father of our Lord Jesus Christ, as he is in process of bringing his Kingdom and, furthermore, to inspire them to desire to do this in their own lives and relationships—to become in a sense the Incarnate Word—to follow in the Master's footsteps.

At the same time, the teacher must realize that this borders on spiritual pride. The goal stated is an impossible possibility. Christ must be seen as God's expression of forgiving grace and loving acceptance of imperfect, sinful men, as well as the Way, the Truth, and the Life. We both are and are not Christian.

A challenge that the curriculum writers and an occasional teacher are responding to is the challenge to teach theology, church history, Christian ethics, and missions as well as Bible. We need these lessons; we cannot be really literate Christian laymen without this content. However, we will never have the teachers to present these materials if we don't move to specialization in lay activity. To teach these things will require study and careful preparation. Where there is a university in the area, I can envision a man or woman who has dedicated himself to be a teacher going to college to take courses in these subjects as part of his stewardship, so he can adequately teach the Gospel and communicate meaning to meaningless lives.

A relevant teaching ministry will not simply emphasize such content courses, however. It will recognize the problems that press in upon God's people—those in the koinonia and those out in the world. The genuine Christian weeps with those who weep. The pain of the divorcee is understood empathetically. The church will provide intelligent teaching about the Christian family. It will provide teaching for all sorts and conditions of men and women, maritally speaking.

A relevant teaching ministry will have special groups for alcoholics and other lost souls. It will seek to bind up the wounds, pour in the healing love of Christian good will and understanding. Such efforts will, insofar as possible, be informed psychologically and sociologically. Much more use could be made of social workers, professors of sociology and psychology, psychiatrists, etc. who live in the community and are willing to share their insights for the common welfare.

Always, the teaching personnel will realize that no real learning is likely to take place unless there is a genuine dialogue—listening and really hearing as well as speaking. Probably a better word would be trialogue, quatrelogue, or conversation. Many a person comes to church humiliated by having taken a wrong turn in his life. He needs understanding, forgiveness, and acceptance. He is willing to make confession, but our churches and groups provide him no chance for confession; so he confesses in secret even if the group knew of his sin. He longs for insight into why he did this and what he can do to avoid doing it again.

Here the type of curriculum and group dynamics present in the Discipleship Series is eminently useful. I was quite interested to sit in such a group out in New Mexico last summer. There were twelve of us, seven regulars and five visitors. Yet, within fifteen minutes, we were really working on the topic the group had chosen in the prepared materials. The lay leader was playing her role effectively, although she was at first threatened by my presence and the presence of the other visitors. When the hour was over, I considered it one of the very rich church school experiences of my life. There is a great need for this type of group to replace the frontier neighborhood, which has vanished. On the average, half the people move every four years. They need, sometimes desperately, to find a group that communicates in a way that is responsive to the things that interest them. The Discipleship materials, under imaginative chairmanship, provide such an opportunity.

The acids of modernity have created a permanent acidity in many lives. They are cynical about self and society. They need a new vision of the possibilities of human life. They need a friendship that is sufficiently Christlike to assure them that Jesus, as the Christ, is not a fairy story but is seeable in the persons involved in Koinonia.

In this context, a zealous and natural evangelism is a normal emergent. It emerges as an expression of understanding love and a gift of redemption proffered to one whom we love and whose misery hurts us as though it were our own. We say Christian teaching is never fulfilled until it brings the love of Christ to the pupil.

How far can this grace reach beyond the front doors of the church edifice? The answer, my friend, "is blowing in the wind," as the popular folk song says. If, like Nicodemus, you can respond to the Lord's insight about "the wind bloweth where it listeth," the Holy Spirit will make a soul restless to remain within the confines of the church. John 3:16 does not say, "God so loved the church." It says, "God so loved the world."

The winds of God are blowing across the whole earth today. God is claiming this whole round orb as his own again. He has had to transcend our missionary enterprise. He moves through the secular world, bringing freedom and dignity to the Negro person through political media, since his Church failed so miserably to do it. If the American church does not want to suffer the fate of the Russian church, it must rouse from its opiate sleep and truly sacrifice for the lost sheep of the world. Let him who has ears, listen!

Christian teaching is quite different from public school teaching. It means being [embodying] the Truth and Love to creating the Koinonia fellowship that acts. Paul Lehmann says that the difference between philosophical ethics and Christian ethics is that Christian ethics involves action, whereas philosophical ethics is content to rationally define the good. Christian ethics reckons with the radical nature of evil. Philosophic ethics does not. I hope he is right. I am not too impressed with the numbers of Christians who act out the implications of the Gospel. But it is obvious that the world desperately needs such Christians. Christian teaching must make this clear, by word and deed. It is not enough to speak the truth, we must be the truth. It is not enough to speak of love. We must be those who love the brotherhood and love our enemies. "If a man say I love God, and hate his brother, he is a liar." Brethren, the primary challenge is the challenge to be the loving Christian brother and to stimulate Christians to create new forms to implement the Gospel as God does God's saving work in the world.

Finally, adequate teaching eventuates in worship. If the foregoing intentions are even partially fulfilled, the student will feel that he needs to worship. He needs it for at least three reasons: he needs to confess his inadequacies, he needs to be together with other Christians who share the Gospel orientation, and he needs it for empowerment to move out into the world as a member of God's army and occupy one of the frontline foxholes, to bring life, not death—to overcome the enemy, the devil, the forces of evil both within and without the individual.

How Come the Bible: The Development of the Canon and Text of the Bible

The New Testament starts with the life of Jesus, who was born about 6 BCE. The Apostle Paul's letters were written about 50–64 CE; the Gospels were written between 64–100 CE. Paul's letters were collected about 90 CE, and the four Gospels were collected about 125 CE. Marcion suggested Luke, Acts, and the ten letters of Paul as the official Christian literature.

The Muratorian Canon (circa 200), discovered in 1740 by L.A. Muratori, was probably written by Bishop Victor of Rome around 200 because of heretical sects which were using other spurious Christian literature to confuse the church. The Canon of Origen (circa 250), who was a scholar in Alexandria, when North Africa was a center of learning, included all of our present twenty-seven books of the New Testament plus two not now included, the Letter of Barnabas and the Shepherd of Hermas. He also expressed doubt about the real inspiration of James, Jude, II Peter, II and III John.

The Canon of Eusebius (circa 325), who was a famous church historian, listed the present twenty-seven books of the New Testament but indicated the following were disputed: James, Jude, "Peter," III John, and Revelation. In 367, Athanasius wrote the Canon of Athanasius in a letter to the churches in his Alexandrian Diocese at Easter in which he listed the same twenty-seven books we now have as the authoritative scripture. He added, "Let no one add or take away aught of them."

The Latin Vulgate of St. Jerome (circa 400) authorized the same twenty-seven books as Athanasius. This Vulgate was the basic Bible Text until recent archeological discoveries brought to light earlier documents. Codex Vaticanus (mid-fourth century) used original Greek texts for the New Testament and old Latin for the Old Testament. It is the most complete. Another ancient manuscript is Codex Sinaiticus, discovered in 1859 by Tischendorf at a monastery at the base of Mt. Sinai. Tischendorf's trip had been financed by the Czar of Russia, so the manuscript went to Moscow. In 1934 the Soviet government sold it to the British Museum for 100,000 pounds, roughly half a million dollars. Codex Alexandrimus (Egypt, fifth century) follow Origen's Septaugent Old Testament and includes some non-canonical books.

The development of the English Bible started with the Wyclif Version (1382). John Wyclif of England translated the Bible, aided by his student Nicholas Hereford, using the Latin Vulgate as the basic text. This Wyclif Version was the first complete English Bible. It preceded printing. Itinerant preachers went about England reading it to the people and explaining it.

Between Wyclif and the next great English translation, three great events occurred. First, Gutenberg invented the printing press in 1450. Second, the Turks took Constantinople in 1453 and scholars fled westward with their knowledge of Greek, bringing about the Renaissance and the Reformation in Western Europe. Third, Erasmus published the first Greek New Testament in 1516. Of course, the Protestant Reformation beginning in 1515 turned people to the Bible as a source of authority and inspiration too.

The Tyndale Bible (1525–36) made the first English translation from the Greek, going back before the Vulgate. His work was received eagerly by the people of England, but the ecclesiastical and political authorities were responsible for his imprisonment after which he was strangled and burned to death in 1536.

Other Bibles include the Coverdale Bible (1535), the Rogers Bible

(1537), and lesser translations. The Great Bible (1539), so called because of its great size, was projected by Thomas Cromwell, the king's minister, and bore a preface written by the Archbishop of Canterbury, Thomas Cranmer. It was so popular that it was often stolen and was always chained to a post near the lectern on which it lay.

The Geneva Bible (1560) was a revision of the Great Bible, done in Geneva, Switzerland, by a group of English scholars in exile. It was small enough in size to become popularly used. It is often called the "breeches Bible" because of its translation of Gen. 3:7. "They sewed fig leaves together and made themselves breeches."

The Bishops Bible (1568) was authorized by Archbishop of Canterbury, Matthew Parker, because the popular use of the Geneva Bible put the Great Bible at a disadvantage. The committee of translators contained so many Bishops that it became known as the Bishops Bible and was the official English translation appointed to be read in the churches until the King James version was published in 1611.

The Rheims-Douay Version was created for Roman Catholics who needed a translation of their own. A group of English scholars working at Catholic Schools in Rheims published the New Testament in 1562. The same school moved back to Douay by the time the Old Testament was ready in 1609.

The King James Version (1611) was the work of six committees of scholars appointed by King James I of England. Four committees worked on the Old Testament and two on the New Testament to revise the Bishops Bible. This translation was never made the official English translation by voice of Parliament but has, in effect, become such. It has had a tremendous influence on the English language and is still the most frequently read translation in all English-speaking countries.

The Revised Version (1881–85) was created from the King James Version because new manuscripts such as Codex Sinaitious (1859) had been found by archeologists and added considerably to authoritative early documents. British scholars invited American scholars to collaborate, but the work of the American scholars was put in marginal notes or appendices. The Americans agreed not to publish an American Revision for 14 years, but they finally did in 1901.

The Moffatt (1921) and the Goodspeed New Testament (1946–52) put the Bible into colloquial English and served to underscore the necessity for further revision They sold millions of copies.

The Revised Standard Version (1946–52) was the result of the American Standard Bible Committee, which was appointed by the International Council of Religious Education (now part of the National Council of Churches) in 1929. It published a New Testament in the fall of 1946 which has been widely received among American Protestants with genuine appreciation. The Old Testament was published in the Fall of 1952 and is having a similar reception. Celebrations were arranged across the country, and Christian groups of all kinds made studies of this new version.

Other translations continue to come out. The work on the New English Bible occurred during 1966–70. Other translations include the J.B. Phillips translation of the New Testament and the Living Bible.

Some Emphases of Fundamentalist Christianity Affecting Youth Movements in the 1970s

Written in April 1972 for the TCU Religion Department Faculty to justify a seminar on Fundamentalism and Liberalism

The late 1960s through most of the 1970s were times of great turmoil in the US, which was engaged in an increasingly unpopular war in Vietnam to prevent the Communist North from taking over the democratic South. The draft was in effect, so many college students were on edge about being drafted or whether they could finish college and pursue a career.

This tension began to manifest in demonstrations on college campuses across the nation. When the war ended and the demonstrations stopped, people reverted to a somewhat fundamentalist point of view that answered their questions and gave them comfort because of strong parameters on their faith. Naturally, the students who came to TCU reflected this cultural shift.

The fundamentalist beliefs included the claim that the earth is only six thousand years old, the rejection of the theory of evolution, and an insistence that the Bible is the literal word of God which is not subject to question.

"Baptists and Johnson grass are about to take over Texas!" "Fundamentalists and Johnson Grass are about to wipe out the liberal and scholarly view of the scriptures." Although this change will affect our churches very definitely, we're concerned about its implication for our classroom approach to the subjects we teach, particularly in 1203 and 3103 (classes listed in the course catalog). "What are the mighty acts of God in the Bible that are primary moments in which God reveals God's will and way?" Creation, Exodus, Kingdom, Prophets, exile, restoration, Christ event, church. "What on earth is God doing now?" Students in both classes came through with a fundamentalist, second-coming-of-Christ-series of answers. "Wars and rumors of wars." "Earthquakes." "Common Market." "Automobiles."

In the 1203 class I could get no other point of view expressed by the students. But in 3103, where I have six honors students, three of them came through with such ideas as: conscientious objectors refusing to go to war, the United Nations as a way beyond international strife, emergence of better conditions for Blacks through civil rights efforts of church and government.

I think it is important to note that there is some awareness of a way to think about such Christian concepts as Kingdom of God that has some social significance and sees the transformation of the social order as the coming of the Kingdom among those who have been in college two years, whereas there is none among the freshmen. Yet, there were twice as many in the 3103 class who took the fundamentalist approach to this matter as there were those who took the liberal view.

The point of all this is that (if I know your theological stances as well as I think I do) you and I are going to have to deal with a predominantly fundamentalist student body for the next period of time. Who knows how long this will last?

You know as much about fundamentalist theology as I do, possibly more. It simply fell to me to remind us of their central concepts. Remember they have a number of differences among themselves. This is obvious in a book by George Eldon Ladd, entitled *The Blessed Hope.* It sets up a straw man, "Pre-tribulationism," advocated in the nineteenth century by S.R. Maitland, who got it from (of all people) a Jesuit, Ribera, and another, Bellarmine, in the sixteenth century. It emphasizes 1260 days of tribulation before the return of Christ. So, these people think that Christ was to come quickly and before the tribulation and the return of Christ. Pre-tribulationists insist that those who expect the coming of the Lord to rapture the Church only at the end of the tribulation really cannot have a Blessed Hope.

This item is something of an aside or parenthesis, but immediately you are in the midst of a process of thinking that involves all the basic assumptions of the Fundamentalists and shows you that there are differences of opinion among them.

My first encounter with fundamentalist thought was in an assignment

H. N. Wieman gave me years ago to read J. Gresham Machan. That was an eye-opener for me. There was a quality of logic and depth of awareness in these writings that I had not encountered in the usual fundamentalist. Then, a decade ago, on the recommendation of William Hordern, I read E. J. Carnell, a Harvard PhD who is a fundamentalist, or as he would prefer to say, an evangelical, about 1959–63. I believe he died in 1966. He was president of Fuller Theological Seminary.

Hordern in his good book, *A Layman's Guide to Protestant Theology*, and L. Harold DeWolf in *Present Trends in Christian Thought* (1960) both recommend a careful look at Carnell.

Back in the 1930s, I thought fundamentalism would be dead now and that some form of liberalism would dominate Christian thought. Now, fundamentalism is stronger than it was then. Jesus Freaks were reported on in *U.S. News and World Report*, March 20, 1972. Jesus People is a group of "reentry from the turned-off people into the main stream of the culture." The Jesus Freaks, whether they know it or not, are undercutting the counterculture. Estimates of their numbers vary from one hundred thousand to one million. Other examples include the Crusade for Christ and the Gerry Craft group. A fraternity sponsored a fundamentalist singer, and another fundamentalist group sponsored a Christian hypnotist or spiritualist, both on the TCU campus. The Hollywood Free Paper prints five hundred thousand to one million copies each week, depending on finances.

Now, what can we say are the basic beliefs of fundamentalists? Look at First Baptist Church in Fort Worth for an example of what is a fundamentalist. Hordern's summary of Fundamentalist Belief follows:

1. Verbal inspiration of the Bible, a need for authority. Polanus is quoted, "even the punctuation marks were inspired" at least in the original manuscripts. A liberal fundamentalist allows that there are some contradictions in the present editions and translations but avers that when we get back to the original message, there will be no contradictions. If you doubt verbal inspiration, soon you will doubt Christ and God and be utterly lost.
2. There is no faith apart from the Bible because God has revealed God's self in the events recorded in the Bible. Now in some sense, all Christians would share this with the orthodox.
3. But the heart of fundamentalism is its concern for salvation. "Are you saved, brother?" is the only really important question.

Starting with Adam's fall, we have all sinned. Guilty, we cannot please God and are doomed to everlasting hell unless God saves man. God has love, mercy, justice. Liberals overlook justice. Liberals think of a God who is not righteous or demanding righteousness, but romantically accepting of anything in the way of human behavior.

Of course, the basic fundamentalist position is the old orthodox position or the classical doctrine of atonement (Hordern),[3] which has been accepted for 1,000 years. Satan gained the souls of men because they had sinned. God made a bargain with Satan that God would give Satan the soul of Jesus, even though Satan did not deserve him, if Satan would release the souls of men who accepted Jesus. Satan agreed, thinking that Jesus was only a good man; but when he received Jesus, he found that he could not hold him, for he was the Son of God. So, Satan ended up with neither Christ's soul nor the souls of those who accepted Christ.

This account is crude, but it communicates to simple minds God's victory over the forces of evil and his concern for the lost. Further implication of this story is this: man has sinned. He ought to pay for his sin. He cannot because he already owes God perfect obedience. He is in a hopeless predicament. Now, in God's love and mercy, God sent God's only Son into the world. He lived a perfect life, did not deserve to die, but died voluntarily in what might be called the perfect death—for others—to save them. Jesus's blood was shed to wash away man's sin, as the blood of animals in the Old Testament cleansed the penitent Jew from sin and God's punishment. The man who accepts Christ as the lamb of God that takes away the sin of the world is assured of heaven and receives the grace of God that enables man to overcome temptation and sin in the remainder of this life. Although fundamentalists accept various kinds of baptism and can be found in practically all Protestant churches, they tend to emphasize believers' confession of faith.

The sixth basic doctrine is that of miracles, which are the seals by which God proved God's activity and presence to men. The Virgin Birth is the most important miracle. It proves that Jesus is the Son of God, born of the Holy Spirit. The physical resurrection is the other most basic miracle, along with the Ascension. Of the miracles to come, the Second Coming is most basic. Fundamentalists believe in miracles easily and thus have no problem with the Red Sea crossing, the axe-head floating,

[3] Hereinafter, numbers in parentheses refer to the page number of the book.

Jesus walking on the water, God consuming the altar and sacrifice for Elijah, the sun standing still for Joshua to slay a few more of the enemy.

Early in the twentieth century, fundamentalists feared scholarship, especially high criticism. But a man like Carnell is at home with scholarship and knows many ways to choose the results he wishes to utilize while laying others aside. In the last analysis, one would have to say that the fundamentalist is not committed to careful investigation no matter where it leads. He is seeking desperately everywhere for supports for his faith structure which simply must stand. Biblically, he prefers lower to higher criticism.

The fundamentalist charges the liberal with dogmatism when he accepts scientific theory, for instance, of a closed or orderly universe, and the liberal says God cannot pass a miracle. A thoughtful fundamentalist might say, "Well, I am more open to novelty than you are." Likewise, regarding the second coming, the liberal will point to the many times the expectant Christians have been disappointed, as in the Millerites of the 1850s and the Adventists in Waco about 1965. But the fundamentalist will emphasize that this points to an unimaginative, impersonal, closed system that denies the Creator's power over this creation.

Carnell and Machen are both good logicians and often ridicule the easy emphasis on love and goodwill that characterizes some sloppy forms of liberalism. The liberal tends to read into the Bible what he wishes—for example, "The Kingdom of God as a socialist state" as in the Social Gospel. Of course, the most obvious answer is that fundamentalists read into the Bible events like earthquakes, common market, and Stalin, etc. as Anti-Christ.

In *The Case for Biblical Christianity*, Carnell puts down Reinhold Niebuhr. "Since he (Niebuhr) is pessimistic about the success of immanence, though not about man's ability to develop a dialectical philosophy, it follows that Niebuhr retains a critical autonomy over the system of Scripture (Bohon's "rational stance"). Whether such autonomy is good or bad depends upon how seriously one accepts or rejects the Bible as a system of thought. Orthodoxy is persuaded that one has no final truth about God until he submits to the Bible's self-testimony. Neo-orthodoxy judges the Bible by dialectical insights; orthodoxy judges dialectical insights by the Bible" (109).

Liberals tend to confuse the church with denomination or institution.

We set up institutions like the Council of Churches. The fundamentalist says the church is present where there is true, orthodox belief and witness to the Biblical word of judgment and grace. So, fundamentalists and liberals as radicals are both outside the church.

Carnell appeals for a return to Reformation doctrine in *The Case for Biblical Christianity.* The question of authority is basic. "If the Bible and Reason are not authoritative, then we Protestants have nothing to say" (171). "Let me give the pith and marrow of what I am trying to say. If Protestants fail to distinguish between apostolic testimony and their own interpretation of this testimony, they corrupt the Protestant principle by slighting the threshold of variable error that attends all Biblical exegesis. They return to the ethos of Roman Catholicism. But, if Protestants make this distinction, and yet refuse to improve their interpretation by submitting to apostolic testimony, they corrupt the Protestant principle by making themselves equal with the apostles. They repudiate the normative elements in Christian theology. The first error overlooks the work of sin in theological inquiry; the second, the authority of the apostles in detecting and correcting this work. If orthodoxy tends to make the first error, liberalism and neo-orthodoxy tend to make the second. At least this is the way it seems to me."

In conclusion, in all fairness to Carnell, I want to illustrate some of the things he has in common with neo-orthodoxy. On p.49 of *The Case for Orthodox Theology*, we read: "The gospel is the good news that God entered history and did something that man could not do for himself. The redemptive events are the foundation of the normative interpretation, and not the other way around. To conceive of the Bible as the primary revelation is heresy! If there had been no redemptive events, there would be no theology."

And finally, a second surprise is in pages 52–53 of *Progressive Revelation.* "The concept of 'progressive revelation' is the key to Biblical hermeneutics. Revelation is not complete all at once. If the light with which it starts is dim, it grows clearer as the ages advance. . . . In the beginning, Revelation has to take up man as it finds him, with his crude conceptions, his childlike modes of thought and expression, his defective moral ideas and social institutions, and has to make the best of him it can. . . . Each stage of divine revelation must be interpreted from within the spiritual and cultural level of the people being addressed. . . . The lower stages have to be read in light of the higher, with the correction which the higher affords. A Christian may uphold the divine authority of the Old Testament, but he will not feel that he is bound by the Mosaic law of divorce. . . . Cultic thinking tends to impose a uniformity on Scripture that Scripture itself disavows."

Five rules govern Biblical hermeneutics:

1. The New Testament interprets the Old Testament.
2. The Epistles interpret the Gospels.
3. Systematic passages interpret the incidental.
4. Universal passages interpret the local.
5. Didactic passages interpret the symbolic.

If any rule is neglected, the harmony of Scripture is disrupted (53, *The Case for Orthodox Theology*).

Now, just a word to start our discussion about what do we do considering the growth of fundamentalism among our students?

The main point is that if you have discussion, they will speak from their perspective and then all your students must try to understand what's going on. Some of them, though a decreasing number, do not have that perspective on reality.

I have one, pretty basic suggestion. I was frustrated with a fundamentalist student last year. I prayed about it. As if in answer to my prayer, I got this vision. Well, first help him state his position in a way that others in the class will understand and get his approval of the statement. Then say, this is the fundamentalist interpretation. Now the scholarly interpretation is this; then go on with your lecture. It was a great relief to my student and to me.

This term, following that procedure, I have had a minimum of difficulty. I put the fundamentalist's position forward as fairly and clearly as I can, and then I put one or two other interpretations before the class. Sometimes I put them on the board.

Now, Friday in my 3103 class, after all the fundamentalist ideas were on the board, I said, "Is there another point of view about what on earth God is doing now?" Glenn Johnson put forward the idea about the conscientious objectors. I put it on the board and related it to Christ's teaching a little more fully than Glenn did. He said, "I notice you elaborated on this idea and present it a little more fully than the others!"

Ministry in the 1970s

I assume full responsibility for the ideas I put forward here, but I must acknowledge the stimulation of my thinking by Reinhold Niebuhr, Paul Tillich, Samuel Miller, Hans Hoffmann, and Ruel Howe in a volume entitled *Making the Ministry Relevant* and also by George G. Beazley, Jr., in his *News on Christian Unity.*

I consider the ministry of the Christ and his Church in the 1970s one of the most significant, demanding, meaningful, and exciting professions that it is possible for man to undertake. The requirements for adequate ministry include: high intelligence and disciplined studiousness that does not end when either the BA or BD or even the PhD degree is earned. It is a life of continuing study. It relates "book learning" to life situations. It requires responsible use of latest knowledge in all the following areas:

1. Psychology as it relates to individual mental health and to theological generalization about the nature of man, sin, and salvation and human destiny.
2. Sociology as it relates to group behavior and institutional effectiveness.
3. Economics as it relates to personal finances, church finances, and corporate management.
4. Philosophy as it attempts to make a rational statement about what can be known rationally and to distinguish this from what must be "faithed."
5. History as it relates for us a record of man's foibles and successes politically, economically, and ecclesiastically.
6. Literature and the arts as they communicate various subtle, sometimes sub-rational, sometimes super-rational insights about man's condition and can be used in sermons, drama, and other ways to communicate with the people for their own salvation.
7. Some knowledge of international affairs so that the church in its missionary affairs be not duped and ridiculous as it enters areas of the world becoming tools of forces far more potent and thus selling the gospel short or distorting it unintentionally.

The above knowledge must be stored or developed in a mind that is in a healthy body and an emotionally stable and mature being so his emotional health will enable him to think clearly and not compulsively.

Furthermore, with all of this equipment, he must be so secure emotionally that he is not seeking wealth for himself and his family, but wishing to be of service to mankind. This would probably be impossible if he did not have a model in his Lord and Savior, Jesus Christ, who emptied himself becoming Servant of All. But, in the Protestant ministry, he does not enter the ministry alone. It is essential that he marry a wife who can share such a vocation, such a life adventure.

He must appreciate the role of Priest and Prophet, of administrator and educator, of Pastor and friend. And he must be willing to assume the responsibility of being "model" for those who demand a model in the pastor.

He must be able to relate past, present, and future of the church meaningfully. He can be no dogmatist who insists that everything be done forever in the same old way with the same old shibboleths, certain of the primary insights and symbols of the "faith of our fathers." He must see the place of creeds, of ecclesiastical order, and be able to work cooperatively with other pastors, with bishops and superintendents. He must not be a "prima donna" who cannot cooperate with others.

In fact, he must have that quality of gladly giving credit to others, such as laymen in his church when they finally catch an idea that he has been germinating in their minds for some time, and encourage them to assume responsibility for developing the implications of it.

Now, how can the Church remain relevant in a primary way in our time? This is an age when secular culture has pushed ecclesiastical culture aside in the swift onrush of technological change. Churches have reacted in two ways: reject secularism or embrace secularism. I think our hope is more with the latter than with the former, but I think our preferred form of relationship is one of dialogue. Obviously, if we simply accept secularism in an uncritical form, we have nothing whatsoever to justify our existence. The church must provide a screen through which we siphon off the stuff of culture. In this sense the church and its ministry, primarily, must be in critical dialogue with culture or secularism or technology. The ridiculous ideas of Christian Science, which in its extreme form will not accept any of the ministries of contemporary medical technology, is not the answer. The church, however, did not accept being excluded from the hospital experience all together. The ministry of the Holy Spirit, though subtle, is real and could not be excluded.

In this area there is an extremely important development taking place in Pastoral Psychology. More about this later.

As Tillich says, man is finite, but he has a certain power of self-transcendence. It is with this power of self-transcendence that we work through education, worship, inspiration, fellowship to help man to work with God in achieving the New Reality, in personal life and in social life.

Every creature is rooted in a creative ground that enables this self-transcendence. From this "courage to be," which takes doubt and threat into the self and frequently experiences the reality of resurrection and new being, the vital power of religious faith is made manifest and human conditions are improved.

This faith is centered in the figure of Jesus as the Christ. The minister will have in his congregation all varieties of Christologies. He must learn the rational and psychological patterns that operate in the various types of individuals to minister, much as a psychiatrist does, depending on his understanding of the syndrome of faith and morals that that individual has, the basic character of the congregation with which he works, and what he thinks is finally true. He taps the resources in that person for the corporate work that he thinks constitutes God's work on earth at this stage of history in this place.

Above all, he will minister to those who have a sense of emptiness or meaninglessness by projecting the image of the Christian possibility for human life both personal and corporate. "We must learn to dream again," said Dr. Gideonse. And it is the ministry which has a rightful vocation of idealism, of helping us to dream great dreams. Where there is no vision, the people perish. The minister must be prepared to be razzed about a lot of things. One of them is that of being "a dreamer and a do-gooder." But, this, above all, is his vocation. He is the source of hope in a culture. He points to a better day, a better condition. He is, above all, a man of faith—faith in God, faith in self, faith in the Gospel, faith in mankind, faith in the possibilities of the crippled individual before him, faith in the Kingdom, faith in the Church, in Christ.

In some ultimate sense, it may well be that "this is a time of waiting, a time of hungering"—a time of "hungering and thirsting after righteousness," but not being able to be righteous because the form and outline of righteousness is not clear, as Dr. Nation Scott said in the Wednesday-night lecture of Creative Writing Week, May 6, 1968. There is a certain kind of "waiting upon the Lord" experience in which the minister can reassure his people that the Lord is not dead, but either he is withholding himself, or men are not looking and listening in the right places or the right manner. All these positions imply a trust that ultimately God will speak and lead and renew and save. Such a ministry requires that the minister be trusting, wise, courageous.

Part of the experience of the Holy Ghost that can be cultivated in such times is the asking of the right questions, the negating of the right disvalues, the refusal to accept shallow answers, often accepted simply because they are traditional. Through use of the arts of painting, dancing, music, and especially literature, the minister and Religious Educator can keep the people questing in an honest and spiritually profound way. In all of this, his trust is in God who made heaven and earth and his assumption that the Creator is also the Sustainer and ultimately the Redeemer.

The minister can help man to evaluate historical events in an "eternal" or "Kingdom" perspective. A Christian will not hope so wildly and dependently for the cessation of bombing in Vietnam, although he will see it as a potential sign of hope. He knows that the sinfulness of man is such that any armistice is merely a temporary halting of hostilities until men make some basic change in their outlook. The same meanness that cropped up in Germany and Japan, then Korea and Vietnam will crop up somewhere else until some basic new conception of appropriate behavior emerges and is committed to by millions of men—some concept closer to the Kingdom—of peace on earth and goodwill among men. This involves eradicating prejudices and false conceptions of people as well as revamping our own motives and goals. So, at bottom, the minister of Christ sees economics and politics, war and peace as decisions grounded in the essential human spirit. These are always going to cause further trouble unless they are truly grounded in the Gospel of God. The minister must keep explaining and redefining in practical terms considering the immediate issues. He can hope for progress but should not be too surprised if the same old issues of Cain and Abel show up in the twentieth century.

Tillich concludes by saying that "to point with inner authority to the eternal is the most relevant function men can perform today" (35). Anyone who does this is ministering in the name of Christ.

As we minister in this manner, we will want to know the difference between neurotic anxiety and existential anxiety. We will want to know when we can minister and when we must refer. We will delight to prepare ourselves for this both by technical studies and careful response to early experiences. We will respect the wisdom of more experienced ministers in these matters. We will work administratively to make available to a neurotic person adequate services at fair cost.

In our counseling, preaching, educational, and pastoral work, we will seek to help persons fulfill themselves, carefully balancing self-denial and self-fulfillment. Neither asceticism nor anti-asceticism is an adequate answer. Between these two extremes and varying with the situation, self-fulfillment through self-giving is certainly the key idea of the Gospel. It is the very meaning of Agape.

Beginning with life in the family, we will endeavor to help parents provide that firm, clear, love-filled atmosphere in the home which will properly nurture the ideological and emotional life of the child so that he has a maximum chance to become a creative Christian citizen. We seek the development of a sane man in a sane society. Niebuhr thinks Freud was absurdly pessimistic about man and that Erich Fromm was absurdly optimistic about man. The true picture lies somewhere between these two extremes.

In relation to the economic situation, both the "profit motive" and the "service motive" must be appropriately recognized and related to the gospel. Freud represents a pessimistic view of man as bent entirely on "profit" or "sexual aggrandizement." Fromm represents a too idealistic view of man as capable of being loving and serviceable to his fellow man. It is particularly important for us to understand the various power structures and to work within them without naïvete. This requires compromise in terms of absolute ideals, but it does not require complete negation of these dreams or ideals or possibilities of new being. We act in love and seek justice. The principles of love are the ultimate norms of human freedom and they can never be structured into norms of justice or law. Yet, we need standards of justice both to arbitrate the conflicting interests of men and to define norms for man as a creature who is something less than a free, loving spirit.

In this process, the Christian is in creative dialogue with the law of the land in which he lives. He criticizes laws made by prejudiced whites which deny his vision of adequate justice to Negroes. He seeks to change these laws for the better. Yet he does not condone the extreme and vicious injustices which minorities do in dramatizing their situation.

We must not go for absolutes like the Catholics have: absolute contraception, for example, no inter-marriage with Protestants, etc. We are forced to be thoroughly pragmatic in our proximate norms, still holding to the general standard of the love commandment for our ultimate norm. "As religious and moral guides in our harassed and perplexed age, we cannot be wisely pragmatic without availing ourselves of every form of knowledge and the social and economic realities in the international realm." We must be "wise as serpents and harmless as doves." We must garner political, economic, and socio-psychological wisdom. And we must apply it at home regarding poverty and abroad regarding peace. This will require joint action. No single one of us is wise enough to be King of the World in the name of Christ. We must take an ecumenical and conciliar attitude toward our moral leadership of the world, but we must not abdicate our Christian responsibility for the quality of life in the world. God loves the world. We are our brothers' keepers. The Kingdom is coming.

The Role of the Elders in the Christian Church

Retreat of Elders at University Christian Church, Austin,
February 29, 1992
Led by Paul G. Wassenich

The role of elders in the Christian Church (Disciples of Christ) has a rich Biblical heritage. There are 188 references to the elders in the Old and New Testaments, sixty of which are in the New Testament.

The basic concept is that age imparts wisdom. When the wise King Solomon had finished building the Temple and was ready to move the Ark of the Covenant from the Tabernacle (tent) into the Temple, "Then Solomon assembled the elders of Israel and all the heads of the tribes . . . in Jerusalem to bring up the ark. . . ." (I Kings 8:1–9).

Ezekiel describes the deterioration of Israel that brings God's judgment. "Disaster comes upon disaster. . . . They seek a vision from the prophet, but the law perishes from the priest, and counsel from the elders" (Ezek. 7:26). When Moses felt he was unable to lead the Hebrew people out of Egypt, he was told to gather the elders together and tell them about his call from God.

After the Babylonian exile, Ezra and Nehemiah rebuilt the walls of Jerusalem and the Temple. Tatenac, the governor, opposed this. "Who asked those elders who gave you a decree to build this house?" (Ezra 5:9). Darius, the Persian king, found the decree of Cyrus approving the release of the Hebrews to rebuild Jerusalem and the Temple. Therefore, the puppet, Tatenac, told his people, "Keep away, leave the work on the house of the Lord alone. Let the Governor of the Jews and the elders of the Jews rebuild this house of God on its site" (Ezra 6:7). Psalm 107:32 says, "Praise God in the assembly of the Elders."

Jesus often included the elders with the scribes and Pharisees in his scorn because they were unable to accept "the new wine of his teachings." Their "old wineskins" broke. So elders can be a hindrance to the creative new thing God is doing.

As the Christian church developed after the resurrection, it had few preachers. Paul was the chief missionary. After Paul was stoned and had recovered, "they appointed elders in every church" and "committed them to the Lord" (Acts 14:23).

The leaders of those churches were the elders. The Greek term is *presbyter; Episcopes* is also translated *elder*, or more frequently *bishop*. They were "overseers," responsible leaders of the church when there were no ministers on the scene.

Paul met with the Elders of the Ephesian Church at Miletus, a port city, on his way to Jerusalem on his third journey. "And from Miletus Paul sent to Ephesus and called to him the elders of the Church and said to them . . . Take heed yourselves and to all of the flock in which The Holy Spirit has made you guardians, to feed The Church of the Lord. . . . I commend you to God and to the word of his grace" (Acts 20:1–30).

Alexander Campbell followed Paul's lead in establishing Christian churches in Pennsylvania, West Virginia, Ohio, Kentucky, and Tennessee. He considered the elders to have ministerial responsibility, acknowledging as did Paul that there are different gifts: teaching, preaching, giving, etc. He referred to himself as a "preaching elder" (I Cor. 12–14).

So he who aspires to the elder's position aspires to a noble task. In Rev. 4:4, John of Patmos envisions heaven as having twenty-four elders sitting in judgment—one for each of the twelve tribes and one for each of the twelve apostles.

Further New Testament references to elders that may be of interest are: I Tim. 3:1, 4:14, and 5:17, also in Titus 1:5. For spiritual inspiration, read Romans 12.

Chapter 19

CHRISTIAN SEXUAL MATURATION

Sermon at First Congregational Church, Fort Worth, December 6, 1970

> "Do you not know that your body is a temple of the Holy Spirit within you, which you have from God? You are not your own; you were bought with a price. So glorify God in your body" (I Cor. 6:19–20).

The basic call of the Christian is to honor God with his whole being. As Paul makes perfectly clear in I Corinthians 6:20, this includes the body. "Your body is the temple of the Holy Spirit within you, which you have from God. So glorify God in your body."

As Sigmund Freud made abundantly clear, love is, at base, sexual in some sense, yet it is pervasive as a motivational force through all our activities as "libidinal drive." It is so complex, so delightful, so frustrating, so frightening, so exhilarating, that adolescents, when they are first aware of the self as one who can "make love," are in a delirious and even a dangerous period of life.

In our memories of where our self-consciousness started, we find ourselves harking back to our adolescent experience as though these were the first ones we had in which our self-image was shaped. To a considerable degree, this is true, although not entirely, as the childhood years have shaping power too. At adolescence, we begin to feel responsible for ourselves and aware of ourselves as beings with sexual desires. Now parents find it difficult to accept this and more difficult to talk about it.

So here is this growing boy or girl with their sexual capacity uppermost in their consciousness, and yet it is something that cannot be discussed with those to whom they would like to feel most close. It is a difficult period for both parent and child; but certainly we Christians should be as intelligently open, informative, and responsive as we know how to be.

Intelligent Christian parents give adolescents as much freedom as they think they can handle without making absolute fools of themselves. They are tolerant and even helpful when adolescents "goof," as they surely will. This is the way we learn to be adults, slowly and painfully. Each one of us is different. Both adolescent and parent should be aware that in this game of life, there is no instant replay. With love and intelligence, the scars of most mistakes can be healed. There will be some scars, though.

An adolescent needs a basic pattern or design of life regarding sex in all its complex exfoliations by which to guide his behavior—even if he simply reacts against it. He needs some awareness of a pattern which represents the best wisdom his elders have to pass on to him.

Now, I am going to undertake to summarize the current Christian sex mores for adolescents and parents of adolescents. That is, this represents the wisdom of the centuries of Christian thought and practice, including some insights from psychology which Christianity has appropriated recently. We are talking particularly about premarital mores.

First, the Christian says life is sacred. All persons are children of God and have a destiny potentially significant before God.

Second, sex is, among other things, the way life is perpetuated, although that is not all it is, Catholic tradition to the contrary notwithstanding. It is also the way we relate to a significant "other" in the most basic relationship of life. It is the way we feel wanted, accepted, and fulfilled or "related." Our "relations," like father, mother, aunt, uncle, grandpa, and grandma, are people with a genetic heritage held in common with us. Genes are passed on sexually. We say, he has grandpa's kinky hair or grandma's brown eyes, etc. It is when one thinks to some depth and across the generations that he begins to get those responsible and reverent feelings about sex.

Third, we must recognize that this genetic factor is also true to a considerable extent about animals in much the same way as it is of humans, although we do not know as much as we would like to know about the genetic sources of brain capacity. The Christian certainly affirms that man is more than an animal. For one thing, we don't just drop our young in a nest or burrow, feed them for three months or so, and then kick them out of the nest. One of the TV programs on animal life showed the life of four young leopard cubs. At the end of three months or so, while the mother cared for them, two of the four were dead. Two remained to go out on their own. Human life is quite different. Parents care for their young for more than twenty years. The primary implication of this for adolescents is THINK! Think of the implications of the sex act in terms of an unwanted pregnancy. Just because one is physically able to create a baby doesn't mean he is mentally, socially, psychologically, or financially adequate to rear that child.

Fourth, all of this means that there is a mental-emotional, even spiritual maturation that must take place before one is really ready to express his sexuality responsibly and to enjoy it as it apparently was intended by God to be enjoyed. At adolescence, human beings begin a long, tortuous process of separating from parents and becoming adults, capable of caring for themselves and their own young ones.

Fifth, parents should, of course, do their part in helping in this maturation process. They should tell their children the "facts of life." If they don't find it possible for one reason or another, they should at least buy a good book, such as Evelyn M. Duvall's *Facts of Life and Love* (NY: Assn. Press), or a fine pamphlet like William Hamilton's "Faith, Sex and Love" (YMCA, 291 Broadway, New York, NY 10007), or *Understanding Sex* by Lester A. Kirkendall (Science Research Associates, 259 E. Erie St., Chicago, IL). Parents should encourage the young people to read these books and pamphlets and then to discuss them together. The Church should also do as First Congregational has done and have an MD lecture to the youth group and answer questions in this area annually. They should also be available for conversations with individuals whenever needed. The public schools are beginning to do some helpful things in this area.

Sixth, in none of these sources do you find what you ultimately need, what I would call "psycho-spiritual" information. Such "psycho-spiritual" information helps you understand that delicate area of feeling and understanding that distinguishes a profound human spirit from one hardly distinguishable from the animals. This kind of insight and information is available through the church in pulpit, worship, Church school, and youth groups and friendships, as well as pastoral counseling.

Seventh, persons are most adequately fulfilled when they can develop emotional stability and skills in interpersonal relationships. Among the young people I have counselled in recent years was a science major who was a brilliant student, leading his classes. He began to fall apart and talked with me about his problem. He was an only child of parents who loved him deeply, but who, in their "gloved fist" way, pressured him to be a scientist. They also had very strict ideas about behavior patterns. He got involved in a group who not only had very loose sexual practices, but also took drugs. He really deteriorated despite anything I could do for him. He switched his major to another field, but the last time I saw him, he was a very miserable human being indeed. This development of emotional stability along with maximum freedom and at the same time responsibility and decisiveness in decision making is one of life's most complex and delicate accomplishments. It requires teamwork by the young person and his mother and father. It is life's most important possession. It is far more valuable than whether one fulfills the dream of being the parent of a lawyer, or governor, or president of the United States.

Eighth, the qualities of character that most Christian parents should seek to engender in their children to prepare them for these difficult years of adolescence when they move into heterosexual relationships are these:

First, "Love others as you do yourself" is the way Jesus put it. That means the capacity to identify deeply with both the immediate feelings and ultimate destiny of long-term goals of that other person with whom one becomes involved. It means to really wish for that person's fulfillment. It means not using him as a "thing" for one's own gratification. If a boy really loves a girl, really loves her, he will care for her in such a complex way that he would not coerce her or rape her. He would think of her well-being as much as his own. This kind of thoughtful empathy is a work of maturity. Adolescence is a time for learning this.

It helps to understand what Evelyn Duvall calls the "involvement process" between a boy and a girl. It moves from meeting to acquaintance to dating to courtship to engagement to marriage. It should take at least two years and sometimes as much as five years, depending on the circumstances. One should never marry without knowing the other person and his family and friends in depth. Love is not just sex, though the sexual factor is important. Love is a whole complex of factors taken very thoughtfully into account.

A second Christian characteristic that one should seek to develop in himself and his adolescent children is gentleness. Blessed is the woman who marries a "gentle" man, and blessed is the man who marries a "gentle" woman. Aggressive, cruel persons make a relationship unbearable for each other.

An enduring relationship must have common interests. Yet there should be room for individuality. Kahlil Gibran, in *The Prophet*, speaking of marriage, says: "Let there be spaces in your togetherness." Each should allow the other space for his uniqueness to flower. Yet they should share as many interests as they honestly can. Before I met my wife, Ruth, I had very shallow aesthetic interests. My art appreciation was about the level of Sallman's "Head of Christ." But the young lady I wanted to marry was an art major at Oberlin College. I followed her literally down miles of corridors of art galleries and really did develop some appreciation for the different artists and schools of art, and she has even walked around a few golf courses with me. No marriage or even friendship will be successful unless one affirms the other in significant areas of his interests. Help the other develop by affirming his significant interests and skills.

Closely related to this, we should note that in our time and culture, as complex as it is, one should really not marry before age twenty-one. Before that time, it is best not to commit yourself irrevocably to one person and to spend endless hours together. It is much wiser to know in some depth many persons of the opposite sex. Each one makes you a wiser and more richly aware person, enabling you to bring a quality of insight to the marriage that you do finally covenant.

The sexual mores of our time are called revolutionary by many. This revolution is seen as closely related to many other complex changes in our technologically oriented urban civilization. It may well be that the sex mores that have been changing rapidly from their Victorian base ever since World War I are about to reach some new ground. I cannot really say. I do know that college students, at least a majority of them, though not all by any means, are talking about premarital sexual liberty in a way that I do not agree with. They say that too much has been made of sex. It is not that important. With the pill, if a good, honest relationship is developing between two consenting young adults in college, then they should go on and express themselves sexually. I cannot agree with this, because I know of too many essentially fine young people who have fouled up their lives and the lives of others that way. They are sons and daughters of ministers, they are preministerial students—all fine people. But their premarital experimentation caused them to marry when they had not planned to marry. In practically every case, the forced marriage lasted only a few years and then divorce followed. The saddest fact of all is the unwanted children in the world. These too-smart people are not as smart as they thought they were, and they are much more irresponsible than they realize. What price society will have to pay within fifteen to twenty-five years for all these unwanted children is frightening to contemplate.

Fourth, when a Christian young person, aware of these factors, and chronologically mature, chooses the one for marriage, he won't be wondering what it would have been like if he had married another. You will be certain, from thoughtful experience, of the qualities which endear your wife or husband to you.

Fifth, if your parents loved you and you knew it, and you really try to "love God with all your being"; and you see loving God as involving loving your friends, parents, and sweetheart or wife in terms of loyalty, trust, and mutual commitment, you have the grounds for a happy friendship and marriage as Burkhart says in *From Friendship to Marriage.*

If during adolescence you are trying to handle the difficult matter of learning how to be intimate in a responsible way but you make a misstep and find the girl pregnant, parents and pastor would both understand and help you "make the most of the rest of your life." Of course, it might mean you couldn't finish college or medical school or law school, but that's just part of the price that you have to pay for your poor judgment.

In conclusion, I have said that

- Christians value life as a gift from God.
- Christians value the quality of life, as separating man from the animals.
- Christians value empathetic and responsible living as the key to human development.
- This knowledge should maximize the possibilities for an adolescent to develop deep heterosexual friendships without premarital intercourse, thus enriching the concept and the significance of marriage.
- But, if in the difficult and dangerous waters of learning to relate to the opposite sex, he flounders on some hidden reefs, Christian and intelligent parents and churchmen will rally to his support and see the couple into the best possible adjustment.

Thus, our Christian emphasis, in trying to implement Christian love in these matters is not primarily negative and judgmental, but educational and supportive.

Chapter 20

TEXAS BIBLE CHAIR, EIGHTIETH ANNIVERSARY

A sermon given April 27, 1986, at the University Christian Church, Austin, Texas

Paul believed strongly in the need for people to have knowledge of the history of the times when the Scriptures were written to help us understand what was happening in those times in order to better understand the Scripture's message. He thought that a well-educated person had to have a background in the history of religious thinking to live fully and productively in the current times.

The Church denominations had begun to set up Bible Chairs at major universities and send ministers to teach courses for college credit on the Bible and the development of Christian thought. These ministers were not considered faculty of the university; they were classified as instructors.

In the 1980s, the approach shifted to a debate on the separation of church and state. The classes were taught as a historical and philosophical review of the times when the Books of the Bible were written. There was no proselytizing. Nevertheless, government officials began to worry, and across the nation universities began to stop giving credit for the Bible courses.

We are all indebted to Dr. Frank Jewett and the many Disciples lay persons who helped him establish the Texas Bible Chair. Without them, we would not be remembering these eighty years of the Bible Chair's service to the university and thousands of students. The major gifts for the two yellow brick buildings that stood on this property from 1909 to about 1960 were given by Mrs. M. M. Blanks of Lockhart. Dr. Jewett occupied this chair for forty-one years. When I came, he encouraged me not only to continue the University Bible Classes but also to help start a Christian Church near the campus. All the other major denominations had such churches and it behooved us to do the same.

At the age of thirty-five in 1946, I succeeded him with fear and trembling. There was a terrific influx of GIs. I taught eight student generations over a period of thirty years. Those GIs were the most interesting and challenging of the lot. Housing was in short supply, so we housed six male students on this property besides the Wassenich family of four. Four of these student residents took a regularly active part in the DSF program that we started. Ruth and I became very fond of the fifty or so students who participated in the DSF program. We could tell some delightful stories of happenings in those early years, but there is insufficient time.

I was pleased to find denominational diversity among my Bible Chair students. That was appropriate, considering our Disciples' ecumenical heritage. None of our Bible chair instructors—Jewett, Wassenich, Cox—ever taught dogmatically. One of Alexander Campbell's favorite sayings was "Christians only, but not the only Christians." Non-dogmatic teaching was and is obligatory in our agreement with the university. It was agreed that the teaching should be objective, scholarly, and consistent with the published results of historical/critical Biblical studies. We should acknowledge here that the same is true in the departments of religion at TCU, SMU, Vanderbilt, Harvard, Yale, Chicago, and most universities in America.

Charles Cox certainly continues to present the scriptures in this critical, historical, contextual manner. He utilizes the enormous accumulation of information that scholars have built over the past hundred or more years of higher critical studies. You can find this information utilized in the great commentaries on the Scriptures.

The Disciples have a history in this matter too. When Alexander Campbell established Bethany College and taught Bible courses there, he introduced the students to a five-finger exercise of questions that proved to be a forerunner of critical Biblical studies. He said we must ask the who, what, where, when and why questions about each book of the Bible. That is, who wrote it, when, why, to whom (what audience), why did he write it, and what did he say? Then comes the interpretative questions: what does it mean to us in our own time, and how is this responsibly related to the context in which the message was originally written?

It makes a profound difference in your understanding of the meanings in the Book of Revelation, for instance, if you know that the background is the Domitian Persecution in 94–96 CE. It was the first empire-wide persecution of Christians. John of Patmos was writing it in his spare time while cracking rocks in the hot sun on the Isle of Patmos, off Ephesus, imprisoned there for his Christian convictions. The "whore of Babylon," which is to be destroyed, is not something in the twentieth century, but the cult of Emperor worship fostered by Domitian.

Back in 1946, I did step over a fine line of distinction for one year when I served as the pastor of University Christian Church in my spare time for the first year of this church's existence. Dr. Jewett had held chapel services for many years, but he had not formed a church. Most of the other denominations had formed university churches. I had attended Dr. Jewett's chapel services while a student in the graduate school here 1934–36. In fact, Dr. Jewett asked me to preach at the chapel service in the fall of 1935, right after my ordination.

Since 1946 the Bible Chair and University Christian Church have worked closely together, but it is particularly important to note that the church has never interfered in the work of the Bible Chair Instructor. The church has never sought to tell him what he is to teach or not teach or what interpretation he is to put on certain Biblical passages or what texts he may or may not use. He has complete academic freedom.

Yet all three of the occupants of the Bible Chair have been active churchmen. They have served in various capacities as elders, members of the board of University Christian Church, and teachers at summer conferences. They have given seminars in various churches across the state and filled pulpits on occasion in churches near Austin. The director of the Texas Bible Chair must walk a well-defined line in terms of his obligations to church, university, and state.

Considering the recent challenge by the Texas Attorney General to the right of the Bible Chairs to exist, let's take a brief look at the development of the Bible Chairs in the USA. There are records of discussions about the Bible Chair concept by the ladies of the Christian Women's Board of Missions (CWBM), a Disciples organization, as early as 1888. Nothing significant was done until 1892, when Mrs. O. A. Burgess, President of the CWBM, urged the founding of a Bible Chair at the University of Michigan in her presidential address. This chair opened in the fall of 1893. However, it was never able to give university credit for its courses.

It continues until today as a student work program, supported by the CWBM, then the UCMS, and now the home missions department of the Christian Church.

In 1905–06, the University of Virginia granted credit to courses taught by a Disciple, Dr. William L. Forrest, and that continues today. Part of the faculty salary is paid from a $50,000 endowment given by a Disciples layman named Cary, and the remainder is paid by the State of Virginia. This fulfills the dream of President Thomas Jefferson which he outlined in his design for the founding of the University of Virginia.

In that same year, Dr. Jewett arrived in Austin and began giving non-credit courses in his home as well as trying to raise money to buy property and buildings. He accomplished this by 1909 with the help of Mrs. Blanks and others. He offered courses and held Sunday services for the remaining years to 1946.

In 1910–11, the University of Texas first granted credit and listed Bible courses in the University class schedule. Other chairs were established at Missouri in 1906, Kansas in 1921, and Indiana in 1910, but credit was not granted until 1953. Indiana now credits fifty-two hours of courses in religion.

The 1985 Directory of Departments and Programs of Religious Studies in North America, published by the Council on the Study of Religion, lists 180 such programs in state universities. It lists nineteen graduate programs in religion studies at state universities. My friend and colleague at TCU, Dr. Ronald Flowers, has his PhD degree from such a program at the University of Iowa. His 335-page dissertation is the definitive study on *The Bible Chair Movement in the Disciples of Christ Tradition,* dated 1967. He continues to do research and to publish significant articles and books in the relation of church and state.

Now, let us look at the State's side of this complex issue and also the University's side of the issue. The State is rightly concerned that it not be accused of fostering sectarian religious teaching. Neither the State nor the State University dare sponsor a church or a dogmatic, evangelistic presentation of any religious point of view, be it Jewish, Moslem, Hindu, Catholic, or Protestant. I am sure we all concur in this and want to protect the students, the university, and the state populace at large from the chaos that would result from such biased presentations.

Yet, at the same time, higher education is incomplete if a person can graduate without some objective knowledge of a phenomenon such as religion which motivates so many millions of people so profoundly. Often they are motivated to be honest, kind, peaceful, and generous. But, in our time, as well as in the time of the Crusades and the Inquisition, some types of religion cause such problems in the world as the war between the Sikhs and the Hindus in India, the Christians, Moslems, and Jews in the Middle East, the Khadafi phenomenon in Libya, the Khoumeni phenomenon in Iran, and the decades long squabbles between Catholics and Protestants in Ireland. An educated person should not be completely ignorant of religious beliefs that affect millions of people so profoundly.

Many state universities find a place in the philosophy department or history department to offer courses in history of religions or, as it is sometimes called, comparative religions.

The Judeo-Christian religion has been basic to the development of American life. We even have chaplains in the Congress and the Legislatures. We have the President sworn in with his hand on the Bible. We have "In God We Trust" on our currency. Yet, we have a heritage of separation of Church and State in some sense, certainly in the sense that there must be no state-sponsored or "established" religion as there is in England, the Scandinavian Countries, Iran, Germany, Egypt, and other nations. We should protect the separation of Church and State in this sense. Just how to balance these two traditions requires continuing careful attention. However, we certainly need to recognize that a person is not educated in the liberal arts sense of the word unless he knows, or has the freedom and opportunity to be informed through courses and literature available to him in the University, about the great religious traditions of mankind.

It behooves us to continue the Bible Chairs. We need to be keenly aware of the difference between university-level, scholarly, critical presentation of the Biblical materials on the one hand and the doctrinal, evangelistic, denomination presentations of the faith on the other hand. We would expect a Moslem scholar to attend the mosque on Friday, the Hebrew instructor to attend synagogue on the Sabbath, and the Christian scholar to attend church on Sunday. However, I have known some great scholars of the Christian faith who did not regularly attend a denominational church on Sunday, and there is no way he can be forced to do so. The twain are separate, except as the individual associates them in his own being.

Around the time of World War I and the 1920s, a great Christian leader named John R. Mott was executive secretary of a very influential movement on American campuses called the Student Volunteer Movement. It worked with most Protestant denominations and motivated hundreds of students to become Christian missionaries of the enlightened sort. Mott had crossed the Atlantic so many times before air travel was possible. Toward the end of his life, he wrote, "If I had my life to live over, I would settle down beside a great university and help students assimilate knowledge and relate it to Christian teachings."

Charles Cox is giving his life in precisely this way. He is presenting a scholarly account of the development of Hebrew/Christian religious and ethical insights. Intelligent and sensitive students who might be turned off by naïve presentations of the Bible are often profoundly helped by discovering how the Scriptures developed and how relevant those teachings are to our contemporary problems. They come to see that the vengeful concept of God held by Abraham, Isaac, and Jacob is altered as it moves through the mosaic period, the kingdom period, the prophetic and exilic period. The prophets see God as just and merciful, and they prepare the way for Jesus and Paul to speak of God meaningfully as a loving and forgiving father, one who loves not just a chosen people but all persons who are children of the one God.

A completely secular education from kindergarten through PhD would not present to our best minds the option to consider the sensitive ethical teachings of the Judeo-Christian tradition. Yet, these have been basic to our understanding of interpersonal relations and personal destiny for the total history of our life in America and beyond that into our European history. An education minus these insights is hardly an adequate liberal education.

Recently, a Dallas paper quoted a study of Highland Park High School students on the issue of cheating. Seventy-seven percent of them said, "I don't see why we shouldn't cheat on exams. Our parents cheat on their income tax reports. Why shouldn't we cheat on exams?" Where in our educational system or culture can we answer that question in a way consistent with "Thou shalt not steal; thou shalt not lie or bear false witness"? How can we reach both parent and child with an adequate understanding of these ideals which are essential to the stability of society?

The American experiment in the separation of Church and State is critically important in world history. A state church is not the answer; that has been tried in Europe and elsewhere. Out of that you are likely to get an inquisition. However, a state which welcomes ecumenical and intellectually respectable religious education is part of the answer. Bible chairs at state universities can help provide the needed antidote to moral anarchy among the intellectually elite who are educated at the University of Texas and other universities. These people will be the leaders of our state and nation in the next generation. We need for them to lead us not only politically and economically, but also morally. They need an enlightened awareness of the concepts of value and how these developed from Abraham to Moses to the prophets to Jesus and Paul.

The eighty years of such service by the Texas Bible Chair have made an important contribution in this regard. I hear it from former students of all three occupants of this chair as I speak in churches across the state. The future needs this complex and vital service just as much as the past did.

Part III

SERMONS AT CHURCHES

The above picture should be of interest to all members of University Church. It was taken when our church was just six months old and still worshipping in the old Bible Chair Chapel. Mr. Wassenich who organized the church was serving as minister. He is seen here speaking on a Sunday morning. Then, as ever since, our facilities were crowded to capacity. Now, with two morning services, and a greatly enlarged worship room, we still face the problem. We sometimes wonder if Texas Disciples know an opportunity when they see it.

Paul preaching at University Christian Church Austin, ca. 1950. Courtesy of University Christian Church, Austin.

Chapter 21

JOYFUL LIVING

Sermon given at Midway Hills Christian Church, Dallas, in 1965 and at First Congregational United Church of Christ, Fort Worth, November 17, 1974

Introduction

In the text found in Matt. 13:44–46, it says "... in his joy he goes and sells all he has and buys that field." Gunther Bornkamm, in *Jesus of Nazareth*, surprised me by emphasizing in his exposition of the Kingdom Teachings, "Joyful Living." I said to myself, "Well, here's a wholesome antidote to the abysmal theological emphases of our time. Will it stand up? Or is it a mere Pollyanna attitude, a shallow positive thinking?"

Frankly, I think there is a church bell that needs to be rung here. I do not want to be naïve. It is certainly true that the far-reaching and deep-going anxiety of our time must be acknowledged, understood, and publicly analyzed by the preacher. It is rooted in personal guilt, economic insecurity, rapidly changing mores, spiritual restlessness, and the threat of the final war.

But note that Jesus does not constantly emphasize the sin of man. He constantly accepts the sinner. He says, "The sick need a physician." He considers sin a sickness. But it is well for us to realize that the surgeon can only create a wound with his knife. God heals. A profound, pervasive power beyond the physician and the patient is the healing force. Jesus was, is, and desires to be understood to be a part of this healing power. He constantly accepts the sinner. He gets criticized by churchmen for being a "gluten and winebibber" who associates with sinners. He says "there is joy in heaven over one sinner who repents" (Lk 15:7). He says the father of the prodigal son who returns, runs out to meet him, puts a robe on him, a ring on his finger, kills the fatted calf, throws a dance and says to all and sundry, "Rejoice with me for this my son was lost and is found." The only unhappy person around the place was the Pharisaic son, who is not oriented in faith, hope, and love to the new possibilities of life. We are not told of what happened to the older son.

Bornkamm generalizes thus: "Again and again in the Gospels, the deep gloom which hangs over the righteousness of the 'good' becomes apparent." With God, the ultimate reality is primarily oriented toward restoration and health.

I. The Need for Christian Joy and Well-Being

The joy that is available to the Christian is not a constant "ball," as the students would say. However, it is closely akin to the "blessedness" of the beatitudes and, in a way, to the eudemonistic "well-being" of Greek thought. It is accepting, balanced, reasonable, whole-being response to things as they have been, as they are, and as they can, by the grace of God, become.

The joyous Christian does not do an Elvis Presley howl and wiggle. But he may step along firmly and hum a tune of faith, or of simple delight "considering the lilies how they toil not" and other evidences of the supporting goodness of God. He has "an attitude of gratitude." He is grateful for the resources of forgiveness and new being that he knows from sin are a part of reality.

Modern man is profoundly in need of this Christian joy because when he is caught in the tolls of guilt, fear, insecurity, and anxiety, the vital processes of his being are blocked. He cannot make his maximum contribution. He is miserable. As Paul puts it in a letter to the Romans, "Their fruitless minds are darkened."

II. The Source of Christian Joy

What are the sources of Christian joy? The grace of God is the source of it. It is a gift. The Christian man accepts it as loving forgiveness and revels in it. He moves out of self to share it. Being loved, he loves. Being accepted, he accepts others. The symbol of angelic choirs singing "Joy to the World, the Lord is come" is meaningful to him. He knows, as personal experience, what the Old Testament repeatedly refers to as the "Steadfast Love of God."

For the Christian, it is an awareness that the Kingdom is coming. It is mysteriously, but truly leavening his life and the life of the world. With

Paul he can affirm that God is able to do exceedingly abundantly above all that we have sense enough to ask or think. The Kingdom coming is seen as God's healing, growing, creative, forgiving forces.

It has the characteristic of creative forgiveness. God is a healing force. With John Engalls, he can say meaningfully and in depth: "Grass is the forgiveness of nature—her constant benediction. Fields trampled in battle, saturated with blood, torn with ruts of the cannon, grow green again with grass, and carnage is forgotten. Forests decay, harvests perish, flowers vanish, but grass is immortal."

With Tillich he can say the rest of our words. *Salvation* is the Latin *salvare*, which means "to heal, to preserve, to deliver." The benison of redemptive love that brings healing hope and quiet joy is the Christian minister's work, and it is profoundly rewarding and joyous to share it. God works through him. This is the ultimate joy. His work is to make himself an instrument of God's love.

III. We Must Become Artists in the Practice of Christian Joy

The day must begin with an affirmation of trust which orients the self anew, such as Psalm 118:24 "This is the day which the Lord hath made, we will rejoice and be glad in it" or Psalm 105:3 "Let the hearts of those who seek the Lord, rejoice." As we meet people, we can say with Bornkamm: "If Jesus's call to salvation is at the same time a call to repentance, the call to repentance is at the same time a call to rejoice" because of our awareness of grace.

So Jesus says, "When you fast, don't look dismal. Rejoice!" Fasting is penitence. It is quite easy to be pharisaical about it.

I am reminded of a sorority at UT one spring when they were preparing a float for a parade. The student group at the University Christian Church were also preparing a float, and I went over to help them. The students worked far into the night. I left about midnight. When I returned early the next morning to get my tools, there were two girls who had toiled all night and were obviously tired. It was Lent, and one of the girls said to her friend: "I'll be so blankety-blank glad when Lent is over so I can smoke," illustrating the deep gloom that hangs over the righteousness of good.

The crowds of am-ha-a-rez, or common people, on Palm Sunday cried: "Hosannah, blessed be he who comes in the name of the Lord." The Pharisees told Jesus to rebuke the crowds, saying that this unseemly joy must stop. Jesus replied, "If they kept their peace, these very stones would cry out."

We could mention many Christian saints to refresh our hope and joy and courage to face a threatening world:

- Bishop Hugh Latimer, the Protestant English bishop who was burned at the stake with another Bishop, Nicholas Ridley, on orders of Queen Mary in 1555, said, as the flames leaped up around them, tied back to back at the stake, "Be of good cheer Sir Ridley. We shall light such a fire in England this day as shall never be put out."
- Or, Dietrich Bonhoeffer, preaching a sermon of quiet and confident faith, forgiveness, and love, just before his execution at the hands of the Nazis.
- Or, Bill Edwards, a missionary in the Congo, who was one of the happiest and most buoyant Christians I have ever known, speaking to my congregation in Detroit. He and his wife were back in the US when World War II broke out. They wanted very much to get back to the mission field. Three times ships on which they were traveling were sunk by the Germans. The first time the Germans captured them, all the passengers were put on a prison ship and then the Germans shot cannons at their ship to sink it. "All I could think of was that typewriter that the Central-Woodward Church had bought me." As the prison ship circled the Atlantic to sink other ships, the dark hold became full of prisoners. On a sunny and calm day, their captors would allow the prisoners up on deck for fresh air and exercise. He would walk the deck, breathe the fresh air, appreciate the sunshine, and open his New Testament. It always fell open to a place in John 16:33 where he read this most helpful word of Jesus: "In the world you will have tribulation, but be of good cheer. Love overcomes the world."

Our lives may not have such stupendous and heroic threats, but they can affirm the basis for good cheer. "In his joy, he goes and sells all that he has and buys that field." Be joyful.

Chapter 22

ROOM FOR GOD

A sermon at TCU Carr Chapel, March 1966
Scripture: I John 4:13–21

Introduction

In our overpopulated world, you wonder if there is "Room for God." Altizer, Hamilton, and others have announced that God is dead. They are echoing what Nietzsche, Sartre, and others have said, including such American figures as Haydon, Krutch, and Overstreet, and such Britons as Bertrand Russell and George Bernard Shaw. Even E. S. Ames, dean of the Disciples House at the University of Chicago, saw God as a symbol for human values—a sort of Uncle Sam, a myth whose reality consisted in the values of a people.

However, for the most part these other men did not get the publicity and did not reach the general populace the way Altizer and Hamilton have. The coverage in some newspapers, but mainly in widely read magazines like TIME, *Newsweek*, etc. has forced every minister to make some response. Dan Williams, in TIME, thought they seemed to be saying "There is no God, and Jesus is his Son."

It is not my primary purpose today to give an answer to "the God is dead" emphasis, except insofar as all preaching has always been an effort to share one's vision of God—to do what Jesus was doing—to point beyond one's self to the Eternal.

I. Where Shall I Find Him?

It was possibly a Jewish Psalmist in the time of the destruction of the Northern Kingdom worship sites, between 734 and 722 BCE, in a period of migration and feeling estranged, who wrote this Psalm: "As a hart longs for flowing streams, so longs my soul for thee, O God. My soul thirsts for God, the living God. . . . I may say to God, my rock: 'Why hast thou forgotten me?'" (Ps. 42:1, 2 ,9). Another psalmist, possibly from the time of the exile, wrote in Psalm 115: "Not to us, but to thy name give glory, O God. . . . Why should the nations be able to say 'Where is your God?' Our God is in the heavens; their idols are silver and gold, the work of their hands."

The Jew knew the experience of being ribbed about his unseeable God from time immemorial. The same kind of ridicule that the Russian cosmonaut hurled at the West a few years ago, saying "I've been in the heavens and I saw no God there," was hurled at the Jews for centuries.

What are you able to say to someone who hurls at you the challenge that God is dead?

II. We Find God between Our Self and Another

In the depth of relation between self and other, we find God, as the Thou, or holy dimension of reality. This holy reality between Jesus and the disciples snapped in the case of Judas. He treated Jesus like an it, a thing, to be sold.

But Thou was the source of the resurrection experience in Peter and the others. Thou was difficult for Thomas, but Thou finally prevailed.

Most of us have seen God in our relation to Jesus. But as Jesus pointed beyond himself to God in one direction, so he pointed us beyond himself to our brother in the other direction. Love God. Love neighbor. You know God by loving your neighbor.

It is amazing that a Jew like Martin Buber, who along with his fellow Jews suffered such horrible things from Hitler and the Nazis, could say that God is to be found in the relation between man and his brother, between man and man. This can only be said by one who is truly humble before God. Buber is a Hassidic scholar, and one of the Hassidic sayings which he includes in his little volume *Ten Rungs* is this one, under the Rung of Pride and Humility: "There is no room for God in him who is full of himself." Or, as I John has it, "If you hate your brother, how can you say I love God?" Why would you hate your brother? Well, because you are so full of yourself or you think the brother threatens the self. There's not room for both of you. So you resent him.

Buber's thesis is that man knows God through seeking to establish that relation between man and man in which the creative love and power of God can do its mysterious, creative good. Precisely what this will be, he cannot say. God is transcendent. Yet, we are not to seek him in mystic trance, but in a real this-world relation. As the Apostle Paul said: "Love seeketh not its own." This outgoing toward the other, seeking to be used of God for the fulfillment of the richest possible relation to the other, is openness to that infinite creative reality we have called God. One's own fulfillment is found in giving the self to the other: whether it be the sweetheart, wife or husband, your child, your professor, your student, your boss, your employee. But this is impossible for him who is full of himself. "He who seeks to save his life will lose it."

In "Criterion, In Memoriam, Paul Tillich," Dean Brauer spoke about Paul Tillich, the teacher. "The real secret of Tillich's appeal for students was that he needed them. He gave himself to them. He needed their questions. No question was too naïve to receive careful attention from him. He took a simple question, developed it into a profound question, gave his answer, indicated the dimension of the question that was unanswerable. The student was flattered by the profundity of the question he had asked." The students responded to him with genuine application of their own abilities to help him solve the unsolved problems of man to which he gave himself (18). One can understand, then, why Tillich would say: "A system should not be a point of arrival only, but a point of departure also" (Criterion, 21).

Implicit in his system is the assumption of its inadequacy; it is open ended. We have arrived at that time in history where all systems had better be open ended. This is acknowledgement of man's finitude. And for anyone who is not "too full of himself," it is acknowledgement of the infinite creative potentiality of Reality—of God if you please. In Biblical language, we say "Underneath are the Everlasting Arms." "In Him we live and move and have our being."

III. The Relations with Holy Significance in our Time

Children are full of themselves. Maturity is that stage when you can relate to someone else responsibly. It sometimes seems that we live in an age that calls for more maturity than we can muster:

- Something must happen between husbands and wives that will firm up the family, produce healthy, emotionally stable children.
- Something must happen between whites and blacks—it is happening—a new sense of oneness as human beings, children of God.
- Something must happen—yea is happening—between Protestant

sects so that the Body of Christ is not the laughingstock of the non-Christian world and can render some ministry to the distraught world.

- Something must happen between Protestants and Catholics—yea is happening.
- Something must happen between Christians and those of other religions—this is just barely beginning to be seen on the horizon.
- Ultimately, something must happen between Americans and Russians and Chinese. This seems a long, long way off. But the ultimate "in between area" is the space between my enemy and me. Where God is made real is defined by Jesus when he says: "Love your enemies." "Do good to those who hate you." "Pray for those who spitefully use you," says the Apostle Paul.

If we know and respond to the other in these interstitial areas, there will be no meaning to the contention that "God is Dead."

Chapter 23

NEW LIFE IN THE CHURCH, OR THE CHURCH: OUR DESPAIR AND HOPE

Introduction

There would be no church without Jesus and without Paul. Our students last summer were amazed at the distances Paul covered and on foot! In Acts 20:20, Paul tells Ephesians at Miletus: "You know how I lived among you, how I did not shrink from declaring to you anything that was profitable, and teaching you in public and from house to house, testifying both to Jews and to Greeks of repentance to God and of faith in our Lord Jesus Christ." Here is a new gospel, new Lord, new church, courageous spokesman, going from house to house, bridging prejudices between Jews and Greeks to form a new church and a new being in Christ, and thus a new society. And by the grace of God, he did it! And so must we!

Look Magazine, in its July 27, 1965, issue, had an article entitled "The Battle of the Bible." The authors noted that "every couple of centuries Christianity breaks out of its institutional container and remakes the human landscape" (17). The early church up to the time of Augustine grew despite persecution by the Romans and the Jews. Both groups were transformed. The church joined with Constantine in beginning, in 315, to develop the Holy Roman Empire.

Then the church took the form of monasticism to become a refuge for some from what was an impossibly evil world. The church worked with popes and kings like Richard the Lion-Hearted and became Christian imperialism. There are Crusader castles in Byblos, Caesarea, and many other places. The church was defined by the brilliant mind of Thomas Aquinas in 1226. It pictured an architectonic "One World," under Christ the King, with the Pope as Christ's Vicar on earth.

Three centuries later, under Martin Luther and John Calvin, it broke in a revolutionary overthrow of institutional authority and established the principle of "the priesthood of each and all believers." When this principle was coupled with the American quest for political freedom in the eighteenth and nineteenth centuries, the church separated from the state and split into about three hundred parts. Yet it has witnessed to the unique divinity latent in every person, and has kept alive a variety of institutional forms, all expressive of the mystical "body of Christ." On the American frontier, it followed courageous men and women to wrestle with the human spirit at its worst and kept alive some semblance of faith and morality.

Today the church is seething with a half-dozen new attempts to express the Gospel and God's will. One is intellectual and has three dimensions:

- Respond to the scientific worldview. Energy is the ultimate concept rather than matter and spirit, evolutionary change rather than rock-like stability, and the world as a tiny speck in an amazingly vast universe (of which the pictures coming through from Mariner remind us—134 million miles out in space), rather than a flat, square earth with four pillars resting on the "deep." (physical sciences)
- Respond to modern man's sense of lostness, alienation as in art and literature, loss of meaning of human life. (psychology)
- Respond to changing social patterns on race, religion, nation, war, economics. (sociology)

Responses of Ministers and Laymen to These Conditions

Some ministers simply give up. One example is the minister who was embarrassed by laymen at international down to state conventions who urged, over his objections, that our denomination get out of the National Council of Churches. Some scientists and literary people are just saying "nuts" to the church. It is never going to change. It is out of touch with the thought of science, the lostness of the artist, and the hurt of the masses of poverty-stricken people. It is hopelessly middle class.

Some worship the Church as an institution and contend the Church can do no wrong. It is wrong to criticize the Church. They naïvely use the Church to reflect the cultural mores. The world rules the Church as in the time of Constantine and the Crusades. Robert Raines, in *New Life in the Church,* says "It wasn't this spirit that enabled the apostles to look on a 5'10", 165 pound, hook-nosed, dark-skinned Jew and see the divine victory over sin, death, and the devil." He also said, "St. means saint and not statistician." Church conventions are full of parliamentary dead works, statistics, and denominational chest thumping. This will never save a bleeding, dying humanity, threatened with loss of meaning for keeping up the struggle to live.

Some react against the Church and in the name of God and the Gospel do all kinds of secular activities, saying the Church has sold out, is washed up, its end is near. This reaction is typical of bright, idealistic college youth. With moral earnestness, they go into social work, education, politics, only to get fed up with compromise, crookedness, boredom, and ignorance.

Be a loyal, participant critic of the Church. Help the Church to do these things and thus recover its sense of mission and develop effective new forms:

- Know and believe the gospel.
- Be, or become the gospel, the ethics.
- Transform the world. Love the world as God loves the world, not like a pagan. We must become new persons to be truly Christian. The Church must become a new Church to be truly Christian.

Conclusion

There are many expressions of new Christian vigor today. You and I should identify with them. Raines, p. 22, quotes Alfred Kazin, "The only kind of change that means anything is that which changes people's thinking—makes them see the world in a different way." Theologically, this means being given new life by God's grace.

There are five very promising new dimensions of Church life that we need to identify with and, indeed, help be expressions of God's gracious new creativity.

1. The ecumenical movement.
2. St. Louis and Paris Urban Ecumenical Church offer recreation, counselling, and suicide teams. They meet people where they work and play. There is a ministry to old folks in Los Angeles.
3. The civil rights movement involves Catholic, Protestant, Jew, white and black, men and women, young and old, government, church, and industry. They cooperate to change the prejudices of Americans.
4. Peace Corps and kindred mission projects.
5. Lay academics, vocational Christian groups (in Europe).

Christianity at heart, is total personal commitment to Jesus Christ. I must ask: What is Christ's will for me now? Then, become involved headlong in the struggles of humanity. It means an all-out effort to see the world through Christ-colored glasses. Paul did it in the first century. We must do it now.

This will continually create new life in the church and in the world.

Chapter 24

GREATER LOVE HATH NO MAN

Sermon at TCU Student Center, June 6, 1968

Scripture: "Greater love hath no man than this: that a man lay down his life for his friends." John 4:13

In the untimely and senseless deaths of John Kennedy, Martin Luther King, and now Robert F. Kennedy, all reasonable men of goodwill have become aware of a sickness in many members of our society and in the world. The man who killed John F. Kennedy was sick and followed, in a confused way, the Communist line which advocates violence to establish order. The man who killed Martin Luther King was sick with racial prejudice, which irrationally resents the rights of minorities and their efforts to get justice.

The Jordanian man who killed Robert F. Kennedy was sick with the resentments that Arabs have against Jews who fled to Israel and, at the expense of Arabs, set up a place of refuge for the Jews who had fled from the irrationalism of Hitlerism. The death of Robert F. Kennedy is the result of a chain reaction of resentment against injustices that go back at least two generations, but, in a way, they go back at least two centuries and are rooted in the basic mistreatment of Jews.

Irrational hatred, leading to violence is the deep, pervasive evil that plagues us—whether in the imperialism of communism, the nationalism and imperialism of Nazism, the racial prejudices of millions of white Americans, the imperialism of the Israeli, or the pan-Arabism of the Jordanians, Egyptians, and Syrians that will not let the Israeli find a place of peace in the world, but plan to drive them into the sea.

People had heard Kennedy say he would support Israel. In the midst of modern man's lostness and confusion, plus man's absurd efforts to settle his problems through irrational violence rather than through reason and goodwill, Robert F. Kennedy, like John F. Kennedy and Martin

Luther King, gave his life in an effort to help the oppressed people of earth to find a new way of life.

Jesus said: "Greater love hath no man than this: that a man lay down his life for his friends" (John 15:13). It was in pursuit of noble goals of peace and a hand up out of poverty that Robert F. Kennedy was felled by a senseless assassin's bullet. Though he was rich, the rich did not like Kennedy, but the common people heard him gladly.

In his California victory speech at midnight on June 4, Robert Kennedy said:

"What I think is quite clear is that we can work together in the last analysis and that what has been going on within the U.S. over the period of the last three years—the divisions, the violence, the disenchantment of our society, the division whether between blacks and whites, or between the poor and the affluent, or between age groups, or regarding the war in Vietnam can be transcended, we can start to work together.

"We are a great country, an unselfish country, and a compassionate country. I intend to make that my basis for running."

He had been warned repeatedly that he might be killed. His response was that he had to be near and among the people. He said, "If they want me, they can take me." President Johnson had offered him a bodyguard, but he declined. This was probably foolhardy. Nevertheless, even with bodyguards, anyone who takes the responsibility to try to lead the American people today must take the risk of assassination.

President Johnson has called on us to "put an end to the aberrations of violence." If we can, this will be a monument to Robert F. Kennedy that we can erect in our hearts and behavior:

1. Seek peace rather than war.
2. Seek justice for black people and other minorities.
3. Seek skill training and job opportunities for the poor.
4. Replace prejudice and hatred with rational goodwill toward all men in our attitudes and behavior.

Like the Christ whom he worshipped, RFK sought "peace on earth and good will among men." He sought it not as a minister of the Gospel, but through the rough and tumble of politics and its harsh realism. His motivations were profoundly patriotic. He was no shallow patriot. He was a patriot who wanted to see the affluence of this great nation used to bless all of its inhabitants and all nations on earth, not for any selfish aggrandizement but to express profound, realistic love and goodwill toward all men.

He really lived the implication of that memorable statement of his brother, John F. Kennedy, given at his inaugural address in 1960: "Ask not what your country can do for you, but what you can do for your country."

He moved about among the people, spending, and being spent, trying to help the American people be worthy of the great wealth and the great heritage that has developed among us. "Greater love has no man than this." "Ask not what your country or the world can do for you, but what you can do for your country and the world."

Bow in a moment of silent prayer.

Amen.

Chapter 25

THE NEW MORALITY

Sermon delivered in Dallas and Corpus Christi—1967 and 1969

Scripture: Matthew 15:10–20; 12:33–37

The Pope said the new morality is an immorality. The term frightens most church people. Jesus talked about a new morality, and it frightened the Pharisees. "You have heard it said by them of old time, Thou shalt not kill, but I say do not be angry. . . ." "You have heard it said, do not commit adultery, but I say to you, do not look with lust . . ." "A new commandment I give unto you that you love one another, even as I have loved you."

It is strange the way mores change. In the Bible, you see sexual mores changing, from polygamy to monogamy, from women as property to women as persons. Other changes go from war as a holy thing, blessed by God, to "love your enemies, pray for those who despitefully use you" and "Blessed are the peacemakers," and from poverty and suffering as punishment from God, deserved by the person (Job) to "Blessed are the poor" and "Blessed are those who feed the hungry and clothe the naked."

When you read Bishop John Robinson's lectures published under the title *Christian Morals Today*, you realize that there is really an attempt here to implement the teachings of Jesus about absolute love. Much Christian morality is puritanism, is Judaism, is legalism. Yet, we have a split mind on this. We do not actually hear much moral teaching from our pulpits.

We are all secularists. The morality practiced today by people in the churches does not differ greatly from the morality practiced by people outside the churches. The secular forces are much more powerful than the Christian forces shaping behavior. What kids do in high school affects young people more than what kids do at church, as a rule. It should be the other way around. Church should lead in setting mores for culture. Christ is the transformer of culture.

However, Christ cannot transform culture unless three things are present. Preachers must read, study, think, and preach clear transformation of cultural patterns of behavior and set new mores. People must enter a meaningful fellowship of redemption in the church where new mores are agreed upon and committed to. The church must have a genuine life together (Bonhoeffer) in which commitment, sin, confession, and renewal are deeply understood and practiced.

Now, let us apply this in a couple of areas, one personal and one social. The personal area is changing premarital sexual mores. The Christian ideal is deep empathy for the other, a spiritual approach which includes physical well-being and mental well-being. There should be no desire to <u>use</u> the other; one should treat the other as a "Thou." In this context, Jesus said, "Don't even look with lust."

Yet, sex is a normal part of attraction between boy and girl. If they are ever going to get sufficiently involved with each other to marry, they will have to have some intimacy. The sex drive is such a powerful thing that it is entirely understandable that two people deeply in love might go on to have sexual intercourse, despite their best intentions. They are not likely to deliberately plan on it; so they don't have contraceptives.

Now, what is the obligation of the Christian churchman, whether parent, pastor, or friend, toward such "sinners"? Jesus clearly forgave the woman found in adultery when men brought her before him to condemn her and to test him. His new morality frightened them. When Jesus invited any of them without sin to throw the first stone, none of them cast a stone because they were sinners too. But they wanted this harsh legal standard and they wanted to use it to condemn others and hide their own sins.

I conclude we should teach our young people how precious life is, including the sex urge, the married relationship, the human personality, and all the reasons why the sex act should be saved for marriage to celebrate the rich quality of love between husband and wife. Teens won't listen to mom and dad; so invite a doctor or a teacher to talk to them. Then, if in their inexperienced, bumbling way, they get fouled up in the fishing lines, we help them untangle the lines and make the most of the rest of their lives. It is terribly important that all through the first twenty-one years of life parents be supportive figures like they are when the child is learning to walk. It is much more difficult to learn how to handle the sex urge than to learn how to walk.

Second, let us apply the Love Morality of Christianity to complex social problems, such as race relations, desegregation, poverty, and war. It should be perfectly clear that both Old and New Testament teach "that God has made of one blood all nations of earth to dwell together in unity." National lines, racial lines, clan lines, religious lines, family lines, color lines are not lines of inferiority and superiority. Like the diversity of the rest of life, they make life interesting, beautiful, and colorful when rightly understood. They are not bases for hatred, but bases for mutual appreciation and total enrichment. It is only ignorant and insecure people who cannot tolerate or appreciate the rich diversity in life.

In Matthew 15:10–20, Jesus tells the am-ha-a-rez who are confused about Pharisaic ideas that it is not what goes into the mouth, but what comes out of the mouth that corrupts a person. That means, when generalized, it is not what happens to you, but how you respond to what happens to you that counts. It also means that the jots and tittles of Pharisaic food laws also miss the point of high religion. High religion is concerned about the character and spirit in which the individual speaks and acts toward others.

There are three critical areas in which Christians just must learn to speak and act in a loving manner. First, we must treat as persons all people of the nations and races. They are children of God. Second, we must not add to the burdens of poverty-stricken people but instead lift them up. Each year our gross national product increases about 2 percent. If we would simply give 1 percent of our national wealth away each year, we could save the starving millions as in India. Our economy expands this much every year. Third, we must avoid war based on our fears that grow out of ignorance and prejudice. "Blessed are the peacemakers."

In conclusion, the New Morality means making the tree good so the fruit will be good. The good man out of his good treasure brings forth good. We must set good new Christian mores to guide the confused secular society. We must not only say but also do them (Matt. 12:33–35). One hundred years ago Christians bought and sold slaves. This is unthinkable today. Pray that 100 years from now these horrible Negro ghettoes will be unthinkable.

Chapter 26

THE SHAPE OF THE TWENTIETH CENTURY CHURCH

Sermon at Midway Hills Christian Church, May 5, 1968

Introduction

We really spend so little of our time thinking seriously and creatively about the Church and acting out the implications of this thought that every sermonic minute should be packed with serious thought. So, I will get immediately to my topic.

Dr. Harry D. Gideonse, eminent educator, Chancellor of the New School for Social Research, holder of ten honorary doctorates, decorated by the Dutch Government, having frequently represented the United States in International conferences, was the Honors Day Convocation speaker at TCU last week. One memorable thing that he said sparked this sermon in my mind. He said: "We must learn to dream again." We have become so realistic and present-oriented that we are forgetting how to project ideals. He quoted the scripture: "Where there is no vision, the people perish." He blamed the clergy somewhat for not stimulating our minds with great visions of human possibilities.

I agree with Dr. Gideonse and I shall give you a vision of the shape that I think the Church should take in the next fifty years or so.

I. Let us begin by a brief summary of the Gospel. As I John says, put very simply, the Gospel says God is love. The ultimate power in the universe is not our enemy, but our friend. God loves us and seeks our well-being.

What is the implication of this primary affirmation? Simply this: "We love because we know that he first loved us." "He who loves God should loves his brother also." "If a man says I love God and hates his brother, he is a liar."

New beyond this simple, central awareness, we must use our intelligence, which is God-given and then developed by our effort, to work out the detailed implications of what the Gospel means in our time. The meaning of the Gospel varies from time to time. When there were no automobiles, you did not have to apply the Gospel to driving, to highway building and repair. When there were no airplanes, you did not have to apply the gospel to flying, landing, taking off, safety requirements by air corporations. When the atom bomb developed with the possibility of destroying whole civilian populations, new thinking became necessary, different than but not unrelated to "Men shall beat their swords into plowshares." When there was no possibility of heart transplants, man did not have this tremendous life-power to use responsibly.

II. Taking these tremendous changes into consideration, what should the church do in the next fifty years? Basically, love means service. The Church, grounded in Christian love, should help the helpless. It should calm the frustrated and the angry. It should reconcile differences. It should help to bring peace on earth and goodwill among men.

No longer can "love your neighbor" be applied only on a personal basis. Today everyone is sitting in everyone else's lap. The Gospel is a social Gospel. God loves us. We must love our neighbors. Love is a social reality. It relates the self to others.

Now, the difficult question is: How can I intelligently love my neighbor? I find my Vietnamese neighbor is being wounded and starved. You may say he is not my neighbor because I don't know him personally. Well, where did we get this neighbor teaching besides this reference in I John? It came from the Good Samaritan parable. Do you have any evidence that the Good Samaritan, a foreigner down there in Judea, had ever seen the wounded man on the Jericho road before? There appears to be evidence that he had not. Did he continue the relationship after depositing him at the inn? Apparently not, except to pay the bill. The point is our obligation is not simply to our family and friends. It is a human need and human resources obligation. We have the resources. Others have the need.

So, to this question of helping my wounded and starved Vietnamese neighbor, how do I help? Do I quit my job, take my $1,000 of savings, spend $700 or $800 of it to get myself to Vietnam, walk down the streets of Saigon or some village until I find a wounded and needy Vietnamese, and give him the remaining $200 or $300? Ridiculous, you say! I agree! Why not work through political means to stop the war? Then, work through political means to help these people to help themselves recover from the war and develop in their own way to take their place in the modern world, as the Philippines are doing? This is one realistic way we can live out our Christian gratitude for God's love in our time. We have spent $90 billion in the past three years in the destruction of Vietnam. What could that $90 billion have done in construction?

Some similar procedure must be applied to rectifying the wrongs our forefathers visited upon the Negro, the Latin Americans, the Indian, and the Jew. Where it can be personalized, all the better. But regarding the huge Negro ghettoes, it cannot be handled personally. It requires Christian imagination applied to complex political and economic thinking to begin the process of renewal. One of the finest happening this summer is the cooperation of "enlightened businessmen" with government to put jobless people to work, training them, going the second mile with them, helping them to help themselves. The ads in various magazines call it "enlightenment." It could also be called "Christian." "The Christian thing" and the "wise and humane thing" are nearly always identical or similar. Christianity is the ultimate wisdom in human affairs. But, the precise application of the Christian guidelines depends upon worldly, realistic knowledge in finance, manufacture logistics, as well as psychological and sociological insight.

The Christian Gospel will never have the impact the world desperately needs until "enlightened businessmen," teachers, politicians, and all kinds of people put their various skills together in a community of goodwill to help the needy of the world to help themselves.

III. So, what is the "mission of the Church" then? Students really get excited about this issue. I am thinking particularly of a group of Honors students in religion at TCU. What is the new shape of mission? Students today are not nearly so interested in foreign missions as students from about 1875 to about World War II. Starting with John R. Mott, Robert E. Speer, Adoniram Judgson and climaxing in a figure like Albert Schweitzer, those persons from England, Germany, the United States, France, Spain, Italy, and Holland and other places took the Gospel to "heathen lands." I am not saying that this movement was not significant. I think that much of our awareness of the rest of the world stems from this missionary movement.

The other factor that makes us aware of the far places of the world is technology: radio, TV, and air transport. Wars have had their role in making us aware of other parts of the world. But, in the process of studying the history of movements of people, including missionaries, over the face of the earth, many scholars have concluded that the cross followed the sword and became an instrument of imperialism. The younger ministerial students want no part of that kind of mission.

However, through that missionary effort, churches have been established all over the world. These are called "The Younger Churches." They want to run their own local churches. They do not want Americans there dominating them. They are glad to have some as technical assistants to teach English or be surgeons, engineers, agronomists, etc. But they insist on controlling the church themselves, just as they are insisting on their own national freedom. That does not mean they do not want to participate with their Christian brothers and sisters in the worldwide, ecumenical church. They do. They want to be heard at the gatherings of the World Council of Churches. We must make loving, intelligent response to their points of view. Just as we must listen to our teenagers empathetically, so we must listen to these younger, less experienced churches.

In this ecumenical dialogue, we hope a catalyst will develop through which the people of the world can be brought to an understanding of each other and the establishment of peace on earth and good will among men. Through understanding each other in the churches, these people can affect the politics of their nations and bridge some of the chasms between nationalities that cause wars.

At home, we will continue to have churches like Midway Hills Christian Church, although I doubt that we should establish a lot more of them. Primarily, we must change our concept from that of constantly multiplying small churches to larger churches that do not spend all their budget on themselves. We should make a building like this serve three thousand people. If we did, we could have multiple staff, including specialists in counseling, youth work, recreation, adult education, and other needed services. We could join with other churches in Dallas, through the Council of Churches and other means, to provide various forms of ministry to the inner-city residents and the minority groups. You should see yourselves as simply a finger of the mighty Body of Christ that is making its loving witness in the total society.

With a much more efficient fiscal operation, we could and should have as an important priority goal: GIVE AT LEAST FIFTY PERCENT OF OUR BUDGET TO OTHERS. This should be standard policy for all churches. Furthermore, every activity of the church need not be at the building. Certain things can be accomplished for Christ in backyards, living rooms, dens, even pool halls, school yards, swimming pools, libraries, and social centers.

"Go ye into all the world and teach all nations" is a complex commission. Mostly you teach by being. What you are speaks more loudly than what you say. You get involved and thereby express the essential spirit that you have decided is the Christian spirit in our time on this problem.

You will need help from your fellow Christians. Thus you will need the Church and the occasions of worship, fellowship, discussion, and education. So, "Neglect not the assembling of yourselves on the first day of the week." But, be sure your Christianity does not end when the assembly is concluded.

Chapter 27

AN AMERICAN DREAM

A sermon at TCU Carr Chapel, 1969
Scripture: Gen. 37:5–21 and Joel 2:28–29

Introduction

I was impressed, as you probably were, last year when Dr. Harry Gideonse concluded his Honors Day address by saying "It is time for us to start dreaming again." I carried that phrase around with me for quite some time. It sort of haunted me.

I was haunted by it as the political conventions appeared on our television screens. I was increasingly haunted by it as the ugliness of our involvement in Vietnam became more and more apparent. I was haunted by it as I saw Congress cut off funds to finance the poverty programs and the ghetto-clearance programs.

I related that phrase to those noble words by Emma Lazarus, carved on the Statue of Liberty: "Give me your tired, your poor, your huddled masses yearning to breathe free, the wretched refuse of your teeming shore. Send these, the homeless, tempest tossed to me. I lift up my lamp beside the golden door."

I related it to those noble words of the second paragraph of the Declaration of Independence. "We hold these truths to be self-evident, that all men are created equal, that they are endowed by their Creator with certain unalienable Rights, that among these are Life, Liberty, and the pursuit of Happiness. That to secure these rights, Governments are instituted among men, deriving their just powers from the consent of the governed."

I related it to those noble words of the Gettysburg Address given by President Abraham Lincoln in 1863. "Fourscore and seven years ago, our fathers brought forth on this continent a new nation, conceived in liberty and dedicated to the proposition that all men are created equal. . . . It is rather for us to be here dedicated to the great task before us—that we here highly resolve that these dead shall not have died in vain—that this nation under God, shall have a new birth of freedom and that government of the people, by the people, for the people, shall not perish from the earth."

And I related it to those moving words of President John Kennedy: "Ask not what your country can do for you, but ask rather, what you can do for your country."

I concluded our dreams must be Christian and universal. But the locus of our power to help mankind is American. You cannot be a man without a country. So, I must apply my Christian faith to the American form of being in the world.

The American Tragedy

Then this summer, I was doing some bibliographical work in the library and ran across the title of an article by Robert Penn Warren. Both the author, who had been on campus for Creative Writing Day, and the title intrigued me. So, I went to the periodical section, found the *Yale Review,* Volume 55, opened to page 1 and guess what? It had been cut out! Some self-centered egomaniac who should be a ditch-digger instead of a college student had cut the first sixteen pages of that volume out and absconded with them. The name of that article? "The American Tragedy."

I was really depressed for days over that. This was done by one of our better people. He was willing to have not only me, but any person who wanted to read that article from now until TCU lies in ruins, to be deprived of it, just so he could have the use of it to write some paper by some deadline, I guess. It is impossible for me to understand what goes on in the mind of an intelligent person who would do such a thing.

I do not know yet what Robert Penn Warren says about An American Tragedy, and perhaps I never will, but I saw a symptom of a profound American tragedy there. It is related to the tragic rise of crimes of all kinds: the thoughtless spreading of trash and filth on the streets, the sewage and chemicals that pollute the rivers and streams, the deterioration of housing in the slums because unbelievably selfish landlords are willing to gouge every penny out of the poor that they possibly can. In our relationships, we treat others with an "itness" instead of a "thou-ness." Some people lack the capacity to love, to be loyal, to be considerate.

Depressed by these thoughts, I picked up Edward Albee's *The American Dream.* That was yet more depressing. It implied that even in the family where some semblance of love, mutual concern and support should certainly reside, there is only hypocritical pretense of love and even outright parasitical living off each other and manipulating each other in America. No genuine love or profound relationship is possible without a profound interpersonal relationship in which the other is treated as a Child of God.

No chauvinism, but genuine idealism, tempered by realism

It is increasingly apparent that our own inner moral deterioration is so complete that the other nations of earth are rapidly losing respect for us and do not feel they can trust us to lead them into a new age of peace and goodwill. We have condemned the Communists so long we have failed to see our own moral deterioration, but outsiders see it. Europeans even fear to come here for vacations because of the high rate of crimes of violence. I have walked at night along the streets and boulevards of London, Paris, Geneva, Rome, Athens, Istanbul, Beirut, Damascus, Cairo, Amman, and Jerusalem and have never been threatened with robbery or violence. But I would certainly not walk alone around New York or Washington, DC, at night. What has happened to the American dream?

When I responded to Dr. Gideonse's statement that it is time for us to dream again, I had visions of our people, both young and old, dreaming dreams of peace on earth—equity among all people—stability in the homes—a beautiful land whose streets and streams were clean, whose people could move about in peace and maximum freedom, where people of all races were respected and given equal opportunity. This is a Christian dream. "Dreams are they all, but shall we despise them . . . God's dreams? That men shall love one another, that white shall call black man brother, that greed shall pass from the market-place, that lust shall yield to love for the race?" (T. C. Clark).

Of course, we will have nothing to do with self-righteous, self-seeking, chauvinistic patriotism. However, if America is to make her appropriate contribution to the "Parliament of Man," she must come with cleaner hands than she has now. I am sure that the word of God speaks to us today and says: "Put your own house in order, O America, before you try to tell the rest of the world how to put its house in order."

In conclusion, I would say that a major theme of the Bible is this. The way of the dreamer is rough and rocky, but his sensitive commitment to new forms of goodness is the means God uses to bless his people. Joseph went through plenty of suffering, sustained only by the hope he had seen in his dreams, and lived to bless both his people and the Egyptian people. In a similar way, in our time, Dr. Martin Luther King was imprisoned, wounded, spat upon, reviled and finally killed, but is already enshrined beside a martyred president as one of the most creative men of our century. It is men like these who can dream great possibilities for the people who bless their time. With Dr. Gideonse, I say "Let us start dreaming again."

Hear the prophet Joel, as he says, after Judah has suffered for her sins:

> It shall come to pass afterward that I will pour out my spirit on all
> flesh.
> Your sons and daughters shall prophesy,
> Your old men shall dream dreams,
> And your young men shall see visions.

Joel expected an apocalypse accompanying a cataclysm. Let us hope that it will not be necessary for streets and home, women and children to lie dead and wasted here at home before a viable vision of a new order can demand our commitment. There has been enough of that kind of violence both at home and abroad.

Let us dream worthy and relevant dreams and commit ourselves to their fulfillment, trusting the God and Father of our Lord Jesus Christ to lead us and all people through the moral confusion of this time.

Let us dream again.

Chapter 28

PRECIOUS PAST AND MEANINGFUL FUTURE

Sermon at Memorial Christian Church, Jan.5, 1969

Scripture: Matthew 13:52. "Every scribe trained for the Kingdom is like a good householder who brings out of his treasure what is new and what is old."

Henry Adams (1838–1918), an American historian and descended from two presidents, said "Young men have a passion for regarding their elders as senile." I might add that old men have a passion for regarding their teenagers as silly. This problem of the generation gap is probably as serious in our time as it ever has been, though there are records of it dating back to early Egyptian times.

On this fifteenth anniversary as a church, you are now a teenager. But I think you are old enough to appreciate the past and young enough to anticipate the new values that will surely emerge in your promising future.

Let us contemplate the lure of the new and the comfort of the old. Borman, Lovell, and Anders (with the help of thousands of technicians) brought us a tremendous burst of novelty this Christmas season. But, Borman said, as they started back from the moon, "We are joyfully anticipating our return to earth, which appears as an oasis in a hostile universe." God seems to have designed us very well. In our youth we are explorative. In our maturity we seek the stable old reality.

A. N. Whitehead, in *Process and Reality* said, "We crave for novelty and yet we're haunted by terror at the loss of the past with its familiarities and its loved ones" (516–7). So the mind seeks to trust in God who remembers and preserves the significant past and supports us, even lures us forward to significant future possibilities. Harry Emerson Fosdick spoke of "abiding experiences in changing categories."

You have sung many times, "Change and decay in all around I see, O

Thou who changest not, abide with me." The only thing that is wrong with that line is that change does not always lead to decay. Just as often, it leads to growth and development. Certainly Midland is a better town and the Disciples a better Brotherhood because Memorial Church has come into being in the past fifteen years.

What things abide? These things abide. Obviously, you have lovely buildings. These may abide fifty to three hundred years. Fifteen hundred persons have united with this church (one hundred per year) by confession or transfer. That is a marvelous record! I hope you can do as well in the next fifteen years.

What is the enduring residuum in each of those lives? Who can say? Who, but God, can say what words and acts said and done here these past fifteen years have had what permanent creative effect on whose lives? Whether we know or not, God knows. God remembers and God orders the significant past and brings it forward to shape the present and the future. This is the Kingdom coming by the grace of God. We are accustomed to saying: "Your past can haunt you." But, if it is a good past, it can bless you and others.

However, a satisfying past can become positively evil if we become self-satisfied. As James Russell Lowell's famous poem, "The Present Crisis," says: "Time makes ancient good uncouth. We must upward still and onward go who would keep abreast of truth." "Behold I make all things new, saith the Lord" (Rev. 21:5). The past is a launching pad to the future. The Christ is the evidence God gives us of the New Being, the New Possibility. The wise old scribe brings out of his treasure things new as well as old.

What are some of the new things that God is obviously struggling to do through us today which we, a strong, mature congregation, are called to help God do? "God so loved the world—redemptively." We, as God's people, are called to love the world, especially "the little ones," the weak ones, those who need help.

We have done such a poor job of missions as Christians. Granville Walker estimated that the US spent more on the moon shot than Christians have spent on missions by all denominations in the total history of Christianity. Personally, I do not resent the moon shot; I glory in it. I do, however, resent the niggardly sharing habits of Christians. We really spend 95 percent of our money on ourselves. This is immature. In our Christian maturity, we must find ways to use our strength to help others.

As mature Christians, we will strengthen those developments in God's world which bring life, not death. "I came that you might have life and have it abundantly." We Americans are the world's most affluent people, and we in the Church are among the most affluent in an affluent society. We are definitely called by God to help the hungry feed themselves, not give a "hand out." We are called to help the naked clothe themselves, not to give charity but to help in such an intelligent way that persons can find self-respect by helping themselves and their fellows, particularly their own families.

Negroes, Latin Americans, poor whites need equal opportunities at public education, religious education, jobs, and recreation. If these people find that it is the state, not the church, that provides them with these things, we should not be surprised if they have no faith in the God the churches represent.

We Christians have the key ideas: All men are loved by God. As God's people, we must find ways of expressing God's love that are new, creative, sustaining, and helpful.

In conclusion, usually the churches spend most of their time, energy, and money on themselves. This is understandable in the childhood of a church; but, as Paul says, "When I became a man, I put away childish ways. . . ."

As Paul Tillich would say, "This is the end of 'dreaming innocence' for you." You leave your glorious childhood as a church and enter the years of Christian maturity. You provide leaders for the state, national, and international and ecumenical church. You put more of your money into missions. You serve the larger community of Midland and West Texas. You become a way-station, and the grace of God flows through you. You will have no doubt about your individual significance or your churchly significance if you do this.

So, may God continue to bless you in your maturity. And may the things you do in the name of God be worth remembering. If they are, you can be sure—God remembers!

PICTURES OF GOD

Sermon at Memorial Christian Church, Midland, Texas, January 15, 1984 and South Hills Christian Church, Parlor Class, February 26, 1984

This situation is quite different from the one I saw thirty years ago when

I preached the first sermon for this church. You and God have done very well indeed. I hope you are grateful to God. I'm glad you invited me for this occasion and that you have given me more than twenty minutes, because I want to share with you some insights that came to me in prayer in the middle of the night last September at our farm near Mineral Wells.

I could not have developed this thesis thirty years ago. It represents a lifetime of reading, travel, reflection, and teaching, plus an inspiration, out of that prayer experience. Like Jacob, somewhat, I was wrestling with God in prayer. I did not feel guilty for cheating my brother, like he did, but I was fussing at God about continual warfare, particularly the Beirut situation. And I said, "I need a picture of you so I can both speak with you and listen to you more clearly."

I immediately remembered the Biblical taboo: "Thou shalt not make unto thee any graven images" (the second commandment, Deuteronomy 5:8). Nevertheless, this yearning for a picture of God remained. I said to myself, "You can handle abstractions. You are a theologian. Why do you need a picture?" "But," I said, "I can picture a spirit, or a process, or an Eternal, or a Sustainer." So, I decided to work on this theme: Pictures of God. No one picture is adequate. It is understood that God who is really God transcends any man's conception of God, much less any artist's painting of God.

First, some historical considerations. Primitive peoples were always animistic. Wind, storms, and volcanoes were feared. In awe, the tribe developed animal symbols for the forces of nature or worshipped the sun itself. Rituals were developed to placate the anger of the volcano, the storm, the drought, and to call forth the activity of the forces of fertility.

Polytheism developed next. There were many gods. Each was worshipped to gain health (Aesclepius) or victory in war (Mars) or to provide unity and prosperity for the city (Athena). Paul thought the only way he could get through to the Athenians was to add Jesus to the pantheon of gods visible in the Agora below them as they sat on Mars Hill in front of the Parthenon. It was not so much the Greek gods that Moses thought of as the Baals of the Canaanites and the Phoenicians and Dagon of the Philistines, and the numerous animal gods of the Egyptians whom they had just left. It was difficult to hold to a clear image of God while Moses was gone a long time; so the people melted down all their jewelry and made a golden calf, like they had seen in Egypt.

Polytheism is still alive in the world. For instance, a picture in *Life* magazine shows some of the 330,000 gods and goddesses in Hinduism in India. There are legalistic, animistic, and mystical forms of worship. For scholars, there is a monotheistic form which treats all these 330,000 gods as mere personifications of one characteristic of the one God.

In contemporary times, we Christians share the Hebrew scriptures with the Jews and Muslims. The Muslims are staunchly, even fanatically, monotheistic (as in the Shiites, some of whom killed 240 US Marines in Beirut in the name of the one God, Allah, and sent six thousand youth into Iraqi minefields).

The God of the Old Testament shows some evolution in the changing conceptions of his character as presented in the Old Testament and the contrasting New Testament.

- Is he Lord of Hosts, that is armies, as in I Samuel 1:3, 1:11, 4:4, 15:2 and in II Samuel 5:10, 6:2, 6:18, 7:8, 7:26—a kind of General Patton, destroying his enemies?
- Is he jealous and vengeful, visiting the sins of the fathers on the sons, to the seventh generation of those who hate me, as in Deuteronomy 32:35, 4:24ff, 5:9, 6:15 and Exodus 20:5, and 34:14?

But even these teachings indicate God to be merciful if you repent and obey (Deuteronomy 5:10). Only in the prophets and the New Testament does God love his enemies. The prophets pictured Yahweh, the one true and only God, to be just and merciful. "What doth the Lord require of you but to do justice, love mercy, and walk humbly with thy God?" (Micah 6:8). Isaiah 9:6 pictures the messiah as "Wonderful Counselor, Mighty God, Everlasting Father, Prince of Peace." "He shall judge between the nations and shall decide for many people; and they shall beat their swords into plowshares, and their spears into pruning hooks. Nation shall not lift up sword against nation, neither shall they learn war anymore." Amos pictures God as a just judge. "Let justice roll down like waters and righteousness like an ever-flowing stream" (5:24). Micah and Hosea add to God's character the quality of mercy and loving forgiveness.

Jesus carried forward these pictures of God, Our Father. "Forgive, as your Heavenly Father forgives, even 70 x 7 times." It means an infinite forgiveness. "Forgive us our trespasses as we forgive those who trespass against us." We forgive others. "For God so loved the world that he gave his only begotten son, etc." (John 3:16). So Jesus is the best picture God ever had taken. The early church developed the trinitarian doctrine. There is some scripture for it. "Baptizing them in the name of the Father, Son and Holy Ghost" (Matthew 28:19–20).

In subsequent Christian theology, we have spoken of God as Creator (Genesis 1:1), Sustainer (Psalms 55:22), Maker of Heaven and Earth "When I behold the Heavens . . ." (Psalms 8:3), The Alpha and the Omega (Revelations 21:6), "The Word" (John 1:1–16).

Nevertheless, there is some validity to the popular statement, "Jesus Christ is the best picture God ever had taken" if you do not press the analogy too far. It does not do justice to God, the Creator and Sustainer of the Universe, nor to God the Lord of History and Arbiter of our final destiny, the Alpha, and the Omega. But, it is helpful in picturing God as he is relevant to human affairs, human suffering and human hope of resurrection and life everlasting.

Of course, all pictures of Jesus, as well as of God, are artists' interpretations. You have a right to conjure up in your mind such pictures if they are helpful in making God or Christ personal and available to you. But, some such conjurings are, in my opinion, unworthy and belittling, as when God is referred to as the "Man Upstairs." It makes God in our own image.

Finally, Albert Outler, the great SMU theologian, speaking to faculty at Brite Divinity School and the Religion Department faculty at TCU some years ago, said "God is ultimately mysterious, that is, transcendent." Thus, we are well advised to honor the God who is really God, and not just some conception or picture of God that we hold at a particular time. In my own lifetime, my conception of God has changed, enlarged, and improved many times.

I admire Blake's "Creator, Above the Sea of Time and Space" and feel that it represents rather well that great scripture (Psalm 8:3), "When I behold thy heavens, the work of thy fingers, the moon and the stars which thou hast established, what is man that thou art mindful of him and the son of man that thou dost care for him?" Nevertheless, I know that Blake's picture, though helpful, is inadequate.

I agree with Outler: "God is ultimately mysterious, transcendent." God transcends all the pictures of God and all the Biblical and theological symbols of God whether it be Lord of Hosts, or Creator, Sustainer, Heavenly Father, or Alpha and Omega. We need these. They are helpful. Different ones help in different ways at different stages of our spiritual journey. But, ultimately, God is God, beyond and above all these human symbols. The Christian revelation affirms that he loves us even when we are prodigals. This we do not know from any other source.

ADDENDA TO "PICTURES OF GOD," January 29, 1984, 5:00 a.m. PICTURES OF REALITY, TIME, ESSENCE OF BEING AND NON-BEING

Call to mind now conceptions of time processes we've studied in this series and the theological series I gave you two years ago.

For Hinduism we have the cycles of reincarnation. They can go up or down, backward, or forward. The forward motion can lead to Nirvana, which is seen as Brahman-Atman—release of the j'wa (individual soul of a Brahmin caste person) who has done all the Karmic law deeds he is supposed to do and his oneness with God is perfected so that he is never reborn into the world again.

In Buddhism, you can accomplish this in your present existence, whatever your caste. What you attain is the release from suffering, from the vicious cycle of reincarnation, but the positive aspects of that are not clarified by Gotama, the Buddha. Nirvana is non-being, no-thing, nothingness, atheism. He says he does not know and so won't speak about God and an afterlife. Zen Buddhism stays with him closely.

Chinese and Southeast Asians tend to think of a heaven, somewhat like the western Judeo-Christian conception of a place or state of being where the soul lives eternally as a Bhodisattva, an angelic being serving fellow mortals by luring them to salvation, being messengers of the deity's grace. The time sequence is more like the western sense. It goes on, for one life of the believer in the bodily form, to the crisis of death of the body, then "the soul puts on an immortal form." As Paul would say, "There are bodies terrestrial and bodies celestial." They endure forever in obedient, useful, peaceful communication with God or gods and are being helpful in doing God's will.

In Chinese thought the time/reality sense is the oscillation back and forth of yang/yin (light and dark). It is oriented to this world. Body and soul are not separated. Eternal life is not contemplated, except as you make inevitable imprint on your descendants.

As I conclude, I will probably lose those of you who did not hear my series on theology in January 1982.

In the process-theology orientation, all of reality is seen as in process and God is seen as the author and ongoing participant, who by lure and pressure guides and develops this coming into being of new goodness. It is seen as progressive development, from the birth of a universe to its transformation, through dying, into other forms. Of course, for individuals, it sees the entity or essence as passing through birth, creative development, dying, and creative transformation into oneness with God—pictured by Whitehead as being caught up into the Unforgettable mind of God (or in Revelation as a part of the angelic Court of God).

For process theologians, the time sense partakes of the yang/yin symbol, but the whole reality system rolls forward and tends to assume the stance of "Lead on O King Eternal" or "Onward and Upward Christian Soldiers." With a profound trust in the One God, who is Eternal, yet lovingly and creatively in every present event, the process theologian believes God is luring and pressuring us onward and upward to our richest and highest potential. The believing individual is using every potential of his whole being (reason, knowledge, emotional maturity) to respond creatively to the upward call of God in Jesus Christ.

Thus, his life has eternal meaning in the now and blesses his brothers and sisters and participates in the upward thrust of the one God who is constantly transforming this person, his fellows, and this worldly universal reality into the Realm of God, or the Kingdom of God, or the Kingdom of Heaven . . . The New Being, The New Reality, The Ultimate Good Possibility.

Chapter 29

SOME PERILS AND SATISFACTIONS OF LIVING IN A CREATIVE AGE

Sermon at the Unitarian Fellowship, March 23, 1969

From time immemorial, we have been aware of two forces: motion and inertia. Analogously, we have been aware of the prophet who speaks for motion or change and the priest who speaks for conserving old values, or inertia. Likewise, in practically all areas of human association and action, both types appear—liberals and conservatives.

However, in the twentieth century particularly, but really in the whole industrial age, change has accelerated. One illustration being bandied about is that whereas human knowledge doubled from 1 CE to 1500 CE, it now doubles every decade. This extent of rapid change is somewhat threatening to everyone.

We need a theology of change very much, and this is available.

First, what are some of the perils of change? Some examples are air and water pollution and the destruction of forests, which not only upsets the life cycle of animals and insects but also causes water to rush unimpeded down mountain sides causing soil erosion, flooding, and destruction of homes. We note California has had whole hillsides crumble away with expensive homes on them.

Admiral Perry forced open the gates of Japan, and as they creaked open on their rusty hinges, a Pandora's box of evils were unleashed, which finally resulted in Pearl Harbor and the extremely costly Pacific War during World War II. A cost still incalculable is the religious change forced on the Japanese by Douglas McArthur when he declared the Emperor was no God. In fact, he forced the emperor to declare he was no God. This drastic revision of the very spiritual basis of a culture is causing and will yet cause repercussions that will not be calculable for at least a hundred years, perhaps five hundred years.

The industrialization of a primitive society, or a backward society, whether it be in Africa or Southeast Asia, often forces complex, rapid changes on people barely able to assimilate them.

In America we have raised our children to think for themselves. We have taught minorities to speak up for their rights. At our Special Course at TCU: Dissent, Protest, and Creative Change, students and blacks are talking very straight and almost harshly to conservative adults. It frightens and angers conservative adults and even some liberal ones—or at least they thought they were liberal.

One of the aspects of this rapidly changing scene that has intrigued me is the way those who hold power, whether in family, church, business, or politics, hate to relinquish it. The will to hold power is a profound, pervasive reality and takes many, many forms.

What are some satisfying or productive ways to respond to change? At a shallow level, we can appreciate dishwashers, clothes dryers, rockets, space ships, and better transportation facilities for air and surface. Presumably when we get over the clumsy growing pains of democratic adolescence in these matters, some degree of relative peace and goodwill will prevail. At least that hope keeps us working on the problems.

One way we might help through religion is to orient theology to creative change instead of to static concepts. We sing "Change and decay in all around I see. O Thou who changest not, abide with me." Not "Fast falls the eventide" but "fast rises the sun." Not "Day is dying in the West" but "Day is dawning in the East."

In this perspective, Process Theology offers the best option. The philosophical work of men like Bergson and Whitehead and the philosophical-theology of men like Wieman, Cobb, Hartshorne, and Williams is promising.

Wieman is the most easily assimilated by most laymen. His central concepts are grounded in assumptions that when something is material, we not try to spiritualize it. He thinks that a certain empirical and pragmatic quality characterizes our thinking. Secondly, he thinks that we need to apply scientific method as far as applicable to our apprehension of reality and its potentiality for creating good as conceived by intelligent people in community. Thirdly, we should ask whether there is a force at work in reality other than or beyond, but yet immanent in the thought-actions of people that is creative of human good.

Yes, he says there is. He calls it Creativity, or Creative Interchange.

Numerous descriptions of it exist. Here are two. God's side of process includes emergence of new values, integration of new with old, expansion of appreciable world, and widening and deepening of community. Man's response that he should endeavor to make include expanding the range and diversity of what I can know and control; increasing ability to appreciate other persons across barriers of estrangement; increasing freedom to absorb antagonism, crisis, shock of change, and reorientation of self and society; and increasing ability of individuals to integrate new facts, persons, experiences into his unique individuality or character. Both are ways that God or Creativity or Creative Interchange operate in life and are observable.

The Church should study ways to make this fact or process known to people and to help them stay sensitive and responsive and to share insights and appreciations with each other.

In conclusion, Wieman says: "The creative event is always working in History, but usually it is ignored" (*The Source of Human Good*, 57). Leonardo da Vinci was a most creative man. In old age and senile, he kept writing in the margin of drawings of creative ideas, "Was anything ever done?"

The creative God is not all powerful, says Wieman. God relies in considerable part on the response of dedicated people.

Chapter 30

ON DOING THE GOOD

Sermon at two Fort Worth churches, 1970

"I'm doing good work and I have a good family." I suppose the power of this simple statement wouldn't have impressed me had I not read *Black Like Me* by John Howard Griffin and developed a profound admiration for this man who is my kind of saint. He and Schweitzer, Grenfeld, Kagawa, and Hammarskjöld represent the spiritual nobility of humans.

For those of us who don't really want to do the good, there is an easy way out. We can simply ask, "Define what you mean by the good." We seem to be saying, "If you can convince me that what you advocate is really good, then I'll feel bound to do it. Otherwise, not." Well, you might as well forget it with that person.

Doing good is a lifestyle, an obsession with some people. Other people seem bent on avoiding the obligation to do the good. Now, presuming we want to know and do the good, how can we proceed?

Kant's moral imperative states that it can't rationally be proved with a physical good. The only ultimate good is good will. His categorical imperative is to "so act as to will your action a universal maxim." He thought we should treat all our duties as divine commands. We cannot rationally prove an ethical absolute or system of morals that everyone must adhere to. The decisions must be made by individuals, invariably. They can be extended to groups as in systems of laws and mores.

Numerous human experiments, such as the Hindu, Jewish, Catholic, Calvinist, and Puritan convince any thoughtful person that legalism and dogmatism enforcement do not provide the answer. In reading James Michener's *The Source* this summer, I was impressed anew with how absurdly cruel dogmatic, legalistic people become whether Jewish, or Christian, or Muslim. So I would say that one lesson people have learned fairly well is that dogmatic moral legalism is not the answer to the question of how do we know and do the good.

As the Apostle Paul told the Romans, neither legalism or libertinism is the answer (Chapters 1–2 of Romans). When there is complete individual, sensual self-gratification, anarchy and chaos result. "God gave them up to the lusts of their hearts." Certain types of existentialism tend in this direction today. If I gratify myself with no concern for the other or by the larger society and everyone else does the same, there can be no social order. The problem is just the opposite with legalism. In legalism, I forego my own fulfillment to conform to the concept of the common well-being.

Neither position is adequate. Philosophically, we can say with Risieri Frondizi in his book on values that the answer lies neither in objectivism nor in subjectivism, but in relational view of values and valuation. That means that adequate valuation procedure, or adequate rational choice of the good is not based merely on my subjective feelings, or merely on the rational conclusion that America is an ultimate value in itself, but upon my intelligent relationship of my own subjective feelings of numerous kinds to the objective geographical, economic, political, religious, and other realities that constitute America.

Every ethical decision is made in a frame of reference in the mind of the decider. Kant's "universal" maxim varies in its universality with the capacity of the decider to universalize, and the extent of his experience. One of the prime reasons that people come together in a church fellowship is that you need the stimulus of the other morally sensitive persons to help you check your universe. Are my decisions adequately aware of the attitudes and special interests of others? Each person who participates in the discussion has a different spectrum of experience and is capable of enriching my awareness. Ideally this fellowship would include persons from different races, colors, national origins, etc.

However, there is the threat of complete relativism. Thoughtful people often become incapacitated for action. The more intelligent and extensively experienced you are, the more difficult it is for you to decide and act with conviction because you see the exceptions. This calls for courage, moral decision and risk in action. Not least among the risks is the risk of looking ridiculous to your other sophisticated friends who didn't act. But, to cop out and not act at all is a gut-less, worm-like adjustment to our total human situation.

You are here because you must act as intelligently as you can and you need loving encouragement from kindred spirits in doing so. Like John Howard Griffin, you must make your commitment, "do good" as best you can, rest in the supportive relation of "a good family," hopefully your husband, wife, children, but also the family of the church, and leave the rest to God and the other good men.

In summary, Harvey Cox in *Situation Ethics* says the goodwill stance is called Christian Love or Agape. The Apostle Paul said, "He who loves his neighbor has fulfilled the Law." This is probably all we can say. The details must be hammered out by fellowships of goodwill in concrete situations and God-given intelligence. Certainly, life is better than killing in all but a very few circumstances. Stable family life which provides children with security is better than sensuality running rampant and free love. Property such as homes and cars and bank accounts need to be safe from theft by other individuals and the government. Beyond this, maximization of freedom to think, speak, write, worship, and associate with a variety of other persons is a high value. We must strive for goodwill, an educated conscience, and a fellowship of sensitive good people.

Chapter 31

THE HISTORICAL JESUS

THE REAL JESUS, PART I

A sermon at First Congregational Church, 1970

Scripture: Mark 8:27–33

I owe this sermon to Pannenberg's *Jesus, Son of God.* You remember the television show of a few years back, I've forgotten the name of it, but after character descriptions came the moment of truth when the announcer said, "Will the real Mr. Markham please stand up?"

In a way you might entitle this sermon "Will the real Jesus please stand up?" if such a title doesn't offend you. I do not intend to be offensive. I intend to explore the problem of Christology from the historical side. There is the historical Jesus and the Christ of faith. Today we are talking about pictures of the historical Jesus that appear in the Scriptures.

Two pictures emphasize the divinity and do not separate the historic Jesus from the Christ of faith. In John 1:1–14, Jesus is the pre-existent Christ, the Logos, one with God, emanating into the world, but the world is hardly aware of how it is being done. He is the response to Gnosticism. In the fourth Gospel, John gives long discourses, like a Greek philosopher, except he adds the incarnational dimension, "The Word became flesh." "I am the way, truth, life." "I am in the Father, and the Father is in me." These words imply oneness with divinity from pre-birth. There is no birth story. He is not baptized by John the Baptist. He does not need it. He is God, an emanation from God, from the beginning. Nathaniel says when he first meets him, "Rabbi, you are the Son of God."

Matthew and Luke have two different forms of the virgin birth story which emphasize that Jesus is not fully God, or an emanation from God, but that he was born of a virgin by action of the Holy Spirit. Luke even traces the divine action to the pre-birth condition, when John the Baptist leaps in his mother's womb at the approach of Mary who is carrying

Jesus. At his birth, according to Matthew, wise men from the East come and ask Herod of his whereabouts. Herod feels his throne shake and asks to be told when they find him. But angels warn Joseph and the Wise Men, and Jesus is taken to Egypt to save him from the wrath of Herod. Herod kills all other boy babies in an attempt to kill Jesus.

The remainder of the Gospels of Matthew and Luke picture Jesus as doing deeds of mercy and kindness, "mighty acts," and being a teacher of the Kingdom of God or Kingdom of Heaven as it is called in Matthew. Matthew has five teaching sections, of which Matthew 5, 6, and 7, The Sermon on the Mount, is the most famous and perhaps the most important.

Jesus teaches the double command, humility, kindness, and love. He illustrates this in many ways, including hyperbole, which says, "Go, sell all you have and give it to the poor and come and follow me." In Matt. 25: "Inasmuch as you have fed the hungry, clothed the naked, visited those who are sick or in prison, ye have done it unto me." Those who have done so, unselfconsciously, will be welcomed into the Kingdom at life's end. Those who have not are cast into outer darkness.

The earliest of the four Gospels to be written is Mark. Here no birth stories have developed; the logos doctrine has not been developed. Jesus hears a sense of call and vocation as God's chosen one at his baptism by John. He is tempted to use this power the way other men do to feed himself when hungry, to rally a following by doing extraordinary things like jumping off the temple without harm to himself, and coming to be a messianic king as the Jews expect. But he says no to all of these and commits himself to follow the leadership of God and his word. Apparently, this means to meet the issues that arise from day to day under the claims of all he knows about God and his will and to make daily decisions.

Tillich says he was absolutely loyal to his ground of being. When someone calls him "good master," he says "Why do you call me good. No one is good, but God." He certainly didn't think of himself as God. He called himself "Son of Man," as Ezekiel had. He identified deeply with man. He performed healing "miracles," such as the raising of the daughter of Jairus, and tells people not to tell anyone about these things.

At Caesarea Philippi he asks his disciples, "Who do men say that I am?" Some say John the Baptist, others Elijah, and others one of the prophets. Then Jesus said, "But who do you say that I am?" And Peter answered, "You are the Christ." And he charged them to tell no one about him. Matthew elaborates on this story by saying that Jesus said he would give Peter the keys to the kingdom of heaven.

Then Jesus told them that he, the Son of Man, must suffer many things and be rejected by the elders and chief priests and scribes, and be killed and after three days to rise. Then, he called the multitude to him and said, "If any man would come after me, let him take up his cross and follow me. For whoever would save his life will lose it; and whoever loses his life for my sake and the Gospel's will save it."

From the cross, he cries "My God, my God, why hast thou forsaken me?" In the Garden, he prayed, "If it be thy will, let this cup pass from me." Both are very human expressions under such severe stress.

It would appear that the historic Jesus would be best reported in the earliest Gospel before the tradition makers had smoothed out the story to fit the final decision about his significance. The Gospel writers all tried to express the uniqueness of Jesus. That picture would seem to be of a very unusual man completely committed to doing the will of God, who went about doing good that struck the people he helped as sheer miracles. He taught loving kindness toward the needy, and he practiced it.

This offended the religious establishment. All four of the Gospels report that he cast the money changers out of the temple and said, "It is written my Father's house shall be called a house of prayer for all the nations, but you have made it a den of robbers." He lived at the poverty level without thought for getting ahead in the world. He taught a very unrealistic set of economic ideas. He told a rich young man that if he was really interested in entering the Kingdom, he would sell all he had and give it to the poor and come follow him. Francis of Assisi later did just that, as have many others.

He blessed the widow who gave her last penny to the temple treasury in contrast to the well-to-do who were giving non-sacrificial gifts out of their plentitude. He taught that freely given love characterizes God's dealing with us. God doesn't give sparingly. He gives in plentitude and even causes his rain to fall on the just and the unjust. He doesn't play a game with his cards held close to his chest. He forgives endless times and is generous like the father of the prodigal son.

This is what should characterize our giving. It should be done generously and gladly, then we will be sons of our Father who is in heaven who makes his rain fall on the just and the unjust. God so loved the world that he gave out of the fullness of his love. Jesus, who became known as the

Son of God, gave himself in this way—even in death, asking forgiveness for those who crucified him. He calls us to be this kind of person; sources of outgoing love, giving of ourselves, our time, our talent, our money to keep alive in the world this saving quality—this awareness of God as outgoing and self-sacrificial love. This is the ultimate hope of mankind. The Church of Jesus Christ endeavors to keep this spirit alive and real in the world.

This is basically the meaning of being a Christian. It has a thousand different expressions depending on the opportunities life puts before us. But I wouldn't want to fail to support the Church, the Body of Christ, which makes real the Love of God in the world generation after generation.

THE REAL JESUS, PART II

Scripture: Matthew 9:1–13

I have found it interesting to endeavor to emphasize the humanity of Jesus and the historically valid incidents, trying to omit the accretions of faith and dogma. Not only do most of the scholarly books on the subject go all too quickly to Paul's statement of faith and meaning, but I find my own mind moving in that direction.

I think this problem arises because the empowerment of Christianity through the centuries, that is, the power it has given to needy men in every age is the clue to the nature of God, of eternity. To have some reassurance or at least a lead idea as to how this human life opens out upon ultimate reality, or how man is related to God, is a hunger of most human beings, especially as they face death, but also many critical decisions of life.

I reviewed three books by three ranking scholars for this sermon: John Knox, *The Humanity and Divinity of Jesus* (Union), Wolfhart Pannenberg, *Jesus-God and Man* (Mainz), and Gunther Bornkamm, *Jesus of Nazareth* (Heidelberg). I think Bornkamm has done the best job of researching the historic Jesus. Both others slip too quickly and easily into the honorific Christ emphasis. That is an important bit of history too, but my present concern is a careful look at the data we have regarding the history of Jesus.

Bornkamm says: "The disciples are concerned with the pre-Easter history of Jesus" (22). The rest of the New Testament is concerned with the post-Easter history of the risen Christ and his imminent return, plus the church which awaits his return. Let us use Bornkamm's own summary of what the Gospels show us of the historic Jesus (beginning in Chapter III, 53ff):

"The childhood and adolescence of Jesus are obscure for us from the historical point of view. The birth narratives in Matthew and Luke, which differ from one another not inconsiderably, are too much overgrown by legends and by Jewish as well as Christian messianic conceptions to be used for historical assertions. The importance and meaning of these texts lie in a different area. The home of Jesus is the semi-pagan, despised Galilee. ("Can any good thing come out of Nazareth?") His family certainly belonged to the Jewish part of the population which, since the time of the Maccabees, had reattached themselves to the temple cult in Jerusalem and the legal practices of Judaism. . . .

"Jesus's father was a carpenter, and possibly Jesus was too. We know the names of his parents, Joseph and Mary, and those of his brothers, James, Joses, Judas, and Simon (Mk 6:3). His brothers, as well as his mother, were originally unbelievers (Mk 3:21, 31; Jn 7:5), but later belonged to the Church and to its missionaries (Acts 1:14; I Cor. 9:5). The tradition occasionally also mentions Jesus's sisters (Mk 6:3; Mt 13:56). Jesus's mother tongue was Aramaic of Galilee, the same dialect by which the servants of the high priest recognized Peter when he denied his Master in Jerusalem (Mt 36:73). Hebrew was at that time no longer a spoken language, but rather only the language of religion and of scholars. He was often addressed as rabbi, and he was asked to speak in synagogue service.

"We find in Jesus no trace of Hellenism—no Greek philosophy, no Greek language, no speaking in Hellenistic towns. Rather he spends most of his time in the small Jewish hamlets of Galilee: Capernaum, Chorazim, Bethsaida, in the hill country and beside the lake of Galilee.

"Luke 3:23 tells us that he began his public ministry, following the work of John the Baptist, at about thirty years of age. His own baptism by John is one of the most certainly verified occurrences of his life. Tradition, however, has altogether transformed the story into a testimony to the Christ, so that we cannot gather from it what baptism meant for Jesus himself, for his decisions and his inner development. But that this event was of far-reaching importance nobody will deny. It is all the more important that Jesus, without ever questioning the mission and the authority of the Baptist, nevertheless does not continue the work of the

Baptist and his followers in the Jordan valley, but starts his own work in Galilee—like John, as a prophet of the coming kingdom of God. The instrument of his activity, however, is no longer baptism, but his spoken word and helping hand. We can no longer say with certainty how long Jesus's activity lasted. The first three Gospels create the impression that it lasted but a year. But they do not give a reliable chronology. We learn a great deal about his preaching, the conflict with his opponents (scribes, Pharisees, Sadducees, Herodians, Chief Priests), his healing and the additional influence help granted to the suffering people, and the powerful influence which went forth from him. The people flock to him. Disciples follow him, but his enemies also arise and increase. The last decisive turning point in his life is the resolution to go to Jerusalem with his disciples to confront the people there with his message in face of the coming kingdom of God. At the end of this road is his death on the cross.

"These meagre, indisputable facts comprise a very great deal. There is little enough in this enumeration, and yet it contains most important information about the life story of Jesus and its stages. But much remains hidden in the obscurity of history."

The Gospel and extra Biblical sources provide us with much information about the world in which he lived, and this helps us understand him a little more. He is a Jew. The Jewish people find their security in their past history and their future hope. It knows no other security (55). Thus the world in which Jesus appears is a world between past and future. It is so strongly identified with these two time dimensions that the present hardly exists. The whole of life is caught in a network of sacred traditions. Jesus's milieu can then be pictured as hardened, encrusted ground (tradition) with a few cracks in it.

Through these cracks, the volcanic erupting fire of a future expectation that restores the glory of the Davidian past breaks forth occasionally. It is the fire of a burning expectation. It will come by the act of God. This is expected by the Essenes, by the Pharisees, by the Zealots. They simply had different programs of just what one should do. John's "Repent for the Kingdom is at hand" is also Jesus's message.

The Jew had a faith in a God who is beyond the world and history, but relevant to the world and history, past and future. This world comes alive and is immediately present in the story of Jesus, as told by the writers of the Gospels. All the characters who encounter Jesus bear the stamp of this world: the priest and the scribe, the Pharisee and the publican, the rich and the poor, the healthy and the sick, the righteous and the sinner. They appear in the story in a matter-of-fact and simple fashion, chosen at random and of great variety, and appearing in no particular order. Yet, all the characters, however great their diversity, present a very human appearance. In their encounter with Jesus—whatever its nature—they come to this encounter as fully real, historically believable people.

"Jesus belongs to this world." Yet, in the midst of it, he is of unmistakable *otherness*. This is the secret of his influence and his rejection. Faith has given manifold expression to this secret. But even he who, prior to any interpretation, keeps his eyes fixed upon the historical appearance of Jesus, upon the manner of his words and works, even he meets with his insoluable mystery. . . . He is a prophet of the coming Kingdom of God (Mk 8:28; Mt 21:11, 46). Yet, he is not completely contained in this category and differs from the customary ways of a prophet. A prophet has to present his credentials by recounting his call. Jesus never speaks of his calling and nowhere does he use the ancient prophetic formula: "The word of the Lord came to me, saying . . . " Even less does he appeal to ecstatic vision and secret revelations. He even refuses to justify himself by performing miracles to prove his authority.

This prophet is at the same time a rabbi who proclaims the divine law, teaches in synagogues, and yet criticizes the law, or at least jot-and-tittle legalism. He dares to say: "The law says, but I say . . . " The Gospels sum it up by saying: "He taught them as one having authority and not as the scribes." "The reality of God and the authority of his will are always directly present and are fulfilled in him." The divine significance of past and future are made real and present in him. It is this uniqueness and the sense of ultimate validity in the man, plus the tragedy of his death and the sense of the eternal significance of the insight that is his life and teaching put together, that is attempted to be communicated in the complex Christology that develops.

In conclusion, when we affirm that Jesus is the Christ, we are affirming many things. Some persons affirm one, some another. They all have elements of hope for the future, a better day coming, good overcoming evil, God bringing God's Kingdom. We are saying I can believe it because there is this brief incident that was historical—the Man from Nazareth. He gave us a glimpse of the possibility of human life. I'm committed to that picture of the human possibilities as the will and call of God.

CHRISTIAN FAITH

Scripture: Hebrews 11:1–3; 35–12.2

After last Sunday's sermon on the historic Jesus I felt it necessary to go on and speak of the Christ of Faith. I've gotten myself in so deep I can't let go of this topic. We concluded last Sunday by saying that we are sure that the people who associated with Jesus considered him an unusual teacher and healer, and some thought him a prophet. Apparently, only a few considered him the Christ; even John the Baptist, while he was in prison, sent a message to ask the question. Jesus did not answer directly. In the synoptics, Jesus does not proclaim himself the messiah as clearly as he does in John. In Matthew he blesses Peter when Peter proclaims Jesus the messiah.

It is the resurrection experience that is basic to the affirmation of Jesus as the Christ. Had it not been for the resurrection experience, it is quite clear that Christianity would not have developed. So, it is not surprising that all the literature including the latter part of the synoptics deal with the resurrection, and most of them try to communicate the meaning and significance of the resurrection.

John Knox, in *The Humanity and Divinity of Christ,* gives three diagrams to attempt to simplify the basic three concepts that have characterized historic christologies (17).

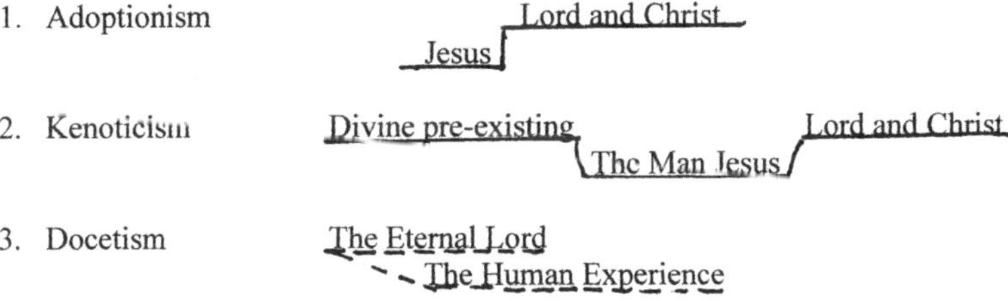

The Human Experience

Now, we should add three more:

1. The Virgin Birth in Matthew and Luke presents Jesus as a Gift from God. He was a God-Man, not fully human from birth.

2. There are many liberal Christians who do not believe in the resurrection. They say the power of Jesus is his uniqueness as an individual in insight and commitment.
3. Paul Tillich speaks of Jesus as "transparently loyal to the ground of his being." He is a window through whom we can see the Divine Being. He is Jesus whom we call the Christ.

Pannenberg summarized various Christologies. In the ancient church, deification came through incarnation. "The son of God has become what we are in order that we might receive a share of his perfection, that will relate us to God from whom we are separated." An early Platonic school emphasized Jesus as the one who strived for and achieved ethical perfection. He is the great example of ethical striving and commitment. In the beginning, the Logos dwelled in Jesus's soul and continued to become more complete.

Anselm of Canterbury (1098) put forward the Christology of vicarious suffering that today dominates fundamentalist thinking. Jesus lived the perfect life which satisfied God's goodness, and then died the death on the cross as a substitutionary sacrifice to satisfy God's justice for those who sin and then repent and believe in God's love, as represented in sending Christ as a propitiation for our sins.

Martin Luther thought that Jesus represents the rest of humanity neither in its striving for the good nor in the offering of works of satisfaction. Rather, Jesus is the representative of humanity before God by humbling himself under God's wrath against sin and thereby being righteous before God. God gives God's grace to the one who is unrighteous in his own eyes and thereby shows himself to be humble before God. But, later in life, Luther added his agreement to the Anselmian idea that Jesus's vicarious suffering on our behalf is a satisfaction to God.

F. Schleiermacher sees Jesus as the prototypal man of sinless perfection who calls forth the Christian community that can still be experienced today and can provide us with a strong consciousness of God. He speaks of the "Body of Christ" and the "Creative Holy Spirit."

Immanuel Kant and F. Ritschl saw Jesus as an ideal of moral perfection who presents to every man a challenge that stimulates his moral consciousness. He not only lives the good himself but spreads good through the community and even sacrifices himself for the good. Jesus is the source of forgiveness of sin, not as a sacrifice to placate an angry God, but as showing that every man can overcome sin. The soteriological emphasis is for this life only. "Thy Kingdom come on earth."

Tillich emphasizes that Jesus finds the courage to be himself in spite of all the threats against the prophets and the pressures to conformity to the established priesthood; and he reveals to people of faith this way of life that enables them to feel "accepted though unacceptable" and to commit themselves to God's will courageously, to see the eternal in the now. Thus, living for the eternal, they participate in the eternal and "death hath no more dominion over them."

Jesus believed in and spoke of the eschaton. He felt that the final word was in the hand of God and that life was meaningful, not meaningless. The way to meaning was the Kingdom Way. Certainly, it meant the way to a better life on earth. It was also the basis on which God would judge our personal and corporate history.

Theologians of Hope are emphasizing today that Christ is our best eternal word of hope both here and hereafter. Pannenberg says, at the conclusion of his book, "Only the eschaton will ultimately disclose what really happened in Jesus's resurrection from the dead. Until then, we must speak favorably in thoroughly legitimate, but still only metaphorical and symbolic, form about Jesus's resurrection and the significance inherent in it."

Many Christians today say they believe in the spiritual resurrection of Jesus and they can relate this meaningfully to the appearance to Saul-Paul, to the appearance to the twelve in Jerusalem, to the appearance on the road to Emmaus, and to the awareness of Christ's spirit as a Holy Spirit abroad in the world today.

Many of our most promising young people today who are morally serious, much more so than many orthodox churchmen, are turned off about the church. They are not sure they believe in God. They find the evidence inconclusive. They are unable to have faith without better evidence than they have been given, but those same young people often admire Jesus. They share the sense of awe and mystery that orthodox Christians feel about him, but typically they speak of him in terms that separate them from the church and often antagonize the churchman, such as "The Naz" short for the Nazarene, etc.

But, when I see them risking their lives to protest the Vietnam War, wearing old clothes and disheveled hair to razz those of us who put too much emphasis on clothing and beauty parlors, it might be well for us to remember that the "Nazarene" was despised and rejected by men, a man of sorrows and acquainted with grief, and that it is recorded that "he had nowhere to lay his head," and he was finally nailed to the tree.

Yet, there is something about the Spirit of God in the Man Christ Jesus that will not stay in the tomb. It just might be God's way of haunting us with the possibility of a warless world and fair distribution of food and clothing, with a loving and forgiving spirit in human relations. And a few thousand other things that we need but can't seem to find anywhere else. This is the ultimate reason for thanks to God, not merely for life itself but for the vision of quality of life that is possible. Jesus Christ is our best vision of this vision of quality of life. He is a gift of God. He continually breaks the molds of history to help us write a new history.

THE JESUS OF HISTORY AND THE CHRIST OF FAITH

Contemporary reading: Wolfhart Pannenberg, *Jesus, God and Man,* pp. 129–131

Scripture reading: II Corinthians 4:1–11

The center of Christianity is the concept of Jesus Christ as primary revelation of God's word for man's salvation. A book published a few years ago was titled *Can the Center Hold?* Well, I have no doubt that the center can hold. I sometimes wonder how many people can hold on to the center as the merry-go-round of life gets faster and more complex. I have some fear that the centrifugal force will throw a great many people off the merry-go-round, that is, clear out of the church and Christianity into a completely humanistic orientation. There is a remoteness of witchcraft in our time, which in my opinion is very regrettable. So, it is important to consider the nature of the center and how it can hold.

Congregationalists have related primarily to the liberal view of Jesus as the best man, or "only" a man, or as ideal man. A second trend called orthodox or fundamentalist has emphasized the divinity of Jesus, sometimes spoken of as "very God of very God," sometimes expressed as "Son of God," sometimes presented as "substitutionary sacrifice" or as "lamb of God that taketh away the sin of the world."

A third trend called neo-orthodoxy usually has presented Jesus Christ either as a third order of being, a Mediator between God and man, the God-Man, as do Emil Brunner in his volume entitled *The Mediator*, Paul Tillich in *Systematic Theology*, Vol. II, and Rudolf Bultmann in *Theology of the New Testament*. It is assumed that we cannot know the historic Jesus, and, therefore, the Christian experience must refer to the faith of the early church which is recorded in Acts and the Letters of Paul. It is assumed that the Gospel writers had likewise been affected by that faith in the development of the Gospels, all of which were written after Paul's death.

A fourth trend is still seeking a bridge between liberalism and orthodoxy. One might even say it seeks to build a bridge between neo-orthodoxy and liberalism. It is the Pannenberg school. Ruth and I listened to and conversed with Dr. Pannenberg in Munich for six hours in June of 1971. I have been presenting his thoughts to my senior theology class for four years.

There are four major emphases of the Pannenberg school that are basic and helpful to Christian faith these days. One is relating again meaningfully the Jesus of history and the Christ of faith. The *New Quest for the Historic Jesus* does not emphasize the difference between the Jesus of history and the Christ of faith. On the contrary, it emphasizes the similarity. The main point of the experience of the apostles, who had forsaken Jesus at the crucifixion, and Paul who had participated in the persecution of Christians, including the murder of Stephen, was that as they encountered the resurrected Christ, they came to understand the historic Jesus. Pannenberg says the Christ reality is impossible without grounding it in the earthly, human figure of Jesus. The two belong together. Separation leads to a gnostic-docetic Christ, a mere "seemism" or a mere "appearance" without reality. The impact of this important and historic emphasis is that the God revealed in Jesus Christ is not merely a spirit on high, but a God interested in the processes of life on earth, even in persons like you and me. God is active in all events of life, struggling to order reality to God's purposes. God appeared in a special, or intensive way in Jesus Christ, not necessarily in a way that is supernatural, but it is extraordinary. Traditionally we say God became incarnate in Jesus Christ. The emphasis is on the manhood of Jesus, however. Through Jesus, God revealed God's Kingdom purposes. Through his teachings, his behavior, his loyalty even unto death on the cross, Jesus was a "man for others," as Bonhoeffer calls him.

The second major emphasis of this school of thought is one that has been dear to the orthodox, even the fundamentalists, that is eschatology. It is the doctrine of the end of history, sometimes treated in terms of the second coming of Christ. What was it that Jesus Christ revealed about God, essentially? It was that God has a purpose in history. God is leavening history. God is working through the processes of history to bring man to love his enemies, to reconcile differences in creative new relationships, to develop new forms for human interrelationship as children of God.

Today it is not difficult to relate this insight to process characteristics of history. Man has evolved, by the grace and purpose of God. Man is in his infancy. He will evolve toward a man of peace. He does not work alone in a meaningless world or universe. He finds meaning in his life by seeing himself as part of the forward aim of God in the world and possibly the universe. He is called to commit himself to emerging forms of intelligent new goodness: women's rights, civil rights for minorities, international cooperation, overcoming poverty, balancing the ecological factors in the total eco-system, unifying the churches, and many other such areas of concern.

The Jesus Christ whom he follows in pursuing these ideals is man all right. "But he is not imitating man. Jesus is man as God would have man to be, and men are to find their meaning in life by seeing in him something of what God calls each man to be. That is to say, Jesus is the end man, the eschatological man or 'true' man." That's what is meant by the "final" revelation. Jesus, living in 4 BCE to 29 CE, is a foretaste of what God is aiming at when he calls this entire earthly history to a halt in the distant future. Or, you may think of it as freezing when the temperature of the sun cools.

Pannenberg, like the liberals, admits that Jesus and the early church made a mistake about when this final eschaton would come. Jesus said, "While some of you standing yet live, you will see the son of man coming in power and glory" (Matt. 16:28; 24:34; Mark 13:30). Well, one can relate that to the resurrection, but not honestly, because Jesus has been talking about wars and rumors of war, but the end is not yet. It will come like a thief in the night or as lightning flashes from East to West. Scholars admit, from Albert Schweitzer forward, that Jesus, the early church, and Paul (I Thess. 4:13–18) expected the end in that generation. It didn't happen. A reasonable theological adjustment is this: Jesus's teachings and life do enable us to foresee the basis of God's judgment, God's loving and creative aim for all God's children, the eschaton, probably far distant in time. We have to have such an aim. It makes this interim we call history and our own individual lives meaningful.

Related to the above eschatology is a third idea which we will treat briefly. Pannenberg says in his book *What is Man?* that medieval Christians stood with their backs toward the future, looking backward to the beginnings to relate to God. This is not adequate to Christian teachings as given by Jesus. It is not adequate to our time, which is pregnant with new possibilities. The stance of the Christian person is, like that of Jesus, future oriented—looking forward. God, who gives us a foretaste of the ultimate future in Jesus Christ, calls us forward into new forms of goodness requiring trust, courage, imagination, and intelligence.

The fourth meaningful and relevant emphasis of Pannenberg's thought is that of Hope. The future is filled with hope. I discussed with you several months ago Moltmann's idea of pro-volution. It is a part of being in which the quality of life is improved for all. This is the hope-filled meaning of "Thy Kingdom come on earth as it is in heaven."

Chapter 32

A GENEROUS SPIRIT

Sermon at South Hills Christian Church, June 7, 1970, one week after Jeff Hassell's resignation from this pulpit and the ministry

This is a difficult spot to fill, but not as difficult as it was for Jeff last week. Jeff said he felt he should leave the ministry because he could not honestly hold to some orthodox ideas. This amazed me for two reasons. This is a generous-spirited congregation. A learned person like Jeff knows that Origen, Arius, Abelard, Hus, Latimer, Nicholas of Ousa, Luther, Calvin all had problems with the orthodoxy of their time. So did Jesus and all the prophets. It is very dangerous at this time in history to set up polarization between orthodox and unorthodox and leave the church to some minority who coercively affirm a particular point of view and resort to some inquisition of greater or lesser cruelty.

That the spirit that is essential is the Spirit of Christ that "loves the enemy." "He drew a circle that sent me out, heretic, rebel, a thing to flout. But love and I had the wit to win. We drew a circle that took him in" (Edwin Markham).

The future lies with the Spirit of Christ, which I shall call a Generous Spirit, or heart. A generous spirit can counteract polarization and set the stage for the operation of the Holy Spirit in establishing new being, a new relationship, a new possibility. The word *generous* does not appear in the scriptures, and yet I chose it because it speaks to us of the essential spirit of Christ who gave himself for us, not counting the cost. The etymology of the word *generous* is from genus to genealogy, meaning a noble heritage and gradually came to mean self-sacrificing, outgoing, giving, without concern for receiving.

Christian love (agape) is the very essence of generosity. "God shows his love for us in that while we were yet sinful men, Christ died for us." A generous spirit is forgiving, empathetic, patient, trusting. I Corinthians 13 describes a generous spirit—very patient, truly kind, knows no jealousy, is never boastful, never resentful, never rude, never irritated, does not seek its own way at the expense of others." Paul had this in mind when he wrote the Romans to "love one another with brotherly affection" (Romans 12:10).

People in a Sunday School class sometimes drop out because they sense that their point of view is in the minority. We need to be the kind of church where the minority point of view is heard, and the person made welcome to express it. That person needs even more to feel loved and accepted by generous-spirited people, but not dishonestly. Granted, it takes a strong faith and strong ego to stay with it when you're in the minority; nevertheless, that is the essence of Christianity. Jesus was a minority of one, and yet he forgave his opponents. The 120 were a minority in Jerusalem; yet, their followers number over billions in human history.

A second characteristic that we must have to be Christian in this chaotic age in which we live is a questing mind, not a closed mind. Allport espouses this heuristic point of view. The Apostle Paul says to the Philippians: "Let each of you look not only to his own interests, but also to the interests of others. Have this mind in you which was also in Christ Jesus, who, though he was in the form of God, did not count equality with God a thing to be grasped, but emptied himself, taking the form of a servant, being born in the likeness of men. And being found in human form, he humbled himself and became obedient unto death, even death on a cross (Philippians 2:5). A questing mind to find new ways to express the graciousness and generosity that is the character of God and the character in men whom God approves is revealed in Christ.

This questing mind is open to transformation and renewal, to new ways of looking at the world, at human life, at human relationships. Forgiveness is not possible for a closed mind. It takes an open mind to forgive. It also takes an open mind to discover a new medicine, or a new friendship, or to see God's work in a new way. Paul says to the Romans: "Don't be conformed to this world but be transformed by the renewing of your mind" (Romans 12:2). The Pharisees were conformists. Jesus was a transformer. The transformers are always threatening to the conformers. Both in Romans 12 and in I Corinthians 12–14, Paul says use your varying talents or gifts to keep open to God's leading into a new life.

The third characteristic which is important to us at this stage of history, both in the world and in this local church, is a firm commitment and trust. The commitment doesn't have to be firm like a rock, unmoving, static, unyielding. It needs to be firm like the love of good parents, like the pull of gravity, like the flight of a seagull in its adjustment to the winds to sustain it, like the tides of the ocean or the flow of a river. It is dynamic, reliable power. This kind of constancy is what I mean by a firm commitment. It trusts in and responds to the power of God.

Paul says in Romans 12:11 "Be a-glow with the spirit." He is referring to the dynamic power of one who is filled with the spirit of Christ, the Holy Spirit. It is firm, clear, and dynamic, like Peter after the resurrection. It is outgoing, seeking new ways to serve God by serving fellow man. It is understanding toward the weaknesses and failings of others but does not use this as an excuse for its own failures.

Above all, it is aware of its dependence upon and sustenance by the loving God made known to us through Jesus Christ and seen by us to be true in nature and our own experiences of reality day after day. It is an attitude of gratitude to this good, sustaining God.

I hope all of you, especially the young people, will stand by the church through this interim and not be either a Judas or a Peter at the time of crucifixion.

Chapter 33

LEGITIMATE SANCTUARY

A sermon given at First Congregational Church, Fort Worth, Texas, 1971

Scripture: Isaiah 40:1–2, Psalm 23, Matthew 11:28–30

In *Future Shock* Alvin Toffler, a sociologist who has taught at Columbia and Cornell, describes the rapidly changing society we will live in from now on. The speed of change will accelerate, not decelerate. He says the mobile ones are the ones on the way up. It is a standing joke at IBM that the initials stand for "I've been moved."

A symptom of the times is Manpower, Inc. They will rent a secretary or a maid, or a plumber, carpenter, or air conditioning engineer for a day, week, or month. If they cannot be rented from Manpower, Inc., they can from similar organizations. This reflects the transiency of our lives. Today, city planning firms are developing to rent their services to cities for special projects. It is likely that the staff permanently maintained by a city's planning department will be skeletal, and these firms will be hired for short term, "ad hoc" projects.

Toffler tells of a Wall Street financier who leaves his office on Friday at 4:30 p.m., takes the elevator twenty-nine stories down to the street, walks six or eight blocks to a heliport, takes a helicopter to JFK airport, takes a jet to Columbus, Ohio, where he is met at the airport by his wife. They drive thirty minutes to their country home where he spends the weekend with his family. He commutes back to New York on Monday morning and spends four nights a week in an apartment in New York. This commuting involves over fifty thousand miles per year and a lot of expense.

Another standing joke at IBM is that it costs so much to move families that perhaps they should just move the man, computerize a matching family at the new site, and relate him to them. It <u>is</u> just a joke. I hope it is not a sign of thing to come.

Such persons need "sanctuary." They need some sense of protection, of loving concern for them as persons. The biblical concept of "sanctuary" means a holy place for worship, but it also means an asylum, a refuge when your life or health is in danger. One example appears in I Kings 2:28. Joab, at the time of David's approaching death, threw his weight behind one of David's sons, Adonijah, who made a bid for the throne. But Solomon and his supporters won the throne. Joab, in terror for his life, "grasped the horns of the altar." Solomon didn't honor the right of sanctuary for Joab; he instructed Beniah, his general, to kill Joab at the altar. The priests had to cleanse the altar after this unholy act.

Legitimate sanctuary means seeking comfort, rest, healing, and security in the holy place. The prophetic side of religion can be summarized as "afflicting the comfortable." The priestly side of religion can be summarized as "comforting the afflicted." Healthy religion must do both things for us.

We are all afflicted—with everything from headaches caused by nervous tension to ulcers and neurotic and psychotic conditions because we can't cope adequately in this difficult age. Previous generations had the dangers of cholera, smallpox, typhoid fever, and scalping Indians. Some of our men have lost an arm or leg in World War I or II or Korea or Vietnam. But most of us do not suffer these physical wounds that we can show and be proud of. Our wounds are psychic, and we get no sympathy for them. In fact, people add to our misery by laughing at us or talking about us. It is an exceedingly difficult age in which to cope. We are marked psychically in one way or another.

How can the Church provide sanctuary for these hurt ones today? Among the unusual things being done is the night ministry in San Francisco, where the Council of Churches hires a man who works all night visiting the bars, the theater district, and similar downtown places where he is available to help the thousands of night people. Other volunteers assist him by answering a telephone service all night and calling him at agreed times and places. He can always get to any person in need within thirty minutes. Depression, threatened suicide, a "bad trip," threatened murder or rape, and other crimes of all kinds find him involved as a healing and helping agent of the church. Similar ministries in New Orleans, Las Vegas, St. Louis, and other places are being experimented with.

Here in Fort Worth we have "Bridge House," "Urban Ministries," "Block Partnership," and other ways of experimenting to help in abnormal situations.

But what about the more normal situation? We recognize that it is a highly mobile culture. Wherever the person moves, there is a church of his denomination or a similar one. He should go and join when he arrives in town. If he waits nine months before he acts and then moves three months later before he can really get deeply involved, he has only cheated himself.

What can the church do for this modern nomad? It can provide acceptance—a profound need that we all have. It can provide affirmation, friendliness, and love. It can provide a fellowship of persons with a similar "life and style." The goals of these people will be like those in the church from which you came. This provides a stabilizing factor in your life and the lives of other members of your family.

The worship, the hymns, the singing of the Gloria Patri and the Doxology, the reading of the scriptures and the anthem provide an aesthetic and emotional balm and reinforcement for the depth of the human spirit. The sermon and the educational program of the church provide mental and spiritual stimulation that keeps us growing and questing after new values in a responsible manner. We are challenged but also reassured. In all these ways, we are reminded of and reassured about the reality of God, that in the last analysis, it is a friendly universe, that "underneath are the everlasting arms."

Of equal significance, we are given a chance to express our talents and skills, to give as well as to receive, to be a part of the answer to the human predicament. And we receive appreciation for this giving of time, talent, and money.

Ruth and I often comment as we get acquainted with the people in a new church, as we have done here: "everywhere you go in the Church, there are some wonderful people whom you would be happy to know in greater depth if there were only time." The person who cheats himself in this nomadic culture is the one who doesn't make deep immediate contact with the church in a new city to which he moves.

Toffler remarks how we make and break friendships. The first year after our friend moves away, there may be a flurry of letters, even phone calls, but gradually the calls cease, then the letters are fewer, and then they cease and perhaps we just exchange Christmas greetings, and after a few years the Christmas card exchange ceases. We need not fret ourselves about this. We have served that person well. We were a psychic, friendly way station. We served an important purpose in their lives while they needed us. When they have found security in a new set of relationships, we should rejoice and send them on their way, saying "there are fine people everywhere." Life is supportive of our best selves. We are reassured.

Even when we stay put, we need sanctuary because the environment is hard on us. We are sometimes hard on each other. If the father, pressured by his work, has ulcers, chronic headaches, tantrums that seem irrational to the teenager in the family, it is likely to be from the pressures at work that frustrate or threaten him. He doesn't want to admit these problems to his children, although hopefully he will feel free to discuss them with his wife. He needs to discuss them with someone and not simply try to bottle them up within himself. Ideally, the home would be a sanctuary for his weary mind and spirit, but if the wife and children don't understand or care, it could be almost more than he can bear.

Today, the same is often true for the mother who may be working outside the home and also trying to do the household chores. We adults need to realize that something similar may be true for the teenager who feels pressures of all kinds at school, at home, from a peer group, or even from a church where he feels unable to cope. Home needs to be "sanctuary" in the sense of a loving, trusting, reassuring refuge. One of the memorable scriptures is Psalm 137 which was written out of the anguish of estrangement of Jewish exiles in the strange land of Babylon around 586 and later. "By the waters of Babylon, we sat down and wept. Yes, we wept when we remembered Jerusalem. Our captors required of us songs, saying 'Sing us one of the songs of Zion.' We said: 'How shall we sing the Lord's songs in a strange land?'" If "Jerusalem" symbolizes that "balm of the soul" that is spiritual well-being, it is very meaningful and speaks of that "estrangement" that we often feel when we think "no one understands, least of all my parents."

Often, the home is an emotional "armed camp" where none of the combatants can establish peace. The church must "comfort the afflicted." Isaiah 40:1-2 are the opening verses of what the scholars call "Second Isaiah." This prophet wrote from Babylonian exile, about 550, some 200 years after the first Isaiah. He saw the possibility of the end of the exile and the beginning of the return to Jerusalem. The words have an ageless majesty and healing quality. "Comfort ye, comfort ye, my people.

Speak tenderly to Jerusalem and say to her that her warfare is ended. Her iniquity is pardoned. She has received double for all her sins." Here and elsewhere the Bible reminds us that forgiveness is essential to health and well-being. We dare not hold grudges against self or others.

Jesus also offered the afflicted soul sanctuary. "Come unto me all you who labor and are heavy laden. Take my yoke upon you and learn of me, for my yoke is easy and my burden is light" (Matt. 11:28). Work that is meaningful, significant in some ultimate sense, and appreciated by those whom we love and from whom we want approval is a healing balm, even to the weary ones.

This aspect of our religion's ministry is captured so beautifully by that most beloved of all Psalms: "The Lord is my shepherd; I shall not want; he makes me lie down in green pastures. He leads me beside still waters; he restores my soul. . . . I fear no evil, for thou art with me, thy rod and thy staff they comfort me . . ."

When the family goes to church together, there can be a cleansing and renewing of the person and the relationships—establishing again the I-Thou relationships which may have been battered in the parent-child relationships during the hurly-burly of the week. The friendly smile and handshake of our fellows in Christ helps renew a right mind within us.

If you are a stranger, often you can talk to a new friend about how hard on you and the children the move from city X to Fort Worth has been and they can sympathize because they have been through it, too. Also, if you can move from this to an involvement of the self at some level of responsibility, this helps bridge the gap between the old life and the new life, the old relationships and the new relationships.

For those who are settled, the Church can be a legitimate sanctuary when they are frightened by growing up or by growing old, by being fired from the old job or beginning a new job—if all members truly seek to care, to help, not to hurt. The Church can be sanctuary. It can combine the "holy" with "refuge" and "renewal."

We should go forth refreshed in our desire and ability to be loving and adequate parents, to be creative members of our corporations, to do our work well, to be kind and helpful to others, to express the Christ Spirit in home and work and school.

This is one of the areas where Jesus's statement: "Give and it shall be given unto you full measure, pressed down, shaken together, and overflowing" really appears to be true. Kindness reaps benefit for the person who is kind if he doesn't intend for it to do so! "Let not your left hand know what your right hand is doing" is the way Jesus spoke of this fact. "He who seeks to save his life will lose it."

Instead of living in fear and resentment, thus worsening the relationship with others, Church should help us to cast off the fears and resentments which often tyrannize us and live in trust and love, in faith and hope. Thus, we live in the Kingdom. We become creative leaven of good will in home and office and school.

THE WORD, THE CHURCH, AND THE WORLD

A sermon preached at First Congregational Church,
Fort Worth, Texas, January 17, 1971
Scripture: John 1:1–14, and L. Gilkey, *How the Church Can Minister . . .* pp. 81–82

Dr. Ron Flowers, a colleague at Texas Christian University, says "Langdon Gilkey is the best teacher I ever had." Dr. Gilkey is the son of Dr. Charles Gilkey, Dean of the Chapel at the University of Chicago for many years and one of my beloved teachers. Langdon Gilkey, after graduating from Yale, went as a teaching missionary to China. He was imprisoned for several years during World War II and has written a book about those experiences. He taught at Vanderbilt Divinity School and is now on the faculty at the University of Chicago Divinity School.

In his book, *How the Church Can Minister to the World Without Losing Itself* (Harper, 1964), he says the Church must carry forward three emphases from the past: (1) from the Biblical heritage, it must see itself as in the great Judeo-Christian tradition of "The People of God"; (2) from the Reformation Period, it must affirm that Jesus Christ is Lord of the Church through his Holy Word; (3) from the Roman Catholic period, it must affirm that the Church is One, Universal, the "Body of Christ."

The great problem is this: how can the church, understanding itself in this way, minister to the world without dissipating its strength, without simply capitulating to the world? There are four basic questions that arise here: (1) How is the Church to mediate the divine authority to men in word, worship, and behavior so that the authority is not merely dogmatic, sterile, irrelevant, and unrelated to the problems of the world? (2) How is the Church to affirm the freedom of its members as cultural beings to live without losing completely the transcendent, holy elements within the Church? (3) How can the Church be concerned with the culture without capitulating to the religions of culture, such as worshipping the nation as the ultimate power and confusing it with the Church? (4) How can the Church be ruled by laymen without surrendering its sovereignty to Main Street? (Gilkey, 58).

We might summarize all this by saying that, as Church, in order to function well, we need: a sense of the holy (transcendent power), a sense of authority, a concern for all men in their daily lives, a sense of relevance in our ethical decisions, action that puts into effect our influence to accomplish good, and dialogue—listening as well as telling—a resilient responsiveness to men in the world and to Christ.

What can we say about "The Word" as our authority? I do not agree with Karl Barth on all points, but I have been helped and stimulated by his conception of the nature of the "Word of God." "Word" means communication, in this case, a communication from God. There are at least three dimensions of "The Word." First, there is the Biblical Word. Somehow the Word of God is there in the Bible, but not in the literal, "verbal inspiration" sense. God did not dictate every word; God did not guide the pen of the writers so that even the punctuation is inerrant. Working on this erroneous assumption, one can make the kind of mistaken judgement of which you may have heard. This fundamentalist approach caused at least one man seeking inerrant guidance from God about a problem to do what the scriptures said. When he opened his eyes, he read "And Judas went out and hanged himself." Well, he thought, there must be some mistake; surely God didn't want him to do that." So, he tried again. This time, upon opening his eyes, he read, "Go, thou, and do likewise." So, that is not the way to elicit the Word of God from the scriptures.

We might use our minds, intelligence and experience and note that Jesus said: "My will is to do the will of Him who sent me." Yet, when his life was threatened in Nazareth, early in his ministry, when the people of his home town took offense at him and sought to cast him headlong down what is now called "The Hill of Offense," he "disappeared from among them." Apparently, he fled. Then, later, he deliberately "set his face steadfastly to go up to Jerusalem, there to suffer and die." We can conclude that he used his mind and his judgment to decide when God was at work in the process in such a way that the giving of his life for the will of God was the right thing to do.

In the second place, the "Word of God" is not merely the words of the preacher, though he is sincerely seeking to speak God's word. These words of God's servant, like the Biblical words, may be media of God's communication, but they must be "screened" by the listener.

Thirdly, the "Word" that comes to the believer in the pew in his life situation can be called "the lively word of God." It is not unrelated to the Bible, not unrelated to preaching, but it is a word with that believer's initials marked on it. It is a word for that person, in the community of faith, under God, driving the person out into the world to witness in action.

So, the Word is a contextual word. It is life oriented. It is changing, dynamic, empowering.

Pardon a personal illustration. I serve on the Committee of Management of the McDonald Branch of the YMCA. It has a branch for Negroes. It is now becoming integrated, and its able secretary is black. We had a meeting of the Personnel Committee last week to choose a young associate secretary. We interviewed three men. Two stood out as of equal merit. One was black, the other white. The white graduated with a 2.8 grade average from the University of Texas. The other graduated with a 2.7 from North Texas State University. The white majored in psychology and minored in physical education. The black majored in physical education and minored in biology.

I had to leave the meeting after we heard their interviews; so I told the other men on the committee, all black, that either one of these men would be fine with me. I thought they had equal merit. I discovered a few days later at the Committee of Management meeting that the rest of the Personnel Committee members saw it as I did, and they wanted the larger Committee of Management to make the decision. The discussion that ensued was one of the most interesting I have ever heard from a group of Negroes. At first a minister said, "I think we should choose the white man, because our present secretary is black. If we hope to minister to an integrated constituency, we need an integrated staff." Then some of those who had been wrestling with the problem spoke up and said, "We agree, but none of the other branches in Fort Worth will hire a Negro. This is the only chance the black will have at a Y job. The white man will have other openings."

The Committee of Management threw the problem back in the hands of the Personnel Committee and told them to act within twenty-four hours, without telling them which one to choose. I thought it was very revealing regarding the complexity of the problem forced upon blacks by our white racial prejudice. How does the Holy Spirit move in this situation? Certainly, more whites need to listen to the Holy Spirit in such matters. Where are the black faces in this congregation?

The World is to be seen as God's creation and the scene of God's continuing action. Our presupposition is evolutionary, as we have said in other sermons. God has been working in the process to bring us this far along the way. God is the creative force who struggles to counteract the destructive forces. God is pro-life, not death. He seeks to overcome death and destruction with new and better life forms. Paul spoke of the "Old Adam" as our sinful natures and the "New Adam" as our redeemed nature. He saw Christ as the "first fruits" of God's action in the human-spiritual realm. Christ shows us that God gives us "the power to become sons of God, born not merely of the flesh, but also of the spirit," and this means intelligent, insightful, sensitive, courageous commitment to new possibilities of goodness for all of God's children.

When we say that the Church is in the world, but not merely of the world, we mean that the Church is people who live in the world as it is, but commit themselves to shaping the world, with God's help, as it ought to be. The Church is a building made with human hands, on a corner of streets designed and paved by human beings, laid up by masons and carpenters and glaziers and heating/air conditioning engineers, etc. But its full reality is something more, something transcendent. It is a Word from God about a New Character for men in the world—a new quality of life—a new bookkeeper, a new computer operator, a new lawyer, a new mother, a new teacher, a new politician.

In this context, it can be said meaningfully: "Now are we Sons of God, and it does not yet appear what we shall become!"

If we are to be the Body of Christ in the world, we need to be less timid about expressing to each other these ideal possibilities that occur to us from time to time. We think of ideal pictures of self, of Church, of social order occasionally. Without the fellowship of God's people, these visions can die within us. "Where there is no vision, the people perish." But, through such visions God's Holy Spirit moves into his world and lures people on to higher goals and purposes that he sees on the path of the infinite. It is vitally important that we have a community such as the church where we can talk seriously about these ideal possibilities and encourage each other to pursue them.

We must be willing to be called "Fools for Christ's Sake," to plant visionary ideals of a new humanity in the minds of practical businessmen and their servants, the politicians. These are the power figures of our time as Pontius Pilate and Herod were in Jesus's time. They need to be confronted by spokesmen for God's Holy Spirit and have their imaginations kindled by the sense that God is at work in God's world. God is not dead. God has not gone to sleep. They need to be haunted as Pilate's wife was haunted causing her to send a message to Pilate saying, "Have nothing to do with that righteous man, for I have suffered much in a dream about him." These secular men need us to make it clear to them that "Jesus is the Way, the Truth, the Life." He is a meaningful symbol of the New and Better Way, a New Reality coming into being, a new possibility for the world, for all of God's children. There will be visions about: the emerging "one world," to use Wendell Wilkie's term; a peaceful world; a democratic world; a world where men are personally responsible in behavior and thoughtful of their neighbors' well-being; a world where there will be a guaranteed annual income given for work a man does, and there will be full employment. No man will receive mere charity, except the seriously ill and handicapped. It will be a world of racial good will and mutual appreciation, a world of international cooperation, where natural resources such as oil and gas and uranium are not squandered in war. It will be a world of expanding Hope, Faith, Love, and Action.

In conclusion, the picture is one of God's word as a lively hope, expressed through God's people, ministering to God's world. We help God in God's creative work. We are a part of the answer, not the problem. "God so loved the world that God gave . . . " In a kindred spirit, we must give. We will preach the gospel by being it. Thus, we will be "The Body of Christ" in the world.

LEARNING FROM GERMAN CHRISTIANS

Scripture: Isaiah 40:12–31

Ruth and I went to Germany in the summer of 1971 to attend an international conference of theologians. This kind of international sharing is essential to the health of Christianity. I have chosen three points to emphasize: the condition of the churches, theological attitudes, and ethics.

In Germany, the church is part of the state and is supported by taxes. Attendance at churches is low. A young Hamburg minister with nine thousand paid-up members had ninety in church and forty funerals in three months. He also conducted marriages and confirmation classes. We went to St. Michal's at the pastor's request and doubled the attendance. The sermon was good; about thirty stayed for communion. One free church we visited was small but packed with about three hundred parishioners. One girl said that if she didn't get to her church early, she didn't get a seat. Another girl went to a church pastored by a very capable young pastor whom we heard speak; there were about five hundred there.

The biggest problem is the history of the relations between church and state. Secondly, they have the same problem that we have in America—secularism. They aren't developing the secular meaning of the Gospel.

There is a gap between theologians at universities and the people. Ministers are not taking their seminary teachings to the people. It is this naïve religion that also sold out to Hitler against which people are reacting. Church is mainly a way to heaven, and the people are losing faith in heaven.

Barth has left his stamp. He says, "God is totally other." Salvation is an individual matter, by the grace of God, in response to the Gospel of God's sending Christ as Savior. Churches often corrupt this idea as they teach people to compromise the Gospel with the secular order. No order is to be confused with God's order. Neither capitalism nor communism, democracy nor monarchy nor oligarch is to have the Christian's blessing as the ultimate form of government. God judges all.

Pannenberg, Moltmann, Gollwitzer, and others whom we heard are emphasizing Jesus as fully human, fully committed to God's purposes, as showing God concerned about people in history and that there is hope in history. Man should look forward to the future as fulfillment of God's purpose in history as well as beyond history.

Closely related to this emphasis is a new emphasis on Ethics. Barth had played down the ethical side of Christianity, feeling that it always got fouled up with the particular culture. You must understand the German situation, especially in Berlin. That horrible wall is always there and just beyond it, East Berlin. We visited it and had a communist guide, of course, by special permission, which he had to get from headquarters of the Christian Democratic Party (one of the four minority parties allowed to function in East Germany). The spokesman, the executive of the party, was a Free Methodist. He had to answer questions with the communist guide sitting right there. It often caused him much travail and he blushed red several times. The guide later told us that he could not agree with many things the man had said and he almost got up and argued with him but restrained himself.

This will help you to understand that any serious ethicist in Germany must know his Marx and Engels. There are many who oppose Communism but find many things they can agree with in Marxism. The impact is that they can't just turn away from Marxism. You have to reason with it and argue with them. Basically, these things are the concern that every member of the community has work, food, housing, clothing and that there not be a great gap between the well-to-do and the poor.

Though we heard some Marxists who shared the communist line that capitalists are imperialists and cause wars for profit, none of the Germans we asked about America's presence in Germany wanted us to leave. I went so far as to ask one man if this was because it would cost Germany so much to defend herself? He said, "Well, yes, that is a factor."

The primary ethical problems that they think Christians should join Marxists or anyone else who will work for solutions are: war, poverty, racial prejudice leading to oppression and injustice, international cooperation to overcome petty, chauvinistic nationalism, and cooperation between the East and West on many great issues such as pollution of the seas, the atmosphere, the stratosphere. Their basic ethical Christian goal is one humanity under God. They will cooperate with whatever government to move toward the realization of these goals.

In conclusion, it was amazing to me to find myself so much at home among German people who were the enemy twenty-five to thirty years ago. I found some satisfaction in knowing that we had helped Germany to rebuild so that it is more prosperous than America on the average. You do not see the slums, the poverty, the crime, the hatred that you see in America. Everything is clean and neat, and building is going on everywhere. Americans, with some self-interest, have restored Germany and Japan, their former enemies, as a bulwark against Russia and China.

A major interest in all of Europe is that through the Common Market and relationships with Africa, they might build a Third Force that will hold the two super-powers, Russia and America, apart so they will not blow up the whole world with a nuclear bomb.

Chapter 34

CHRISTIAN HOPE

A sermon at South Hills Christian Church, Fort Worth, October 17, 1971

Scripture: Psalm 42:1–5, 9–11; Romans 5:1–5, 15:13

The Hopelessness and Despair of Modern Youth

Most youth generations provide the idealism and hope for the entire population. We have come on strange times when the youth are more despairing than the adults. We can overstate and falsify this, so we must be careful. I do know a minority of youths who can't believe in business, or businessmen, in politicians, teachers, preachers, doctors, lawyers, or their parents. These youth see all of them as subtly blessing the evils of the present society which oppresses the poor, is prejudiced against minorities and oppresses them, will not give women equal pay for equal work, and is willing to send thousands of its young men to die in a war about which they have not given serious thought. "It's just a minor incident off there on the other side of the world," they think.

Another reason they're despairing and hopeless is that at the same time they see these evil acts of the older establishment types, they do not have a visible and relevant faith in God, either because it wasn't presented to them well, or they couldn't believe the sincerity of those who presented it. Possibly the reason that they couldn't believe in God as their hope was that God's name and the Christian Gospel were used to bless the established order, which they are convinced has these evils just mentioned, and these are not condemned by those who speak in the name of God but rather are justified.

Also, they see billions spent for planning and pursuing wars but practically nothing spent to plan and establish peace when the adults claim they're peacemakers. And all this at a time when the planned wars will end human civilization. You would think that there would be a world-wide sit-down strike against such plans by the people of all nations, led by the Christians. But, no. We all dumbly acquiesce, feeling the whole thing is above us, beyond our capacity to cope. So, youth ask, where is there any hope?

I think it is critically important for all people to point as realistically as they can to sources of hope. Everyone needs it. Cynicism and negativism are too pervasive in our time. They are ultimately destructive, causing creeping paralysis.

Knowledge of History Provides Us with Hope

The Psalmist 42 says: "Men say, 'Where is your God?'" Why doesn't God do something? "My soul is cast down," on the one hand, and on second thought I see that God has been doing something all along—"Like streams of living water. God is my defender, my resuscitator. I shall again praise God." God is my hope. God is our hope. God is mankind's hope. There is a power not of ourselves that creatively works to save us when we are planning to kill ourselves. Jesus said: "My Father works to this end. And so will I."

Teilhard de Chardin says our awareness of history must include Paleontology—the science of ancient and early forms of life—and an awareness of how man has evolved from the amoeba and the paramecium, through intermediate forms to higher forms. God is the creative force bringing this to pass. It is not all an accident. It is our primary basis for hope and meaning. Man is the first self-conscious, reflective form of life to emerge. He becomes co-creator with God, made "in the image of God" as Genesis says. Man can even reflect on the emergence of a new form of life in Jesus Christ and meditate on the implications of Jesus Christ as a vision of the end to which God is luring and pressuring us for our own fulfillment. That end we call the coming of God's Kingdom.

This end has peace and harmony and goodwill among people. A time, says Paul, "when God will be everything to everyone." As Romans 3 says, "Our hope is in having our being flooded with the love of God." This means love of neighbor as Christ and I John make clear. "If you love God, you will love your neighbor." Such a person uses his intelligence and his power to act and influence reality, like an Albert Schweitzer, thinking of ways to help needy people, ways to bridge the chasm between Europe and

Africa, between black and white, between rich and poor, between the "have and the have-nots," between those with the tools of technology and those without them. Such a person sees himself and all his intelligence and action power as a tool of God. As Jeremiah put it, he is clay in the hands of God, the potter or better yet, he is the space rocket steered by God.

As I watched the marvelous *Today* show on Iran's 2500th birthday Friday, I became aware of two generalizations I want to share with you that are apropos to our theme that God is at work in history, but we have spent an awful lot of time trying to foul up God's work. As I watched those legions of soldiers march past representing the armies of Persians and those whom they fought over these 2500 years, the first thought I had was how tragic that history is mostly a record of wars. There has been at least one war every two years throughout recorded world history. Think of all the wasted energy and the brain power of the dead young men killed in these wars! What outrageous behavior! How much grinding hate is involved! How antithetical to the word God has been trying to give us. The second thought was this: At almost precisely the time (2500 years ago) that Cyrus and his legions put the Persian empire together and dominated the Middle East and the Eastern end of the Mediterranean, God sent a prophet whom we call II Isaiah who spoke to the Jews in Babylonian exile whom Cyrus soon released, giving us that marvelous vision in the fifty-third chapter of Isaiah.

> He was despised and rejected by men, a man of sorrows and acquainted with grief. . . . he was wounded for our transgressions. . . . by his stripes we are healed.

The only way we can be healed by the stripes of Christ and other persecuted people and millions of young men who died in battle across these 2500 years is to learn something—namely that wars are ridiculous, crude, primitive behavior patterns—that the latent intent of God is what I Isaiah said: "Men shall beat their swords into plowshares, their spears into pruning hooks. Nation shall not lift up sword against nation, neither shall they learn war anymore." God gave us that lead idea in 740 BCE by the prophet I Isaiah. It has been lying there all these centuries like a time capsule ready to be discovered by some people whose brains have evolved sufficiently to see how ridiculous have been our wasting wars and how promising is creative peace. These people can hear the words of Christ: "Love your enemies; turn the other cheek, go the second mile; return good for evil." Think what the world would be like if the creative energy, wealth, and lives of young men wasted in war had been used in life-saving and life-enriching activity? Why do we in the US not have a peace budget of $15 billion instead of a war budget of that amount? Sure, we need defense at the present stage of man's adolescence, but how long will we go on being so adolescent? When do we start maturing? When do we start investing in international understanding and goodwill? When do we become mature people in Christ?

Christ Pointed beyond Crucifixion to Resurrection

He pointed man's inhumanity to man to God's transmutation of our evil into good.

God is indeed bringing God's Kingdom on earth—the signs of it are everywhere for those who have eyes to see! Negatively, the young people are turned off at affluence, at the expense of war, cruelty, and injustice to the masses of people. Positively, we see the emergence of the United Nations, the amazing move by a Republican President to do business with communists whom just a few years ago he wouldn't do business with. Perhaps more importantly, we see the commitment to peace of figures like Dag Hammarskjöld and Ralph Bunche. These are the new heroes. Their day is yet to come. They are the men whom God is using to do a new thing—"to beat swords into plowshares."

At the end of World War II, most of us wanted to see Germany and Japan crushed into nothingness. But somehow better realities developed, in spite of us, and today they are better allies than France and Russia, who were then our allies. Like Teilhard de Chardin, I am convinced there is a power not of ourselves that works for righteousness. It is God. God is our hope.

God was at work from the beginning. God brought man out of the earlier forms of life. God is not through. God is not dead. God is at work in us now. God is at work in you. Are you aware of it? How can you possibly obstruct God's attempts to do some goodness—goodness which you didn't have the courage to do? God is the source of courage. Hope thou in God!

Chapter 35

GROWING OLD GRACEFULLY

A sermon at First Congregational Church, Fort Worth, November 24, 1974

Contemporary Reading from Paul Tournier, *Learn to Grow Old*

My first attempt at this subject was at the age of twenty-two, when a graduate student at the University of Texas. I knew it was presumptuous, but it intrigued me! Every stage of life is interesting and requires a certain grace in maturation. That is certainly true of adolescence. I was in late adolescence when I preached that sermon. Today people mature at twenty-eight to thirty, according to Robert Kastenbaum, a sociologist.

Personally, I like the stage of life I'm in now as well as any of them. I have no desire to be an adolescent again, nor a young father, nor a middle-aged man. I like it right here, and I'm looking forward to retirement. Robert Browning's Rabbi Ben Ezra said it this way:

> Grow old along with me.
> The best is yet to be,
> The last of life
> For which the first was made.

We shouldn't dwell on old age and/or death, but we should occasionally reflect on that stage of life just as we do on childhood, adolescence, or the middle years, as we are all here together, people of all ages, constituting the church.

Death is a fact of life. We should not be morbidly obsessed with it, but we should learn to put a friendly face on it. Martin Heidegger, the existentialist philosopher, says: "Man is a being unto death. As soon as man live, he is old enough to die." Rilke says: "We always act like men who are going away."

Life is more basic than death. When we were in Kiev, Ukraine, Soviet Union in June 1972, our guide, while showing us the tomb of the unknown soldier, told us that half the population of Kiev was killed in the German attack on Kiev in World War II. Then the Kievites battled the Russians to get their freedom from Russian domination and lost. Over three hundred thousand people of that city died. Yet the place was teeming with life! When we were in Moscow, at Red Square, I thought of the millions of people who had died here and in Russia in the revolution, the two world wars, the Napoleonic invasion, and the oppression of the Czars and Stalin. Yet, Moscow was teeming with life.

There are two ways in which death is swallowed up in victory. In sheer numbers of people who are born to take the places of those who die, and in the Christian sense of "This is the victory that overcometh, even our faith. Death is swallowed up in victory." For the Christian life is more basic than death. He can trust God with his life, including his death.

Robert Kastenbaum quotes several studies in *New Studies in Old Age* which indicate that adolescents think only of the intense present. If they think of the past, it is to say that they were in a period when they were confused and inept, "kinda dumb." The future is too pallid and vague. The present is real and vital. Old people are a bore.

One of my colleagues at TCU was quite depressed at coffee this week because it was his fortieth birthday! Kastenbaum's studies showed that few people in their forties had many goals out ahead of them. I was surprised. Not all, but most of my significant work was done after forty.

Another friend said: "In thirty-six hours, I'll be sixty years old!" I said: "You appear young to me—more like fifty." "Well," he said, "maybe during the day, but when I first look at my visage in the mirror in the morning, I look every bit of sixty."

It is possible to look forward to retirement. I think it is worth trying to do so. Planning for a different style of life that will keep in touch with what you have done, but allow you to do it much less intensely and to intensify your interests in new activities that are more appropriate to your new stage of life is worth the effort.

Or, if you are very happy in your work and are your own boss and don't have to retire at sixty-five, then cut your schedule back and do as some other friends I know who work about four hours per day, five days a week, and then have time for more leisurely hobby activity. This can make retirement a real joy.

Certainly, all aging persons need to plan for appropriate exercise, appropriate meaningful work, enjoyable hobbies, and, by all means, try to keep up with friends even if you move to a new town. In that case, make a special effort to make new friends. Tournier says, "Solitude is the most serious difficulty. . . . " Loneliness aches.

Prepare your will so that, if possible, it won't have to go through the courts and cost your heirs a major portion of your estate to clear title to the property. Plan your funeral. Tell your children and/or spouse what kind of funeral you prefer and what you want done with your body. Write it out. One good thing to do with the body is to donate it to a medical school, thus serving your fellow men in death as well as life. Perhaps it can be arranged to use some of your organs for preserving another life through transplants.

Currently, if both husband and wife live, enjoy your marriage. You'll have time to yourselves for leisurely living, no children underfoot, or requiring babysitting, when you want to go to the symphony. If the husband travels, the wife can go with him and avoid the loneliness both have previously known.

Most churches do nothing distinctive for the aged. They need ministry just as much as children and adolescents. A Golden Year Fellowship such as that which meets at University Christian Church might well be active in every church. It might need the sponsorship of a couple in their forties or fifties and some attention from the pastor. For the most part, the leadership and planning could be done by the members themselves. They could see to it that not one of the elderly members felt neglected by the church.

For the most part, the enlightened planning for old age that is evidenced in social security, Medicare, and pension funds has eradicated the opprobrious "poor house" of forty to one hundred years ago. Thank the Lord. But with inflation, there are many elderly who can barely make it on their Social Security and pension money. Some churches and other groups are providing "Meals on Wheels" or having inexpensive group meals at the church. All pay a minimum charge. It supplements inadequate diets and provides equally important fellowship and breaks the lonely monotony. Often youth groups go to homes for the aged to sing or put on a play for the elderly and to visit them, bringing a fresh viewpoint.

The aged sometimes get dogmatic and don't want to listen, but only to tell. However, I find that if you can hear them out on a few things they're hipped on and just not argue with them about that, then they're interested to know what you think about what is going on in the world. The mind will remain vivid longer if there are conversations with vivid younger people, at least occasionally.

Just as young life has to feed off of older life when it is born into the world and for the first twenty-one years or so, so older life has to feed off of younger life as it goes out of the world from about sixty-five to eighty. If the young man can be considerate of the old as the old are of the very young, it will be a more beautiful world for all.

Certainly, everyone should be seriously saving money for the exigencies of old age from fifty to sixty-five. They should plan to take care of themselves as long as possible and allow their children to have their homes for themselves and their families insofar as possible. It is a reasonable elderly person who, when he sees he can't handle his or her affairs anymore, says to his family, now it's time for me to move into a new phase of life. Arrange for me to go to a retirement home or a nursing home, as the case may require. When one enters there, do it, not in resentment, but in the spirit of a new adventure. Seek out new friends. Be friendly. Learn a few more things about life and about the courage that enables most people to face the great transition to the next with courage and faith. There are many wonderful Scriptures and poems to give us faith and courage to face death, such as "The Eternal Goodness" by John Greenleaf Whittier.

Chapter 36

"DID WE NOT FEEL OUR HEARTS ON FIRE?"

Address to the United Church of Christ of Texas annual convention at TCU May 19, 1979

Ruth and I practice Unity. She was a Congregationalist and became a Disciple. We've thoroughly enjoyed the two interim ministries at First Congregationalist Church. If we Disciples and the United Church of Christ could bear united witness to the Christian life, so many of life's woes would vanish.

1 Corinthians 1:10–17 expresses Paul's disgust that, as Paul puts it, some of them are saying "I am Paul's man, or Apollo's man, or Peter's man." Even while Jesus was on earth, James and John were arguing about who would sit on his right and left when he came into his kingdom. At his crucifixion, when Peter was taunted by some of Jesus's assailants, Peter said: "I never knew the man."

The natural man or woman cannot be one in the Lord, as the hymn claims. There are times when it appears that we are very early on in the human evolutionary process. God is the one who calls us forward. In *God and the World,* John Cobb describes Kazanzakis's picture of God struggling with man (53). In our time, as in the first century, God calls on us to move out into new forms, new places, in Antioch, Ephesus, Rome, Paris, London, New York, Fort Worth. As Christians, we have taken the forms of the Greek Church, the Coptic Church, the Methodist Church, the United Church of Christ. Surely it is time for us to hear a different drummer, one who will answer Jesus's prayer in John: "That they might all be one, Father, as Thou and I are one."

It is the "new order in Christ" that can join us with others to be one in the Lord. Cleopas and the other disciple said to one another and to the risen Christ, as they walked along the Emmaus Road: "We had hoped that it was he who would deliver Israel." The ultimates Jesus brought were, as

Paul said: "More than we can ask or even think." They are infinitely creative, calling each generation of committed Christians to do more than they are willing to do.

The dream of Disciples of Christ and United Church of Christ uniting is just a ridiculously small bit of the action that should be going on among Christians, and yet it is so difficult to bring about. The leadership of Christ's Spirit calls for so much self-abnegation that few, if any, of us are up to it. Peter Ainslie said the ultimate thing is that the Disciples of Christ and all other churches should die and be resurrected in a new and surprisingly beautiful form—the living "Body of Christ." But we'll not do it soon. So the best thing we can do is to move toward it piece by piece. The Disciples-UCC unity movement is a sensible and feasible one.

"When anyone is united in Christ, there is a new world; the old order has gone, and a new order has already begun." In Christ, when we really are a part of that resurrected reality that is like the man Jesus, we are extremely capable of creative goodness, a new being in Christ. The resurrected one means confessing, repentance, forgiveness, grace, renewal. This means infinite creative possibilities. Also it means dropping all bragging about who we are and how great we are. It emphasizes that we are not what we ought to be. We are not "One in the Spirit, one in the Lord." It emphasizes we do not belong to Peter or to Paul, but to Christ alone. It means we can open up to new forms of church, new forms of social service, new forms of worship, new friends in Christ, new concern for the lost and wandering populations; therefore, new forms of ministry and gospel communication.

The first century Church was not like the Roman Church, the Eastern Orthodox Church, the Presbyterian, Congregational, Baptist, Christian, or United Church of Christ. A Church precisely like the first century church could not minister in the twentieth century. At this point, it behooves us to hear the prophetic and eternally true words of John Robinson as he saw the Pilgrim Fathers off to the New World from Holland in the seventeenth century: "God hath yet more light to break forth from his Holy Word." This is what First Congregational Church engraved on a pen holder after my first interim with them. I guess I could have taken it to mean that they hadn't learned much from me and my ministry! But I took it to mean that they had found this excellent, historical, Congregational summary of the dynamic character of Christianity that I had preached about to them.

In conclusion, I want to summarize my central theme by quoting from A. N. Whitehead's *Process and Reality*, pp. 243–46.

> There are four creative phases in which God and the Universe accomplish the actualization of the new dimensions of reality.
>
> 1. Conceptual origination, deficient in actuality—Isaiah: "swords into plowshares."
> 2. Physical actuality originated—Jesus: "Blessed are the peacemakers."
> 3. Perfected actuality in which the many are everlastingly merged and participate in the new form—much as Church, or United Nations.
> 4. Love passed from heaven to earth and back to heaven.
>   Through it all, God is the Great Companion of man, the fellow sufferer. Jesus the man is the inalienable necessity to help us see the eternal significance of suffering goodness as key to the character of God and God's Kingdom.

It is going to take some self-abnegating, even suffering commitment to Christian unity to get even our two groups together, much less the thousand and one other sects of Christianity. But the only way life has any real meaning is to be at work as a steward of God's grace. And you know that infinite, competitive sectarianism is not God's will. The new world, new being, can set our "hearts on fire with the Holy Spirit, the God who call us forward. Unite!"

Chapter 37

SERMONS AT TRINITY TERRACE, FORT WORTH

GOD IN NATURE; GOD IN CHRIST

A sermon at South Hills Christian Church, Fort Worth, 1980; Lake Buchanan, 1984; and Trinity Terrace, Fort Worth, 1992

On several occasions, Paul spoke at Chapel or to the residents on the nursing floor at Trinity Terrace, a retirement community in downtown Fort Worth.

Scripture: Ps. 8; Matt. 5:43–45; II Cor. 5:16–20

I have problems with the God in Nature Emphasis or Natural Theology. There are times when I can look at the starry heavens, the beautiful sunrise or sunset, the flowering peach trees, and say with the Psalmist: "How majestic is thy name in all the earth" (Ps. 8:1). Or with the poet Browning, "Morning's at seven, the hillside's dew-pearled . . . God's in his Heaven, all's right with the World!"

There are other times when, with Amos, I can see some sense in saying grasshoppers and drouth which eat up the grain and grass are a punishment of God. And other times when a late freeze that kills half my peaches by destroying the blossoms and a hailstorm that destroys the remainder of the peaches seem very unjust, even ridiculous. And then to follow that with a summer that is the hottest in recorded history and to bring a plague of grasshoppers that threaten to destroy even the fruit trees themselves, it is practically impossible to see the hand of a loving, forgiving, creative God in the midst of that scenario.

When I was selling peaches at the Dallas Farmers Market, I got to talking to the lady in the next spot. I happened to express this thought about why these bad things happen to someone who is trying to provide food for people and wondered why God let that happen. She responded that maybe God was trying to tell me something!

Over the years I've wrestled with this problem quite a bit in a rather theoretical way, but never at first hand in 113-degree heat—and above 100 degrees heat for fifty days in a row and no rain since May—seventy-five days without rain.

Jesus helps me quite a bit when he says in Matt. 5:43–45 "God's rain falls on the just and the unjust." Rain doesn't start and stop at the barbed wire fences of the good and bad families, nor does drought, nor do grasshoppers.

Yet, in some profound way, I do affirm God to be Creator and Sustainer of this vast and marvelous universe. I was reminded of this when Ruth and I took our grandsons to the Fort Worth Museum of Natural History and saw the show at the planetarium, tracing the history of our universe from the "Big Bang" beginning to the potential "black hole" ending.

Also when we studied the marvelous functioning of the blood cells, glands, muscles, reproductive system, etc. with the aid of an excellent model of the human body, I cannot believe that the entire evolutionary process of development that has brought forth this amazingly complex and sensitive reality that is a human being can possibly be "a tale told by an idiot, full of sound and fury, and signifying nothing." It would be more appropriate to say "created in the image of God" although there are problems with that generalization. There are times when, if nature is God or God completely controls nature and a tornado or hurricane comes along and destroys property and takes lives, I have a problem with that.

Similarly, I have problems with black widow spiders and rattlesnakes and water moccasins and copperheads, and night ants that strip a peach tree of all its leaves in a night. In early June I was having trouble with night ants, so I went out at dusk to see where their hold was and put some poison around it. (I suppose from the ant's point of view, they wonder why God created someone like me.) As I was returning to the house after dark, flashlight in one hand, peaches in the other, I met a four-foot rattlesnake head-on. I veered right. He veered left. I shouted for Ruth to bring the gun. She got there with it much quicker than I thought she would. She took the peaches. I kept the flashlight on the snake which was now about ten to twelve feet away. I had to take the gun out of its case. Fortunately, it was loaded. I took three shots to hit him while at the same time holding the flashlight on him. When I did hit him, he jumped a foot in the air and coiled. I hit him again. He slithered off in the high grass, and I decided to leave good enough alone for the night. The next day I couldn't find him. He had apparently found a hole to crawl in.

We used to enjoy sitting out in the front yard at night and watching the stars. Now, we think constantly of snakes. So, rattlesnakes are a theological problem for me. The enmity between man and snake in the story of the Fall is borne out.

I conclude that I can be grateful to God for the facets of nature that create, support, and develop the higher forms of life. I think I must realize that mankind is in nature, but not completely of it. As the Genesis story of creation puts it, people are to rule over nature. Some of the most revolting aspects of Hinduism are their confusion of aspects of nature such as cows, monkeys, sex, and rivers with the divine.

Consequently, I conclude that the ultimate relation of man to God and God to man is seen in Christ, not in nature. You really can't see with any consistency that God loves world by sorting out rattlesnakes and hummingbirds, scorpions and honey bees. You can see only that God loves mankind by rightly interpreting the actual human/divine event of Jesus Christ and seeing that God was in Christ, reconciling the world unto Himself.

By seeing across the pages of history how very creative has been the startling, sweet spirit of Jesus in St. Paul, St. Francis, Martin Luther, Pope John Paul XXIV, Martin Luther King, Albert Schweitzer, and others, we can see that amazing strand of grace creatively at work overcoming the demonic spirits like Napoleon and Hitler and Mussolini, the rattlesnakes of the human world. God was and God is still in Christ reconciling the world unto God's self. Jesus is the best picture of God that we have.

Then there is something we can do. We can try to imitate Christ and confess and accept his forgiveness when we fall short. We can use our patience and intelligence and courage to overcome the devastation of hurricanes, volcanoes, hailstorms, droughts, and grasshoppers. And we can keep a wary eye out for rattlesnakes.

TRINITY FOR THE ELDERLY

A sermon at Trinity Terrace, Fort Worth, November 15, 1986

Scripture: Psalm 90, Psalm 118, Matt. 25:31ff

First, wake up surprised and grateful. Psalm 118:24 says "This is the day which the Lord hath made. We will rejoice and be glad in it." Verse 1 says "O give thanks to the Lord for He is good, His steadfast love endures forever." Meland wrote "The difference between the religious and the irreligious is an attitude of gratitude," as exemplified by these two views of the Grand Canyon: "Golly, what a gutter" vs. "What a marvelous thing God has wrought."

Refresh your mind and spirit about the eternal. With your life nearing its end, think often about time and eternity. Read Psalms 90:1–2, 10, 12, 16, and 7; all of Psalm 8; and Revelations 21:5–6, "I am the Alpha and the Omega, the beginning and the end. . . . Behold, I make all things new. To the thirsty, I will give the water of life. My four-score years are but as a watch in the night, but I am a part of the Eternal. God knows me, remembers those actions of mine that were worth remembering. They become a part of his good creation." St. Simon's memoirs speak of Light Times and Dark Times.

Try to be worth remembering by God. Look for opportunities to do something for a neighbor, like the Good Samaritan. There are plenty of opportunities here at Trinity Terrace. Do something for your church, even if you can't go to church. Do something to "feed the hungry, etc." as Christ says so clearly in Matthew 25:31ff. Do something for the Presbyterian Shelter, Loaves and Fishes, Salvation Army, Gospel Mission, Bridge Association, UNICEF, etc.

GOD

A sermon at Trinity Terrace, Fort Worth, January 30, 1994

The most basic concept of any religion is its concept of God. Nelson's concordance of the Revised Standard Version of the Bible has 3,680 references to God and 7,000 references to Lord. That's over 10,000 references to God in the Bible.

Sometimes in the Gospels, Jesus is referred to as Lord. The Gospel of John speaks of Jesus as God. Christianity finally developed the Trinitarian concept of Father, Son, and Holy Spirit. These are presented as different persona or aspects of God. I think it might be helpful to you for me to lift several concepts of God that we often take for granted. It may deepen our worship and devotion.

"In the beginning, God created the heavens and the earth." The last book of the Bible, Revelation, quotes God as saying, "I am the Alpha and the Omega," the beginning and the end. God is creator and final destiny of each of us and all of us.

Through the time of Abraham, God cares about God's people and leads them though their many ups and downs. God, through Moses, is lawgiver and judge of morality and immorality. All of God's children are answerable to God. In the Old Testament, that is the Jews. In the New Testament, that is everybody. According to John Calvin, that means only "the Elect." According to Wesley and Campbell, it means everyone. Jesus said, "Go ye into all the world and preach the Gospel to every living creature," and "Lo I am with you always even to the end of the age."

In the time of Saul, David, and Solomon, God established his Kingdom, but it divided and then fell. In the time of the prophets, he explained through them why the kingdom would fall. The emphasis on our relation to God began to shift from the social and political to the individual.

The prophets developed individualism in religion. They heard the word of God as different from kings and temple priests. Isaiah 6: "In the year that King Uzziah died, I saw the Lord, high and lifted up, and his train filled the temple. Above Him stood the seraphim; each had six wings. With twain he covered his loins, and with twain he did fly. And one cried to another and said, 'Holy, holy, holy is the Lord God of Hosts, the whole earth is full of his glory.' Then Isaiah responded, 'Woe is me, for I am undone. I am unclean and I dwell amid a people who are unclean, for mine eyes have seen the King, the Lord of Hosts.'"

There follows a picture of Isaiah's cleansing and his commission to tell the people of their sins and how they can be cleansed. Although this takes place within Judaism, it awakens the prophets and other thoughtful people to the necessity to straighten out their individual lives. Micah says, "What does the Lord require of thee, but to do justice and to love mercy and to walk humbly with thy Lord."

In the New Testament, Jesus spoke of God as both Judge and loving Father. The law he approved, but he put it positively. Thou shalt love the

Lord thy God with all thy heart and mind and strength, and thy neighbor as thyself. Jesus speaks of God as both Judge and loving Father. God has two hands—love and judgment.

The Apostle Paul spoke of God as the Father of our Lord, Jesus Christ, requiring of us penitence, faith, hope and love. He also taught that Jesus would return soon and the quick and the dead in Christ would rise to be with God forevermore.

Many philosophers and theologians from Plato to Paul Tillich spoke of God as Being—Being Itself or Ultimate Being, also Ultimate Reality, the Really Real, behind all our inadequate concepts of what's real.

Another group of philosophers and theologians, such as Whitehead, Wieman, Hartshorne, Cobb, spoke of God as Creative Process—creating and recreating at all levels of reality from the atom and the amoeba, to humans, in their bodies, minds, and souls, a new being in Christ, or a "born again Christian."

Finally, an SMU theologian, speaking to the faculty of Brite Divinity School and the TCU Department of Religion on his concept of God, said, "Finally, no concept of God is adequate. The God who is really God transcends human and earthly concepts. God is ultimately divine, transcendent mystery, before whom all sensitive souls bow."

FREEDOM AND DESTINY

A sermon at Trinity Terrace, 1993

Scripture: Romans 8:1–4, 9, 28–30

Theme: "There is a divinity shapes our ends, rough hew them how we will."

Shakespeare, *Hamlet*, Act V

Thanksgiving morning, I awakened about 6:00 a.m. and was too lazy to get up; so I climbed back in bed and began a meditation, going back over some of the critical events of my life. This line from Shakespeare came to mind: "There is a divinity shapes our ends, rough hew them how we will."

I'm not a Presbyterian or any kind of Calvinist, but as I told a class I taught at First Presbyterian a while back, I do believe in the Providence of God. There's a difference in Predestination. Your freedom is taken away. You don't choose; God controls every event of your life. In the providence of God, God leads you, stimulates you, picks up the pieces when you foul up your life, and helps you make the most of the rest of your life, as Harry Emerson Fosdick said in one of his great sermons.

The most important passage of scripture regarding this matter is in the eighth chapter of Romans, particularly verses 28–30. It includes this key verse: "We know that in everything God works for good with those who love him."

At the risk of boring you with personal history, I am going to share some of that meditation from that Thanksgiving morning.

I never received a call to the ministry like a bolt of lightning, but as I look back across the years there was a divinity guiding me in various ways that I did not comprehend at the various critical moments of my life.

Soon after my baptism, I considered becoming a missionary. Cammie Gray, missionary to China, had given a series of talks at First Christian Church of Beaumont; and at the age of twelve or thirteen, I thought I would become a missionary.

At age fifteen at a Christian Endeavor convention at our church, we were given printed cards if we wanted to sign up for full-time Christian service. At the time, I was much involved with the YMCA, and Y work was listed as one of the types of Christian service. I signed up and ever after considered myself a Christian Service student. At TCU I worked part-time at the Y. It made college possible for me.

During my senior year at TCU, Granville Walker and Perry Gresham took me out for a cup of coffee and urged me to consider the ministry instead of Y work. They offered to write Dean Ames of Disciples House, University of Chicago, recommending me for a scholarship. I pondered the matter and said OK, assuming that my grades weren't good enough to get a scholarship to a prestigious university like Chicago. Lo and behold, Ames accepted me!

At the same time, I had a letter from "Block" Smith, executive secretary of the Student Y at Austin. He offered me a job paying $108 per month. He also said I could take one course per day, that is two per week, to work on a MA degree. It was his hope that I would decide to stay with the Y movement, in the College Y work.

Since I owed $200 to my mother which she had loaned me in the depths of the Depression, I saw a way to pay her back while taking a master's degree. I told Block I'd like to, but I couldn't see turning down this marvelous scholarship at Chicago. Block got in touch with Frank Jewett, the minister of the Disciples Bible Chair at UT. Jewett had taken a BD degree at Chicago, and he knew Dean Ames. He wrote to Ames to see if he would promise to give me that scholarship two years later if I took an MA at Texas. The answer came back, "Yes!"

I went to Austin, worked at the Y, paid off my debts, bought engagement and wedding rings to give to Ruth in due time. I finished the MA degree and took off for Chicago. Ruth was not happy about this year delay in our courtship. She was in Ohio, attending Oberlin College.

Dean Hall at TCU invited me to be ordained along with some other TCU people. Jewett asked me to preach in Bible Chair Chapel and then said he wanted me to succeed him in the Bible Chair.

I finished two degrees at Chicago. Ruth got a scholarship to Chicago School of Theology, and we were able to marry. In 1939, we accepted a call to a small-town church in Ohio, spent twenty months there, and then were called to a church in Detroit where we spent five years.

One day in 1944, the head of our Missionary Society, Dr. Robert Hopkins, appeared in Church. I asked if he wanted to preach. He said, "No, I came to hear you preach!" After the service he took us out to Sunday dinner and said that Dr. Frank Jewett was to retire from the Bible Chair at Austin next fall and that he had designated me to succeed him. Ruth and I were flabbergasted. We were happily settled into a significant ministry in Detroit and had no desire to leave. We turned him down. I had never considered teaching. My vocation was ministry.

But after a few weeks, Dr. Hopkins came back to me and insisted that I reconsider the Austin position. Now this time Ruth and I considered it very prayerfully. This impressed us as a call! We answered "Yes," and Ruth cried the whole night through.

We asked for a year of study to refresh my mind and prepare the courses. We arrived in Austin in August 1946. I started my classes, University Christian Church in Austin, and the Disciples Student Fellowship all that first year. I really wanted to become pastor of University Christian Church, but the board chose another pastor. I applied myself to my classes.

They grew, and I became a successful college professor. TCU awarded me an honorary doctorate. The time came as our boys were growing up that we had to admit that the home missionary salary was too low to send them to college. I called a minister friend and asked him to watch out for a church opening for me. I needed more money for this next stage of life.

His response was, "Paul, you are an excellent teacher. Students tell me that frequently. Let me contact Dean Moore at TCU to see if he can find an opening for you at TCU."

So it was in the fall of 1957 that I began teaching at TCU. At the end of the first year, the students elected me Outstanding Professor. I was amazed! But, from then on, I was sure that I had finally found my calling. Later three churches in Fort Worth, Austin, and Dallas approached me to become their pastor. I was clear that my calling was in teaching and turned them down.

In conclusion, perhaps you can see why I can say: "There is a divinity shapes our ends, rough hew them how we will." And, with the Apostle Paul, "We know that in everything, God works for good with those who love him." You are all God-bearing, God-loving persons.

Now, I hope you will think on your life during this week and decide where God has laid God's hand on you, and you can now say in retrospect it was the providence of God that led you hence.

THE BOOK OF RUTH

For Nursing Floor Residents at Trinity Terrace, February 29, 1996

The Book of Ruth is one of the best loved stories of the Old Testament. It has to do with international marriage. We need to get some geography in mind. Israel is the land of Judah with the city of Bethlehem. Moab is another land.

We need to think about a Jewish couple who lived in Bethlehem, the City of David. When this story took place, David had not been born yet. The Book of Ruth appears in the canon after Joshua and Judges, which is when the story happened. It was written around 400 BC after Ezra and Nehemiah and the return from exile, when there were strict laws about social and international marriage. The author of Ruth disagrees. He reaches back in history to present an opposite point of view.

Elimelech and Naomi flee drought in Bethlehem, Israel, and go to Moab, east of the Jordan and the Dead Sea. Their sons, Mahlon and Chillion, marry Moabite women, Ruth and Orpah. The three men die; so we have three widows. Naomi decides to go back to Bethlehem and her people. The girls say they will accompany her. She says, "No! I don't have sons in my womb. You stay here and marry Moabite men." Orpah agrees to do so. Ruth says, "Entreat me not to leave you or to return from following you; for where you go, I will go and where you lodge, I will lodge;

your people shall be my people, and your God, my God. Where you die, I will die and there will I be buried."

So Ruth and Naomi return to Bethlehem. Naomi told Ruth to go and glean in the field of Boaz, a relative of Elimelech. Boaz came to the field and asked his superintendent who is that young woman? He said she is the Moabite daughter-in-law of Naomi, the widow of Elimelech. So, Boaz told Ruth to glean in his field, not others, and to stay close to the maidens who worked his fields. He said, "I have charged the young men not to molest you." She asked, "Why have I found favor in your eyes?" Boaz replied, "Because of your loyal care for my relative, Naomi; and you're a relative by marriage."

When Ruth went home and told Naomi about all this, Naomi said, "Take a bath and anoint yourself with perfume. Put on your best clothes, return to the threshing floor. Boaz works the harvest too. When he has eaten, note where he lies down to sleep. Go sleep at his feet." She did so after dark.

Boaz said, "Who are you?" "I am Ruth, your maid servant and next-of-kin." He said, "There is one next-of-kin closer than I. Do not fear. I will take care of you." Boaz went to the gate, sat down, and waited. The closer next-of-kin came. He was offered the field owned by Naomi and the servant Ruth. He declined it.

So, Boaz, being the next of kin, told the elders of the city he would assume responsibility for Ruth and Naomi. He purchased the land that would have belonged to Elimelech, Mahlon, and Chillion and brought Ruth to be his wife.

When this story was told in the 400 BC period in the time of Ezra and Nehemiah, it had a humanizing effect against the too-strict laws against marrying foreigners. Finally, when the Jews canonized the books of the Law and the Prophets around 150 BC, they included Ruth with its liberal teaching as well as Ezra and Nehemiah with their conservative teachings.

FORGIVE AND YOU SHALL BE FORGIVEN

A sermon at Trinity Terrace, Fort Worth, June 16, 1996

Scripture: Luke 6:27–38

Last Sunday's sermon by Dr. Danny Stewart, pastor of Central Christian Church, Fort Worth, was one of the most stimulating and thoughtful sermons I have heard from this pulpit. His sermon title was "Principalities and Powers: The Problem of Evil." I said to him after the service that our next sermon should be on forgiveness. He agreed; so when it fell my lot to preach today, I felt I must fill that need.

Jesus's teachings and his whole life were an attempt to reveal that God, the Ultimate Reality, was the very essence of forgiveness. Jesus's last words from the cross included: "God, forgive them for they know not what they are doing." He was speaking of the rough soldiers gambling over his clothing and cursing as they did the dirty job of crucifying Jesus and the two thieves. He also included the Chief Priest and the Saducees.

One thief joined the mob, saying to Jesus: "If you're the Christ, save yourself and us." He didn't see any difference between himself and Christ. The other thief was more sensitive. He said: "Do you not fear God? You and I suffer justly, but this man has done no wrong. Jesus, when you come into your kingly power, remember me." Jesus replied: "This day you shall be in paradise with me."

One of the most persistent interpretations of the meaning of the cross is called "substitutionary sacrifice." Jesus paid it all, all to him I owe, for my salvation. I cannot earn salvation by my good works. Jesus suffered for our sins, not his.

The Apostle Paul presents the Gospel as a Gospel of reconciliation. Our sins estrange us from God, and we cannot do anything to restore a saving relation with God. It is done for us by God through Christ. God in the Christ event presents a means of reconciliation. We are saved by grace through faith.

In a similar vein, Jesus said: "If you have aught against your brother, first go and be reconciled to your brother, and then come and offer your gift at the altar."

Jesus's teachings about forgiveness include the following:

1. The Prodigal Son story is about a father who forgives his younger son who had left home and squandered his inheritance.
2. The Golden Rule, "Do unto others as you would have them do unto you," is about empathy.
3. "Forgive and you will be forgiven."

In my lifetime, I have had some experience in forgiving and being forgiven. One evening, when my sons were young and living at home, one of the boys was acting strangely. I gave him a whipping. Years later,

I told him I was sorry for whipping him. He didn't even remember the incident.

Another example was a colleague who spread an evil tale about me among friends and colleagues. I really didn't know anything else to do than to keep on being my essential self. One day he wrote me a letter, agreeing with a letter I had published in our national journal. After that, we resumed our friendly ways, and the issue faded away. You don't just forgive and forget. You forgive, and the significance of the issue fades away. It is remembered in a different way.

It even works at the socio-political-economic level. Our attitude after World War II toward our former enemies, Germany and Japan, was to build them up, and now they are partners for peace in the United Nations. After World War I, our attitude was to punish our enemy who were defeated, and the outcome was another war.

Love your enemies; do good to those who hate you; pray for those who despitefully use you. This is our best answer to evil. It ain't easy! God help us! Amen.

THE ROLE OF WOMEN IN THE CHURCH

A sermon at Trinity Terrace Chapel, September 25, 1994

Scriptures: My text is Galatians 3:28, "Those who were baptized into Christ have put on Christ. There is neither Jew nor Greek, neither male nor female, neither slave nor free, for you are all one in Christ Jesus."

Acts 16:14 and 16:40 speak of Lydia, the seller of purple goods, as a convert who was very helpful. II Tim. 1:5 Paul to Timothy, "I am reminded of your sincere faith, a faith that dwelt first in your grandmother, Lois, and your mother, Eunice, and I am sure now dwells in you."

Romans 16:1 "I commend to you our sister, Phoebe, a deaconess in the Church at Cenchreae, that you may receive her in the Lord as befits the saints, and help her in whatever she may require from you, for she has been a helper of many, and of myself as well."

Romans 16:5 "Greet Mary who has worked hard among you."

Of course, we dare not overlook Paul's statement in I Cor. 13:34–35. "As in all the churches of the saints, the women should keep silence in the churches. For they are not permitted to speak, but should be subordinate, as the law says. If there is anything they wish to know, let them ask their husbands at home. For it is shameful for a woman to speak in church."

So Paul left us a mixed picture. We have to choose. Most churches are choosing these days, two thousand years after Christ. It's about time!

The role of women in the church is changing rapidly these days. About half the students at Brite Divinity School and other seminaries are women these days. Such enrollment has been increasing since about 1970. I think it is about time the churches were acknowledging the profound Christian qualities of women. Women have played a gracious subsidiary role in the churches for nearly two thousand years. It's about time they were being recognized and offered leadership roles.

Women are achieving roles as pastors, Elders, deacons, board chairpersons, as well as the long-established roles of teachers, choir members, etc. It will be for the best interests of the Church.

This change makes us think deeply about God. If you use a pronoun for God, you usually use He, but why not She? One of our women Elders has refused to lead the Lord's Prayer when she serves as the Lord's Table, because it says, "Our Father." But when we stop and think, we know that God is not a man or a woman. God is above these divisions. We just don't have any pronouns that apply. So increasingly you will find ministers and those who lead worship saying God, Lord, Ruler of Heaven and Earth, etc. and avoiding a masculine or feminine pronoun.

Nevertheless, there are problems! Some women have three careers: wife, mother, and career woman. Men as well as women will have to develop new habits and behavior patterns. Already large corporations are providing on-site day care for their employees' children and allowing women time off with pay when a child gets sick. The process for a man who has responsibility for a child to take leave has not been worked out and has not reached the corporate level yet.

There is a very popular book that is a best-seller, *Men Are from Mars; Women Are from Venus.* One of the main points is that men never listen, illustrated by what happens when a man comes home from work. However, this problem can occur with anyone at any time or any age.

Part IV

CONTEMPORARY THEOLOGY

"Man's ultimate thought is—GOD." Paul teaching upper division theology. Courtesy of *This is TCU 1962.*

Chapter 38

SOME THEOLOGICAL TENDENCIES TODAY

An address to the Women's Club, Fort Worth, October 1, 1970

Paul was a scholar of Christian thought, but what he probably enjoyed most was teaching students, Sunday school classes, people at a church worship service, people at conventions, church groups gathered for a special seminar, and community groups who wanted to learn about current trends in Christian thought. As research revealed more about the history of Christianity and how some ideas became the dogma of the church, he wanted to share what the more recent theologians and scholars were saying about the nature of God and Jesus, especially in relation to how we love God and our neighbors as ourselves in our contemporary world.

You are aware of the rapid change taking place in institutional patterns through a rapprochement between Eastern and Western Catholic Churches when Pope Paul embraced the Greek Archibishop in Jerusalem in 1963? You're aware of the National and World Council of Churches? You're aware of the Consultation on Christian Unity? You may have heard of the new emphasis on secular Christianity and of the "death of God" theology. This last idea is extremist, headline catching, and ridiculous. The nearest serious thought to that position is a rather old set of ideas called religious humanism.

I wish to talk to you about dominant trends in serious theology, which I think will interest you. I reference Perry LeFeure's *Philosophical Resources for Christian Thought*, in which he discusses process theology, phenomenology, linguistic analysis, and existentialism. Of the major trends among serious theologians, neo-orthodoxy is the closest to traditional orthodoxy, although it is important to say that Fundamentalism and Evangelicalism or the new conservatism might dispute that statement.

The great names in neo-orthodoxy are Karl Barth and Emil Brunner in Europe as well as Gustave Aulen, Reinhold Niebuhr, and others. They differ among themselves in precise matter, but basically they emphasize knowledge of God through revelation, primarily through Jesus Christ as a God-man but functioning to reconcile God and man, known through faith, with no emphasis on Natural Theology (Barth, Brunner). They accept high criticism and tend to be Pauline in emphasis on faith and grace. (See Galatians and Romans.) Regarding man, they accept a modified concept of "original sin." Speaking in psychological terms of alienation and estrangement, man is fully man and is God-conscious. The Universal Church is the body of Christ and not identical with the institutional church. Neo-orthodoxes react against liberalism and the social gospel. They emphasize eschatology and individual response to God, according to Pannenberg. They believe the final determination is by God, not man.

Paul Tillich is a major proponent of Existentialism. He offered the principle of correlation or philosophical theology. God is Being Itself, not a being. Existence is estrangement from essence. We experience the threat of non-being as well as New Being. Christ as the man was absolutely loyal to his ground of being. His existence and essence were unified. He overcame the threat of non-being in the resurrection and revealed the eternal hope of the new-being character of reality that overcomes the threats of non-being.

Adherents of Process Theology include H. N. Wieman, A. N. Whitehead, John Cobb, and Hartshorne. They emphasize reason more than faith and acknowledge the venture of faith in the collaboration with creativity in establishing new possibilities of value. Process theologians see Jesus as fully human, accepted by believers as the expression of full commitment to creativity and cooperation with God. The resurrection and the developing community of faith is evidence of God at work as a leaven in history.

Many efforts have been made to recapture the Jesus of history, whom Bultmann has threatened. (See Pannenberg's *Jesus, God and Man* and Moltmann's *Theology of Hope.*) Both liberals and conservatives are bent on this quest, although Bultmann and Tillich both think it is impossible and an unnecessary quest.

The historical validity of the faith has been proven through the centuries, and that history, including the Bible and especially the New Testament, is clear and recoverable. God has worked through his people's faith and will continue to do so. However, the new emphasis on history puts more focus on eschatology. Jesus believed that the end of history is in the hands of God, and this is essential. It is in history that God has revealed God's self. It is by studying history (both Biblical and Church as well as secular) that we can sense what God is doing in history. The historical Jesus is at the center of history. God is the clue we have to the Alpha and Omega of history. God is at work in history bringing God's kingdom, which God will clearly declare in the Eschaton.

John Cobb says we must have the Biblical faith of the Neo-orthodox, the existentialist's insight about the depth of the individual soul, the liberal's concern for the transformation of society, and the historical theologian's trust that in the end, God will make sense out of it all. The age ahead of us has been characterized in two different ways theologically. It will be impossible to write a system for the foreseeable future. We must "hang loose" and communicate with each other about our revelations, our insights and convictions. We need to create an understanding and loving community of faith. The other point of view (Cobb) says we must take the elements of insight we have into nature, revelation, and individuals, and write a correlated, systematic theology for the late twentieth century. It will have as its natural theological base process theology which sees God as growing, developing, bringing new things to pass, so it will never become a static, dogmatic, closed system by which men exclude other men from church or heaven. Certainly, they will not torture or kill them as they have in the Middle Ages and the Reformation.

Chapter 39

CREATION AND CREATIVITY

A lecture in San Angelo, June 1973

When you put God's word together with God's act, you get creation. The main theme of the Bible and of contemporary Christian thought that we're trying to state clearly is that God creates. God continues to create. It is God's nature to create. God is not destructive. In the Bible when God destroys as in the flood story or in the destruction of Jerusalem or the ten tribes of Israel, it is always like a gardener getting weeds out of his garden so he can plant some good seed and get a good harvest. In the beginning, God created. And God continues to create.

Process Theology

Ancient man thought of a more static universe, two-tiered and later three-tiered. Today, we know, with the help of astronomy, of the vast distances and millions of stars and planets in the universe. The Palomar Glass in California has shown us that two hundred million light years out there, there are still stars and other celestial bodies appearing. Radio telescope "sees" even farther.

Our little earth is just a tiny dot in the tail of a spiral nebulae. Such awareness we usually put away from our minds, as it is too threatening to us as individuals. The real question arises how can God care for me if God has so much territory to cover? Our science and religion must be brought together into one coherent weltanschauung insofar as possible. It is not possible in a real clear, neat way.

Good religion does not deny scientific fact to try to protect some ancient dogma. As the leaders of the Christian Church (Disciples of Christ) have always said, we must wed reason and faith.

Creative change is going on all the time. The great process philosopher of the twentieth century is Alfred North Whitehead. His greatest work is *Process and Reality.* Another book of his is *Religion in the Making.* Other great process philosophers are Charles Hartshorne, who wrote *A New Natural Theology;* H. N. Wieman, *The Source of Human Good, Man's Ultimate Commitment,* and *Intellectual Foundations of Faith*; and John B. Cobb, who wrote *God and the World* and *A Natural Theology for Our Time.* Others include Norman Pittenger, Dan Day Williams, and Teilhard de Chardin, the Catholic, who wrote *Philosophy of Man, Future of Man,* and *Divine Milieu.*

The main point for us to think about is how do we get our Biblical theology together with our modern, scientific understanding of the world? Dedicated Christians think this is terribly important because all too many people are becoming completely secular in their outlook. That is, the moral, ethical and salvation teachings of the Bible are not "where they live." Cobb wrote that the loss of the vision of the world as God's creation destroys the context in which Christian theology is possible.

It is important to understand that science is not the enemy of religion. Science is simply exploring the nature of certain segments of reality. It makes certain assumptions that are difficult for religious persons, like theologians or the average Christian, to deal with in areas such as the miraculous. The theologian is not completely stumped by this problem. He sees God working through those creative aspects of the natural process and as a rule, the "miraculous" is the name for the unexpected, the surprising. God is always acting. The primary concern of religion is to get man to see it and respond.

Paul says to the Romans: "Pray constantly" or "Pray without ceasing." Be God-conscious in every event. One's whole life should be lived under the shadow of God's wing, as it were. The poetic language of theology used here is a way of saying memorably that God is always at work creatively in our lives. Attend; open your eyes. Respond creatively to God's nudging.

Chapter 40

CURRENT TRENDS IN CHRISTIAN THOUGHT

Sermon at First Unitarian, Fort Worth, November 14, 1973

There are six major trends in contemporary Christian thought. They are:

1. Resurgent Fundamentalism or Evangelicalism
2. Resurgent Liberalism: Cobb and process theologians
3. Agnostic or Secular trend: Christian atheism
4. Neo-orthodoxy continues to be significant.
5. Paul Tillich, the bridge theologian between Liberalism and Neo-orthodoxy
6. The theologians of Hope: Pannenberg and Moltmann

Fundamentalism emphasizes the verbal inspiration of scripture, the Virgin Birth of Christ, substitutionary sacrifice and forgiveness of sin, the imminent return of Christ and a final judgment, hell for unbelievers, and heaven for believers. I think it is important to try to keep communication open with these people because occasionally they cross over into rational discourse.

The Liberalism that was sheer humanism/optimism has been considerably tempered since World War II. Social concerns continued to be brought forward by several types of developing thought. I'll give attention in this brief perspective to John Cobb of Claremont and Hartshorne of Texas. Their theology was grounded in A. N. Whitehead and the process theology of H. N. Wieman. They emphasized rational theology based on natural creative order. In contrast to the Creator, King, Judge, Destroyer God of the Old Testament, they present "the One who calls us forward into a potentially better tomorrow"; not all powerful , but powerful; the creative lure and co-worker with people in established appropriate new forms of goodness; and Jesus seen as the example instead of savior.

Christian Atheism and secularism says simply that modern man can no longer live with God of the gaps, or God who works miracles, so let's just say God is no longer viable; "God is dead." Altizer, Hamilton, and Van Buren are examples from this group. All three admire Jesus for his sensitivity to human need, his self-sacrifice for others, and call on all men of good will to follow Jesus, until perhaps a Christ-like God forms in our minds.

The Neo-orthodoxy of Barth and Brunner continues to be significant. Man is a sinner through and through so that when he uses reason to try to understand God, he makes God in the image of something human, such as culture, economic system, or a political system, like "Uncle Sam." God is *Totaliter Aliter.* God completely transcends these relativities of human reason and culture involvement. God can only be known by faith, which is in response to grace given by a power from beyond at some crisis in life in which one faces some abyss of despair.

Thus, the man of faith moves through life in dialectical fashion, walking a ridge between dogmatism on the right and self-criticism on the left, saying yes and no to the issues that arise in daily life, seeking to hear the Word of God which is a Christ-like word that is relevant in the midst of all the secular words that are thrown at him from every direction. Men seek to hide from God in the state, in the church, in corporations, in pleasure; but God in Christ calls for the individual man to hear a new, dynamic Word from God to transform the quality of life around him.

Paul Tillich continues to be the Ground of Being for many. Calling himself a bridge theologian, bridging the space between liberalism and neo-orthodoxy, Tillich developed a metaphysics, or ontology, which utilized the insights of existentialism and spoke a meaningful message to modern man. The individual man feels "the threat of non-being" in many ways: war, joblessness, the atomic bomb, and the knowledge that he will die someday someway. He also feels estrangement because he has to move every three years and leave old friends and familiar places, learn a new trade, etc. Existentialism art and novels and plays, like Camus's *The Stranger* and *The Fall*, show man's lostness in the twentieth century.

Christ as the New Being is the answer to this Threat of Non-Being. The resurrection, interpreted spiritually, in terms of the new dimensions of life that developed out of the Christ event, is the answer to this estrangement. A call to new life, new hope, new being in Christ and the

Church is a call to a proper relationship of Love, Power, and Justice. God is not dead. Only certain concepts of God are inadequate. God is the Really Real, behind and beyond all inadequate conceptions of reality.

The theology of Hope is presented by Wolfhart Pannenberg and Jürgen Moltmann. They were stimulated by Barth. They accept higher criticism but are more concerned with reason. They were interested in the New Quest for the Historical Jesus, thus correcting both Barth and Tillich. They explored eschatology as a word of Hope for the future for modern man who finds the future threatening. They related past, present, and future in a continuum of meaningfulness to counteract the despair that results from the existentialist's inward look.

The most hopeful thing is that there is a seething of thought in theology as everywhere else. Some wish that Theology would give some final authoritative word that would provide a safe haven in this storm-tossed area. Personally, I prefer the dynamism of process thought, where God is seen as the power of creative, changing, emergent new goodness. *God calls on you and me to see that "Time makes ancient good uncouth.* We must upward still and onward who would keep abreast of truth" (Teilhard de Chardin, *Phenomena of Man: Divine Nature*, 33).

Chapter 41

FIVE LECTURES ON CURRENT TRENDS IN CHRISTIAN THOUGHT

Lectures based on Hordern's *A Layman's Guide to Protestant Theology*

Introduction

We will divide the material for the five sessions as follows:

1. What was Christian Orthodoxy to begin with?
2. The threat to Orthodoxy—in the Renaissance, rationalism, in Hume, Locke, Kant, and in Schleiermacher's romanticism, as well as in Freud and Marx.
3. The liberal remaking of Orthodoxy, with some attention to fundamentalism.
4. Neo-orthodoxy—Barth, Brunner, Niebuhr
5. A bridge between Neo-orthodoxy and Liberalism, which Hordern calls "Orthodoxy as a growing tradition," rooted in Tillich's boundary line theology between liberalism and neo-orthodoxy.

I. Christian Orthodoxy

The following seven doctrines, experiences, and emphases were basic for the developing orthodoxy:

1. The resurrection is the sine qua non. At the depth of despair from the cross, Jesus was known to be alive, so hope is given for man. Resurrection meant to the Disciples that Jesus was the Messiah after all, even though Jesus didn't fulfill the expectations exactly, and even though Jesus had been crucified. God, thus, proved God's self more powerful than the worst and most powerful earthly forces of evil as found in the Roman government, the Jewish religion, and the Greek sensuality. The spirit of Jesus proved more powerful than the spirit of evil in man. They looked forward to the second coming of Jesus and the final judgment. A decisive battle had been won, but the final

battle remained to be fought. In Jesus as Christ, God had spoken, God had acted, God had revealed his nature to man. "God was in Christ, reconciling the world unto himself" (II Cor. 5:19). Gradually, they called Jesus Christ, Messiah, Lord, Savior, "only begotten Son," and finally in the creeds "very God of very God." Jesus was God, God at work in the life of man.

2. Paul established the doctrine of "Salvation by grace through faith," particularly in Romans. Legalism was transcended. Man, like a child in a healthy home, was loved by God not because he deserved it, but because God was gracious. For Paul, Augustine, and Luther, faith is not belief in a dogma, though some beliefs are inevitably involved, but Faith is a loving, trusting response to the love of God known primarily in Jesus Christ. Philippians 2:5 says, "Have that mind in you which was also in Christ Jesus." John says Jesus is the Way, the Truth, and the Life. The Christian makes a whole-being response to this man Christ Jesus as revealing the love of God. Such grace responded to in faith frees a man from evil habits, the lures of the world, and gives him power to become all that God calls him to become, and at last to know eternal life in God's presence. The Christian feels that all of this is a gift from God, not something to be earned. The Grace of God "frees man from fear and sense of guilt."
3. The Council of Nicea in 325 CE declared that Christ was Homoousios, of the same substance as God. He was not homoiousious, a substance like unto God. He was very God, and he was very man. The Apostles' Creed says "born of the Virgin Mary," emphasizing born far more than Virgin, to counteract the Gnostics who thought God could not be anything other than spirit. The same Creed also says "God, the Father, Almighty, Maker of Heaven and Earth." The emphasis is that this is the good earth. God made it. Jesus was incarnate in it. God loves it. "God so loved the world" is John's answer to the Gnostics. Also, "the resurrection of the body" in this creed emphasizes man is one whole, not a dualistic body and spirit.
4. Having said in the Nicene creed that God and Christ were of the same substance, this pressed Christians to define the Trinity more sharply. Jews, Muslims, and Unitarians razz Christians about having three Gods. This is shallow. The "God in three persons" must be understood in terms of the Latin word *persona* meaning a "mask" as

in Greek drama. God shows three elements of God's being to man in Father, Son, and Holy Spirit.

Augustine sought for adequate, meaningful symbols for these three. He spoke of lover, love, loved, which I think is not as good as another: "memory, understanding, will." God, as Creator-Sustainer, as Redeemer, and as Ever-present love, are elements of the Christian's awareness of God that the Trinity communicates, though it has never been defined in detail in a creed. Of course, the Disciples have said weakly, "We are neither trinitarian, nor unitarian."

The problem of how Jesus could be both human and divine led to a strange doctrine called Apollinarianism to the effect that "the second person of the Trinity took the place of the physical personality of Jesus, but it was his body." Nestorianism argued against Apollinarianism. Jesus, the man, had two natures, human and divine. The human Jesus gave himself over completely to the divine so that he achieved moral unity. It seems to leave him with a split personality. It was never accepted officially. The Council of Chalcedon declared him fully human and fully divine. Tillich uses the Nestorian idea. Jesus was completely loyal to the depths of his being and thus to God, and God in the resurrection experience makes it clear to believers that Jesus is the Christ, the revelation of God's nature and will for man.

5. Augustine had a depth in psychology 1,500 years ahead of his time. In *Confessions* he analyzes the depths of his own involvement with his mistress and with the flight from God's claims. As in the original sin, man seeks pridefully to fulfill his own desires. Adam was free; he had everything in Eden. But he desired one more thing; he desired freedom from God. He resented his dependence on God and wished to take the place of God. This is pride. Man's refusal to take his rightful place as creature leads him to seek to be equal with God his Creator.

The result was concupiscence, the unrestrained lust after the things of this world. Greed, robbery, murder, sensuality, and selfishness naturally follow. Thus far, we can agree, possibly, with Augustine. He says that the sin of concupiscence is passed on to all men because they can be born in no other way than through sexual union, and this union itself is evil, though necessary to life, and thus all men are born in sin.

6. Predestination never became orthodox for all Christians, but Calvin picked it up from Paul and Augustine. For both Augustine and Calvin, the center of theology is God, not man. Man does not earn God's grace. Grace is a free gift. For Calvin, faith in man was faith in a bruised and broken reed. Faith in Almighty God, as our Trustworthy Helper amid futile strife, was man's only real hope. The doctrine of predestination acknowledges man's dependence, God's power, and man's need to cast himself upon God, in trust and faith, and then to thank God for the capacity to trust and to have faith.
7. Sinful man breaks fellowship with God and fellow man. Christianity is the only religion that teaches that God has performed the atoning work. Through Jesus, he has brought man back into fellowship.

In the beginning, Christian Orthodoxy held that God has performed a sacrifice in the crucifixion that atoned for man's sins and restored man to fellowship with God. There are three classical forms of this idea. First, the primitive doctrine is that man sinned, and Satan gained their souls. God made a bargain with Satan: he would give Satan the soul of Jesus, even though Satan didn't deserve him, if Satan would release the souls of men who accepted Jesus. Satan agreed, thinking that Jesus was only a good man. When he received Jesus, he found that he could not hold him, for Jesus was the Son of God. Satan ended up with neither the souls of those who accepted Christ, nor Christ himself. The only continuing value of this idea is that evil tricks itself. Hitler was an example.

In the eleventh century, two new modifications were suggested. Anselm said that man owed obedience to God, but man had failed to obey God. Hence, he fell into debt to God and dishonored God. To clear God's honor (a feudal concept), either the debt must be paid, or Man must be punished. God did not want to punish man eternally, for his purpose in creating man was to have fellowship with him. Man could not give God satisfaction since man owed God perfect obedience to begin with. If God simply forgot the debt, his honor would be despoiled, and his prestige and moral order weakened. Man owed the debt, but only God could pay it. So God sent the God-man, Jesus. Because he was God, he was adequate to the debt. Because he was man, he could pay it for his fellow man.

Jesus did not deserve to die, since he was sinless. When Jesus, the sinless, gave himself up for sinful man, the debt was paid, God's honor was vindicated, so God could forgive those who, through faith, claimed the substitutionary sacrifice of Jesus. The value is that forgiveness is costly.

The third and liberal view comes from Abelard. There was nothing on God's side that made forgiveness impossible (which differs from Anselm). You cannot forgive a man who does not want to be forgiven. Forgiveness means restoration of a broken fellowship. So God acted. He sent his Son to suffer and die for man as a manifestation of God's great love.

When men see this, at least the elect are moved to shame and repent; so God is able to forgive them. The value is that in the death of Christ, we see the love of God in such a way that we are moved to repent. Abelard emphasizes that Christ's sacrifice moves man to repent.

II. The Threat to Orthodoxy: Rationalism and Romanticism

The theme is Protestant thought; so we are not treating Thomas Aquinas. The Renaissance phenomenon dates to the thirteenth century. It was the result of Crusades bringing languages and documents back to Europe. The Renaissance spirit was Greek: rational, man-centered, this world instead of heaven. Its interest in religion was ethical. It was also interested in restoring the original manuscripts of the Bible as well as Greek classics. Erasmus's publication of an improved Greek New Testament text that exposed inadequacies in the Vulgate caused a furor in the Church, but Luther in translating the Bible made use of Renaissance scholarship.

The eighteenth century's rationalism, called the "age of enlightenment," can be thought of as bringing strong secular blows against orthodoxy. Man's hope was thought to be in reason, in politics, in freedom, in ordering his life on earth through his rational use of freedom in political and economic life.

Some of the great rationalists, like John Locke, were strong opponents of atheism. The rationalists like Locke and Kant wanted a religion within the bounds of reason only. Immanuel Kant (1724–1804), in pursuit of knowledge by "pure reason," found the Themistic five "proofs" for the existence of God which were based on Aristotle's thought, to be inadequate. All knowledge is temporal through and through. Because all knowledge is based on man's experience, time and space are dimensions of experience. They are not absolutes. If time and space are not absolutes, then God must not be absolute. God, the ultimate being, must be temporal since God cannot be "proven" by pure reason.

In terms of practical reason, man must project to the universal level. There he needs a vision of God as the Ultimate End, the Ultimate Good.

Man must give himself to the highest universal good, as unto God, and expect immortality based on commitment to this. So act as to rule your action and universal maxim. But, of course, this is hardly the God of orthodoxy, as Hordern says.

Furthermore, eighteenth century rationalism was developed by a Scottish philosopher named David Hume (1711–76) who attacked orthodoxy at the vulnerable point of its emphasis on miracles. He did not argue that miracles were impossible, but that they were improbable. It became next to impossible for Orthodoxy to "prove" the truth of the faith by pointing to the miracles.

The rationalists were concerned about evil but were opposed to any doctrine of original sin. Man's rational choice of evil was the sin, and man's mind was not corrupt. It was man's hope, so they sought the cause of evil in ignorance, or in lack of discipline.

The struggle between science and religion began with the Copernican revolution, which proved mathematically that the earth moves around the sun and not the sun around the earth. Later the Newtonian modification that even the solar system is not the center of the universe shook traditional theology to its foundations. Man had to shift from the teleological way of understanding nature or quizzing it, to the mathematical way or physical way. God could be seen perhaps as a great Mathematician, but not very well as a loving Father, because there didn't seem to be any preference on his part for this tiny ball, the Earth. This type of thought is still developing, as in Fred Hoyle's recent book on the expanding universe, showing that the Crab Nebula has expanded constantly since first careful observations in 1054.

Add to this finitizing of man by physics and astronomy, the animalization of man by Darwin, the materialization of man's motivations by Marx, and the sexualization of man's motivations by Freud, and you see four very basic reasons why, though man has in one sense become his own god, one says there is no god except the gods men set up by reason. At the same time, man has become disillusioned with himself, and his universe has seemed meaningless. He is led to despair because there is no ultimate God who guarantees the victory of the moral values he once thought to be revealed by God, guaranteed by his work in nature and beyond nature.

In Darwin's careful work in *The Voyage of the Beagle*, wherein he observed myriads of species and phyla and classified them, in his *Origin of the Species* wherein he projected the theory of evolutionary process in the development of species, and in his theory of the survival of the fittest, the law of the jungle seemed to take over again. Man seemed puny against brutality. Why develop the sensitivity of morality and religious faith when the brutal superman type won out in existence.

However, this was not exactly what Darwin meant. The "fittest to survive" were not necessarily the largest, witness the demise of the dinosaurs. Intelligence was an adaptation process, a sort of protective coloration to enable survival.

Also, in the nineteenth century and into the twentieth, Sigmund Freud developed an elaborate theory of man's rationalization process so that the good word of the 1700s becomes the bad word of the 1900s. Man's rationalization of his subconscious and inadmissible wishes is a deep, dark mystery, in which man's emotional and libidinal drives coerce his reason and cause him to think what he wants to think. Particularly in a patriarchal culture, the benevolent father image is desired to bless rather than to threaten, and the whole elaborate development of Jewish and Christian theology is a wish-fulfillment, a rationalization. Religion is an escape into a dream world, a flight from reality. It is used, much as Kant said it should be used, to bless a moral order that does violence to the individual. The sexual desires especially, but also many other natural desires, are suppressed and sublimated, and a guilt feeling arises which causes all kinds of havoc in personality.

Psychoanalysis was Freud's answer to this problem. Let the individual dredge up out of the depths of his being his desires that he had suppressed, look at them, in many cases express them, and the guilt feeling will disappear. Rationalism and Freudianism have had enough influence on Christian thought that liberals and even some neo-orthodox speak more of fulfillment than of salvation. Harry Emerson Fosdick summed this up by saying: "Man no longer desired to die and go to heaven. He wanted to live a hundred years and see what new wonders the inventive genius of man would bring forth."

Thus, the impact of philosophy, physics, math, and psychology had proven terribly revolutionary for man and his theology. Now come Economics and Sociology and the picture of man as merely the product of socio-economic forces. Karl Marx, another nineteenth century mind, pictured man's motives as primarily materialistic. He developed in *Das*

Kapital a theory that acknowledged this and set an economic production unit as basic in establishing an economic democracy which he called the dictatorship of the proletariat. All capital gains made by profit reinvested that did not really represent human productive capacity, mental or physical, was invalid capitalistic profiteering. The leisure class, by keeping wages low and profits high, worked the capitalistic slaves to death. Religion was the opiate of these common people, employed consciously by the profiteers to keep the masses by promising them "pie in the sky when they die."

Religion was used to keep people conservative in all things, to bless the present status-quo of society, and to create sanctions for the present and fear of change to a new order. Thus, "come the revolution" there will be an atheistic society in which the superstition of religion will be ridiculed into nonexistence, and a stage in man's evolution toward a fully rational being will have been passed.

While these secular minds, growing out of the Renaissance, were threatening the faith from without, there were related threats from within the church. First, the Reformation itself was a tremendous threat to Roman Catholicism. Its emphasis on the priesthood of all believers was anarchic, scandalous. Authority would disappear. True, Protestantism needed an authority. so they appealed to the Bible as the authority, to the extent that it began to be called the "paper pope" of Protestantism.

The separation of the church from the state, the kindred rise of the merchant class, the development of democracy, and the need for strong taboos to responsibility led to four types of Protestant response:

a. Lutheranism with its separation of Church and State, or Church dependent on the State, with the Church preserving for itself only the area of "salvation" into another life, otherwise keeping its hands pretty much off of state ethics (witness the Hitler fiasco).
b. Calvinism, wherein the Church leader is the dominant figure in a republican state. Our New England colonies were patterned after Geneva.
c. Anglicanism, where a modified Roman Catholicism acknowledges the head of the State as the head of the Church.
d. The sectarian reaction from the Quaker "inner light" to Unitarian Deism, the latter growing out of Socinianism (1600ff).
e. The Socinians and later Unitarians argue that religion must be rational and free from a reliance on claims to revelation as au-

thoritative. The Deists like Herbert of Cherbury (1648), Thomas Paine, Emerson, Channing, et. al., who background our Unitarians, affirmed:

(1) God can be proven to exist by the world's need for a creator (this is a resurrection of Aristotle-Aquinas' Prime Mover and First Cause arguments in a new form).
(2) Such a God deserves the worship and obedience of man. This means man must live ethically (rationally) to the glory of God.
(3) When we fail to do this, we must repent and try again.
(4) Since this life does not adequately regard the righteous and punish the evil, there must be another life in which accounts are straightened out.

This religion has never reached the common man; it was a religion for intellectuals only.

Comparative Religion questioned the uniqueness of Christianity. Strauss and Schweitzer, et.al., established the historicity of Jesus but found him an eschatologist. Friederich Schleiermacher (1788–1834) spoke in a milieu of Romanticism (feeling) replacing Rationalism. He insisted that the great debates over proofs of God, the authority of Scriptures, miracles, and the like, were all on the outside fringe of religion. The heart of religion was and always had been "feeling," not rational proofs. God, to the religious man, is not a theory devised to explain the universe. God is an "experience," a living reality.

Religion is based on feeling or "intuition." Schleiermacher analyzed this feeling in terms of "Dependence" upon the universe. Every man must come to terms with his dependence upon the universe, the source of his individual being. Not only religion, but also great art and literature acknowledge man's dependence upon the universe. This is the base of all religion, but creeds, etc. have obscured it with minutiae of priestly ritual. Religion is essentially ethical for Schleiermacher.

We need the forms of religion to remind us of this, but if the forms become ultimate and obscure this basic fact, we must have a fresh vision of our basic ethical insights. Sin occurs when man isolates self from fellow man and ultimately from God, or the universe. Selfishness is sin. The misery of man under these circumstances is proof of it. Losing self in service of God and others is the only answer to sin. God sent Jesus Christ as the Mediator to restore separated man. Jesus is the real miracle, not the Virgin Birth. Jesus, as the God-filled man, can communicate complete obedience to committed man. In Schleiermacher, the center of religion shifts from the Bible to the believer. The criticized Bible speaks more clearly to the informed, committed believer.

Albrecht Ritschl (1822–89) continued this development. He is the father of the Social Gospel in Europe. His emphases were practical. The individual asks: "What must I do to be saved?" not in heaven but in this life. How can I be saved from sin, selfishness, fear, guilt? Ritschl emphasizes man's own sin in contrast with Augustine's "original sin."

Science tells us the facts, but religion weighs these facts and makes value judgments, which empowers us to act in terms of the value judgments made. For Ritschl, God is not known intuitively as God is for Schleiermacher. Nor is God known rationally, as with the Deists. God is necessary to postulate an explanation of the sense of worth or value that man has, somewhat like Kant's ideas.

The conflict between religion and science begins when religion tries to make statements of fact, or when science tries to make value judgements, such as, "Because man evolved from the lower animals, man is worth more than the lower animals." Religion and science are two basically different, yet interrelated approaches to reality. Religion is more subjective; science is more objective.

III. Liberalism and Neoliberalism: Attempts to Relate Christian Revelation to the Impact of Nationalism

Liberalism is sometimes called "modernism." It represents "liberation" and progressive adjustment to new depths of understanding. Related to the philosophical idealism of Royce and Hegel, it assumed the ultimate rationality of Creation, and thus that God was some form of rationality of creation, often called Mind. Like the Greeks, particularly Plato, the idealist sees as man's goal to use his God-given mind to see the essence of reality, through application of science and reason to all matters.

While trusting Mind to discover Truth, and God is Truth, the liberal is quite tolerant. Minds may differ but will ultimately agree, corrected by ultimate Truth-reality. The idealist-modernist is primarily optimistic.

Liberals, modernizing, say the world has changed drastically since the Bible and creeds were written. We have to re-think and re-state Christianity in thought-forms that are meaningful to the modern mind. Harry

Emerson Fosdick put it this way: "abiding experiences and changing categories." We must not forget the abiding experience of man's dependence upon a creative God, who is friendly and loving, but he need not be conceived in anthropomorphic terms.

Evil is threatening but need not be personalized as the Devil. Judgment is real but need not be motivated by fear of a literal burning hell. Heaven is symbolic of enduring goodness but need not be conceived as an actual space entity with golden streets and pearly gates. God is reality but need not be conceived as an elderly grandpa with a long white beard sitting on a throne with 144 angels around him, as in Revelation. God will triumph over evil, but eschatology need not be in the form of a literal Second Coming.

Fundamentalism emphasized the continuity of literalism. Fundamentalists believe in the verbal inspiration of Scripture. E. J. Carnell, of Fuller Seminary, a graduate of Wheaton College, is their best spokesman now. He is wooden in his Biblical literalism. He has a PhD from Harvard. Billy Graham is one of this type. Even Chad Walsh says the Anglican Church ought to open conversations with this type of Fundamentalist.

Fundamentalism is the faith by which millions of Americans really live. Actually, many liberal preachers use the Bible somewhat like a fundamentalist—leaving that impression with their listeners. They quote Scripture and thus cinch an argument, whether their argument is reasonable or not.

For fundamentalists, the Virgin Birth is essential to "prove" the supernature of God, and the Divinity of Christ as an authoritative messenger from the supernatural God. For the liberal, there is something divine in the birth of every child, and God comes to man in each of these events. Christ's birth is thus a symbol of the creativity of birth itself.

The main ideas of liberalism are the immanence of God and the transcendence of God. Liberalism is not a complete capitulation to Idealism. Liberals find God in the whole of life and not just a few spectacular events. Liberals deny that some things are caused by natural forces and others by supernatural forces. God works in and through all that happens or is.

Many liberals retained their faith in the transcendence of God. Their statement of it was usually hazy. Rufus Jones, the Quaker mystic, says God is Spirit; and it is the essence of spirit, even in the form of spirit we find in man, to transcend itself. So, an immanent Spiritual God must transcend the space-time universe. "He is more than the universe, but he is not basically separated from it."

Evolution is difficult to swallow with this kind of conception. So is Freudian behaviorism, and economic materialism is an anathema. The liberal's adjustment was essentially "Some call it evolution, and others call it God." In Hegel's thought, the thesis, antithesis, synthesis dialectic leads ultimately to a Synthesis in Absolute Spirit.

For the liberal, God becomes humanized, not that God is a mere human being. God is not anthropomorphic, as in the ancient religions of the early Old Testament that have been ridiculed as unworthy of belief by enlightened man. Liberals require that God be at least as Good as a good man. "Having been raised on a grim creed of Calvinistic determination, I was relieved to find that God could be at least as good as some of the elders of our church."

So, the "Kingdom of God" with its assumption of the absoluteness of God's will threatened some liberals. They really preferred to talk about the "Democracy of God." Some assume that man can demand certain "inalienable rights" from God! (It is primarily at this point that Neo-orthodoxy takes issue!)

An important form of liberalism is process theology (H. N. Wieman), which we will treat more fully in a moment, but suffice it to say here: "If God is found in (immanentism) world process, we do not need special acts of divine revelation." (Tillich tries to take account of this on his liberal side.) Man, at his best, is a revelation of God and his purposes. All liberals agree that revelation must be treated by reason and experience.

The liberal welcomed "higher criticism" of the Bible, which showed God's "progressive revelation" as an evolutionary process. Some liberals consider Jesus as divine revelation of God, others consider him "one of the great leaders" of religious and ethical thought. At this point, there is great disagreement among liberals. William Adams Brown says Jesus has been authoritative for the Christian in three ways: Jesus is the clearest illustration of "The Way" Christians should live. Jesus exemplifies the spirit of love and self-sacrifice that is creative of the good society. Jesus was flooded with divine insight, fortitude, and love at every crucial period, including the cross, which shows that all men who live this way can count on God's love and victorious power.

Liberals joined gladly in search for the historical Jesus and consider Paul the culprit for hiding Jesus behind a smokescreen of theology. Jesus represented the simple Galilean prophet. "Christ" represented the corruption of this figure by the mind of Paul. As to what kind of man this historical Jesus was, it was generally agreed that as Harnack indicated: "He was a simple Galilean ethical teacher, whose emphasis can be summed up in the term 'Fatherhood of God and brotherhood of man.'"

The fundamentalists cried in alarm that the liberals were losing Jesus. The liberals replied they were rediscovering Jesus. (Note Jack Finegan's recent book of sermons.) The liberal said: "all the fundamentalist has is the Jesus of the cradle, cross, and tomb. The fundamentalist was concerned with theological doctrine to the exclusion of following Jesus' teachings" (86). The liberal said: "Jesus was one with God in that he completely lived the will of God in all things," rather than the Nicene Creed's emphasis that Jesus was of the same substance with God.

Fundamentalists charged that liberals were unrealistic about Sin. Liberals countered that concern with the total depravity of man makes the individual so hopeless he will give up, but concern with the more recent sins of the fathers and of the self that can be corrected is creative. The liberal has less to say about sin in general and more about sins in particular.

Ethics is a primary concern of liberals. Liberals like E. S. Brightman and H. N. Wieman were more concerned to be philosophers than theologians. If revelation is denied, there is no realm of reality that cannot be handled by reason, according to Tillich on philosophical theology.

Rauschenbusch in the Social Gospel reflects on the impact of "higher criticism" in sociology and economics and reaches back to the prophets. He considers Jesus a prophet, skips Paul and the early church for the most part, except to note the new community that was developing in the early church "had all things in common." His primary concern was that the "Kingdom of God" was in conflict with the "Kingdom of Evil." Catholicism had a social gospel, which is found in Medieval Society. Calvinism influenced nations and affected the development of democracy.

The Reformation was concerned about establishing a Christian social order. The insights of social psychology are included in Rauschenbusch's thinking. He sees that "there is no use trying to save individuals out of a society by preaching a kind of fire insurance gospel. The whole of society must be saved. Since man is molded by his environment, a corrupt society corrupts man."

What Jesus meant by "Kingdom of God" was not "afterlife" or a "society on earth set up by a superman in the Second Coming." Jesus did mean "that society on earth in which men are brothers, living in cooperation, love, and justice together." This ideal society is one that man himself, with the help of God, can build.

God progressively leads man on in the development of this Kingdom on earth. Members of the Church are the forward leaders. Rauschenbusch was aware of a "Kingdom of Evil," social forces organized against such progressive development, like Governor Faubus in Little Rock. Rauschenbusch did not identify fully with Socialism or the New Deal or any particular program, but many Christians did. Some identified with communism in its earlier, more idealistic days, but they are deeply chagrined and disillusioned now. Liberals tend toward pacificism, labor justice, racial justice, slum clearance, projects like Hull House, etc.

Naturalism, as described by H. N. Wieman, takes a non-transcendent view of God. It focuses on the natural, scientific, and rational. Creativity comes in two forms. For society, it is in the emergence of new values, the integration with old values, the expansion of the appreciable world, and the widening and deepening of the sense of community. For the person, creativity manifests as the integrated self, shaken by experience of reality, then reintegrated; action to give self to others in commitment; and the emergence of new relationships of self to others.

Naturalism requires an all-out commitment of self to apply new knowledge for the welfare of all. There is a process of reward and judgment in nature that checks us and from which we can learn.

IV. Neo-Orthodox Reaction Against Liberalism: Kierkegaard, Barth, Brunner, Niebuhr

To over-simplify, natural theology or liberalism speaks of man's search for God. Neo-orthodoxy speaks of God's search for man. Liberals used the method of reason and experience to emphasize natural theology as the only theology. Neo-liberalism (Dan Williams, for example) represents a new trend to give theology a new hearing without abandoning natural theology. Neo-orthodoxy repudiates natural theology almost completely, especially Kierkegaard and Karl Barth.

Soren Kierkegaard (1813–55) was an Existentialist, which he described as "existence as it is existed by an existent" or "true thought must begin with the fact of a concrete man in a concrete situation." "Abstract truths about men might be true of all men in general, but they would describe no man in particular." Whereas Descartes started his system alone, withdrawn from life, saying "I think, therefore I am," Kierkegaard begins with man as he exists in relation to God, the universe, and other men. He revolted against abstract thought in philosophy and religion. The aim of true thought is to bring man to commit himself to a way of life to answer the question, "What ought I to do?" It is an either/or decision that involves aloneness with God and God's will to be used by Him to bless man.

In objective thought we think coldly and rationally of objects separate from ourselves. We are not vitally concerned with them in our whole being. But it degrades God and man to make them objects. God is subject and not object. When man acts in response to God, he is subject and not object. Man is a self, not a thing. Thus, man must be seen as an individual, not en masse. Kierkegaard was reacting against Hegel primarily, but he enabled Barth's reaction against the Social Gospel. Man can cease to be truly human by conformity to the crowd, by becoming a mere cog in a wheel. Existentialism fights to preserve man as "The Single One" who makes his own decisions in concrete situations with integrity. The individual should capitulate neither to State nor Church, but only to God. Yet, God does not ask for capitulation, but for realization.

What does it mean to be Christian? Most Christians are only nominal Christians. Kierkegaard says we are not saved (i.e. we do not become Christian and fully human) by coming to know something that we did not know before. Rather, we are saved by the transformation of our existence through divine grace. The Gospel is not a new philosophy; it is the act of God which comes to solve the problem of man's despair. Man does not become a Christian. He simply strives to become one.

Man's reason comes up against a boundary it cannot penetrate. The reason which can prove things in science is incapable of using the same methods to understand God, for God can never be just an object whose existence can be proved or disproved. When God is known, he appears paradoxical to our reason. The God that men claim to find in their philosophies is just an image of themselves. The real God can only be found insofar as he reveals himself—makes himself known. But God makes himself known only to faith. Faith is a leap into the unknown, involving trust. But man never makes this leap as long as he thinks he can save himself.

It is only when he is in despair about himself and his adequacy by reason to fathom life (*The Razor's Edge* made famous by Somerset

Maugham) that he will grasp the salvation that God offers. Man can flee from God in sensuous eating, drinking, making merry. But as soon as he takes seriously the ethical life, he will see his inadequacy, be ridden with anxiety and brought to despair about his condition, and reach out toward God in trust.

Man's doubt is never completely overcome, but in the leap of faith where he chooses to follow Christ, man finds the only significant certainty possible for him—betting one's life on the God in Jesus Christ. Such faith is not dogma, but a state of being, an all-out whole-being commitment of self in constant either/or choices for Christ or against him.

Kierkegaard's God is always transcendent, not over against the immanent God of the liberals, but over against the individual man, separated from God by his sin. Man cannot lift himself to God; God must come to man. Even when man leaps in faith, God must act. Christ is the picture of the God who acts in man's behalf—reaching toward man through the tragic depths of sin and estrangement.

Karl Barth (1886–1968) began as a liberal, social gospel theologian but shifted during World War I. He published *Romerbrief* in 1919 and became head of a theological movement. Christianity can be saved only if it disassociates itself from a dying culture. This is a time of *krisis,* or crisis-theology. Man must make decisions in daily life, but they are not simply between man and man. God is always there. God makes a crisis; then man must choose between man's way and God's way.

Barth criticizes liberalism because the liberal starts with himself, building his *weltanshaung* around man. Using reason, natural theology, and mystical experience, he builds a system in which God can be found. But the God found there is merely a pale reflection of ourselves. Secondly, the liberal is optimistic. He forgets he is part of a dying culture (European pessimism). Instead of this man-centered faith, we need to be confronted to the point of crisis so we will no longer trust our power and our reason, but trust God, and wait for him to speak to us.

Preaching must no longer appeal to the strength of men with a "push-em-up" attitude, but to confront them with reality and show them their helplessness and God's power revealed in Christ. Man lives in Time; God lives in Eternity. God is *Totalite Aliter* and cannot be known by an analogy with anything we possess or are.

Since God is Totally Other, God's relation to man cannot be expressed in neatly logical terms, but only in paradoxical statements, such as: Jesus is both God and man; "In revelation God is both revealed and hidden." When Barth calls God "Wholly Other," he is emphasizing that God is not just idealized man, or "the spirit of humanity" or "the value-producing aspect of the universe." God exists independently of man and the world. Barth, like Kierkegaard, says God is transcendent, not immanent.

Nevertheless, he says God is at work in the world, and he denies any division between sacred and secular. God works in all events. He works to reveal himself as transcendently Other. The gulf or "abyss" between man and God is a gulf dug by man's sin.

When man seeks for a God, it is always an idol of his own making. It is only through God's search for man that man can have communion with God. Man can never have any kind of control over God. God is free, like the wind, as Jesus tells the Sanhedrin member, Nicodemus. The gulf has been bridged by God in Christ. Religions often veil God instead of revealing Him. The early Christians were called atheists because they destroyed the man-made gods of their time and were killed by the emperor-worshipping Romans and the Yhwh-worshipping Jews. Christians have also created gods, instead of listening to God.

Since God is this living, unpredictable God, we must not identify the words of the Bible with the Word of God. We have made the Bible a paper pope. The words of the Bible and Jesus are tokens. One may look at both without being encountered by God. However, the "Word within the Word" comes to us through these tokens. Some days, as we read or look at some aspect of Jesus, the word may come alive to us. Thus, the word is always spoken to a particular person in a particular situation. The Christian revelation is not like a proposition of logic which is unchangeably true to all persons in all times and places.

History is the story of man's sin and, thus, of separation from God. God cannot be found in nature because sin blinds man's eyes to God's presence in his creation. But Grace is more abundant than sin! Sin has already been overcome and defeated by Christ. The Christian knows the victory of God forgiving sin. Yet, Barth speaks little of new moral strength which enables the Christian to live without sin. Barth makes extreme statements, such as "Faith takes reason by the throat and strangles the brute." He wants man to use reason but also to recognize its corruption. By reason, man finds the God he wants to find, not the God who really is. Secondly, the God who reveals self as an "I" to a "Thou," not as the "Supreme Being" of philosophy, forces man to decide and act.

Originally, Barth said it is not the Christian's role to reform society, and he tried to be oblivious to Hitler. However, he had to flee and told his fellow Christians to take to the catacombs rather than capitulate to Hitler. Since then, he has taken essentially Niebuhr's position that the perfect social order can't be built and God's full blessing cannot be asked on any social order; nevertheless, the Christian must help build the best possible social order.

Regarding eschatology, Barth thinks we are living at the end of an age. This time must be taken up into eternity. He speaks often of the Second Coming. For him, the Second Coming is not the same as for the fundamentalists. It is like the resurrection—visible only to the eyes of the faithful. It is the victory that God brings over the old order as a new one is born. The Christian must live in the world and use force and coercion as wisely as possible, though this is unchristian, because the Kingdom has not come. The Christian must serve the state, but it is spiritually dangerous because it is implicit disloyalty to God. This is further evidence of the present sinful state of man. Our only hope is in Christ, who promises that God may yet do another deed—the Second Coming—as miraculous and redemptive as the deed he did in Christ. In this hope we live.

Emil Brunner (1889–1966) shared Barth's ideas until the 1930s, when they sharply disagreed on the issue of natural theology. Brunner denied that the image of God in man had been completely lost through sin, as Barth said it had. Brunner believed there was some revelation of God, outside the Bible, in nature. He charged that Barth leaves no room for the new nature of the redeemed man to grow out of the old nature. Barth responded: "Nein!"

Brunner is no liberal. Man does have a natural knowledge of God, but it is always blurred and distorted by the sinfulness of man. In this sense, man's natural knowledge of God cannot save man. Both Barth and Brunner agree that Scripture is the only source of knowledge about God. Brunner says Scripture is the primary criterion by which we can judge the truth of knowledge about God that arises elsewhere.

Barth cannot even talk with a philosopher because there is nothing in common between revelation and natural reason. Brunner, though, can recognize truth in the philosopher, atheist, or member of a non-Christian religion and thereby enter in meaningful debate with him. Brunner will say the other man has some knowledge of God, but it is incomplete and from this point a meaningful discussion can ensue. Brunner accepts

Augustine's analysis of original sin (concupiscence), but denies his idea that it is inherited. Sin arises out of free decision. Original sin is a result of man's choice, not his heredity. Man is created by God for a life to be lived in harmony with God, but instead he lives a life centered around himself. Man withdraws into his "I" castle and can only be brought out when God comes to him with love and, winning his confidence, overcomes his anxiety and enables him to give himself away.

Brunner uses Buber's "I and Thou" concept. The knowledge of God is to be contrasted sharply with "objective" knowledge. Objective knowledge has as its purpose to get power over something and to manipulate it. The known has no vital concern for the knower; there is no communion between knower and known. The primary form of objective knowledge is scientific knowledge of limited areas of manipulative reality.

Over against this objective knowledge is the "I-thou" relationship; it is not merely subjective. It is relational. It is intelligent and loving, empathetic identification of self with the other. By losing self, one finds self. This is the creative, redemptive relationship. Sin makes an "it" or a "thing" of a Thou. When we feel this Thou possibility in a relationship, we reveal the depths of self to another. There is now communion, and it changes a person to the depths of his being. We truly know God only in an I-Thou relationship, where we give or reveal the depths of self to God and God reveals the depths of God's self to us. We cannot manipulate, possess, or control God through saying mass, or paying tithes, or being baptized.

Revelation does not give some bits of knowledge about God. It is God giving God's self, and God can only give God's self in a Thou relationship. God can be revealed only to faith. Therefore, natural theology or philosophy can never give an adequate picture of God. In philosophy, God is an "it," a concept, a generalization, not a vital communion experience. When a philosophy class discusses the "proofs" for God, it may have a pleasant time and learn something about the use of logic, but it can learn nothing about the God whom Christians worship. God is always known as the Lord of one's life. God breaks the laws of logic and justice as God reveals God's forgiving I-Thou nature and relationship in the Christ event.

In the *Divine Imperative*, Brunner says man's "sense of ought" calls him to do what does not come naturally. Whence comes this sense of ought? What can "thou shalt" mean unless it come from God? And Kant's rational imperative is really colored by his Christian training. If we have no divine imperative, we can only say to Hitler: "I don't like you." The only authoritative ethic arises out of that man who is no longer self-centered because he knows God's love has lifted him out of himself. He lovingly obeys God's will. "Obedience is not the fruit of 'ought' but the free act of love. God does not give commands to slaves; he gives instructions to sons."

Society is organized in certain "orders of creation": State, family, Church. They give stability to society. But, though God-given, they are tainted with sin. A Christian judge may have to enforce unjust laws because legal order is a value. But he can also work for the reform of that law.

V. American Neo-Orthodoxy: The Boundary between Liberalism and Neo-Orthodoxy, Reinhold Niebuhr and Paul Tillich

Reinhold Niebuhr returned to orthodoxy, not fundamentalism, as more intellectually valid than liberalism to describe man's predicament and possibilities. He used the term "myth" to describe the relation of finite man to infinite God that cannot be expressed in any other way than myth. He thought that theology is an attempt to express the dimensions of depth in life. Myth is necessary. As examples, he spoke of the myth of creation, the myth of the fall, the myth of the Virgin Birth, and, in a sense, the myth of resurrection.

God is transcendent but also immanent and active in the world. Our earth-born and bound logic cannot speak of this except in myth. Myth is not a fairy tale but a profound truth. Fundamentalism takes the myths literally and thus enters conflict with science over evolution, in contrast to neo-orthodoxy.

Niebuhr criticizes both the anti-rationalists like Kierkegaard and Barth and the rationalists like Origen, Aquinas, and Wieman. If, on the one hand, revelation has nothing to do with what we know, how can we understand it? On the other hand, the rationalist who claims to know everything about everything and does not acknowledge the limitations of his knowledge and logic is dishonest. Life comes to us full of "paradoxes. Life is full of contradictions. Simple rational explanations are oversimplifications." Niebuhr has pointed at man's pride and over-reaching and recalled man to an appropriate humility but not servitude.

The necessity in natural order does not carry over to the historical order of man. Man has "freedom" and responsibility. Social sciences cannot predict events with the certitude that the physical sciences can. As we see in the depth of another being, as he reveals himself to us in events, qualities that surprise us, and develop a certain reverence or respect, so it is with God in history. Revelation is awareness of depth experiences with Reality, which are intimations that this world in its history points beyond itself. We cannot know this dimension of reality except as it is revealed to us. Christianity is based on the faith that God has spoken in the events of the Bible and particularly in the life of Jesus. This faith cannot be proved rationally. It can only be accepted with love, trust, and faith, like Aquinas; but this does not leave us helpless, as Barth thinks. Given the revelation and a faith-response, reason then can show that it gives a more adequate picture of reality than any alternative. He believes that the hypothesis of Biblical revelation is the most adequate explanation of depth in history.

Although Niebuhr emphasizes original sin, he does not believe that we inherit Adam's guilt, but it means that man does fall naturally and inevitably into the sin of claiming for himself and his interests more than their objective importance would warrant. Sin arises because man is capable of thought, dreams, morality, and the ability to stand outside himself and judge himself. The meaning of life is threatened by man's dependence, man's animal drives, and man's death. Man longs for perfect knowledge, freedom, behavior, justice, but what he attains is always less than these.

Because man is spiritual in that he can participate in God, the Infinite, to some extent, he needs to have and yearns for meaning in life. Yet, every meaning he finds is threatened because he is finite. His knowledge is limited, his integration of self is limited, and he dies. This dual nature of man leaves him split, torn, anxious, anxiety ridden.

To overcome his anxiety, man tries to grasp some ledge of security where he can hide safely from the vicissitudes of life. Sometimes, he seeks to affirm himself in sensuality: sexuality, many friends and popularity, conspicuous consumption. Other times he asserts himself in pride that is closely related: bragging about his accomplishments, or the institutions with which he is related, or the wealth he has, or the favor God has shown him; pride at the expense of others; refusing to recognize his limitations, his claims for himself what belongs to others or to God.

Thus, man is a sinner. This does not detract from man's basic dignity. It simply points to his responsibility. Only one who can choose to be something higher than an animal can be held responsible for behaving like an animal. Three forms of pride are pride of power, pride of knowledge and the failure to recognize relativities, and moral pride in which religion may lead men to confess their sins or to thank God that they are so virtuous.

In moral relativity, we are rarely faced with a clear good and a clear evil. Individual acts, though not perfect, can be conducted on a higher level than social acts. Institutions corrupt moral persons by forcing them to act as though an institutional decision (organization man) is completely good and no part evil. "My country right or wrong." Reforms are never made simply because they are right, but persons have to be shown some "profit" in it.

Thus, all our goodness is soiled slightly, like an old cabbage. We are all dependent on the forgiveness of God and of each other. Church must make decisions realistically and act realistically in the light of this.

Chapter 42

WHITEHEAD AND *PROCESS THEOLOGY*

First, one might say that process philosophy (as in Whitehead) is empirical. It recognizes that all we have to work with is the world and our actual experience of it.

Not only obvious objects like table, building, dog, but more subtle realities such as personality, and even a power hard to describe in detail, God, are all "actual entities," and they can be called "events or occasions." An event is always in process of change, of becoming or dying, of coming into being, progressing in being, falling away into concretion, or deadness. This is true of electrons, protons, atoms, worms, fish, frogs, dogs, cats, persons, and nations, but not of God.

We analyze reality in terms of events that may be complex or simple and actual occasions that are relatively simple. The asking of a question is an actual occasion, set in a larger occasion of a lecture, set in the larger occasion of a college term, set in a larger occasion of four years in college leading to a degree, set in a larger context of a whole life, set in a larger context of family, nation, and finally the life of God.

Every actual occasion and event can be analyzed from several different perspectives—physical, chemical-biological, psychological, sometimes mathematical, philosophical, theological. Philosophical and theological perspectives are the most inclusive.

Each event or actual occasion is a part of a series of past, present, and future. Its meaning can be declared only by some reference to past and future.

Beneath all this flux of change is Creativity—the endless coming into being of actual occasions and events. In Whitehead and Cobb, this is not God. This is the raw material of reality on which God works. Wieman uses the term "creativity" in a different way.

God is identifiable in our experience as a trinity of Primordial,

Consequent, and Subject-superject. The Primordial nature of God is almost like Creativity, but not quite. Wild creativity makes no distinction between a jungle and a garden, between normal cell growth and wild, cancerous cell growth, between the birth of billions of fish and fish eggs being destroyed by spilled oil. It is a growth process, but it makes no value judgments. God makes value judgments.

The Primordial nature of God is always struggling to inject the eternal forms into actual occasions, to make real the eternal in the temporal. Types of eternal forms are of the objective type, redness or roundness, or of the subjective type, beautiful, good, true. Both are responded to by sense-feelings, a feeling-awareness. Reason and emotion can be seen as a moving toward or a moving away.

The Consequent Nature of God is a catch-all that reckons with the fact of God remembering, taking into God's self the essence of all experience, and being shaped by it and responding to it.

The Subject-Superject nature of God refers to the fact that God enters as a subject with a purpose into every actual occasion and event. This is pan-en-theism, not pantheism, according to Hartshorne.

John Cobb (*Living Options in Protestant Theology*) and Charles Hartshorne (*A Natural Theology for Our Time*) say that a major reason for the theological confusion of our time is that the wedding between Jewish and Greek thought attempted in Christian orthodox theology never quite came off. The concepts of forms and substance in Greek thought plus the transcendental emphasis that pictured God as Perfect, Complete, Omnipotent, and often unloving, in the sense that he had no need of man's love, or man's goodness, was really alien to the God of the Bible who was deeply involved in give and take with his people and responsive both to their goodness and their evil, to their problems and their triumphs.

The God of the Bible is quite personal. The God of the Greeks was impersonal. The God of the Bible was responsive; God could "repent God's self" and make a covenant involving response from God's people. God was purposive in the sense that God was working out a kingdom in and among God's creatures, and men found fulfillment in responding to the God who cared for them both individually and as a people of God.

In no system of Christian theology is this element ever completely absent. One might think of it as the process of interaction between God and man, or the cooperation of God and man in the creation of the world, or the kingdom. Men are always pictured as being called to be co-laborers with God. However, God became ever more distant as men sought to "prove" his existence, to force the non-believer to believe.

Of course, the evidences or "proofs" for God's existence put forward by Thomas Aquinas (1225–74) have stood for centuries as important to those who do have Christian faith and seek a reason for the faith that is in them. But also, many have (especially among twentieth-century philosophers) held that Hume demolished them. They had been crumbling since the late Middle Ages.

As science developed, both Catholics and Protestants were blind to its implications, for the most part. Theologians continued to work with Greek philosophers, particularly Aristotle, to establish their natural theology. But the line between natural theology and revealed theology is always blurred. Usually, Christians take their stand in revealed theology to nature as understood by non-Christians and the secular community.

Both the Protestant and the Catholic theologians met a hardy adversary in David Hume (1711–76). This important Scotch philosopher transformed the concept of causation into "impressions" and associations. These fade off into mere ideas. They have no unity or coherence except by customary form of thought and association of ideas. Causation is regularity in the flow of impressions, a habit we expect to continue. This subjectivism, which continues its effect until today, denies that man can know an objective principle of causation, but it does not deny the objective reality of the object. We cannot infer a divine mind as the cause of the world order. Yet Hume was almost deterministic. Causality is inexplicable, but it apparently has absolute sway forbidding any freedom of choice or open alternatives. We can only work with probabilities.

We know no explanation for the orderliness we seem to experience. If there is a divine source that gives order, then the problem of evil is insoluble, for that source orders that too. There is empirically observable, limited goodness, so any deity presumed to exist would have to be limited in power. No alternative is suggested, save a crudely finite deity. Some might think that the deity we find in Wieman, and in different forms in Whitehead, Hartshorne, and their followers, is a development of this crude finite deity because this God is certainly not the Omnipotent God of Orthodoxy, or the eternal, perfect, impersonal God of the Greeks.

One other impact of Hume's thought that is relevant is that process theology is a natural theology with no place for miracles. Hume's argument against miracles can be found in Hume's *Enquiry Concerning Human Understanding.*

"A wise man proportions his belief to the evidence. . . . if his past experience provides uniform evidence of a regular happening, he assumes it to be natural law. . . if it does not, he tests it on the basis of probability as evidenced by tests or experiences. He speaks of a miracle as a 'violation of the laws of nature' and, as 'laws of nature' have been established from our experience, proof against a miracle is as entire as any argument from experience can possibly be imagined."

He concludes that there really are no miracles, because there is not to be found, in all history, any miracle attested to by a sufficient number of men of unquestioned good sense, education, and learning as to secure us against all delusion in themselves. We may observe in human nature a principle which delights in the surprise and wonder and awe and mystery of enlarging strange experiences to miraculous proportions to elicit the admiration of other gullible persons. Miracles abound chiefly among the ignorant and unlearned.

Having said these devastating things, Hume then says that faith cannot be established by reason, and those who seek to do so are enemies of the Christian religion. Mere reason is insufficient to convince us of its veracity, and whoever is moved by Faith to assent to it, is conscious of a continued miracle in his own person, which subverts all the principles of his understanding and gives him a determination to believe what is most contrary to custom and experience. This viewpoint is acceptable to Protestant thought, particularly to Karl Barth.

This subjectivism that Hume espoused was also espoused by Immanuel Kant. Hume had said at the conclusion of his *Enquiry on Human Understanding* that the existence of a being "can only be proved by arguments from its cause or its effect, and these arguments are founded entirely on experience. . . . If we reason *a priori*, anything may appear able to produce anything. The falling of a pebble may, for aught we know, extinguish the sun, or the wish of a man may control the orbit of the planets. . . . Divinity or theology, as it proves the existence of a Deity, and the immortality of souls, is composed partly of reasonings concerning particulars, partly concerning general facts. It has a foundation in reason so far as it is supported by experience. But its best and most solid foundation is faith and divine revelation. Morals and criticism are not so properly objects of the understanding as of taste and sentiment."

Immanuel Kant (1724–1804) pursued this idea further and more systematically. In his *Critique of Pure Reason*, he found that *a priori* proofs for God were indefensible. Science deals only with the world of phenomena. There is a dichotomy between phenomena and noumena, or appearance and reality. Kant agrees with Hume that this world consists entirely of the flow of experienced qualities that cannot, in themselves, explain or justify our ideas of substance and causality, and Kant argues that Hume should have seen that our ideas of space and time are also experienced in like manner. They are functions of mind in grasping events or objects in relations.

We gain knowledge not of objective reality but of contents of our own minds. Mind and sensation are posited as noumena, but of these noumenal realities nothing can be known except their existence. The categories of thought appropriate to phenomena cannot be applied, so metaphysics and cosmology are almost wholly eliminated, and their relevance to belief in God is ended, as Cobb has said. "Since natural theology has always consisted in metaphysical or cosmological arguments for the existence and nature of God, the Kantian argument confirmed Hume's refutation of metaphysical proofs." Philosophy must cease claiming its capacity to rationally order total reality. It must give up all attempts to penetrate behind appearances. So the impact of Kant was the elimination of natural theology; ultimately, he drove theology to extreme revelational bases of self-justification.

Kant didn't fully understand this and set out in his *Critique of Practical Reason* to say that the mind must seek a rational belief in God based on ethical experiences. Creative mind can see that man must so act as to rule his action by a universal maxim. This requires a belief in God and in immortality. Man seeks happiness. He cannot have it alone. He must seek rationally the universal well-being of all men. Kant, like the deists, rejected belief in revelation as a source of knowledge to guide our ethical behavior.

Hegel continued the attempt by reason to establish a religion without revelation. It became an absolute idealism that became a substitute for theology. It has a sense of flow about it. The dialectic of thesis, antithesis, and synthesis led to the absolute. Some sought to use it as a natural theology, but it was never successful. However, as the evolutionary theories of Darwin became known in the nineteenth century, some attempted to relate these and say that there is a creative force at work in the universe that transcends all Newtonian categories.

Certainly the impact of evolution, first in the biological sphere, then in the planetary, then in the sociological, and finally in practically all areas, was tremendous and finally forced the development of process theology as an explanation of the dynamic, changing character of reality as it is experienced by modern man.

One of the philosophic figures who tried to rethink all of man's understanding of reality in terms of evolution was Herbert Spencer (1820–1903). An English engineer, his work made no important continuing contribution to philosophy, though he enjoyed a great vogue in the late nineteenth and early twentieth century. He thought evolution arose from the principle of the conservation of energy. Thus, evolutionary progress was possible, and good is conserved. This is related to Darwin's concept of the survival of the fittest. Although Darwin, tutored in Christian concern for the weak, favored human charity, he felt that this was likely to delay the creation of the process of natural selection by which progress has been possible. Both he and Spencer accepted the ideas of laissez faire. Spencer thought that private enterprise in open competition, unhampered by government regulation, fostered human welfare, just as the stern disciplines of vegetable and animal natural competition for life fosters the survival of the fittest.

T. H. Huxley, taking issue with both Darwin and Spencer, held that valid ethical norms cannot be derived from evolution. In his *Evolution and Ethics* (1896), he rejected both evolutionary ethics and revealed religion. He said, "The practice of that which is ethically best—what we call goodness or virtue—involves a course of conduct which in all respects is opposed to that which leads to success in the cosmic struggle for existence. In thrusting aside or treading down all competitors, it requires that the individual shall not merely respect, but shall help his fellows; its influence is directed, not so much to the survival of the fittest, as to the fitting of as many as possible to survive. It repudiates the gladiatorial theory of existence."

Another figure in this philosophical line of development who had an important impact on the thinking of Wieman, was a brilliant French Jew, Henri Bergson, who lived from 1859 to 1941. In his *Creative Evolution*, he maintained that creative evolution is a process developing spontaneously under the guidance of a life-force that he called *élan vital* that is active within nature itself. He ascribed genetic variations not to chance or to divine influence but to an immanent creative urge striving toward higher forms. The life-force moves toward freedom and integration and is hindered by matter, which is deterministic and tends toward randomness. He therefore attacks what he calls mechanistic views of evolution, but he is equally emphatic in rejecting any idea of teleology, which postulates a fixed plan in the mind of God or in the vital force itself.

Bergson sees evolution as guided, but not completely controlled, novel and unpredictable, groping its way and modifying its course as it proceeds. Contrary to both natural and divine determination, the world is spontaneous and the future is open. Such purpose-impulse is a creative immanent force that transcends individuals, but it is not conscious and does not transcend nature. It pushes blindly along divergent lines, with no definable end in view. Problems recognized by later writers in Bergson's work are that the *e'lan vital* is a rather vague notion, his dichotomy of life and matter are inadequate—the vital force is working on matter, and overall, there is romantic intuitionism. But the enduring value of his work was his emphasis on creative, evolutionary change as characterizing the natural order.

In summary, Bergson moved away from a static view of absolute perfection of scholastic theology toward a God manifest in concrete events and in the intimate history of individuals and organisms. He plainly rejected the absolute deity of Aristotle for a dynamic personal God of love, and he rejected the *a priori* method for an empirical approach.

Bergson conceived of God not as complete but as growing. God is that in process which alters and in altering remains God's self. Being the subject of change, God endures and escapes the ravages of time. The vital impetus is God operative in evolution and present in all life and reaching a higher level of attainment of God's purposes in man. The reality of time, the waste in the onward movement of the vital impetus, the importance of freedom, novelty, and struggle, connect God with the thought of a limited but ever creative cosmic force.

Religion has had a conservative effect through customs, mores, taboos, and institutional forms, but it has also had a creative effect through its prophets and mystics who respond to God in ways which transcend these forms and enable a reformation of them.

Chapter 43

INTRODUCTION TO PAUL TILLICH

Paul Tillich was a citizen of Germany and served as a Chaplain in World War I. After the war, he returned to teaching but was forced to leave Germany in 1933 by Hitler. He came to the US under the sponsorship of Union Theological Seminary and the support of Richard and Reinhold Niebuhr.

Tillich conceived of Bridge Theology, the boundary situation. He worked on the bridge between Liberalism and Neo-orthodoxy, between Philosophical and Theological, secular and sacred, God is immanent and God is transcendent.

Ontology is the method of understanding reality. God is whatever is ultimate—the really real. God is being—the Ultimate Being. God is eternal subject, never object—no "itness" about God. To know an object is not to know God. The object is the creation, not the creator. Man is a participant with God in Being and therefore never an it, properly, but a Thou. The vocation of man is to have the "Courage to Be" in terms of the depths of being known to God. His knowledge is always finite, but it is the only knowledge available. All of man's knowledge is finite.

Man must not confuse himself as a finite being with God, an infinite being, but he must seek to respond with his whole-being, mind and emotion, to what he knows of God's Being. Within the categories of Space, Time, and Being, man must seek being and not non-being. This requires courage and that is very much like faith. But faith is as reasonable as man is capable of making it. The ontological elements of man's response are Individuation and Participation, Freedom and Destiny, and vitality (Dynamic) and Intentionality (Form).

Jesus, as man, was so transparently loyal to the claims of God that in the figure of Jesus as the Christ, men can look through him and see God, as through a wonderful transparent picture window. Jesusology is a sin, a finitude made infinite. Precisely because Jesus never made himself an end but always lived dynamically in all-out commitment to and trust in God—the God who really is God—he became the Christ, the picture of what God would have all men do and be, the one who reveals God's nature to man.

This is not to say that men can know nothing of God anywhere else. The Bible, understood as the scholars understand it, is the record of men committed to God and the creative, open-ended goodness that results. There is dynamic ontological faith present even in some secular movements and certainly in some other religious movements, as in Gandhi. But Christ is the definitive picture of whether a thought or movement is in touch with reality, transformative, redemptive.

Love, Power, and Justice is the book that speaks primarily to the issue of ethics. God is Being; as Being, God is Power and Vitality. Something of Being and, therefore, Power is present in every man. Where men form community, there is power, although it is always referable to the individual. Groups can corrupt power more easily than an individual. When this power is used immorally, God is known as justice in the social structure, and in the inner confusion of an individual. Justice is a corrective factor amid reality. It is the "Judgment of God."

Judgment even expresses something of the love of God. "The Shaking of the Foundations" is an essential ingredient before "The New Being" can emerge.

As in all systems of Christian ethics, Love is ultimate—Agape Love. Man never perfectly mirrors agape love. He is caught in eros love, but his eros love can be qualified and developed as he is aware of Agape love. He can be an honest member of a community of love and faith in all orders of existence: family, church, and state. The Kairos is the Greek New Testament term for crisis moments in history of individuals, groups, and states when judgment and new being are possible.

In such moments, man must open his mind and his emotions, his whole being, to the creative possibilities of goodness and live in all-out commitment. This is Faith. It is dynamic being: facts, reason, love, hope, and commitment to creative new possibilities, primarily Trust that the loving, forgiving, creative God known in Jesus Christ is sovereign Lord of history. The best picture of the kind of community that God is endeavoring to build on earth is "religious or Christian socialism." It is democratic, seeking the welfare of all, providing corrective institutions for the handicapped, obstructing the selfishness of the grasping, providing education and other media so all persons may fulfill themselves most completely.

He classified the church in three ways. Heteronomy is illustrated in Catholicism, Communism, and National Socialism. Autonomy characterizes rugged individualism and selfishness. Theonomy reflects Protestantism in its ideal form.

LOVE, POWER, AND JUSTICE by Paul Tillich
Lecture Notes

God is Ultimate Being, Ultimate Reality, Unconditional Being. God is the Power of Being.

Man has being. Man participates in the being of God as he is "grasped by the power of being and by conforming his being to his understanding of the Being of God." His existence is shaken in its foundations when he is separated from the center of his being. To understand his own being in depth and to be courageously loyal to the core of his own unique being is to have the basis for self-realization, to be grasped by the Power of Being.

It is to be neither autonomous ("self-sufficient finitude")—concerned only for self and one's own selfish or egocentric ends, nor to be heteronomous, that is to be merely a meaningless robot in conforming to various heteronomies such as society, church, school, government, organization, etc. It is to live theonomously, that is, to bring all of one's self and one's participation into conformity with the claims of God.

To be autonomous is to be alienated, to overdo individuation at the expense of participation. To be heteronomous is to overdo participation at the expense of individuation. To be theonomous is to balance these two in relating self to God, self, and other. It is to trust the power of God to work in and through the self and the group for creative purpose.

Does this mean, for example, to be a Capitalist, or a Socialist? Neither, necessarily. Ultimate Reality judges both. One is too individualistic; the other too heteronomous. The true or valid stance is theonomous.

God, as Ultimate Being, is Power. To be as a man or any being is to have power. The being of a man involves power. It is to demand lebenaraum, to push for food, housing, clothing, attention, and education, etc. Being is, in a sense, power. This power, in the raw, is egocentric. We push each other around.

When this is the case, we must qualify each other's power with justice. Justice is the act of love qualifying power for the best interests of the group—a form of heteronomy. Yet, higher than justice is love.

The basic power of being is rooted in love. Tillich says: "Life is being in actuality and love is the moving power of life. . . . Being is not actual without the love which drives everything that is towards everything else that is. In man's experience of love, the nature of life becomes manifest. Love is the drive towards the unity of the separated. Reunion presupposes separation of that which belongs essentially together" (Augustine: "Thou hast made us for thyself...").

"Estrangement presupposes original oneness." "Every self is self-related and a complete self is completely self-related. It is an independent centre, indivisible and impenetrable, and there is aptly called an individual. Love relates one individual centre to another individual centre and a depth of each self is found in relation to the depth centre of another person. Neither individual is destroyed or belittled in the process but is enhanced."

All forms of love are attempts of the individual to reunite the self with Being from whence he came, to whom he belongs, whether they be *Epithymia* (desire) or *Eros* (love). Self-love is a more elaborate involvement in physical love, as in libido (desire to rid self of tension), but this is a perversion resulting from an inadequate understanding of the nature of being and love, or a crippling childhood experience. There is *Epithymia* in every *eros*, but *eros* transcends *Epithymia. Eros* is in polar relation to *philis* (individuation and participation). Beings without a personal centre are without *eros*, though they are not without *Epithymia.*

He who cannot relate himself as an "I" to a "Thou" cannot relate himself to the true and the good or to the ground of being in which they are rooted. He who cannot love the friend cannot love the artistic expression of ultimate reality.

Philis is dependent on *eros.* If individuals do not have a healthy *eros* (self-love), they do not make healthy members of a group. And this *eros* is rooted in libido. "There is an element of libido even in the most spiritualized friendship. A saint without libido would cease to be a creature."

Agape is the transcendent revelation of love of God that is Ultimate and Unconditional and shows us the relativity of all lesser loves. *Philis* and *eros* are related to *Agape,* which is love cutting into love from beyond.

Agape runs in and through all these lesser loves. It is our necessity that we have the courage and discipline by use of our reason to allow *Agape* to structure all our lesser loves.

Ontology is the never-ending rational task of describing being as being, or the depths of being. Here at the heart of being, we find *Agape.* Ontology is the use of reason to organize the self, its emotions and habits, and responses and structure of being to allow this Power of Being to be fulfilled in our persons and our relations. "Ethics is the science of man's moral existence, asking for the roots of the moral imperative, the criteria of its validity, the source of its content, the forces of its realization."

Christian ethics consists in seeing in Jesus as the Christ, the man who was thus completely loyal, courageously, to the depths of his being, so that he was willing to go to the cross, to let the Ground of His Being, namely God, have his way completely. The Resurrection is the power of being, as The New Being, emerging out of this apparent tragedy to prove it no tragedy, but a victory, the victory of Being over non-being, of good over evil, love over hate.

"The power of being is real only in its actualizations." Here we are reminded of Thomas Aquinas's central emphasis that God is potentiality become act. The meaning in Tillich is that Ultimate Being or God is realizing himself in the act of finite being like ourselves when we are completely committed to the integrity of our own being.

God as Love and as Truth is known in the depth of our involvements which are always ethical; they always have the promise of new being, or the threat of non-being. We must say yes to being and no to non-being, yes to the light and no to the darkness, yes to Truth and no to error, yes to Theonomous reality and no to autonomy and heteronomy.

But we are never so alone in this. As Kierkegaard said, we are not only individuals but participants. We are social by nature, but if the self's autonomy is completely lost in a heteronomy, we have non-being. The validity of the self and the group is not lost, however, in theonomy. It is realized, fulfilled.

"One draws another power into oneself and is either strengthened or weakened by it. One throws the foreign power of being out or assimilates it completely. One transforms the resisting powers or one adapts oneself to them. One is absorbed by them and loses one's own power of being, or one grows together with them and increases their and one's own power of being. These processes are going on in every moment of life, in all relations of all beings. They go on between the powers of being we call nature, between man and nature, between man and man, between individuals and groups, between groups and groups."

"There is a hierarchical structure of life. The more centered a being is, the more power of being is embodied in it. The completely centered, self-related and self-aware being, man, has the greatest power of being. He has a world, not only an environment, and with it infinite potentialities of self-realization."

Each person has power. Power actualizes itself through force and compulsion. It is being actualizing itself over against the threat of non-being. If compulsion overreaches and becomes inappropriate, it has a backlash that undercuts the power of being.

Love is the foundation of power. It is being taking all the threats of non-being into itself, like Jesus taking the cross into himself, and God taking the cross into himself and responding with the resurrection. Nevertheless, the unity of love and power is difficult. How can the compulsory element of power, as in war, be united with love? "Nobody felt the weight of this question more than Luther, who had to combine his highly spiritual ethics of love with his highly realistic politics of absolute power. Luther answered that 'compulsion is the strange work of love.'" Sweetness, self-surrender, and mercy are, according to Luther, the proper work of love; bitterness, killing, and condemnation are its strange work, but both are works of love. What he meant could be expressed in the statement that it is the strange work of love to destroy what is against love. Love must have the security of power from which it can perform its works of charity and must even do these works sometimes through the structures of justice by judging and punishing.

"In order to destroy what is against love, love must be united with power, even compulsory power." What are the limits of this wedding of love and compulsory power? "Love, through compulsory power, must destroy what is against love. But love cannot destroy him who acts against love." It will seek to redeem him. Note Bonhoeffer's tragic decision to kill Hitler.

Compulsory power represents the tragic price which love must pay for the reunion of the separated. God does not enjoy his role as judge.

Forms of justice must constantly be changed so that they allow the fullest possible realization of reunion of the criminal with society and his loved ones—so love can be most fully realized. Punishment for punishment's sake, done in hatred, is not corrective, but spoiling.

Equality before the law is an essential if justice is to express love—reunion, correction, restoration of being at the individual and social levels. And this is the end in view. But actually there are many differences within the basic equality and adequate justice informed by love. We must endeavor to take account of these and provide distributive justice. A $1,000 fine for a wealthy man is just, and a $10 fine for a poor man is just.

The relation of equality and justice depend on the power of being in a man—his emotional stability, his financial power, his educational power, his physical health, his family circumstances, his history of good or evil, etc. The proper union of power, justice, and love, there, will work for the creative renewal of being in persons and groups.

Theonomous ethics includes ontology, and we approach three different spheres of life with different ones of the great trilogy: love, power, and justice. We approach human or personal relations in terms of justice, love, and power. We approach social institutional relations in terms of power, justice, and love. We approach the relation to God, the Ultimate relation, in terms of love, power and justice.

First, in personal encounters are justice, love, and power. Man's powers are unlimited, or the limits are not known, until he meets another man. He only knows he has an ego when he meets another ego that tells him to limit his power. The other one is a "thou" who cannot be removed, penetrated, or used. To do so is to destroy the self.

To try to make a thing out of a "thou" is to destroy both other and self. Tillich thinks even the Golden Rule is inadequate. We are not to do for another what we would have done for self. We should do for another what the other needs done for him. Man is never without a treasury of ethical wisdom which prevents him from destroying himself. It is in the conscience, in the morés, in the law, in the church, in revelation.

Law is externalized conscience. Rules of justice are created by the interplay of law, new situations, conscience, and creative reason. What is the purpose of it all? To provide the best ontological situation for persons—both the other person and the self. How is this best done? When love is the motive, which by reason structures power to provide justice, which is the fullest possible freedom for the individual, limited only by this ego's threat to that other ego.

Love transcends justice as revelation transcends reason. Love can be called justice in ecstasy as revelation can be called reason in ecstasy.

Creative or love-filled justice has three functions: listening, giving, and forgiving. Creative justice seeks to understand what is in the dark recesses of the other person so it may act redemptively. We listen, in order to understand. From this understanding, we give whatever we can to the other that will be redemptive.

Ultimately creative justice is forgiving. When the corrective action, whether imprisonment, fine, or scolding, has been administered, we forgive and restore to fellowship. Deep beneath it all, we love, and love means restoration to a healthy state of being.

Second, groups are power structures. Power is their prime concern. They rush for space. As old functions are outlived, they seek for new functions to preserve the self. They try socio-egocentrically to extend themselves. They pridefully build themselves up before other threatening groups. They coerce weakness which does not contribute to the power structure.

Groups can rarely love. The best level of goodness that groups attain is justice, equity. Power structures must be rationally turned into such forms and relationships that maximum justice can be established which will make possible maximum realization of love in personal relations within those structures of justice.

Can this be done by:

- Continental power structures, like Europe, North and South America, Asia?
- Domination by one great nation, such as Russia?
- A world organization?

Here is the place where the creative, loving individual constantly needs to humanize the group to keep it sensitive and empathetic.

Third, theonomy is the unity of Love, Power, and Justice. The depth of these three qualities of love, power, and justice are in the depths of God's being. If we throw them in faith into the depth of God, we can expect them to be transformed and retransformed. God is ultimate love, God is ultimate creative justice, God is ultimate power. God is the unity of the three. We have a trinity here. Historical, chronological order of discovery was Power, Justice, and Love.

In conclusion, sometimes we get angry and say either God is not all powerful or he is not loving. "As an emotional outburst, this question is very understandable. But as a theoretical formulation, it is rather poor. If God had produced a world in which physical and moral evil were impossible, the creatures would not have had the independence of God, which is presupposed in the experience of reuniting love. The world would have become an infant's paradise, but neither love, power, nor justice would be real. Actualization of one's potentialities includes, unavoidably, estrangement from one's essential being, so we may find it again in maturity. Only a God who is like a foolish mother, who is so afraid about the well-being of her child that she keeps him in a state of enforced innocence and enforced participation in her own life, could have kept the creatures in the prison of a dreaming paradise. (Role of literary art is to show estrangement; why not renewal?) As in the care of the mother, this would have been hidden hostility and not love. This would not have been power either. The power of God is that God overcomes estrangement, not that God prevents it. God takes it, symbolically speaking, into God's self (crucifixion).

This is the symbol of the cross—God participating the creaturely suffering. This is the unity of love and power in the depth of reality itself.

Love, power, and justice are unified in God and in the new creation of God in the world (the new being that comes upon man). Man estranged from the ground of his being is still man, but he is a lost man, a seeking man, a miserable man, reaching out for reunion with God, the ground of his being. This yen for reunion is the power of being that resists non-being. It is the drive to all kinds of ethical behavior both personal and social. It drives for the Holy Community, the community where agape transcends all lesser forms of love, as well as power and justice.

This agape Community transcends the individual but does not destroy the individual. It fulfills and redeems. It transcends the nation and all other heteronomies but does not destroy them; it helps them to appropriate self-realization. It transcends the church but in the sense of helping the church to realize itself as the vehicle of God's gracious Agape. Only in the light and power of the love from above can man appropriately love himself.

In *The Religious Situation*, Tillich says if you do not have a concrete program of social action, then you end up blessing whatever is. We must turn away from "self-sufficient finitude" and take a stance of "belieful-realism" open to the transcendent.

Chapter 44

KARL BARTH ON NEO-ORTHODOXY

A seminar given in October 1974

Karl Barth (1886–1968) was born in Basel, Switzerland. About 1935, having taught at the University of Bonn, Germany, for five years, he was forced to leave Germany by the Nazi government. He became Professor of Systemic Theology at the University of Basel and remained there until he retired in 1962.

It was while he was preaching in Safenwil, a village in north-central Switzerland, in 1911–21 that he had to think through the horrors of World War I, the fallacies of the Social Gospel, and respond to a new interpretation of the Gospel which he got started in his great work on Romans. Prior to doing this (while in Geneva as an associate pastor, 1909–11), he considered himself a follower of Albrecht Ritschl and that form of the social gospel, Justification and Benediction.

He says that his discovery of Dostoyevsky, with the help of a friend, Edward Thurneysen, was necessary to his writing of *Romans.* He also said that the writing of *Romans* and the preaching he did in this vein startled him with its effectiveness. He presented himself as climbing the church stairs to look from the belfry only to stumble, lay hold on the rope, the bell rang, and everyone came to church.

He became convinced that all attempts to know God through reason were not only futile, they were sinful. They blocked the possibility of knowing God. He says, in *Church Dogmatics: Selections,* "The logic of the matter demands that, even if we only lend our little finger to natural theology, there necessarily follows the denial of the revelation of God in Jesus Christ. A natural theology which does not strive to be the only master is not a natural theology. And to give it place at all is to put oneself . . . on the way to giving it sole sovereignty" (56).

To know God is man's primary business. This he cannot do through natural reason, but only by faith. "Faith takes reason by the throat and chokes the demon."

Also, religion (church) can obstruct knowledge of God and his will. "In religion, man bolts and bars himself against revelation by providing a substitute, by taking away in advance the very thing which has been given by God" (54).

Through the centuries, man, as theologian, has tried to also show God through reason, conscience, emotion, history, nature, and culture. But, now we can see that the "also" demanded to be "only."

Faith

We know God by faith or we do not know God, but some false god. This faith is a response to the objective reality of the incarnation of God in Jesus Christ. "He exists, not only inconceivably as God, but also conceivably as man; not only above the world, but also in the world" (*Word of God and Word of Man*, 45).

We begin with the assumption (positivism) that this God revealing himself in Jesus Christ is Sovereign Lord. He is *totaliter aliter* (19). Though he is a creator of nature, he is not nature, nor any aspect of nature. He is infinitely beyond nature. We must make this leap of faith. Without it, we cannot make sense of any kind out of our life, the world, man, God, sin, salvation, or last things.

The Word of God

The only thing for the preacher to preach is the word of God. What is meant by the word of God? For Barth it certainly is not the literalistic words of the Bible, though the Bible as Scripture is terribly important as the locus of the Word of God. Barth is a highly educated man who is profoundly aware of higher criticism.

There are three ways to speak of God: Dogmatism, Self-criticism, and Dialectic. We will enlarge upon these in just a moment, but first we must say that the man who attempts to enter into dialogue with God is a "saved" man, an elect man, a man who is aware of his sin, has gone through the narrows of the crisis and been called late into the dialogue by God's grace. We will develop this doctrine of man later. You must note that instead of beginning with man, as most liberal theologies do, he begins with God, revelation, Christ.

We are human and cannot speak of God. To speak of God seriously is to speak in the realm of revelation and faith. To speak of God would be to speak God's word. It is the word that God becomes man. This is the theme of "The Humanity of God." The only answer that possesses genuine transcendence and so can solve the riddle of immanence is God's word. There are three ways, then, to try to speak God's word. They've been named a moment ago: Dogmatism, Self-criticism, and Dialectic. What does Barth mean by these?

1. Dogmatism: "When the minister is given the final insight that the theme of the ministry is not man becoming God, but God becoming man—even when this insight flashes only occasionally upon his mind—he acquires a taste for objectivity, and he ceases to view objectivity as a mere psychic instrument for use in analyzing the Bible and dogmas. He finds a world which previously he had despised and hated as 'supernaturalistic,' slowly but surely becoming reasonable and purposeful. He understands it, so to speak, from within. He sees that what is written must be written. He gains assurance and freedom of movement in corners of that world so remote and strange that he had not allowed himself to dream he could ever be at home there. And at last he is perhaps able to find in the Apostles' Creed, with all its hardness, more truth, more depth, and even more intelligence than in any other that short-breathed modernism would put in its place.

   "But obviously one cannot speak of God even in the most powerfully and vividly conceived supernaturalism. He can only witness that he would like to do so. The weakness of orthodoxy is not the supernaturalistic element in the Bible and the dogmas. That is its strength. It is rather the fact that orthodoxy, and we all, so far as we are in our own way dogmatists, have a way of regarding some objective description of that element—for instance the word 'God'—as the element itself. We have our myths and accept them pragmatically—a working faith! We have all come upon those places in Luther—in his teaching about the trinity, for instance—where we are simply left standing with instructions to give up thinking, lift our hat, and say Yes. We feel, in spite of ourselves, that it will not do, thus to slay the harlot, Reason. And we remember with dismay how often we who are not Luther, have done so, in public, and even more often in private.

   "Why will it not do? Because by this kind of answer, a man's question about God is simply quashed. He no longer has a question. In place of the question, he has an answer, but as long as he remains a man, he cannot let the question go. He himself, as a man, is the question. . . . Man cannot believe what is simply out there before him. He can only believe what is both before him and within him. He cannot believe what does not reveal itself to him and have the power to penetrate him" (201–202).

2. The second way to speak of God is by self-criticism (203). Seeing this revelation of God in man, we say "woe is me, for I am a man of unclean lips, etc." We have here a disturbingly clear account of God's becoming man to die, to surrender all his uniqueness, his selfhood, his ego-hood, and to become still, unassuming, receptive. . . . God is not this or that; God is no object, no something, no opposite, no second; God is pure being, without quality, filling everything, obstructed only by the particular individuality of man. Let this latter finally be removed, and the soul will of a certainty conceive God. This is the way of mysticism that must be reckoned with. . . . The mystic knows that man really desires One who is not himself. I call this the way of self-criticism, though it may also be called the way of idealism—because by it a man places himself under judgment and negatives himself because it shows so clearly that what must be overcome is man, as man.

   Mysticism is strongest where dogmatism is weakest. Here something happens; here we are not left standing with instructions to believe; here we are seriously attacked; here God becomes man with such vigor that there is nothing of man left over, so to speak. Yet, even this is better, infinitely better, than the pagan cults of the intellect and the human will.

   The Abyss. "But even here we cannot speak of God. The mystics, and we all insofar as we are mystics, have been wont to assert that what annihilates and enters into man, the Abyss into which he falls, the Darkness to which he surrenders himself, the No before which he stands is God, but this we are incapable of proving. The only part of our assertion of which we are certain, the only part we can prove, is that man is negative, negated. Thus, man thinks of nothing from which he came, and he thinks of death as a not beingness. He is faced with a gigantic question mark beyond life's boundary. This is disquieting!

"To experience this abyss, this boundary, this is not to experience God, not quite. God has not become God, but man has become man, with a vengeance! There is no salvation in that. God may be spoken of only (in that objectivity of which Orthodoxy knows all too much) when God himself become man and enters with his fullness into our emptiness, with his Yes into our No."

3. The third way to speak of God is in dialectical fashion, often spoken of as paradox. This is the most inclusive way. It sees the relative values in dogmatism and in self-criticism. The dialectical way is by far the best. It is the way of Paul and the Reformers. This way undertakes seriously and positively to develop the idea of God on the one hand and the criticism of man and all things human on the other. They are not now considered independently but are both referred constantly to the common presupposition, to the living truth which, to be sure, may not be named, but which lies between them, and gives to both their meaning and interpretation. Here there is an unwavering insight into the fact that the living truth, the determining content of any real utterance concerning God, is that God (but really God!) becomes man (but really man!). God is the thesis; man is the antithesis (206).

"But how now shall the necessary dependence of both sides of the truth upon this living Center be established? The genuine dialectician knows that this Center cannot be apprehended or beheld, and he will not if he can help it, allow himself to be drawn into giving direct information about it, knowing that all such information, whether it be positive or negative, is not really information, but always either dogma or self-criticism. On this narrow ridge of rock, one can only walk; if he attempts to stand still, he will fall either to the right or to the left, but fall he must. There remains only to keep walking—an appalling performance for those who are not free from dizziness—looking from one side to the other, from positive to negative and from negative to positive, from dogma to self-criticism.

"Our task is to interpret the Yes and the No by the Yes without delaying more than a moment in either a fixed Yes or a fixed No; to speak of the glory of God in creation, for example, only to pass immediately to emphasizing God's complete concealment from us in that creation (as in Romans 8); to speak of death and the transitory quality of this life only to remember the majesty of the wholly other life which meets us at the moment of death; of the creation of man in the image of God simply and solely to give warning once and for all that man as we know him is fallen man, whose misery we know better than his glory; and, on the other hand, to speak of sin only to point out that we should not know it, were it not forgiven us.

"According to Luther, God's justification of man is to be explained only as sin justified. When a man realizes that he is a sinner and nothing more, he awakes to the fact that as such he is a justified sinner. When a man becomes really aware of the inconsistencies of all human work, the only response he can make to this awareness is to go eagerly to work, but when we have done everything we are responsible for, we shall have to say we are unprofitable servants" (207–208).

Barth predicted precisely what has happened. Onlookers will first bewail your supernaturalism and next your atheism. You do not fit the categories of dogmatism or the categories of secular knowledge.

We should speak of God and yet cannot; and if anyone knows God, we should by all means give God the glory (212).

What Is the Word of God?

We have indicated how one responds dialectically. But, what is it to which one responds? It is certainly not the literal word-for-word inspired text of the Bible in the fundamentalist sense. Barth accepts the scholarly, critical view of the text.

The Word of God is threefold: revealed, written, proclaimed (*Church Dogmatics: Selections,* 136). Yet the Word of God, which is from this Totally Other, comes from the Bible, into a Christian man, listening in the Holy Spirit in a congregation of believers. It is not any precise word that the preacher says. It is not any particular word that the preacher reads from the Holy Scriptures. It is a Word that comes when God confronts man. It is a Word of encounter. It is a word of destiny to men.

It is a word that comes in crisis: personal and social crisis. The crisis of Western Civilization and, relatedly, the crisis of this man—the sensualism, evil, idolatry, sin, and alienation of this man in this culture. "We need to see that in the view of God, all our activity is in vain even in the best life; i.e. that, by ourselves, we are not in a position to apprehend the truth, to let God be God and our Lord. We need to renounce all attempts even to try to apprehend this truth. We need to be ready and resolve simply to let the truth be told us and, therefore, to be apprehended by it. It is

God who arranges for each creature its end and ends. He coordinates all the ends into a totality" (153).

"But this is the very thing for which we are not resolved and ready" (51). This is precisely our sinfulness. It is revelation: "The majesty of God in his condescension to the creature" (31). God is known to us as Father, Creator through Jesus, not natural theology (148).

Man as Sinner

Inextricably related to sensing the word of God and one's need for grace given therein, is one's awareness of one's self and all men's condition as that of sinner, alienated. God created man in his own image. Man utterly defaced this image (this is the meaning of Adam's fall). Barth's doctrine of the Fall and Reinhold Niebuhr's are similar in that every man finds himself ultimately an enemy of God, deeply involved in evil, unable to extricate himself, thus dependent upon a gracious God if he is to be saved, ultimately.

In his Scottish lectures, Gifford speaks about that phrase in the Scottish creed: "The image of God was utterly defaced in man," and he comments: "Man has now become a tarnished mirror in which the glory of God can no longer be reflected. To be man means now to be an enemy of God and this means to be the destroyer of one's own proper glory" (*Knowledge of God,* 50). "To make use of the existence, dignity and freedom given us means now that we go farther along the well-trodden by-path, in our life as a whole and in all its details, and thus become ever more deeply and completely involved in our own corruption. To be in the world now means to be lost in the midst of powers, figures, and events, which, after we became men without a Lord, they ceased likewise to have a lord and so to have any significance for us" (*Knowledge of God,* 51).

"It is impossible for man to undo or to make amends for his sin itself. Why can he not? The reason is that it is sin against God, not merely of acting, but of being against God, in all his actions. It is this that he can neither undo (hopelessness of this statement) nor make amends for. God's revelation in Jesus Christ tells us this unambiguously. It consists in God Himself undoing and making amends for our being against Him and for our sin. If we believe this, it discloses to us the final horror of sin and with it the impossibility of setting ourselves free from it" (*Knowledge of God,* 51).

Now, it is at this point that Barth's Calvinism is too extreme. It drives man to utter hopelessness and despair. This is like Jonathan Edwards's extreme Calvinism. It seemed too extreme to Brunner and finally even to Barth himself, for he says in *Humanity in God:*

"It must now be quite frankly granted that we were at that time only partially in the right. . . . What expressions we used—above all the famous 'Wholly Other' breaking in upon us 'perpendicularly from above' and the no less famous 'infinite qualitative distinction' between God and man, the vacuum . . . that only one way appears, that from above downwards, the problem of ethics was identified with man's sickness unto death. Redemption was viewed as consisting in the abolition of the creatureliness of creatures, the swallowing of immanence by transcendence, and, in conformity with these, the demand for a faith like a spring into the abyss, and more of the like! All this was said somewhat severely and brutally—our critics said, even heretically.

"How we cleared things away! And we did almost nothing but clear away. Everything that smacked of mysticism, even remotely of mysticism and morality, of pietism and romanticism, or even of idealism was suspected and sharply interdicted . . . ! What should have been only a sad and friendly smile was a derisive laugh. . . . Many contemporaries probably thought we had taken Schleiermacher and stood him on his head . . . made God great at the cost of man.

"Where did we really go astray? . . . We worked almost exclusively with the concept of diastasis, only seldom with the complementary concept of analogy. . . . The alienation that we were teaching that God is in everything and man nothing, was bad. . . . It is true that it was pre-eminently the image and concept of a 'wholly other' that fascinated us. What if the result of the new hymn to the majesty of God should be a confirmation of the hopelessness of all human activity. . . . God forbid!

"But did it not appear to escape us by quite a distance that the deity of the living God—and we certainly wanted to deal with Him—found its meaning and its power only in the context of His history and His dialogue with man, and thus in His togetherness with man? Indeed, and this is the point, back of which we cannot go—it is a matter of God's sovereign togetherness with man, a togetherness grounded in Him and determined, delimited, and ordered through Him alone. . . . It is a matter, however, of God's togetherness with man. Who God is and what He is in His deity. He proves and reveals not in a vacuum as a divine being-for-Himself, but precisely and authentically in the fact that He exists, speaks, and acts as the partner of man, though of course as the absolutely superior partner. He who does that is the living God, and the freedom in which He does that is his deity. . . . It is precisely God's deity which, rightly understood, includes his humanity.

"How do we know this? Only in Jesus Christ where God reveals Himself not as a God separated in splendor, but as God together with man. . . . Jesus Christ is in His one Person, as true God, man's loyal partner, and as true man, *God's* loyal partner" (*Humanity of God*, 43–45).

Perhaps this quote from *The Word of God and Word of Man* will make it clear to you how subtly sin can operate. "The same happy gentleman of culture who today drives up so briskly in his little car of progress and so cheerfully displays the pennants of his various ideals, will tell you apprehensively tomorrow, if the matter comes up, that men are small and imperfect and that one may not expect too much from them, that one may not be too decided about it anyway.

"But we are apprehensive about the Word of God because we feel much too small and too human for anything so different and so new to begin in us and among us (diastasis). This is our despair. We cannot make a very decided answer of Yes or No to a whole new world of life" (17).

The heart of the Christian message is "God with us" (6). It speaks of the unifying or reconciling factor between God and man (8). The meaning of this event consists in the fact that it has to do with the salvation of man.

Salvation

Salvation is fulfillment, the perfected being which is not the being of creation. Salvation is eschaton. So the saved being can only come from God, not from self. The coming of this salvation is the grace of God in the narrower sense. In the wider sense, creation is grace also, but the person who has not received grace in the narrower sense does not see it. But the "God with us" of the Christian message does not refer to this general grace. It means the redemptive grace of God which was revealed in the second person or mode of the trinity (9).

As Barth gave up on Schleiermacher, he turned to Kierkegaard. Søren Kierkegaard had a tremendous influence on Barth. Man cannot be saved by the Church, by the Bible, by culture, or reason. He can only be saved by grace through faith in Jesus Christ. In his *Knowledge of God*, he says that God has revealed himself to man in two ways: in the Chosen People community, and by becoming man, identifying himself profoundly with man, in Jesus Christ. Jesus is the saving word.

It is important at this point to note that Barth can be misunderstood in his emphasis on God as Wholly Other. It does not mean for Barth, as some insist it must, that God cannot have anything to do with man, cannot even save him, communicate with him, etc. God's relation to man is a logical paradox, the paradox of the Incarnation. In Christ, God comes near to man to speak a word of eternity into time. In Jesus, we see God's identity with man. Jesus Christ is God-with-us. He speaks a Perfect Word into the imperfect world.

This is Barth's way of witnessing against the easy Schleiermacher-Wieman emphases upon "value-producing aspects of the universe" or the "spirit of humility" as God. Or, as Wieman sometimes puts it: "That character of events to which man must adjust himself in order to attain the highest and avoid the greatest evils" (Hordern, 92). This is a special revelatory event.

Barth is clear that he wants to witness against this "Baalism" or "Emperor Worship" of our time (we often really worship the democratic process, for example). But this does not mean that there is no analogy or similarity between God and man. God is an objective reality and not merely subjective concept. He is really there. He really encounters and confronts man. He is not merely man's best self. This is a miracle that God has opened his eyes to atoning love through incarnation or saving love.

The Bible can be the Word of God for man when he looks for the Word of God therein. "To suffer in the Bible means to suffer because of God: to sin, to sin against God; to doubt, to doubt God; to perish, to perish as the hand of God. In other words, that painful awareness of the boundary of mortality which man acquires with more or less certainty in life's rise and fall becomes in the Bible, the order of the God of holiness. It is the message of the cross; and from It, in this life, there is no escape. . . . But as the Bible forces persons, no matter what question they ask, to turn it to the question about God 'one simply cannot hear the "question" without hearing the answer. The person who says that the Bible leads us to where finally we hear only a great "No" or see a great void, proves only that he has not yet been led thither. This No is really Yes. This judgment is really Grace. This condemnation is forgiveness. This death is Life. This hell is heaven. This fearful God is a loving father who takes the prodigal in his arms. The crucified is the one raised from the dead. And the explanation of the cross as such is eternal life. No other additional thing needs to be joined to the question. The question is the answer'" (*Word of God and Word of Man*, 120).

God's election is relevant to all men. Saying "no" to it simply proves it ultimately, whether Hitler, or an alcoholic, or a rapist. The chaos brought on is judgment in the midst of reality which is designed to turn the person back to God. Salvation is seen as an act of God's grace.

Grace

At the abyss of despair, God decides to come to needy and sinful man through Jesus Christ. "To know Christ is to know God." God lets nothing but the strictest Justice befall us in order that we might be able to accept his election of us in Jesus Christ. The election of us takes place as the judgment takes place or at the time we become conscious of it. Thus to know Jesus Christ means to know a new man, the elect man. At this point, too, we are dealing with God's action, when we consider it in the light of its result in man upon whom God acts, appears as free mercy, as a miracle wrought by God, as Grace.

God became man in Christ, and suffered the death that man suffers for his sin, and even perdition and hell, on man's behalf. (Now a weakness of Barth appears here: A questioner said: How could God die such a humiliating death? His answer: "This is the death that is spoken of in the Bible." Many times he resorts to a Biblical literalism or proof. Yet in his more careful and thoughtful moments, he does not approve this.)

The Redeemed Life

Jesus becomes Lord of our lives. Because he is our future, he determines our present. "To accept Him as our judge means to believe in Him today and, therefore, to acknowledge Him as our righteousness and our life" (100). "Man is the creature who is for God." God shows us in Christ he is for man. The Christian says yes to being a creature of God. We are self-consciously in the Kingdom as we, in faith, acknowledge Christ. This encounter judges us and redeems us. A free man realizes freedom is God-given. He does the good when he acts in accord with the imperative inherent in his freedom. He acts in a Christian manner in the concrete event.

The Real Christian Life is an ordered life which grows out of naming Jesus as Lord. God opens up to us works to do and give us grace to walk in his way as we name Jesus Christ as Lord. There is no separation of faith and works. When we daily acknowledge our sin and daily receive God's forgiveness mediated by Jesus Christ, we are daily involved in the real struggle of the spirit against the flesh and endeavoring to follow the leading of the Holy Spirit and by it to overcome the evil in our own lives.

The Ten Commandments describe the elements of our relation to God and to fellow man. But these are not a demand for a particular morality or for exceptional achievements. "Christianity is not morality." "We are not intended to be benefactors or instructors, much less Gods, to one another. We are not doing anything special when we love one another. In doing this, we are simply doing the one thing most natural for those aware that they have been chosen and saved in Jesus Christ. We are doing the one thing natural which we owe as brothers in Christ. In doing this, we are simply being obedient. And once again, our obedience will not be something special, but only the natural expression of the freedom which is bestowed upon us by God Himself, becoming our brother in Jesus Christ (*Selections,* 165–66).

"What is the true Christian Life? We are on a razor's edge. Is Jesus Christ our life? It should be so. But this is often merely a pious phrase. . . . So we often just give ourselves up to frivolity, thus signing our death warrants; or bury our heads like ostriches, we persuade ourselves that the law to which we are subject is in no sense Perfect and Majestic Law, but merely a law code, culture-bound, and we think we are able to fulfill it 'to a certain extent' and that this will suffice.

"But Jesus is the true fulfillment of our life—the true fulfillment of the law. Our own lives are poor by comparison. Our only hope is to identify our lives deeply with the Life of Jesus Christ and to live in gratitude and loyalty. Freedom of the Christian man is freedom to give obedience to God in various ways. He tries to avoid setting a new 'law' to keep it dynamic. Don't confuse pen-ultimate things with the ultimate" (*Knowledge of God,* 139).

Again, the weakness is that Barth rarely ever, in his writings, grapples with precisely what this means. You never see him, as you do Niebuhr, really grappling with ethical problems in the light of this above-indicated position, except a few instances like his 1962 statement that the church is as well off under Communism as Capitalism.

The Church

The Church is the Body of Christ, vertically related to God, and horizontally ministering to the world. We cannot seek God and shun his people. God lives in his church (154). Religion may be a private matter, but faith cannot be. Real service to God takes place in the fellowship of the one holy church or it does not take place at all. Real service of God does consist in our believing in Jesus Christ and in accenting that He lives His life in our stead and for our sake. His life as the life of the Head is not to be separated from the life of the body, nor is His life as the life of the One free from the life of the many. If His life is our life, then our life must be the life of members of His body. We, too, cannot remain without, but because He is within his church, we must likewise be within and with Him. We must guard against very easy but false analogies. One can be a good citizen without belonging to a political party, etc. But one cannot hold the Christian faith without holding it in the church and with the church. The church is neither a party nor a society nor a movement. She is the form in which the Christian faith exists because it is faith in the One who died and rose again for the very many. Such a content must have and can only have this form (155)!

The State renders a minimal, but necessary service to God. A certain order, peace and justice is required as the condition in which the Church and Jesus Christ can best work, so the Christian renders what service he can in bringing about these conditions in the world. Yet, this is by no means his ultimate vocation.

His basis for criticism of any State or Political order is whether it allows freedom for the Church to preach the word of God. This word always has ethical relevance (creative good possibilities), although it may threaten present structures and forms. The Church is the ever-present reminder of God's activity in the world.

Last things. Nature is fallen. In Christ, a new divinely restored order is announced—announced, not made perfect. We live in an in-between time. It is not the time of prophets or of apostles or of fulfillment. It is an in-between time. We hopefully await the fulfillment. It will be the time when God will fulfill history based on the revelation of the Kingdom in Christ. The work of revelation has always a future dimension. In the eschatological hope, it will sometime operate fully on man. It does not so operate now, but we live in confident hope because God has so announced in Christ. Our time is the time between the Ascension and the Return of Jesus Christ.

As Easter is the beginning of his coming again, he is continuing to make his presence known in the world. He will finally manifest himself. "God is post-temporal. God is before and over time. He is also after all time and he is after each time or event. All movements or roads that lead away from or beyond time lead to God. God is the Last as he was the First. He is the Absolute, the unsurpassable future of all time and of all that is in time. All parts of time will ultimately make sense as part of time is completed time. As God looks back upon time from the end, He will decide what it has been. Man cannot know; he has only the Word of God to guide him in the present moment of involvement and a promise on the basis of which he can trust eternity.

"As we exist in time, God embraces time from a position in front of us. Thus, in having Him in faith, we have everything. He is the Kingdom, now and evermore" (*Dogmatics*, vol. II, 1, 629). Of course, you understand that he means based on faith and trust and not based on man knowing now all that God ever will know.

Summary of Barth's *Humanity of God*

God is human in the sense of Fatherhood of God, Brotherhood of Man.

1. Out of all this, all human dignity arises.
2. This is not blotted out by the Fall of man.
3. Man is elected to communion with God, despite the Fall.
4. We can meet God only within the limits of our humanity. He does not reject the human.
5. God affects man in the context of culture.

God is human. So theological culture is concerned with God's encounter with man and with their dialogue in history, where fulfillment take place.

Since God is human and yet eternal, this calls for a dialectical theology that never rests in any particular moment.

1. Humanity at any one moment is no adequate image of God. There is a shift from humanity to divinity.
2. Christ is the image of the eternal love of man by God.
3. Theology can be no fixed system, but it is a sermon and a prayer, the worshipping congregation, where the Word speaks.

4. The sense and sound of our Word must be primarily positive, not opening the abyss.
5. It means involvement with the church. The word that is critical of the church can be creative only when it stems from insight.

Summary of Arguments between Brunner and Barth on Natural Theology

The exchange originally took place in 1933 and was published in German in 1934 but not in English until 1946. Brunner lists Barth's "false conclusions."

1. Since man is a sinner who can be saved only by grace, the image of God in which he was created is obliterated entirely without remnant. Man's rational nature, capacity for culture, and humanity contain no traces or remnants whatever of that lost image of God.
2. Since we acknowledge scriptural revelation as the sole norm of our knowledge of God and the sole source of our salvation, every attempt to assert a "general revelation" of God in nature, in the conscience and in history, is to be rejected outright. There is no sense in acknowledging two kinds of revelation, one general, one special. There is only one kind, namely the one complete revelation in Christ.
3. Accordingly, there is only grace in Christ. There is no grace of creation and preservation active from the creation of the world and apparent to us in God's preservation of the world.
4. So, there is no such thing as God's ordinances of preservation, which we could know to be such and in which we could recognize the will of God which is normative for our own action. Such a law of nature can only be introduced into Christian thought as a pagan thought.
5. So, it is not permissible to speak of a "point of contact" for the saving action of God. For this would contradict the sole activity of the saving grace of Christ, which is the center of the theology of the Bible and the Reformation.
6. And the new is in no way a perfection of the old, but comes into being exclusively through destruction of the old and is a replacement of the old man by the new.

Barth says these ideas of Brunner's are: unbelievable, Thomistic and

Roman, and derived from the Renaissance Enlightenment and, therefore, against the Reformation.

Brunner's counter-theses are:

1. I agree with Barth in teaching that the original image of God in man has been destroyed and that with it the possibility of doing or even being willing to do that which is good in the sight of God and, therefore, the free will has been lost. But man as a sinner has not ceased to be the central and culminating point of creation. God has created man to bear his image, and this special purpose has not been destroyed. Man has an immeasurable advantage over other creatures. He is called by God to be responsible. And he has capacity for words and thoughts. Not even as a sinner does he cease to be one with whom one can speak. He has defaced the image, but he is not beyond speaking to.
2. The world is the creation of God. In every creation the creator is somehow recognizable, whether by fiat or by evolution. God leaves the imprint of his nature on what he does. Therefore, the creation of the world is at the same time a revelation, a self-communication of God. This is not a pagan statement but a Christian one.

   The revelation in Christ and in Nature are related. Sin dulls a person's awareness. Man in sin tends to turn God's presence in his creation into idols. Only the man who stands within the revelation in Christ has the true natural knowledge of God, but it is visible there in Nature. It is not known in such a way as to provide salvation. That is only through Christ.
3. God is present in nature in a third way—as gracious observer. God is present even to his sinful creature which is far removed from him. The way God is present to his fallen creature is through his preserving grace. Preserving grace does not abolish sin but abolishes the worst consequences of sin. The grace of preservation for the most part consists in that God does not entirely withdraw God's grace of creation from the creature despite the latter's sin. The state, for example, is a function of God's preserving grace to check the worst consequences of sin.

   Preserving grace is a biblical doctrine and may be called general grace. It includes the natural life and the historical life. In man these two are inseparable.
4. So, within the sphere of this preserving grace belong those "ordi-

nances" which are the constant factors of historical and social life, which form a basic part of ethical life. Such ordinances include matrimony and state. Both give some grace to men unaware of God's grace in Christ. "But—and this is the critical point: only by means of faith can their significance be perfectly understood. Therefore, it is only by means of faith that they can be realized according to the will of Him who has instituted them. . . . Nevertheless, they are and remain divine ordinances of nature. Yet, only by faith, through Christ, can their relation to the loving will of God be rightly understood."

5. All who agree that persons, not sticks and stones, have the image of God, will have to agree that this point of contact is not lost in the sinner. The fact that man is man with this sense of responsibility in him and thus his potential receptivity to the Word of God, his candidacy, the possibility of being addressed by God. This is the critical point. This is presence of God in the creation, in nature, even in fallen man. His knowledge of sin, his potential for repentance, and his possibility of being addressed are all necessary presuppositions of his capacity to receive the divine message of grace. The grace of God is comprehensible only to him who already knows about sin.
6. The death of the old Adam does not mean that this is to be taken materially, but spiritually. The subject as such is not destroyed by faith. The personal God meets man personally. That involves the continuance of self-consciousness. As Paul said, "Nevertheless, I live; yet not I, but Christ lives in me" (Gal. 2:20).

   Similarly, if we say we have faith as a gift of the Holy Spirit, nevertheless it is I who believes through the Holy Spirit. The self, natural self, is still there and aware and responding. The Holy Spirit is within us.

Brunner then goes on to argue with Barth and say this is Reformation doctrine. He quotes Calvin at length, the essence of which is: God can be known from nature other than man, but also from man himself—from experience. But the knowledge of God to be gained from nature is only partial. Metaphorically, from nature we know the hands and feet, but not the heart of God" (38). "But this imperfection of the natural knowledge of God is no reason for underestimating it. Not even he who has been taught by the Word of God can dispense with it and is bound to acknowledge it. Moreover, he is greatly assisted by it." "Through Scripture, the revelation in nature is both clarified and complemented." "If you reject natural theology, you do not stare at the serpent with the result that it stares back at you, hypnotizes you and is ultimately certain to bite you, but you hit it and kill it as soon as you see it. . . . Real rejection of natural theology can come about only in the fear of God and hence only by a complete lack of interest in this matter" (76).

Chapter 45

EMIL BRUNNER

The Divine Imperative
An Example of "Neo-Orthodoxy"
Lecture notes

Emil Brunner spent most of his life as Professor of Systematic Theology at the University of Zurich in Switzerland. He was an early, eminent disciple of Karl Barth, but split from him over details of natural theology—whether God is known at all in nature. Barth wrote his explosive address, "*Nein!*," against Brunner.

The Divine Imperative is one of a dozen or more books Brunner published. It was the key presentation of his *Christian Ethics*. Other books by him are: *Revelation and Reason, The Mediator, The Divine-Human Encounter, The Christian Doctrine of God, The Scandal of Christianity.*

The heart of the problem is the contrast between philosophical ethics and Christian ethics. Philosophical, rational, culture-oriented ethics stand over against relational, God-oriented ethics. The Kantian ethic offers no link between the world of what is and what ought to be. He presumes the reason and influence of the individual can attain it. Of course, Kant projects a God and immortality, but this is not the Creator-Revealer-Redeemer God of Christian faith. Brunner says Kant subconsciously actually relies on this faith but does not get it explicated in his system. Kant's God is a project of the human mind; so "is" and "ought" do not get connected.

The Creator-Revealer-Redeemer God of Christianity does link "is" and "ought" in being. Christ *is* what man *ought* to be. God stands over against reason and rationalization in judgmental love. In Kant and most modern theologians, the sense of ethical duty is always eudaemonistic. The necessary antithesis or "over-againstness" is not present. The Categorical

Imperative loses its force. The Good is no longer a command; it is "value." Thus, conduct is no longer controlled by duty, but by inclination.

In an adequate ethic, happiness has a place and not merely duty, love and not only obedience, the individual as well as the universal, law as a minimal guide but not as final and closed. Christian revelational ethic is the only ethic that provides these elements.

Is Christian revelation a basis for value judgments and behavior? Revelation is only known in faith. Where and what revelation is, is a statement which can only be ventured upon as a confession. Here the Christian church comes forward with her confession that God has spoken to her in God's Word. Science and reason cannot pass judgment on the claims of faith in revelation. They can only be effectively criticized from within the circle of faith. As believers, we are never wholly convinced but striving to clarify and order our faith.

There is a present revelational or "existential" experience by the believing individual. The many antitheses (good and evil, body and spirit, individual and community) are really one single antithesis, which can only be perceived personally in one's own existence. The true statement is not "Man is sinful," but "I am sinful." It is in this personal experience of being the fallen or alienated one that the person of faith can know the experience of grace. Christian ethics begin here.

The Good (Value) is based on the sense of the Holy. "Ye shall therefore be Holy, for I am Holy" (Leviticus 11:45; 19:2). The Holy means God as the unconditionally sovereign Lord of the world. The holiness of man consists in knowing that he belongs to God. No one has a claim on a man or a people save God alone. God's claim permeates all the relationships of life. God's claim is the only valid norm. Hence the religious element is also the ethical element and vice-versa. The relation of God and man is based on the covenant and is therefore a matter of loyalty. Man's goodness can be nothing other than response to the goodness of God.

This theonomous ethic is also human and social. God's will fulfilled means fulfillment for the individual and the development of community among persons. There is no other way to fulfillment. Love God. Love neighbor as self. Neither religion nor morality is autonomous. Both are theonomous.

In drawing man to God's self, God does not draw him out of the world. God comes to men in the Incarnation. The Cross of Christ means the revelation of God's character as reaching toward man in love. Man is, thereby, called to Agape, which has no limits and makes no demands. There is no basis for "I will love you if . . . " Love is unconditional. The Good is simply and solely the will of God. The New Testament message of Incarnation is "What God's will is wholly a will for humanity." The message is that "in Christ" we can become fully human.

In the cross the Christian sees evil and its cost clearly. He sees his own guilt condemned and ceases to judge others. He becomes equal with his brother—forgiven, reconciled, prepared for "New Being in Christ." He understands he belongs to his brethren. Moralism (the legalism and self-righteousness of works) is at times the worst enemy of true morality. In love to God, through neighbor, the antithesis between happiness and duty is removed.

The Christian "New Man" always sees a contradiction between his new self and an "Old Man," or old self, a previous view of God, self, good, and evil. Faith exists in a polemically critical atmosphere. The believer lives amid this conflict to the end of his life. Theological heuristics (a combination of apologetics and polemics) characterizes the Christian. He is constantly trying to state the faith to the outsider and preach to himself so his life and that of the community will be more valid. He seeks to speak to the outsider helpfully.

From the point of view of faith, how are we to understand natural morality? Man is created in the "image of God" and designed for "freedom in God," yet "fallen." Sin has perverted his relation to God. Sin is expressed in "autonomy" (egotism) or in a false "theonomy" where man calls the world God. He then constructs a self and/or world-oriented set of values. The result is a confused reverence that mixes the Holy and the unholy. It is an easy step to calling God an impersonal law. (Is this Wieman's fallacy?) A next step is a culture-ethic, but no leverage for a creative transformation is provided.

Here we see stages of degeneration. "The more profound the forgetfulness of God, the more deeply does human existence sink down to the level of animal immediacy." This degeneration is accompanied by, or caused by, loss of meaning and therefore motivation in life. Devoid of God, man leans toward formal, legalistic ethics or toward eudaemonistic materialism. The latter degenerates toward hedonism and vitalism and fights against legalistic moralism. Vitalism justifies life in its immediacy and instinctiveness. Here the bare level of human existence has been reached, which, if it could be realized by all men, would erase utterly every trace of humanity; for man is only man by virtue of the claim made upon him by God. Finally, when men no longer know that evil means the severance of the mind and soul from God, he may try to construct a legalistic, synthetic ethic, but this is hopeless. It does not have the power to motivate profound, whole-being commitment.

Christian faith is the response of penitent man to the Divine Word revealed in Christ and his act of redemption. The restoration of the individual and the community to wholeness is not an idea grasped rationally, but an action of God recognized in faith. It is not a principle, nor a process, but a divine act.

On the other hand, natural ethics is an attempt to achieve self-security. This is a dead-end street. Security does not live in a sense of self-righteousness, but God-righteousness. "The worst state of man is that in which he has complete confidence in himself." The essential fight is not against lawlessness, but legalism. Both Christ and the existentialists of today are anti-legalistic. The legalistic person finds it impossible to come into real human, personal contact with his fellow man. Autonomy and legalism both obstruct God's activity. The Bible does not speak of the God who demands and the man who is blindly obedient, but of the God who acts and the man who receives the Divine gift.

This is the great inversion of existence. Previously, the person's life at its best was directed toward God; now it is life from God. God graciously contradicts the contradictions of life. The splitness of life is healed by grace. However, this "new life" is not bestowed in a magical way. In this real historical event, God is present as Spirit and Word. Even the word made flesh is still Word. It is something which must be heard, known, recognized, responded to (Prodigal Son).

After that, man knows his life is a gift from God, not a straining after God. He no longer wants to be interdependent. He understands his dependence. He no longer has to do with law, but with God. Love is not only the fulfillment of Law but its end, and thus, the end of all ethics as law. Faith is the relation to God which enables response to his love. Faith enables obedience without resentment. It is an act that pulls the self together and gives earnest determination to do the will of God which will bless your brother—mankind.

Natural ethics is the science of conduct which is distinguished from all that is accidental (and not based on principle) by ultimate principles which characterize it as "right." "The Christian conception of the Good differs from every other conception of the Good at this very point, contending that it cannot be defined in terms of principle at all. Christian ethic is the science of human conduct as it is determined by Divine conduct." Scientific ethic would demand absolute impartiality. This is absurd when enrolled to ethics. Ethics means involvement, concern. "A scientific ethic would remain embedded in a morass of biology, psychology, sociology." It would not motivate action.

An ethic free of presuppositions has never existed. The question is: what presuppositions? As shown above, ethics based on causal or normative reason is full of contradictions. So, why not try an ethic within the church, the fellowship of faith? Faith and reason are not in opposition. Faith in the Word of God does not exclude reason. Faith penetrates through reason by realizing itself through reason. It is not the existence of reason, but only the perversion of reason which is in opposition to God. One who does not believe cannot understand the conception of the Good. The organ of reason is placed at the disposal of faith for its clarification.

Neither ethics nor law can tell us finally what we ought to do. They can only prepare the way for the hearing of the divine command.

THE DIVINE COMMAND by Emil Brunner
Lecture Notes

The Divine Command answers four questions:

- Why we act?
- Who acts?
- To whom we ought to do so and so?
- What are we to do?

Briefly, the answers are as follows:

- Why we act? Because God has acted in love.
- Who acts? The believer who hears God's word as command.
- To whom do we do what? The needy brother or brothers who meet us in some present event. We serve God by serving brother.
- What do we do? No man can tell another precisely what to do. Law guides our decisions but is not ultimate. "Do not kill, nor covet, nor

lie" are helpful guidelines. So is "love your enemy." However, they are not to be followed slavishly. Intelligent response to the love of God in the present moment and event is God's demand.

The sixteen propositions which follow in pages 114 to 288 are Brunner's development of his answer to these four questions. For purposes of this summary, we will lift the main propositions.

1. We know God's will only through God's revelation, in God's Word.
2. The divine command is absolutely concrete and cannot be formulated in general terms adequately. Loving obedience is such a generalization.
3. The basis of the divine command (Love the God who has loved you and love your neighbor), but the content varies with varying circumstances.
4. The divine command presupposes law in a three-fold sense: (a) the law which requires simple legal obedience, (b) radical law which leads to repentance, (c) guidance for faithful behavior.
5. God alone is good. God alone can be the subject of good human conduct. All conduct of the "new being in Christ" is addressed to God.
6. The command of God requires of the believer only one thing—existence in love. But this implies the existence of every "virtue."
7. God's command requires thankful acceptance of our given individual existence, coupled with denial of egocentric, self-seeking behavior. When man is living off the Ego alone, he is a living lie.
8. Though the divine command is love, it can only be apprehended through law which requires three things: (a) life on the level of ordinary morality, (b) renunciation of all claims to virtue, (c) striving after virtue, even perfection.
9. The prime response and the prime requirement of the divine commandment is "Serve God," not for God's sake but for humanity's sake. God is revealed in the Incarnation as "God for humanity."
10. Thus, God gives us our calling and requires from us the fulfillment of the duties of our calling. It is personal and concrete.
11. As Creator, God requires us to recognize the orders of God's creation. As Redeemer, God orders us to ignore the present order and inaugurate a new order—the Kingdom of God—which redeems this fallen order.

12. The divine command can be only perceived if we note these three forms of law: (a) the laws of official duty by which external community in the world is maintained, (b) the absolute law that all men are one in God the Father, by whom we recognize the lack of genuine, ultimate community in the world, (c) the law of love, whose function is to instruct the believer in his right personal relation with his neighbor.
13. God graciously gives and justly demands the right coordination of the means necessary for the attainment of a true end. "We could not act at all if we were determined to act only in opposition to the accepted code of behavior; but we could not act as Christians if we were always to conform to the accepted code, that is, if we were unprepared to strike out on a new line of our own."
14. The Command of the Creator-Redeemer requires and hallows the use of the means, which in reality are Divinely created and yet sinful but offer successful action. At the same time, God's command demands that all means which are contrary to the purpose of God shall not be used, but definitely rejected, at the price of possible rejection of what the world calls "success."
15. In view of this work which has to be done, the divine command must be understood in the light of the following threefold law: (a) it requires cooperation with secular society in accordance with practical righteousness, (b) As absolute law, it is critical of society, as are the prophets, (c) it guides the extraordinary action of the Church in preaching and in philanthropy.
16. Success and progress. On the one hand, the divine command makes a manifold demand: a progressively fruitful realization of good works; on the other hand, God demands one thing only: to turn in faith to the only action that is fruitful—God himself.

Brunner then applies these propositions to the orders of existence (291–562).

The man of faith sees himself as a sacred "Thou" in which the divine image is present. He sees other men similarly. To be responsible to the "Thou" means to be bound up in the bundle of life with the "Thou" by God himself. Thus, are we created in his image.

Thus do we approach our participation in the orders or social forms of our existence:

- Marriage and the family
- Community of labor
- The state or the people and the law
- The community of culture—science, art, and education
- The community of faith—the church

Chapter 46

RICHARD NIEBUHR

Summary of *Christ and Culture* by Richard Niebuhr Lecture Notes

One of the great classics of modern times is *Christ and Culture* by the memorable Christian theologian of Yale University, Richard Niebuhr. He gave these lectures at the Presbyterian Theological Seminary in Austin, right after World War II, in 1949. I got to hear one of them. Now, I would say I should have given my classes a holiday and gone to hear all of them.

Let's be clear that by "Christ," Niebuhr means the whole Christian understanding of all that Christ taught and all that he was and is. That is to say, he meant the Church's understanding of Christ as seen through some of the dominant points of view.

By "culture," Niebuhr means the state, the mores, the customs, the laws, the economic systems, the church, etc. He means the way men live their lives together in a given area, such as Europe during the Medieval period, or America in the twentieth century. You can see in paintings of the period that medievalist saw Christ as a medieval man, a monastic, and almost separated from the world. Twentieth-century men tend to see Jesus the man almost to the exclusivity of his divinity. Bruce Barton saw him as something of a good moral executive businessman.

One of the main things we must recognize is that persons in different ages appropriate different values from Christ and relate them to the culture of their time. This shows the boundless spiritual resourcefulness of Jesus Christ.

There are several views of Christ:

- Great teacher and lawgiver who persuades the mind and attaches it to his way.
- A revealer of truths through himself in incarnation, death,

resurrection, and living presence, shows us God, and claims man's faith, thus raising the lives of men he encounters to a new level.

- Christ, who establishes a new community, the Holy Catholic Church, which mediates his grace through word and sacrament.

In all these, Jesus Christ was a real man, with a real history. Extreme views of his nature and significance can be corrected by historic fact, even though the records may not yet be fully understood as to their verity.

The Christ who teaches the new law is the Christ who lives it and dies and is resurrected and through whom the Church is founded. His ethic is Love of God and man, not love of love. His love is all inclusive, but concrete.

Bonhoeffer said, "There was an extremeness in the hopefulness of Jesus that sets him apart from all other men who expect lesser glories or more frequently, no glory at all. Average morality presupposes complacency tempered by a little cynicism, or resignation qualified by moderate expectation of good. Intense anticipation of supernal good must result in a transformation of ethics."

His trust is in God. His eschatology and his ethic are rooted in this fundamental trust in the sovereign God. Obedience to God and God's commands for this man are basic. It is an involvement, deep, profound, possessive, eliciting whole-being response.

There is also structure and content in God's Will: the ten commandments, mercy not sacrifice, obedience to God's self, also love and faith in God and love toward the neighbor whom God also created. It is not obedience to an impersonal principle, but a son's obedience to his Father.

Jesus is a great skeptic about man. He believes that he is dealing with an evil and adulterous generation, with a people who stone their prophets and then erect monuments to them. He puts no trust in the institutions and traditions of society. He shows little confidence in his disciples; he is convinced that they will be offended in him, and that the sturdiest of them will be unable to stand by him in the time of testing. Only a romanticist would say he saw the goodness in men and sought by trusting this to bring out more goodness. Despite this skepticism, he is amazingly free from personal anxiety. He is heroic in his faith in God.

Yet, he is inordinately humble. He lived with the ill, the poverty stricken, the tax-collectors; all needy persons sought him out. His humility, though, is toward God, not men. He had confidence and a sense of authority. "There is no condescension in his life toward the sinners, such as might mark an insecure or apologetic man."

Jesus is the Mediator between God and Man, not half-god, half man. "He exists rather as the focusing point in the continuous alternation of movements from God to man and man to God, i.e., God's *Agape* and man's *eros*, God's authority and man's obedience, God's promise and man's hope, God's faithfulness and man's trust."

Niebuhr says there are basically five ways that Christ has been understood in relation to the world or culture.

I. Christ Against Culture

Tertullian (150–225 CE) interpreted Love of Neighbor to mean love of fellow Christians basically. Withdrawal from those associations in the world that would compromise one's association with Christ was basic. In his *Apology*, he said "As those in whom all ardor in the pursuit of honor and glory is dead, we have no pressing inducement to take part in your public meetings; nor is there aught more entirely foreign to us than affairs of state" (38). He thinks there is an inner contradiction between the exercise of political power and Christian faith. Military service is to be avoided not only because it involves participation in pagan religious rites and the swearing of an oath to Caesar but chiefly because it violates the law of Christ, who, "in disarming Peter, unbelted every soldier." "How shall the Son of Peace take part in battle when it does not become him even to sue at law?"

Trade cannot be prohibited with equals, and there may even be some righteousness in business. Yet, it scarcely is "adapted for the Servant of God." Apart from covetousness, which is a species of idolatry, there is no real motive for acquiring, or doing business (54).

Well, that is rather extreme for us, isn't it? But this is not only the thought of an early Christian; it has characterized much of monasticism, puritanism, and related Quakerism. Keep yourself unspotted from the world. Christ said, "My kingdom is not of this world. If my kingdom were of this world, then would my servants fight" (John 18:36).

Another Christian of this type in more recent times was Leo Tolstoy (1828–1910), the Russian Christian. He found himself tormented by the hypocrisies and cruelties of daily life. Though wealthy, he lived a monastic life on his own estate. He believed that the law of God given by Christ in the fifth chapter of Matthew was to be our guide to good life on earth. He summarized it thus:

- Live at peace with all men and never consider your anger against any man justified. Try in advance to destroy any enmity between yourself and others that it might not flame up and destroy you (59).
- Do not make the desire for sexual relations an amusement.
- Never make an oath to anyone about anything.
- Do not submit to the stupid and bad social order in which you have to live. "Never resist the evildoer by force; do not meet violence with violence. If they beat you, endure it; if they take your possessions, yield them up; if they compel you to work, work; and if they wish to take from you what you consider to be yours, give it up."
- Love your enemy. Do not make distinctions between your own and other nations; don't bear enmity to foreign nations and people; do not take part in war; do not arm yourself for war; but behave toward all men of whatever nation or race as toward your own people.

Tolstoy thought that evil was not resident in individual persons, but in the culture. So, this is clearly a Christ against Culture position. (See p.66 ff and p.75.)

II. Christ of Culture (or accommodation to culture)

Persons in this category of Christian belief are believers in the Lord Jesus Christ, but they seek to maintain community not only with all believers, but also with the larger community. They feel no great tension between Church and World. They think "This is my Father's world." They think Christians should help improve the quality of life in the world by applying Christ's teachings and life style to the culture, both political and economic.

The Gnostics of the first three centuries sought to relate the spirit of Christ to the knowledge of the Greek and Roman worlds. Gnosis means mystical knowledge of spiritual things. Our fourth Gospel, John, was written with the gnostics in mind. Unlike the Christ against Culture monks and others, the gnostics sought to correlate essential Christian teachings with secular knowledge.

If a Christian was too enlightened to take seriously the popular and official worship of idols or emperor worship, he was also too enlightened to make an issue out of its rejection and he scorned martyrdom. He thought knowledge of Jesus Christ was an individual and spiritual matter, which had its place in the life of culture as the very pinnacle of human achievement. He selected from Christian beliefs and cultural beliefs what he considered valid and integrated them into a theological position that enabled him to live meaningfully in his world. Pierre Abelard was persecuted by the more orthodox Christ Against Culture power figure Bernard of Clairveaux and died on his way to Rome to explain his position (essentially Aristotelian instead of Platonic) to the Pope.

Abelard had a broad and charitable spirit toward non-Christians. He offered a kindly and liberal guidance for good people who wanted to do right. All conflict between Christ and Culture was gone. He thought the Church failed to understand Christ's love for the world, and God's love for the world.

In the 1700s and 1800s, several figures who emphasized the reasonableness of Christianity had great influence. John Locke wrote *The Reasonableness of Christianity.* Immanuel Kant wrote *Religion within the Limits of Reason.* Thomas Jefferson edited the Gospels, choosing the teachings of Jesus that he thought could stand up to contemporary reason. He saw Jesus as the great enlightener, who seeks to establish a peaceful, cooperative society achieved by moral training.

Friedrich Schleiermacher in his *Speeches on Religion* sought to speak to the cultured despisers of religion, saying what they find offensive is not Christ, but the Church with its teachings and ceremonies. He said: "This Christ of religion does not call upon men to leave homes and kindred for his sake; he enters into their homes and all associations as the gracious presence which adds an aura of infinite meaning to all temporal tasks" (93).

In the early twentieth century, Albrecht Ritschl, in Germany, and Walter Rauschenbusch, in America, presented what became known widely as "The Social Gospel." From the New Testament, we conclude that God and Man have the common task of realizing the Kingdom. God works within the human community to establish the Kingdom. Christ is both priest and prophet. He ministers to the needs of persons through prayer and sacrament, but he also works through the culture inspiring persons to ethical striving in many institutions, such as hospitals, YMCAs, Social Centers such as Hull House, or today's Presbyterian Night Shelter or

Peace groups. He also applied this ethical striving, following the teachings of Jesus, to businesses, political parties, recreational life, certainly family life, and more (98).

The effort of these spokesmen for the Social Gospel was to get not just the church members, but all members of society to work together to establish the Brotherhood of Man under the Fatherhood of God.

Fundamentalists in the early twentieth century used to condemn Social Gospelers for their concern about political and social affairs. Now the Fundamentalists are socially active on issues like abortion, Medicare, Affirmative Action, etc. They are opposed to these issues, whereas liberal Social Gospelers favor them.

The Christ of Culture spokesmen attempt to make effective the universal meaning of the Gospel, plus they present Jesus as savior not of a little band of ingrown, self-righteous persons, but as the Savior of the World (John 3:16).

Later we will find that too close identification of Christ with culture can make an idol of a nation and confuse its goals with the purposes of God. It can blind one to the fact that there are Christians in other nations, even some of the nations against whom we have been at war. (German soldiers in WWI had "Gott mit uns" or "God with us" on their belt buckles.)

We are not immune to making the connection of Christ and culture. Some churches have the American flag at the front of the sanctuary. We had prayer in the public schools. We recognize that only by engaging in civic work for the sake of the common good by faithfulness to one's social calling is it possible to be true to the example of Christ (97).

In this position, Jesus is the savior, not of a selected little band of saints, but of the world. Those who know and love him are the means through which he loves and saves the world, or the culture. Jesus is the great teacher, leader. It's easy to confuse Christ and culture, to become secular. Most people advocated a socialism as the earthly form of the Kingdom. Herbert Marcuse, in an essay on liberalism, and Tielhard de Chardin and Jürgen Moltmann do. Man is a social organism.

III. Christ Above Culture

Here culture is not seen as evil, nor is it seen as ultimate. The best spokesman for this point of view is Thomas Aquinas.

He thought monasticism was okay, but not only monks are saved into heaven. Those who try to make the world a better place for their fellows, who try to be Christian in their family and vocation, are also saved. All men are ultimately saved by grace, for all fall short of perfection.

The Christian must answer the question about what he ought to do by asking and answering a previous question: What is my purpose, my end? He will seek to lay aside all immediate wishes and try to determine his ultimate reason for being. I am a part of the creation of God. Reason is given to help me realize my fullest potentialities and dedicate them to God. This will bless all men. Creation is not ultimate; only God is ultimate. Hence, God alone can fill the heart of man (131ff). The thought of God can alone satisfy the mind of man. St. Augustine said, "Thou hast made us for thyself."

There is a double happiness for man, one in this life and world and one in God and the next world. The steep climb toward the other world by bringing my daily life into harmony with God's purpose as understood by me is where a leap of faith and trust is necessary. Here we are aware of the otherness of God. God is not merely in culture, God is beyond culture also. Here we know ourselves as in need of grace. The seven sacraments (baptism, confirmation, eucharist, matrimony, penance, holy orders, extreme unction, or last rites) minister this grace to us. We receive it from God's servants and the church as means of ultimate salvation (133ff).

Thomas Aquinas combined natural theology and revealed theology into a synthesis. But the culture is not ultimate; Christ and his gift of grace are above culture. Culture is neither to be despised nor worshipped (140–44, 148).

IV. Christ and Culture in Paradox

This idea is probably the most difficult to understand because paradox is itself an admission of non-understandability. These Christians are called dualists. They are not the same as Tertullian and the Christ against Culture people. They emphasize, with the Christ against Culture people, the evil nature of culture, the contention that nothing in this world can be truly Christ-like or truly satisfy God. Man is steeped in sin, culture is man-made; so culture is steeped in sin. But we must live in the culture where we are (156–57).

All human action, all human culture is infected with godlessness, with the attempt to live without God, to live as though God were dead, or as if

I were the captain of my own ship, my own soul. Any time I act as though something on earth, even the church, were ultimate, I err sadly. Though the earth and the institutions of earth are in some sense the creation of God, they are not to be confused with God. God is totally other, as Karl Barth put it.

The ultimate paradox for the Christian is Jesus Christ himself. He is man, but not only man. He is God, or as Emil Brunner says, The God-Man. He is the Mediator between man and God. This does not fit any of our categories of reason. The person holding this position sees all of man's culture-building as like the Tower of Babel, as cracked and slightly askew. He is called to "hear another drummer," to put his trust in God alone, yet live in the culture wisely.

Yet, paradoxically, he is called to do what he thinks is right in this world, even to giving his life to oppose Hitler, as Dietrich Bonhoeffer did. Yet, he does not consider that this will neither assure him of heaven, indicate that he doesn't care about the order of life in the world, nor assure that there won't be any other Hitlers. We might recall Jesus's statement in John 16:33: "In the world you will have tribulation, but be of good cheer. I have overcome the world." In a sense, this point of view emphasizes that statement of Jesus: "My kingdom is not of this world," rather than his other statement, "Thy kingdom come on earth."

As Bonhoeffer puts it, everything the human mind can conceive and the human being can seek and attain is "pen-ultimate, it is the thing before the last thing." The last things are beyond this order of being. They are of God in his own transcendent way. Our trust is ultimately in God and God's purposes. In the meantime, we do the best we can on earth, sure of his love, grace, forgiveness. We are very careful not to confuse our government, our economic system, our denomination, with the ultimate will and purpose of God.

Martin Luther is an illustration of Christ and Culture in Paradox. "The life of Christ and the life in culture, in the Kingdom of God and the kingdom of the world, are closely related. The Christian must affirm both in a single act of obedience to the one God of mercy and wrath, not as a divided soul with a double allegiance and duty. Luther rejected the synthetic solution but was equally firm in maintaining the unity of God and the unity of the Christian life in culture (172ff).

"As long as man mistrusts his Creator, he will in his anxiety for himself and his goods be unable to do anything in all his service for others but serve himself. He is involved in the vicious circle of self-love, which leads him to look for credit for every apparently altruistic action. . . . Christ, by his law and his deed of redemption, breaks this circle of self-love, and does make men righteous—not within themselves, but in the response to Him of their humbled and grateful hearts. . . . When the self found its security in God, it was delivered from anxiety and thus set free to serve the neighbor self-forgetfully.

"Luther affirmed the life in culture as the sphere in which Christ could and ought to be followed; and more than any other he discerned that the rules to be followed in the cultural life were independent of Christian or church law. For instance, though philosophy offered no road to faith, yet the faithful man could take the philosophical road to such goals as were attainable by that way. In a person 'regenerated and enlightened by the Holy Spirit through the Word' the natural wisdom of man 'is a fair and glorious instrument and work of God.'

"A Christian was not only free to work in culture, but free to choose those methods which were called for, in order that the objective good with which he was concerned in his work might be achieved. As he cannot derive the laws of medical procedure from the gospel when he deals with a case of typhus, so he cannot deduce from the commandment of love the specific laws to be enacted in a commonwealth containing criminals.

"We may say then that the dualism in Luther's solution of the Christ-and-Culture problem was the dualism of the 'How' and the 'What' of conduct. From Christ we receive the knowledge and the freedom to do faithfully and lovingly what culture teaches or requires us to do. . . . The drive to action on the part of man comes from our God-given nature; its direction and spirit is a function of faith; its content comes from reason and culture" (176).

The paradox is obvious when the Christian is committed to love the enemy and yet kills him in war as an agent of the state. Both can be valid in this paradoxical situation.

V. Christ, the Transformer of Culture

Niebuhr calls these people "conversionists." "Augustine not only describes but also illustrates in his own person the work of Christ as converter of culture. The Roman rhetorician becomes a Christian preacher, who not only puts into the service of Christ the training in language and literature given to him by his society, but, by virtue of the freedom and illumination received from the Gospel, uses that language with a new brilliance and brings a new liberty into that literary tradition.

"He had been a Neo-platonist and continued many of those emphases, but this wisdom was humanized and given new depth by his attention to the Christian incarnation. Augustine wrestles with the culture problems of the demise of the Roman Empire with its many values and the role of Christ in bringing to birth a new empire more humane in his *City of God.*

"Christ is the transformer of culture for Augustine in the sense that he redirects, reinvigorates, and regenerates that life of man, expressed in all human works, which in present actuality is the perverted and corrupted exercise of a fundamentally good nature, which, moreover, in its depravity lies under the curse of transiency and death, not because an external punishment has been visited upon it, but because it is intrinsically self-contradictory.

"Man is essentially good, but when he turns away from God, he is lost. In turning back to God, he is saved and is used by God to transform society. But society is not the ultimate order of goodness. That, of course, is heaven, which is beyond the world.

"Christ is God's picture of our end, our way, and God's love. Christ restores what has been corrupted and redirects what has been perverted. Christ transforms the emotions of men, not by substituting reason for emotion, but by attaching fear, desire, grief, and joy to the right object. . . . The reasoning of the redeemed man begins with faith in God and love of the order which he has put into all his creation; and is thus free to trace out God's designs and humbly to follow his ways. This man rejoices in all God's creatures and serves and blesses them in his actions. His actions seek to reflect the love and glory of God in his creation." "Thou hast made us for thyself alone, and our hearts are restless until they find rest in thee" (208).

Calvin is like Augustine. He adds dimensions such as a dynamic concept of vocation. Man should glorify God in his vocation, as a calling. Also, the state is God's minister not only in restraint of evil, but also in positive promotion of the welfare of man. Though he takes the fall of man very seriously, the elect are called to acknowledge God's sovereignty and to rule as they think God would rule in ordering the society. This is what Calvin did in Geneva. The Christian seeks to convert the kingdoms of this world into the Kingdom of God. There is temporal and eternal dualism, heaven and hell. God over against man.

As Niebuhr says in conclusion, any thoughtful Christian can see that there is some validity in each of these positions. He can, probably, say that I tend to be basically a Christ of Culture man, or a Christ against Culture man, or a Christ above Culture man, etc. However, I think most of us best fit into the position that Niebuhr seems to prefer. It is called Christ, the Transformer of Culture. This position recognizes that Christ does care about culture and many teachings and actions of Jesus could be quoted here, such as the Good Samaritan.

Yet, at the same time, the fact that the very priests in the Temple of God did not recognize the Messiah when he appeared and could not accept his rebuke gracefully when he overturned the tables of the money changers makes us conscious that we probably could not receive his rebuke if he came back among us either. We need to hold ourselves and the church always under the sovereignty of God in Jesus Christ. We need to continually realize that our goodness is pen-ultimate and subject to review by God, including our churches which we sought to erect to the glory of God.

And so, the last note of these lectures is like unto the first. God is continually, dynamically judging and renewing, bringing creative new things to pass, including new persons, new churches, new nations. One can live in a time of judgment or a time of growth and renewal. It behooves us to try to understand the answer to the question: "What on earth is God doing now?"

Our ultimate security is in God who transcends the institutional forms of life. Not money, not job, not church, not even our good works are our ultimate security. Ultimate security is in the loving grace of God revealed preeminently in the gift of Jesus Christ. "God showed his love toward us in that while we were yet, Christ died for us sinful men."

RICHARD NIEBUHR, *THE MEANING OF REVELATION* (Macmillan, 1941)

Notes for a lecture at Meadowbrook Methodist Church, September 1996
The rationalist view opposing revelation was developed by Kant, Hume,

Butler, Schleiermacher, and others, such as Ames and Wieman. The higher critical view of the scriptures opposed divine inspiration of the scriptures and revelation as a source of inspiration for the scriptures. The Deists were opposed to the concept of revelation.

Both Catholics and Protestants have tried to hold on to revelation. Catholics fled the twentieth century into the thirteenth; Protestants shunned the adventure of the social gospel and ran away from historical and psychological criticism. It is either reactionary or antiquarian.

But closer acquaintance with the thought about revelation that is developing in our time will not allow such generalizations. The thought is part of a revolutionary movement.

Changes in religious and moral thought begin with the remembrance of something superficially forgotten, yet real in a transcendent or social mind. It returns to original sources for new fountains of inspiration, but it is not necessarily reactionary. It does not seek to maintain customs established in the past.

The problem has been set by historical relativism: We realize that the point of view that a man occupies when he views reality is of profound importance. Remember Christ and Culture.

VI. Historical Relativism and Revelation

Spatio-temporal relativism plays the same important part in twentieth-century thinking that idealism did in the seventeenth and eighteenth century and evolution did in the nineteenth (7). Theology is concerned with relativity as it has influenced history and sociology, and then philosophy and theology.

Earlier idealists, as in Schleiermacher, decided they could not describe God as God is in God's self but only God in human experience; yet they were able to work within those limits with an effectiveness greater, if anything, than any time before....They found that empirical theology left as much room for faith as rationalistic theology.

History and sociology have continued the human self-criticism which psychology began. Critical idealists and realists knew themselves to be human selves with a specific psychological and logical equipment; their successors know themselves to be social human beings whose reason is not a common reason, alike in all human selves, but one which is qualified by inheritance from a particular society. They know their theology like their politics changes with time. We have resisted this self-knowledge and continue to do so.

All reality has become temporal for us, but our historical relativism affirms the relativity of the subject even more than the object. Not only is man in time, but time is in man. And the time in man is particular and concrete, not abstract.

Sociology of language has shown us that there can be no universal concepts when there is no universal language. Language is always particular and historical. Theologians have been reminded in the last 150 years of the relativity of Biblical language to historical setting. The nineteenth century liberal could not claim biblical authority for his point of view because the language and concepts of first and nineteenth centuries were so different, with the eschatological thought of the first century being a major point. Value scales have a history, as mathematical systems have (15). No observer can get out of history; so his historical context must be considered.

But there is no sense in attempting rational suicide in skepticism or egoistic totalitarianism.

Yet, since all stand in some historical sequence that provides meaning. Theology can seek, within the history of which it is a part, an intelligible pattern. It can undertake to analyze the reason which is in that pattern of history and to assist those who participate in this historical life to disregard all that is secondary and not in conformity with the central ideas and patterns of the historical movement. Such theology can seek to state the grammar, not of a universal religious language, but of a particular language, in order that those who use it may be kept in true communication with each other and with the realities to which the language refers (18). Relativism does not imply subjectivism and skepticism. Admitting my stance as a Christian, I do not have to doubt the reality of what I see. If I know my concepts are not universally held, I do not have to doubt that they describe the universal reality. This approach affirms intellectual stubbornness or toughness in the face of opposition.

It is not necessarily true that since all traditions are historical, nothing is mediated through history.

The acceptance of the reality of what we see in psychological and historically conditioned experience is always something of an act of faith, but such faith is inevitable and justifies itself or is justified by its fruits. To be in history is to be in society and to be subject to correction by other participants in the society (20).

Christian theology must begin in Christian history because it has no other choice (22); in this sense it is forced to begin with revelation, meaning by that word simply historic faith. But this is the beginning and not the end of inquiry.

When a Christian speaks (thus) of revelation, he means not only that religion, like politics, is subject to its finite historic point of view, but also it can rightfully say that in the historic Christian faith a reality discloses itself which invites all the trust and devotion of finite, temporal men. Such a theology of revelation is objectively relativistic, proceeding with confidence in the independent reality of what is seen, though recognizing that its assertions about that reality are meaningful only to those who look upon it from the same standpoint (22).

VII. Religious Relativism and Revelation

As Luther, Schleiermacher, Ritschl, Barth, and many others have seen, one can make meaningful statements about God only from the relativistic stand of faith in him (23). When a Christian says God, he does not mean first cause of cosmos, etc. He means a being infinitely attractive which by its very nature calls forth devotion, "my God" (25). Ritschl's insistence that belief in God represented a value judgment indicated why intellectual approaches to God brought no sense of repentance, prayer, etc. Schleiermacher emphasized that philosophy and theology are two different approaches to reality.

It is not fair to Luther or Schleiermacher to imply that faith itself saves. They both believed that it is God who saves.

But Ritschl developed an inconsistency that killed his viewpoint's effectiveness. Having said that the relation of man to God is the ultimate value relation, he sets up a prior value-relation, man's relation to nature, as more basic. He interprets man to himself as he appears not in relation to God, but in relation to lower forms of nature. He regards himself as the crown of the natural development. So Ritschl did not approach God as a Christian who values God as infinitely superior to man, but from the standpoint of man's confidence in his own worth as superior to nature. (And, of course, this is dead as a do-do bird today with man in despair as to whether he has any value per se. The optimism of the late nineteenth century is dead.)

At any rate, the anthropocentrism and self-idolatry of the nineteenth century is apparent in Ritschl, and this age-old view has a flaw at its center as the Jews knew (31). In trying to prove Christianity superior, he did not rely on the character of God revealed in Christ but the faith in man as a superior being.

Ritschl really developed a theology with two foci—God and man. The resulting confusion in which a church emphasized either a high and exalted God or became an ethical culture society and didn't seem to be able to get the two together was hard on the church.

Christianity seized upon the opportunities offered by the leaders of thought to abandon the standpoint of Christian faith and to take up another point of view. Churches became national or cultural societies. Faith in the God of Jesus Christ is a rare thing and faith in idols tends forever to disguise itself as Christian trust (34).

The lesson of history is that the only point of view from which the God of Christian faith may be understood is that of Christian faith itself (35). A theology which abandons the point of view of faith in God does so because it does not permit theology to follow another interest—the defense of civilization or man or Christianity itself before culture.

God cannot be apprehended save by a willing, feeling, responding self (35). And this person must live in a historically relative community. Because God and faith belong together, the standpoint of the Christian theologian must be in the faith of the Christian community, directed toward the God of Jesus Christ (37). There is no absolute freedom available for the theologian in the sense of being completely uncommitted to any supreme value. But, there is considerable freedom in the bondage of Christian community and historical relativities.

VIII. Revelation and Confessional Theology

Our apologetics for Christianity are often attempts to justify our behavior and ourselves rather than to put men in touch with God. The idea of revelation may be employed, not for the greater glory of God, but as a weapon for the defense and aggrandizement of the church or even of the individual theologian. We must not substitute the sovereignty of the Christian religion for the sovereignty of God (40). Jesus himself emptied himself and refused to claim the kingly crown.

We can proceed only by stating in simple, confessional form what has happened to us in our community, how we came to believe, how we reason about things and what we see from our point of view (41).

Revelation (in Christ) is not something that the Church can possess like a property and dispense like hot cakes. The confessional form of theology tries to avoid this. It puts the individual on his mettle to stand before God and be encountered by him in a revelatory event. Then he shall know the meaning of the historic revelation.

This revelatory event (Christ) exposes human sin no less than divine goodness. Religious response to revelation is made quite as much in a confession of sin as in a confession of faith . . . and the theologian must recognize that he speaks as a sinner, not as a saint (42).

This is the sum of the matter: Christian theology must begin today with revelation because it knows that men cannot think about God save as historic, communal beings and save as believers. It must ask what revelation means for Christians rather than what it ought to mean for all men, everywhere and always. And it can pursue its inquiry only by recalling the story of Christian life by analyzing what Christians see from their limited point of view in history and faith (42).

IX. The Story of Our Life

When early preachers were asked what they meant by their theological jargon about salvation, etc., they replied essentially, "What we mean is this event of Jesus Christ which has happened to us in history." They spoke like the prophets, which is the way Judaism has always spoken.

Whitehead: "Religions commit suicide when they find their inspiration in their dogmas. The inspiration of religion lies in the history of religion" (47). We are in history as the fish are in water. The revelation of God can be seen only as we look through the medium in which we live (48). If we develop natural theology, we do it through the mind of Christ and the Christian interpretation of history. Scripture is in the same position. If not interpreted through what God has done through Christ in history, it is meaningless (49).

As Protestants we have discovered that we inevitably must interpret scriptures from a community point of view. We cannot know an historical Jesus save as we look through the history and with the history of the community that loved and worshipped him. A Jesus of history apart from the particular history in which he appears is as unknown and unknowable as any sense-object apart from the sense qualities in which it appears to us (52).

How do we relate God to history and not lose him in past or future? The particular historical events (biblical, counciliar, etc.) can be studied just as objectively as any other events.

If revelation means history, it cannot also mean the object of faith, save in this purely factual and wholly opaque sense that certain people have attached transcendent value to certain events, as Bultman says (56).

If revelation means history, is it not necessary to concentrate on a past event and not the here and now? Such concentration has called forth revolts by men of piety who said God lives in the here and now also. Faith for them was confidence in an abiding, ruling will of love. Struggling with contemporary evil, such men have rebelled against identifying the faith with the past. They have insisted on the present reality of the Holy Spirit (57). Also, emphasis on a God who meets us in the future, but not now, has led to revolt.

History seems always to lead to doubt rather than to faith. So many are tempted to a "Christ of faith" instead of a Jesus of history. But faith is a strange thing; it is not sufficient to itself and will not work alone. Like the eye, it needs a mate to sense depth. Philosophy, as historical in all its forms as religion, can share and strengthen the life of faith, but only when it speaks out of a mind that has been filled with Jewish and Christian memories. . . . Gilson reminds us that the God of modern philosophers is more than the God of their philosophies; God could not mean so much in their thought if God did not mean more than their thought expresses about God. God is always transcendent, the God of history—Abraham, Isaac, and Jacob (58).

X. History as Lived and Seen

History as we mean it is not seen at a distance, objectively. It is our inner history as lived. It is an existential view of history. Niebuhr contrasts Lincoln's Gettysburg Address as it idealizes our forefathers bringing forth a nation dedicated to liberty and the proposition that all men are created free and equal, with the *Cambridge Modern History* account of the Declaration of Independence: "The doctrine of the equality of men, unless it be qualified . . . is either a barren truism or a delusion" (60–61). Difference in sentiment can make this wide difference of idea in interpreting an historic event.

Lincoln was speaking from within our history. The Cambridge historian was speaking from without (62). The data are I-Its, as Buber would put it (65). While in inner history, they are I-Thou relations. The I of the I-It and the I-Thou relation differs.

In external history, we try to abstract all subjective accounts. In internal history, on the other hand, we are not concerned with the primary and secondary elements of external historical perception, but with . . . values. These are not private and evanescent, but common and verifiable in the community of selves; yet they are not objective in the sense in which the primary qualities of external perception are said to be objective. . . . There is a descriptive and normative knowledge of history, and neither is reducible to the other (66–67).

In external history, value means power, strength, influence of an event. In internal history, value means worth for selves (68). . . . The valuable is that which bears on the destiny of selves.

As with value, so with time. In our internal history, time has a different feel and quality from that of external time. . . . In external history, it is a scale of dates; in internal history, our time is our duration. What is past abides in us as memory; what is future is present in us as potentiality. Time here is organic or social (69).

When we become a member of a community, such as the Christian Church, we adopt its history as our own past. We think like poets—of persons, purposes, and destinies (71). It is like Job and Hamlet rather than a procession of kings. It is the history of drama, where the valuations of the characters are exposed.

When the evangelists told of the Christ event, it was internal history they were recording—the starting point of their faith, the personal history, their reorientation of self (72).

The inspiration (revelation) of Christianity has been derived from history, but not from history as seen by the spectator; the constant reference is to subjective events, that is to events in the lives of the participants.

One must look with Paul, not at Paul, to see the risen Lord. Paul cannot promise to take you to a place on the Damascus road where anyone who wishes may see the risen Lord. I have been there and I didn't see him, but I appreciate Paul's "I have seen the Lord."

XI. Faith in Our History

How is it possible for revelation to point to history and to God, also? Well, not by the traditional method of pointing to miracles and inserting them in secular history. Or to support scriptural infallibility by pointing to the miraculous. That supposed a process which suspended the natural processes and guaranteed inerrancy (75). The result was a natural and a supernatural system set side by side. Revelation took place in the supernatural. Reason operated in the natural.

History as seen from without by "pure reason" and from within by "practical reason" can be allied. An inner history is always an affair of faith. As long as a man lives, he must believe in something, for the sake of which he lives. Without belief in something that makes life worth living, man cannot exist.

Most men have man gods and so do many communities. Without a single faith, there is no real unity of the self or the community. Inner history and inner faith belong together (78). To be a self is to have a god; to have a god is to have a history; to have one god is to have one history.

XII. Relations of Internal and External History

When we've found that revelation is implicit in our internal history, we cannot refrain from asking ourselves how this history is related to the external accounts of our life. We face a dualism.

First, the event as it really is the event as seen by God, who sees it from within and without at the same time. Finite man cannot do this, except through confessional faith (84). In faith he can sense the event-for-God. An external history of Christianity can become an internal event for Christianity to which it must respond. A new interpretation of its history which it must declare in faith to be true or false. Such external histories have helped to keep the church from exalting itself as though its inner life rather than the God of that inner life were the center of its attention and the ground of its faith. Thus external history has contributed to internal history.

Secondly, just because the Christian community remembers the revelatory moment in its own history, it is required to regard all events even though it can see most of them only from the external point of view, as workings of the God who reveals himself and so to trace with piety and disinterestedness so far as its own fate is concerned, the ways of God in the lives of men (86). It is necessary for the Christian community, living in faith, to look upon all the events of time and to try to find in them the workings of one mind and will. The God who reveals himself in inner history is the creator, the universal God, the creator of all other happenings, too.

Faith cannot get to God save through historic experience, as reason cannot get to nature save through sense experience. But as reason, having learned through limited experience an intelligible pattern in all other experience, so faith, having apprehended the divine self in its own history, can and must look for the manifestation of the same self in all other events (86–87).

An external history finds its starting point or impulsion in an internal history (88). We don't write external histories unless a lot of people find them meaningful based on internal history. Without the Bible and the rites of the institutional church, the inner history of the Christian community could not continue . . . (89).

Though we cannot point to what we mean by revelation by directing attention to the historic facts as embodied and as regarded from without, we can have no continuing inner history through which to point without embodiment (89–90). External history is the medium in which internal history exists and comes to life. The nature of Christian life and history is duality in union. The sphere in which revelation takes place is internal history, the story of what happened to us, the living memory of the community (90).

XIII. Reasons of the Heart—Imagination and Reason

Revelation means to Christians "history as it is remembered by participating selves" (92). "Revelation means for us that part of our inner history which illuminates the rest of it and which is itself intelligible. . . . Whitehead . . . has said 'Rational religion appeals to the direct intuition of special occasions, and to the elucidatory power of its concepts for all occasions.' The special occasion to which we appeal is called Jesus Christ, in whom we see the righteousness of God's power and wisdom. But from that special occasion we also derive the concepts which make possible the elucidation of all the events in our history. Revelation means this intelligible event makes all other events intelligible. Such a revelation, rather than being contrary to reason in our life, is the discovery of rational pattern in it" (93–94).

Revelation means the point at which we can begin to think and act as members of an intelligible and intelligent world of persons (94). The affections of the soul come to us through and in our social body almost as much as in our individual structure (98).

XIV. Interpretation through Revelation

By revelation in our history, then, we mean that special occasion which provides us with an image by means of which all the occasions of personal and common life become intelligible (109). . . . It illuminates other events and helps us to understand them. It is an event in our history which brings rationality and wholeness into the confused joys and sorrows of personal existence and allows us to discern order in the brawl of communal histories. Such revelation is no substitute for reason. The illumination it supplies does not excuse the mind from labor, but it gives the mind the impulsion and the first principles it requires if it is to do its proper work (109). It is revelatory because it is rational.

The revelatory moment makes our past intelligible (110). Reasoning based on revelation means the heart not only understands what it remembers but is enabled to remember what it had forgotten (113). The revelatory event is not merely intellectual, but moral (116). To remember the human past as our own past is to achieve community with mankind. It constitutes a moral conversion. This is an indispensable part of the soul's conversion (117). Such conversion is a permanent revolutionary movement (118). Without revelation, reason is limited and guided into error; without reason, revelation illuminates only itself. The heart must reason not only about the past but also in the present too (121). We do not call those events in our history revelation which cast no light upon the things that are happening to us . . . (121).

In interpreting our present, we use the life and death of Christ as a parable and an analogy (124). But even more than an analogy, a rational image . . . we try to understand what our actions and sufferings really are.

Theology tends to generalize, lose contact with the existential meaning of the revelatory event, relate revelation to doctrines—such as original sin, grace, salvation. The preacher's use of the dramatic image comes nearer the requirements of the reasoning heart than does the theologians application of a conceptual pattern (126).

Revelation is like a classic drama which, through the events of one day and place, makes intelligible the course of a family history. Or, it is like a decisive moment in the common life of friends. In the community of faith, we turn to a critical point in man's conversation with God (129). We try to understand the present as a continuation from that beginning.

In the light of revelation, we see the end because we discern the beginning of the end in the present. Prophet and New Testament apostles do not predict immortality without judgment (cross) intervening. The possibility the new Christian discerns is not his own. It is the possibility of the resurrection of a new and other self, a new community, a reborn remnant (131).

Thus, the heart reasons with the aid of revelation. All reasoning is painful and none more so than that which leads to knowledge of the self (131).

XV. Progressive Revelation.

Revelation which furnishes the practical reason with a starting point for the interpretation of past, present, and future history is subject to progressive validation (133). Revelation is not progressive in the sense that we can substitute some other moment in our history for the revelatory moment of Jesus Christ and interpret the latter through the former (135). The God who revealed himself continues to reveal himself—the one God of all times and places (136).

We do not easily change first principles, but as we move back and forth, dialectically, between revelatory event and experience which illumines the meaning of it in life, the meaning of the revelation grows progressively clearer. Hocking illustrates: a mountain at the distance gives no hint of all the richness of streams, deep valleys, high forests, snow banks, and steep inclines which one encounters as he lives with the mountain in climbing it (136).

Revelation requires of those to whom it has come that they begin the never-ending pilgrim's progress of the reasoning Christian heart (137).

XVI. The Deity of God—God Reveals Himself

When we speak of revelation, we mean that something has happened to us in our history which conditions all our thinking and that through this happening, we are enabled to apprehend what we are, what we are suffering and doing, and what our potentialities are. What is otherwise arbitrary and dumb fact becomes related, intelligible, and eloquent fact through the revelatory event. To the extent that revelation furnishes the practical reason with an adequate starting point, it may be said to be validated (138).

Revelation is like the kingdom of God: if we seek it first, all other things are added to us, but if we seek it for the sake of these other things, we really deny it. . . . Revelation proves itself to be revelation of reality not only by its intrinsic verity but also by its ability to guide men to many other truths.

Revelation is personal. A self must reveal itself. A self must respond. Buber's I-Thou relation expresses it best: meeting with such a Thou, the I is changed (146). The Thou meets me, but I step into direct relation with it.

But what is revealed? Jesus? "Revelation in terms of the person of Jesus is manifestly inadequate. . . . how can we have personal communion with one who exists only in our memory, monuments, books, and sentences?" (148).

Others say it is not the person of Jesus but the fellowship of the church which is revealed. But in this way lies disaster. The self-worship of non-Christian communities is enough to warn us that communal self-exaltation is an evil imagination of the heart leading to destruction of self and others (149). Also, if we say that the central insight of Jesus is that human selves have infinite value, we end with self-worship (150–51).

All revelation points beyond the historic event to that which is revealed through the historic event—to God. All revelation is the self-revelation of God. . . . God reveals himself in that he forces us to trust him wholly. Revelation is the activity of God in which he unveils his hiddenness, his giving of himself in communion (152).

Revelation is the moment in which we find our judging selves to be judged not by ourselves or our neighbors but by one who knows the final secrets of the heart; revelation means the self-disclosure of the judge (153). Revelation means that we find ourselves to be valued rather than valuing and that all our values are transvaluated by the activity of the universal valuer (153).

When a price is put upon our heads, which is not our price, when the unfairness of all the fair prices we have placed on things is shown up; when the great riches of God reduce our wealth to poverty, that is revelation. When we find out that we are no longer thinking of God, but God first thought of us, that is revelation. . . . Revelation means the moment in our history through which we know ourselves to be known from beginning to end. . . . It means the self-disclosing of that eternal knower, the one who cares! (152–53).

One problem is that revelation in Protestantism has meant scriptures or doctrinal content of scriptures such that Jesus Christ was the Son of God or God forgives sin. In Roman Catholicism, revelations meant supernatural knowledge about man's supernatural end. Also, isn't our concept so mystical that its content is totally irrelevant to our discursive knowledge and to our moral standards? No, I think not.

Another problem is that revelation means divine self-disclosure. How can we be sure it is God who discloses God's self when we have no previous meeting by which to judge the disclosure? We have in Jesus.

XVII. Revelation and the Moral Law.

Revelation does not come through moral law because moral law is finally a social concept (Kant, as quoted on p. 163). The deity we can deduce from moral law is no more absolute than that moral law and no more unified than we know it to be. We may have intimations of immortality, but these are merely a great yearning.

The moral law is changed in the process of God's divine self-disclosure. One does not transgress the old law blatantly, but seeing the insufficiency of it, responds to God's self-disclosure in such a way that the eternal earnestness of a personal God is made manifest. It transcends culture and the usual human boundaries. Revelation of God's person is not revelation of law, but of law's sin or inadequacy. It is thus a criticism of the law as well as a validation of the law. Obey the law and go beyond it in love. In Christ we have a replication of the moral law in a personal edition.

Revelation may involve radical reconstruction of our beliefs, but it imparts no new beliefs about natural or historical facts (172).

We don't have to glorify the self. We can study the world disinterestedly. Emergent evolution in nature is no adequate counterpart to revelation of God as divine being (174). Pure reason does not need to be limited in order that room be made for faith, but faith emancipates the pure reason from the necessity of defending and guarding the interests of selves, which are now found to be established and guarded, not by nature, but by the God of revelation whose garment nature is (175).

XVIII. Human Value and the God of Revelation

The second set of difficulties is that "revelation is not the communication of new truths and the supplanting of our natural religion by a supernatural one. It is the fulfillment and the radical reconstruction of our natural knowledge about deity through the revelation of one whom Jesus Christ called Father" (182). It is a new meeting of one we have met before in nature.

Revelation is revolution, creative change, in religious knowledge. We sought a God to bring unity, by being beyond the many. But God has met us not as the one beyond the many, but as the one who acts in and through all things, not as the unconditioned, but as the conditioner" (183).

Through God we see our disorder and our lack of unity; and through God we find unity flowing into our world in another manner than we desired (184). Revelation is a revolution in our thought about morals, about self, about unity, about divine power (185).

The God revealed to us in Jesus is not other than the God we meet in nature and in history. God's reality and power is the reality and the power of the world. God is the life-giving and the death-dealing power. The power of God is made manifest in the weakness of Jesus, in the meek and dying life which through death is raised to power. God's power is seen in God making the spirit of the slain Jesus unconquerable (187).

With revelation, we must begin to rethink all ideas about deity. Revelation is the beginning of a revolution in our power thinking and our power politics.

Deity must be value, good. The goodness we expect from deity must be both intrinsic and instrumental. If deity is one, deity must combine with power an adorable and a ministering goodness. The God who reveals God's self in Jesus Christ is precisely this—an adorable and a ministering goodness. The value we see here is the simple everyday goodness of love—the goodness which exists in pure activity. It surprises us and puts our expectations to shame. All our ambitions to be ministers of God are humbled. God is our minister. We had sought to keep our sense of virtue in the center of the picture. Now we stand shamed by God's surprising simple goodness.

Revelation is not the development of and not the elimination of our natural religion; it is the revolution of the religious life. God ministers to all our good, but all our good is other than we thought.

This conversion and permanent revolution of our human religion through Jesus Christ is what we mean by revelation.

"I do not say to thee, seek the way. The way itself is come to thee; arise and walk" (191).

Chapter 47

ERICH FROMM

Psychoanalysis and Religion, by Erich Fromm
Yale Press, 1950
A lecture

Looking at the Creation, modern man can say "it is good." But looking at himself, he can't say "created in the image of God." Ours is a life not of brotherliness, but of schizophrenic madness.

We pray for rain in churches while at the same time hiring scientific rain-makers. Merchants listen to sermons on love and charity, then go out and sell people items they do not need and cannot afford. In fact, all the animal hungers of naïve men are used to create the desire to buy.

We hear no voice telling us where to go, or that it will lead us through the wilderness, as the children of Israel did. Priests and ministers seem to be the only group concerned for the soul and expressing love and affirmation. In some cultures, philosophers and physicians have also been friends of man.

Those who affirmed man's independence of Church and political shackles in the Enlightenment did so in an attempt to discover the roots of human happiness. Reason to discover truth and the essence of things has been replaced by intelligence to manipulate things. Man has ceased to believe that the power of reason can establish the validity of norms and ideas for human conduct.

Academic psychology has dealt (through weights and measures) with everything except the soul. Psychology became a science lacking its main subject matter, the soul. (Manning seems to endeavor to overcome this.)

"I want to show in these pages that it is not true that we have to give up the concern for the soul if we do not accept the tenets of religion." Studying both religious and non-religious symbol systems, he finds that the question is not whether man returns to religion and believes in God, but whether he lives love and thinks truth. If he does so, the symbol systems he uses are of secondary importance. If he does not, they are of no importance.

Freud considers religion an illusion—an obsession—a regression to childishness to handle the threatening forces without and within that he does not understand. When a child, he felt protected by a father. He tries to return to that childlikeness in maturity with God, the Heavenly Father. Religion is a collective neurosis, caused by conditions like those that create childhood neuroses. Freud does not say because an idea fulfills a wish of man, it does not automatically mean that the idea is false. It may mean that. Some rational basis for decision must be established. Many, like Schleiermacher, emphasize that the feeling of dependence or powerlessness is the core of religious experience. Freud does not agree.

Jung says he will avoid philosophy. Freud, William James, John Dewey did not avoid philosophy. Jung will be phenomenological. Stick to observation of events. For instance, regarding the Virgin Birth, the psychologist is concerned with the fact that there is such an idea and not whether the event took place objectively. Fromm disagrees. He says we must test ideas for truth. A practicing psychiatrist could not function were he not concerned with whether the idea held by the patient accords with truth, reality.

Jung thinks that if whole groups believe something, it is "true" or objective. But if only one individual believes it, it is delusionary. Fromm reminds us of the "folie de millions."

Jung defines religious experience as being seized by a power outside ourselves. Therefore, for him, the concept of the unconscious is a religious one. It is not a part of the individual's mind, but is a power beyond our control intruding upon our minds. When we assume responsibility for it and say it is our own, we are overstating it. It is ours, but more. It is God's.

Both Freud and Jung appreciate religion. But Freud emphasizes the positive ethical values: knowledge, truth, logos, brotherly love, reduction of suffering, independence, responsibility.

Jung emphasizes emotional surrender to a higher power, whether this higher power is called God or the unconscious. Both are types of religious experiences. William James, like Jung, compares the unconscious with God.

Fromm understands religion to mean "any frame of reference or system of thought and action shared by a group which gives the individual a frame of orientation and an object of devotion . . . (21). In this sense, all cultures have religion. Man needs this because self-awareness, reason, and imagination have disrupted man from his original, animal harmony. . . . Devotion is an expression of this need for completeness in the process of living. . . . We must understand every ideal, including those which appear in secular ideologies, as attempts to restore man's equilibrium and harmony in his world" (25).

The question is not religion or not, but which kind. Most formal religions are veneers laid over more primitive forms of behavior-religion: ancestor worship, nationalism, totemism, fetishism, ritualism, the cult of cleanliness, etc.

Calvin emphasizes "I do not call it humility if you suppose that we have anything left. We cannot think of ourselves as we ought to think without utterly despising everything that may be supposed an excellence in us. This humility is unfeigned submission of a mind overwhelmed with a weighty sense of its own misery and poverty; for such is the uniform description of it in the word of God" (*Institutes, P&R*, 35–36).

This authoritarianism is present in all Western ideologies in one form or another—Pope, King, Hitler, the Presidium or Politburo of Russian Communism, in the military. All of these strip the individual of his responsible self-fulfillment.

Humanistic religion, on the contrary, emphasizes man's strength and elicits its use to develop his power of reason to understand himself, his relationship to his fellow man and his position in the universe. He must also recognize his limitations. He must develop his powers of love for others as well as himself and experience the solidarity of all human beings. He must have principles and norms to guide him in this aim. Religious experience in this kind of religion is the experience of oneness with the All, based on one's relatedness to the world as it is grasped with thought and with love. Man's aim in humanistic religion is to achieve the greatest strength, not the greatest powerlessness. (This idea is really Nietzsche's Superman concept.) Virtue is self-realization, not self-abasement. The prevailing mood is that of joy, not sorrow and guilt. When humanistic religions are the "istic," God is a symbol of man's own powers which he tries to realize in his life and not a symbol of force and domination, having power *over* man.

He says the following illustrates this humanistic religion: Buddhism,

Taoism, the teachings of Isaiah, Jesus, Socrates, Spinoza, certain trends in the Jewish and Christian religions (particularly mysticism), the religion of Reason of the French Revolution. This attitude cuts across theistic and non-theistic systems.

"Life itself must be grasped and experienced as it flows, and in this lies virtue" (40). In Spinoza, God is the totality of the powers of the universe (true in Schleiermacher, too), akin to Wieman.

Fromm quotes Rabbinic stories about man forcing God to keep his promises and bear his share of the blame for sin, evil, suffering in the world (45–48). He thinks this is better than Abraham's sacrifice of Isaac (especially as interpreted by Kierkegaard) and better than Calvin's fearful obedience. (Now, I think loving obedience is a different matter.)

Christian man projects the best he has onto God and impoverishes himself. His only access to himself is through God. In worshipping God, he tries to get in touch with that part of himself which he has lost through projection. After having given God all that he has, he begs God to return to him some of what originally was his own. . . . This not only enslaves him to God but makes him a bad man. He has no faith in his fellow men, or in himself.

Fromm says to live without love is to live in sin. The more Calvinistic man praises God. The emptier he becomes, the less able he is to regain himself. What people think and feel is controlled by their basic characterology, by the socioeconomic and political structure of the society. Whenever religion allied itself with secular authority, it had to become authoritarian. Judaism rarely did so, says he! Has he forgotten Ezra and Pharisaism, the Chief Priest and the Sanhedrin?

To understand how limited our power is is an essential part of wisdom and maturity. To worship it is masochistic and self-destructive. The one is humility; the other is self-humiliation. Man creates God because he needs a figure outside himself to love. Does it follow that God exists, just because man needs him? (55). Just because a man thinks something doesn't mean it is true. Man once thought the world was flat. It isn't. Man once thought disease was caused by demons. It isn't. Men once thought they should duel to death for the slightest provocation. It was absurd. Once man thought they honored God by killing unbelievers. It was absurd.

The split between our sheep (or herd) nature and our human or rational nature is our problem. Reason is not our real guide; we are sheep.

But we rationalize and pretend that there is a reason for our behavior when we have committed it. Very few individuals can say the truth despite the threat of losing touch with the herd. For example, two questions asked in the South are: (1) "Are men created equal?" (2) Are the Negroes equal to the Whites? Even in the South, 61 percent answered "Yes" to #1, but only 4 percent answered "yes" to #2. In the North, those percentages were 72 percent and 21 percent.

We must give ourselves to the understanding of the reality behind the human thought systems. "The God who is really God, behind the gods we call God." Therapy cures by helping the person to self-understanding and thus to find the courage to assert himself and pursue his self-fulfillment. Adjustment therapy helps the person to be like everybody else in the culture, but this is no adequate cure.

Physicians of the soul free the soul to be valid, integral, a free self, creative, productive. The adjusted person has often made himself into a commodity. Fromm thinks the person of integrity will have an inner strength that makes him less reliant on the good will of others, less vulnerable to changing fortunes. Man must recognize the truth, be independent and free, an end in himself, and not the man for any other person's purposes. He must relate himself to his fellow man lovingly. If he has no love to give, he is an empty shell.

The Buddhist Tibetan precepts of the Gurus enumerate ten ways in which one may err:

1. Desire may be mistaken for faith.
2. Attachment may be mistaken for benevolence and compassion.
3. Cessation of thought-processes may be mistaken for the quiescence of infinite mind, which is the true goal.
4. Sense perception may be mistaken for revelations of Reality.
5. A mere glimpse of Reality may be mistaken for complete realization.
6. Those who outwardly profess, but do not practice religion may be mistaken for true devotees.
7. Slaves of passion may be mistaken for masters of Yoga who have liberated themselves from all conventional laws.
8. Actions performed in the interest of self may be mistakenly regarded as being altruistic.
9. Deceptive methods may be mistakenly regarded as being prudent.
10. Charlatans may be mistaken for Sages.

Psychoanalysis is a therapeutic method to help man discern truth. The truth shall make you free. Analysis therapy is essentially an attempt to help the patient gain or regain his capacity for love. This requires truth. When Judaism and Christianity teach Love God and love neighbor as self, this position is one of healthy, creative strength.

Psychoanalytic cure of soul aims at helping the patient achieve an attitude which can be called religious in the humanistic though not in the authoritarian sense of the word. One aspect of religious experience present in the psychoanalytic Cure of Souls is Wonder, Marveling, becoming aware of life and of one's own existence, and of the puzzling problem of one's own relatedness to the world. Another quality of religious experience is what Tillich calls "Ultimate Concern," which is connected to this wonder about the meaning of life, its fulfillment, self-realization, a sense of oneness—mystical with THE ALL.

We experience our individualized selves, then, as a drop in an infinite ocean of myriad drops of water, inter-related and inter-dependent. Repression is replaced with permeation and integration. You can't take too much time to help an individual find himself. He is the ultimate in values.

The language of religion is the language of myth and symbol. It is the only language we know to speak of these ultimate concerns and mystical feelings of oneness with each other and the All. God is the Ultimate I Am (Moses). We know God more in terms of what God is not than what God is. No man has seen God. No man knows God completely. God may reveal something about God's self, but never Godself.

THE ART OF LOVING by Erich Fromm
A Lecture

Love is the art to which one must bring all his intelligence and emotional security. The positive emphasis must be on loving, more than being loved; on relating to another person rather than considering them to be "objects." You do not "fall" into love, and love is not a commodity on the market.

Love is the answer to the problem of human existence, not animal love, which is present only instinctually, but rational, intelligent love, a conscious effort for a new harmony of being, to replace the harmony man knew when he was an instinctual animal and which is irretrievably lost. (Fromm's interpretation of the Garden of Eden story.) Man's separateness arouses anxiety. He must relate himself or go insane or die.

Early man had orgiastic primitive rites for union with the tribe and the tribal god. Modern man's equality means sameness; it does not mean deep unity. Unity in work and play is provided in modern society by "conformity." Some unity is achieved in creative work for the group.

However, "the unity achieved in productive work is not interpersonal; the unity achieved in orgiastic fusion is transitory (e.g. a football crowd); the unity achieved by conformity is pseudo-unity. Hence, these are only partial answers to the problem of existence. The full answer lies in the achievement of interpersonal union, of fusion with another person, in love" (18).

Symbiotic union, the living together in close union of two dissimilar organisms, is either dominant-sadistic or passive-masochistic.

Mature love is union under the condition of preserving one's integrity, one's individuality. Love is an active power in man, a power which breaks through the walls which separate man from his fellow man, unites him with others. Love makes him overcome the sense of isolation and separateness, yet permits him to be himself, retain his integrity. In love, the paradox occurs that two beings become one and yet remain two.

Love is primarily active—a giving, not a receiving, although it has its quiet moments of meditation and felt union in which there appears to be no external activity. "Giving is more joyous than receiving, not because it is deprivation, but because in the act of giving lies the expression of my aliveness" (23). "Love is care, responsibility, respect, and knowledge" (26).

"Know thyself," the Delphic oracle, is the basis of all psychology. "Love is the only way of knowledge, which in the act of union answers my quest. In the act of loving, of giving myself, in the act of penetrating the other person, I find myself. I discover myself. I discover us both. I discover MAN" (31).

Likewise, man can never know God, except in the faith-act of love (32). He is describing what man has called "knowing God. In other words, we do not know God as an object, but subjectively. There is a male-female polarity in all of us. We find fulfillment only in the union of these two." Sexual desire is not merely an itch, as Freud said, else masturbation would be the ideal sexual experience. Sexual desire is a desire for union with another who is in some sense self. It expresses the bipolar nature of the self and fulfills the self.

Childish love can be expressed thus: "I am loved because I am." Adult infantile love says: "I love because I am loved." Mature love says: "I am loved because I love." Immature love says: "I love you because I need you." Mature love says: "I need you because I love you" (41).

Brotherly love underlies all mature love—responsibility, care, respect, knowledge. If I have developed the capacity for love, then I cannot help loving my brothers. Brotherly love is the experience of our essential oneness; we have a central relatedness (47).

Mother love communicates infectious confidence and love of life or infectious anxiety. One can tell which children got only "milk" and which got "milk and honey."

In erotic love, two people who were separate become one. In motherly love, two people who were one become separate. Mother helps child grow up. Erotic love is exclusive, but it loves in the other person all of mankind. Its premise is I love from the essence of my being, and I love the other person in the essence of his being (55). If one loves only others, he does not really love at all. Love of others is rooted in healthy self-love. As long as you love another person less than yourself, you will not really succeed in loving yourself, but if you love all alike, including yourself, you will love them as one person and that person who, loving himself, loves all others equally (63).

Worship in religion moves from animism (worship of nature) to totemism (a clan God usually in the form of an animal) to idolatry (as Baal or the Ark). In totemism, the clan warriors wear animal masks, etc. that have totemic power to save. In idolatry, the works of one's hands are worshipped. Man projects his own power into the things he makes. Later, men are worshipped, as the Greek gods who are manlike myths. In Roman culture, the emperor was worshipped, usually after he has died but sometimes while he is living.

The earliest religions are mother-centered religions. Mother loves the child whether he is good or bad. The children of mother earth are all equal. Then, the Father-type religions developed. Mother is dethroned. Father structures life by principles and laws and requires obedience. The development of private property accompanies the development of patriarchal religion. Then hierarchical forms of government, priesthood, and inheritance develop.

In Luther, the simple mother-love type of faith has been replaced by a father-love type of faith. One hopes against hope that the father will accept one. If God is a father, my love for God and God's for me is father-like. If God is like a Mother, her love is mother-love.

The degree of maturity of the individual determines the level of love he has for God. The stage beyond the father-image is when God ceases to be the father-person and becomes a symbol of principles, or a process of creative goodness. Most people live at the father-stage, pleasing or displeasing the Father.

The mature man sees God as a symbol of the unity of the world in love and truth and justice. He has faith in these principles and he has an ultimate concern about them. To love God means to long for the full capacity to love both one's self and others (71).

The Ultimate Power in the Universe transcends both the conceptual and the sensual sphere. Man cannot know what God is, but he can know many things that God is not (Meister Eickhardt).

The only way the world can be grasped ultimately is not in thought, but in act, the experience of oneness, as in some act of love. All of life is devoted to knowledge of God, not in right thought, but in right, loving action (78). This emphasis upon the transformation of man develops. This is characteristic of the paradoxical thought of the Orient.

In the West, emphasis on right thought (science) and right belief (dogma) transcended right deeds. So here the man who thinks right and does wrong is more approved than the man who does right and thinks wrong.

Paradoxical thought in the Orient and in Eckhardt, Hegel, and Kierkegaard led to transforming goodness, while Aristotelian thought led to science and the atom bomb as well as Catholicism and structured dogma. "In the dominant Western religious system, the love of God is essentially the same as the belief in God, in God's existence, God's justice, and God's love. The love of God is essentially a thought experience. In the Eastern religions and in mysticism, the love of God is an intense feeling experience of oneness, inseparably linked with the expression of this love of God." In Meister Eckhart, we read: "By knowing God, I take him to myself. By loving God, I penetrate him."

"Man's form of love for God is inevitably related to the culture in which he grows up. If the social structure is one of submission to authority, overt authority or the anonymous authority of the market and public opinion, his concept of God must be infantile and far from the mature concept . . ." (82).

Love has deteriorated to many forms of pseudo-love in western society. Capitalism demands men who feel free and independent, not subject to any authority or principle or conscience, yet willing to be commanded, to do what is expected of them. He must fit into the social machine without friction, be guided without force, led without leaders, prompted without aim—except the one to make good, to be on the move, to function, to go ahead (85).

Love cannot be merely sexual satisfaction, as Freud mistakenly believed. But love, says Fromm, involves elaborate security arrangements. These provide for both parties validation of self as worthy, and for a growing number of mutually shared satisfactions.

The practice of love, like the practice of any art, requires discipline, concentration, patience, and supreme concern. It requires time alone for reflection. It involves reason. The emotional counterpart of these is humility. And the growth that accompanies this state requires rational faith. What matters in relation to love is faith in one's own love, in its ability to produce love in others, and in its reliability.

Man for Himself by Erich Fromm
Rinehart & Co., 1947
A Lecture

Humanistic ethics need affirmation against authoritarian ethics. Man needs not the guilt feelings and self-renunciation that religions like Judaism and Christianity lay upon him, but appropriate self-love and self-confidence. He needs to be able to take upon himself that true perspective of molder and shaper of his own destiny.

Fromm endeavors to affirm humanistic ethics—"to show that our knowledge of human nature does not lead to ethical relativism, but, on the contrary, to the conviction that the sources of norms for ethical conduct are to be found in man's nature itself; that moral norms are based upon man's inherent qualities, and that their violation results in mental and emotional disintegration."

He says Virtue equals the decisions of, and thus the character structure of, mature, integrated personalities whom he calls "productive" type individuals. "VICE" he calls self-mutilation, or indifference to one's own self. Vice negates the individual's valid self-fulfillment. Virtue affirms the individual in his valid self-fulfillment.

In humanistic ethics, moral principles are always subject to rational reevaluation. In authoritarian ethics, inviolable norms of behavior are set down by a transcendent norm giver. Emphasis in the religious cult is put upon blind and fearful or loving obedience. "Theirs is not to reason why; theirs is but to do or die."

Our indoctrination into patterns of behavior as children rests upon the fear of disapproval and the need for approval. "Good," when analyzed rationally, however, seems to mean approved by the person speaking. An employee is "good" if he advances the interest of the employer; a child is "good" if he makes life comfortable for his parents.

Fromm says "Unless the authority wanted to exploit the subject, it would not need to rule by virtue of awe and emotional submissiveness. It could encourage rational judgement and criticism, thus taking the risk of being found incompetent. For self-protective reasons, the authority pressures for conformity to its wishes, and the worst sin is rebellion. The rebel is accepted again when he exhibits 'a sense of sin' or a feeling of guilt, for this affirms the authority's superiority" (12).

"Love is not a higher power which descends upon man or a duty which is imposed upon him; it is his own power by which he relates himself to the world and makes it truly his" (14). Are we driven then to some subjectivist (individual) basis for ethics if we oppose all authoritarian ethics? Hedonism?

Fromm says no. Norms in arts, medicine and science are arrived at by rational discussion, criticism, and agreement. It is discovered and generalized that to accomplish its purpose an art object, or a bridge, or a surgical operation must conform to certain criteria of success.

Life itself is an art, the most complex and difficult art. It is the art of developing one's highest potential. Humanistic ethics is the applied science of the art of living. The excellence of one's achievement is proportional to the knowledge one has of the science of man and to one's skill and practice.

Every applied science is based on the assumption that the end of the activity is desirable. Medicine and surgery, for example, assume that it is desirable to cure disease and prolong life. Man cannot help wanting to prolong life. The real choice he has is between a good life and a bad life. The art of living is the most important of the arts but neglected in our century. Man makes himself basically miserable in pursuit of other goals—money, prestige, power, related to the grim sense of duty to work.

Everything is important to him except his life and the art of living. He is for everything except himself" (19).

The first principles of an objective, humanistic ethic are: affirmation of life, the unfolding of man's powers. Virtue is responsibility toward his own existence. Evil constitutes the crippling of man's powers; vice is irresponsibility toward himself.

The Science of Man, growing out of the enlightenment, assumes man to be malleable in nature, not unchanging as the authoritarian points of view do. Neither is man predetermined to be evil, nor is he a blank sheet of paper on which his environment writes, as the psychological behaviorists say. Man can adapt to slavery, sexual denial, etc., but in doing so, he becomes less than himself, neurotic or psychotic. Human evolution is rooted in man's adaptability and in certain indestructible qualities of his nature which compel him never to cease his search for conditions better adjusted to his intrinsic needs.

The science of man does not start with a preconceived definition of human nature, but seeks such an understanding as its purpose (24). Psychology investigates the nature of man and ethics and thus is applied psychology. The psychologist traces the tradition of humanistic ethics through Aristotle and Spinoza to Dewey.

Aristotle said that virtue (or excellence) is activity, the exercise of the functions and capacities peculiar to man. Happiness or well-being is man's aim and is the result of activity or use of his capacities, not a quiescent state of mind. In the Olympic Games, not the most beautiful and strongest are crowned, but those who put their abilities to work, to win and fairly—the noble things of life. The free, rational, and active (contemplative-active) man is the good and accordingly happy man.

Spinoza, as a naturalist, says to act in conformity with virtue is to preserve our being and to persevere in becoming what one potentially is. Man is to be man, neither horse nor angel, but man. Potency is the fulfillment of that and for our human nature that God has set before us. Happiness is not an end in itself but is what accompanies the experience of increase in potency, while impotence is accompanied by depression. Man is an end in himself and not a means to an authority transcending him (27). Value can be determined only in relation to his real interests, which are freedom and the productive use of his powers.

John Dewey is opposed both to authoritarianism and to relativism in ethics. Authoritarian ethics, based on revelation, divinely ordained rulers, commands of the state, convention, tradition, and so on "assumes there is some voice so authoritative as to preclude the need of inquiry."

Mere enjoyment, though important, is not absolutely definitive of value. It must be checked by evidential facts. Value can be arrived at by the power of human reason. The aim of human life is the growth and development of man in terms of his nature and constitution.

"The science of man can give us a picture of a 'model of human nature' from which ends can be deduced before means are found to achieve them." Utopias are not meaningless. They are visions of ends before the means to achieve them are worked out.

Empirical inquiry is necessary to the establishment of an adequate humanlike ethics. Psychoanalysis, beginning with Freud, has developed into this science. Through him we learned to study the total personality and to understand what makes man act as he does. This method is the analysis of free associations, dreams, errors, transference. Private data are made "public." Access was gained to phenomena not otherwise available. Also repressed emotional experiences which could not be recognized even by introspection were uncovered (32).

At first, only neurotic behavior was studied, but gradually it became apparent that this could only be understood in relation to the character structure of the individual. The neurotic character became the subject of study. Psychoanalytic characterology, though in its infancy, is indispensable to the development of ethical theory.

A virtue isolated from the context of character may turn out to be nothing valuable (as for instance, humility caused by fear, or compensating for suppressed arrogance) or a vice will be viewed in a different light if understood in the context of the whole character (for instance, arrogance as an expression of insecurity and self-depreciation).

Ethics and psychoanalysis (30–37) reviews Freud's thought about Id, Ego, and Super-ego—characterology, rational pursuit of goals that will prove satisfying to self and others. Therefore, this means a conscious effort to live as an ego. The Super-ego, insofar as it is an authoritarian, father-image instilled conscience, is to be overruled by the rational ego, and a clear character formed around concepts of appropriate behavior will lead to the realization of rationally projected goals.

There is a dichotomy between man's body, with its various drives and demands, and man's mind. In his mind he is aware of death and the claims of his body, but he is also aware of compelling ideals that transcend death and animal desires of the body. In pre-human existence, he lived in a state of harmony with nature. Now he must, by his mind, become the master of nature and of himself.

His mind drives him forward to find answers to the blank spaces in his knowledge. This is his effort to reestablish harmony between himself and nature from which he feels split. These dichotomies between man and nature, man and man, man and himself are existential—by the very nature of his existence. These dichotomies are between life and death, between what he is and what he dreams of becoming, and between his individuality and his relatedness to others. Then there are certain historical dichotomies: his desire for freedom but caught in institutions of slavery, and contemporary ability to create material wealth, but inability to use it for peace.

By such contradictions, the mind is stimulated to find an answer. All progress is thus stimulated. Here is a memorable statement: "Man can react to historical contradictions by annulling them through his own action; but he cannot annul existential dichotomies, although he can react to them in different ways. He can appease his mind by soothing and harmonizing ideologies. He can try to escape from his inner restlessness by ceaseless activity in pleasure or business. He can try to abrogate his freedom and to turn himself into an instrument of powers outside himself, submerging his self in them.

"There is only one solution to his problem: to face the truth, to acknowledge his fundamental aloneness and solitude in a universe indifferent to his fate, to recognize that there is no power transcending him which can solve his problem for him. Man must accept the responsibility for himself and the fact that only by using his own powers can he give meaning to his life. Meaning does not imply certainty; indeed, the quest for certainty blocks the search for meaning. Uncertainty is the very condition to impel man to unfold his powers. If he faces the truth without panic, he will recognize that there is no meaning to life except the meaning man gives to his life by the unfolding of his powers, by living productively. Only constant vigilance, activity, and effort can keep us from failing in the one task that matters—the full development of our powers within the limitations set by the laws of our existence. He must be himself and for himself and achieve happiness by the full realization of those faculties which are peculiarly his—reason, love, and productive work.

"When man has fulfilled his sexual, hunger, and thirst strivings, he is not satisfied. He strives for power, love, and destruction. He risks his life for religious, political, or humanistic ideals, which is peculiar to human existence. Man does not live by bread alone."

This has been interpreted to mean that man needs God. Fromm thinks it only means that man needs an all-inclusive mental picture of the world which serves as a frame of reference from which he can derive an answer to the question of where he stands and what he ought to do next. He must strive for the experience of unity and oneness in all spheres of his being to find a new equilibrium. A system of self-orientation implies not only intellectual elements, but elements of feeling and a sense to be realized in action in all fields of human endeavor.

Fromm calls such systems of thought, whether theistic like Christianity or humanistic like early Buddhism, "frames of orientation and devotion." In the process of living, man relates self to the world by acquiring and assimilating things, and by relating himself to people and himself. He can acquire through purchase, gift, or production. He can relate through work, defense, sex, play, for the upbringing of the young, etc. He relates by love, by hate, by cooperation, by competition. He can build a social system on equality, or authority, liberty, or oppression, but he must relate in some fashion.

These orientations, by which the individual relates himself to the world, constitute the core of his character. Character can be defined as the "relatively permanent form in which energy is canalized in the process of assimilation and socialization." This character structure takes the place in man of instinct in the animal. Man could not possibly make a fresh decision about every new item of experience. It would be too consuming of time and energy.

He develops the dynamic concept (as against the behavioristic) of character and personality types. There are four negative types: (1) Receiving (which includes all authoritarian types, especially religious), (2) Hoarding, (3) Exploitative, and (4) Marketing.

Over against these is the productive type of character orientation. It is (in the Freudian sense) genital oriented rather than oral or anal. It is productive as in mother-love, or the scientist seeking answers to unnecessary death from disease, or the social scientist or ethicist seeking answers to war and death in new conformations of society, such as the United Nations.

Productive love is quite different from shallow romantic love, which assumes that if the right person would only come along everything would fall neatly into place without effort or rational discipline. Productive love is characterized by Care, Responsibility, Respect, Knowledge. It wishes for the other person to grow and develop. It is the expression of intimacy between two human beings under the condition of the preservation of each other's integrity.

There follows a chart of the affinities between various orientations regarding assimilation and socialization:

Assimilation	*Socialization*	
I. Nonproductive orientation		
a. Receiving	Masochistic	Symbiosis: bringing together of opposite types
(Accepting)	(Loyalty)	
b. Exploiting	Sadistic	
(Taking)	(Authority)	
c. Hoarding	Destructive	Withdrawal
(Preserving)	(Assertiveness)	
d. Marketing	Indifferent	
(Exchanging)	(Fairness)	
II. Productive orientation		
Working	Loving, reasoning	

In reality, we always deal with blends of these types (112). Fromm thinks the receptive type blends most frequently with the exploitative. I think that healthy, liberal religions are usually a blend of the receptive and the productive. One tends to dominate, as he says, but it can be either. Many a preacher is essentially receptive-exploitative, as he says. And many a person (as contemporary physicians) are productive, exploitative, or productive-marketing types.

The remainder of the book discusses in detail the meaning of self-fulfillment love as basic to love of others. It develops some of the ethical implications of such love.

Selfishness and self-love, far from being identical, are actually opposites (131). Selfish persons are incapable of loving others, but they are not capable of loving themselves either.

Many "unselfish" people develop neuroses whose symptoms are tiredness, depression, inability to work, failure in love relationships, etc. Such people have only (often) this one redeeming character trait of "unselfishness." He does not "want anything for himself," he "lives for others," is proud that he does not consider himself important. He is puzzled to find that despite his unselfishness, he is unhappy and that his relationships with those closest to him are unsatisfactory. He wants to have what he considers all his symptoms removed, but not his unselfishness. He is really pervaded by a hostility against life. His unselfishness is a façade.

Appropriate love of self and acceptance of self as legitimately needing and pursuing certain fulfillments makes one capable of appropriately loving others. Love, in principle, is indivisible as far as the connection between "objects" and one's own self is concerned. "Genuine love is an expression of productiveness and implies care, respect, responsibility, and knowledge" (129). "To love is an expression of one's power to love, and to love somebody is the actualization and concentration of this power with regard to one person" (129).

Conscience is man's recall to himself. There is an authoritarian conscience which is an internalization of an external authority. A good conscience pleases this authority; an evil conscience displeases it. Disobedience and rebellion is the prime offence. Even progressive education has not overcome this. Teachers say: "You will not like to do this." In a way, it is more oppressive. It is harder for the child to rebel.

Humanistic conscience is Fromm's preferred term for a conscience that is the reaction of our total personality to its proper functioning or dysfunctioning. It is effective (emotional) but it is rationally oriented. Actually, everybody has both kinds of conscience (165). "Often guilt feelings are consciously experienced in terms of the authoritarian conscience while, dynamically, they are rooted in the humanistic conscience. In this case, the authoritarian conscience is a rationalization of the humanistic conscience."

Enlightened pleasure and happiness is the goal of life, coupled with moral responsibility, which means appropriate help to others in the attainment of such pleasure and happiness. This cannot be fulfilling when pursued on a neurotic basis, but only on what Fromm calls a productive basis—the full development of his productiveness.

Pleasure and happiness involve both means and ends. If all emphasis is put on ends and none on means, the ends become abstract, unreal, usually mere pipe dreams. If one is going camping, he has to put emphasis on transportation, tent, cooking equipment, finances, maps, locating good camp sites, etc. The entire concatenation provides the pleasure. Pleasure and happiness disappear when there are contradictions in man which he does not understand.

If faith cannot be reconciled with rational thinking, it must be eliminated as an anachronistic remnant of earlier stages of culture and replaced by science dealing with facts and theories which are intelligible and can be validated (197).

When faith was too structured, skepticism had its place as a tool of research, but now "lack of faith is the expression of confusion and despair." Skepticism and rationalism are now rationalizations for relativism and uncertainty. Tillich says that faith is a centered being regarding an ultimate concern.

Man cannot live without faith. Without it he becomes sterile, hopeless, and afraid to the very core of his being. Faith in Hebrew (Emunah) means "firmness." It denotes a quality of human experience, a character trait, rather than content of belief.

Humanistic faith means a man has faith in himself, in the creative order of nature, in the creative possibilities of the culture, in his friends, family, co-workers, in the capacity of man to solve problems personally and corporately. It means his whole being (mind, body, emotions, wealth, and all) is committed to the creative, responsible purposes of the human enterprise (200–09).

Faith is not some passive, waiting state, but a dynamic, active state of involvement. "Since rational faith is based upon our own productive experience, nothing can be its object which transcends human experience." It must be rational, not irrational (209). Faith in God is usually rooted in man's conviction of his own powerlessness and in his fear of God's power, a kind of symbiotic masochism.

Humanistic faith is rooted in man's rational trust in the productive possibilities of human activity. Man is not necessarily evil. He becomes evil only if the necessary conditions for his growth and development are lacking. However, when that occurs, it is evil and somebody's fault. Evil has no independent existence of its own. It is the absence of good. Evil brings misery and discomfort. God brings happiness, well-being, and productivity.

Goodness involves man's fulfillment of his desire to love himself and persons and objects whom he wants to love—ultimately a universal love. Evil involves blockage of this love and fulfillment, for one or more of several reasons. For example, the over-solicitous person may have a sadistic tendency. But this fact can cause a potentially sadistic person to develop character habits of kindness which protect him from his sadistic behavior tendencies.

The productive orientation of persons is based on freedom, virtue, and happiness. "Man's main task in life is to give birth to himself, to become what he potentially is. The most important product of his effort is his own personality. We can judge one another on this basis. If he failed to realize his potentialities, we should not blink the fact. It is his moral failure. If one fully understands all the circumstances, one knows why he failed. Understanding a person does not mean condoning. It only means that one does not accuse him as if one were God or a judge placed above him" (237).

There are relativistic and absolute ethics, or better, universal and socially immanent ethics. Universal ethics are rational norms for the unfolding and development of all men. Socially immanent ethics are norms necessary for the functioning of a segment of society. An example of a universal ethical norm is do not kill. Love thy neighbor as thyself.

The function of the ethical system in any given society is to sustain the life of that particular society. Such socially immanent ethics is also in the interest of the individual. There is still a place for the prophetic kind of behavior which does not submit to the socially immanent ethics, but is rather committed to the universal norm which can transform the socially immanent ethics. A rationally good man can find his satisfactions in this kind of behavior.

Chapter 48

A MATTER OF VALUES

A Response to Geraldine Dominick's Session on Values at the Honors Retreat

TCU Monthly, Vol 6, No. 3, November 1974

Dr. Dominick, a TCU accounting professor, spoke to the students at the Honors Retreat and asserted that each student enters the university with a set of values, whether or not he or she knows, understands, and had voluntarily and deliberately assented to that set. Her presentation sparked a discussion that continued in the Honors Program. She wrote a follow-up piece that appeared in the TCU Monthly, *which was followed by a response from Paul Wassenich.*

I appreciate Dr. Dominick's reflections on values, as a continuing discussion from the Honors Retreat.

I wish to relate to her articles some reflections that hark clear back to 1966–68, when I led the Values Colloquium. We studied numerous value positions, including insights from literature, the fine arts, religion, and philosophy. Then, assuming pretty much the position espoused by Dr. Dominick, I sought to get each person to state his own value hierarchy and bring relevant illustrations to bear out of the literature we had shared and/or other sources known to him.

I was always puzzled, even amazed sometimes, at the resistance of students who were juniors and seniors to taking such a position. Now, six years later, I am more convinced than ever that this is an exercise that would be most appropriate in a good program of higher education. We should encourage, perhaps we should force it upon the student. Require it! Wow! This should get a reaction!

With Gere Dominick, I would not see the role of the instructor, or the Honors Program, or the University, or whoever was assigning the exercise, as one who insists that particular conclusions about value be reached. The assignment should simply insist on serious encounter with the issues involved in making value decisions. The purpose, as I see it, is to bring more reason and reflective wisdom to bear on choices on some basis other than habit that has been structured by authority figures such as parents, teachers, ministers, the state, etc. Hopefully, junior-senior level college honors work on this subject would enable the person to develop new and wiser value awareness and choices than his childhood conditioning structured into him. However, it is conceivable that mature reflection would sustain some of those earlier value orientations.

As I have remembered the difficulty I had in this area with students six and seven years ago, I think their main concern was to rebel against authority. I have noted this in other students subsequently. I did it myself in college. This I consider healthy in the college classroom situation. The point is that hopefully they will not simply do something learned by rote, but will be creative and state new and better values. This was my hope in the Value Colloquium in 1967–68.

However, the stance that many took troubles me. They said, "I can't or won't, or it is impossible." Basically, my answer from my present perspective is "You do, you can, you will." People do act upon values they have been taught, or emotionally structured to hold, as Dr. Dominick says. What she and I are both saying is that from the standpoint of a senior honors student, "the unexamined life may be tolerable, but it is not really worthy of you." You can do better. You need to give responsible reflective value leadership to your society. You won't do this through coercion, of course, but you will do it (with a greater or lesser degree of consciousness) through direct and indirect forms of influence upon other lives.

To state such a value position does not mean that you are saying: "This is final. I will never deviate from these values." Quite the contrary, it is saying: "This is the way I see the higher qualities of life now; hopefully, as I mature further I will find this inadequate, and like the chambered nautilus, move into a new dimension of awareness and practice." Creative change, openness to new values can be the most basic, dynamic value concept held by an individual. It is valuable to be open to the emergence of new values rather than uncritically holding on to old values.

Chapter 49

SUMMARY OF JOHN COBB

Notes

God is not terrible, judgmental, or a destroyer. God is creative-responsive love. As in Christ, God is suffering love. God doesn't blast his enemies. The conversion of Saul to become Paul the Apostle is a prime example.

Jesus Christ is the best picture of God as creative-responsive love. Believers are called to imitate Christ, to be "in Christ" as Paul says, thus to be a "new being." Jesus afflicts the comfortable and comforts the afflicted. He opens us up to creative transformation. As the image of God is in each of us, so also is the image of Christ in each of us. We ask "What would Jesus do?" in an attempt to transcend the Old Testament law.

The Church is the body of Christ. It holds itself answerable based on Christlike behavior. It is unity with Christ that constitutes true church membership. Jesus Christ is a real event that shows the potentiality of other events. God is both immanent and transcendent. God in Christ is present in all loving, responsive, creative events as the Holy Spirit, the Christ-like spirit that operates in the world through the church and beyond the church.

Scripture says "Where there is no vision, the people perish." Basically, Christianity says that the end is in the hands of God, which is good. It is not meaning less; it is meaning full! My body is not ultimately separated but part of the Body of Christ. Everyone is members, one of another; we are one in Christ. The future on earth and in heaven is open. So, we act in the present in such a way as to make an ideal Christian future. Think the eternal, ideal hope. The end is not Nirvana. God is eternal. He takes our temporal good and transmutes into an Eternally relevant good. We contribute through our good deeds to the eternal joy of God. God remembers. The ultimate condition is peace.

The Church is in creative transformation. Science has lately been providing for creative transformation of the Church. (See *Secular Meaning of the Gospel.*) The Reformation was a courageous transformation of the Church, but churches have since lost a lot of their nerve. "Religion is tending to degenerate into a decent formula to embellish a comfortable life." Openness to Christ is feared as a threat to a comfortable life. Issues such as equal pay for equal work for women and blacks need attention. Caesar, male, king concepts must give way to "the tender elements of the world, which slowly and in quietness operate by love" (PR 520).

As we face the Global Crisis, we seek a theology of survival. On the spatio-temporal scale, astronauts' view of the earth prompted them to declare, "That's my home." But there is already so much trash in space that it is a threat to recently launched space vehicles. A similar condition can be found on earth, as our air and water are fouled. The church can help teach ecological sensitivity. We must be aware of the impact of over-population and using up finite resources and learn to reuse paper, metals, and plastics.

JOHN COBB'S CONCEPTION OF THE ONE WHO CALLS
Notes from *God and the World* (Westminster, 1969)

All of us are aware that though theologically traditional churches, such as Church of Christ, Assembly of God, and Baptists, are growing and serving thousands and even millions of people today, that millions of thoughtful people are deciding to bypass the church in their attempts to be morally responsible, to remake the world. They find the church irrelevant. Its activities are irrelevant, but deeper than that, its thought is irrelevant, they think.

In this context, J. J. Altizer, Hamilton, Van Buren, and others have followed Nietzsche and Sartre and other in declaring God is dead.

While John Cobb is appreciative of them and their project in a certain way, he disagrees. He thinks that what Altizer is really saying is that the first person of the Trinity is no longer motivational, no longer meaningful for man, but that the second person is and hopefully the third will be. Christ is divine redemptive reality, wholly immanent in history.

Cobb says he has four objections to belief in God understood as the Creator-Lord of History-Lawgiver-Judge. He says the traditional approaches to God, seen in this sense, have little point of contact in the modern sensibility; that they have no distinctive grounding in Jesus Christ; that they lead to doctrines which make God responsible for evil; and that the resultant imagination tends to represent God as a restrictive and repressive force over man.

What he proposes to set over against it is a picture of God as "The One Who Calls" us into a new future and who is free from doing evil, who is not restrictive and repressive, but who is Christ-like and lures us to new good.

God has functioned all too often to sanction what has been prized by the past and to discourage, if not actually destroy, creative efforts to bring goodness into being. Cobb's ideas relate to the future emphasis of Moltmann and Pannenberg.

It was this awareness of how institutions used the name of God to wage wars and bless numerous obstructive movements which coerce the movement of the Holy Spirit in its Christ-like attempt to free people to love and good will in new forms of life, that caused Bonhoeffer to declare himself for a religion-less Christianity. As Cobb put it, "He saw that the age-old attempt to persuade man to his need for God by pointing to man's limits as manifest in guilt and death has operated against man's maturation." Cobb's concept is related to Eric Fromm's original concept of "return to the womb" and the idea that belief in God is man's weakness and failure, an attempt to drive man to his knees and return him to the dependency of childhood. Now that man has "come of age," this approach in the name of Christianity is futile and wrong. "Mature man has no need of this kind of God, which Bonhoeffer associated with religion."

As Dick Gregory spoke to the students at the University of Alabama (recorded on Channel 13, January 9, 1970), this fact was poignantly clear. He appealed to morality and complimented the young on their moral sensitivity, but it was a revolutionary morality that would be as frightening to a staid Alabamian as Amos's statements were to the "cows of Bashan" or the strange pacifism of Bonhoeffer that finally plots the death of Hitler is frightening to all militarists everywhere, and with them to the whole established order.

Cobb thinks that Altizer's atheism, which is not cynical like that of much contemporary atheism but is called Christian atheism, may serve to break open to us the urgency of moving forward to the realm of the creative spirit in responding to the creative ground of being that, as Holy Spirit, seeks to lead us forward to the Kingdom of New Order, an order of love and good will and maximal freedom. Accordingly, he agrees with Bultmann's summary of Jesus's message: In faith we are set free from our past and made open to whatever new reality comes to us in each moment.

Cobb points out, however, that the complete openness of Bultmann is falsifying and threatening. It expresses no hope. The openness to whatever future there may be is not the New Testament picture. That picture is the coming of the Kingdom in which people will know God and be known of God, who is Christ-like love, and will accept each other as brothers in the Kingdom. The hungry will be fed, the naked clothed, the imprisoned visited and renewed, the sick cared for. Mutual concern and care will know no bounds of race or age or status.

So Cobb doesn't think that we must agree with Altizer to be benefitted by his analysis. Cobb prefers to believe in God as Christ-like. Instead of autocratic power, declaring laws and passing judgments, God is, like Christ, one who comes among us meek and lowly in heart, limited in power, but giving what power he has to the needy ones, in fact to everyone in every event, or actual occasion.

Actually, Marxism, as interpreted by Ernst Block, in his *Das Prinzip Höffnung (1959)*, challenged a whole generation of Christian thinkers to see in Christian teaching a hope for man in a new society, where there is no hunger and all who want work can find it, and the rich do not oppress the poor. This hope for a transformed future stimulated all kinds of future-oriented thought among Christians.

Of course, the social Gospel of Rauschenbusch, the process theology of Wieman and others had already expressed a hope of this kind, and even Tillich's "new being" does. Even the theology of Wolfhart Pannenberg is a future-oriented theology. He maintains that faith is to be directed only toward the God revealed in Jesus and that this God is to be contrasted with the God of traditional theism. Pannenberg believes that existence in any moment is determined by its relation to the future. It derives meaning from this relation and its very content is dependent on its anticipation of what is to come. Ultimately what is anticipated is fulfillment. The Biblical image of this fulfillment is the Kingdom of God, and Pannenberg believes that the thrust of Jesus's message identifies God with the Kingdom of God, which is coming. Thus, the locus of God is not primarily past, but future. He is, that which is to be.

Even Tillich put emphasis on the New Being, the new possibility, and the courage to be despite threats of non-being. Also, John MacQuarrie emphasizes God known as the dimension of Being. "Letting Be" is a variation on this theme, putting the responsibility on man to respond to Being in such a way as to be the creative new forms and, in a sense, emphasizing what Bonhoeffer called our standing with God with his weakness and suffering.

So far, Cobb had made it clear that he wished to speak from a Christian stance. The Christ event is primary in structuring his thought of a new possibility for man. In fact, Christ is expressive of what God can do and the primary characteristics of God in God's relation to people. The Incarnation is centrally important in doctrine. And it is clear that God is no autocrat. God is limited in power. God participates with man in the struggle to bring the Creative good to pass.

Whitehead points out that where the church went wrong was using Aristotle's image of God as the Unmoved Mover and creating God in the image of Roman, Egyptian, and Persian rulers. The church gave God the attributes which belong to Caesar. But, says Whitehead, there is in the Galilean origin of Christianity a strand that does not fit well with this autocratic picture. It does not emphasize the ruling Caesar, or the ruthless moralist, or the Unmoved Mover.

It dwells upon the tender elements of the world, which slowly like leaven or seed in the soil in quietness operates by love. It finds purpose in the present immediacy of a kingdom not of this world. Love neither rules nor is unmoved; also it is a little oblivious as to morals. It does not look to the future, for it finds its own rewards in the present and the relevant future.

So, the implication of the foregoing is that "God viewed as Creator-Lord of History-Lawgiver-Judge has functioned all too often against the full maturation of people. In the light of all this, it appears that faith in God must and will be abandoned altogether unless the Christian radically reconceives God in the light of the revelation in Christ he has always affirmed."

Cobb's way of speaking of God is as "The One Who Calls." What is the nature of the call? We cannot be called back to the details of Jesus's life and situation. It is a call forward in our situation. Cobb puts forward three questions: First, can we identify the call forward in our experience as something distinctive? Yes, it is a call to a distinctive kind of responsible freedom. If it is freedom to break priestly laws about the Sabbath, it is a call to a more profound worship. If it is a freedom to break the morés and laws of racial order as imposed by a society, it is a call to create a more profoundly satisfying and creative order among man. It is a call forward to fulfillment and enrichment of personal and social life. Two characteristics of the responsible use of freedom are TRUTH (recognizing the problems of relativity) and DISINTERESTED CONCERN (or Agape) at its highest level.

In expressing disinterested concern we can view the situation humanistically and say with Dewey we do so by projecting ideals and seeking to attain them. We assume that the power resides in the ideals themselves or in the person.

To quote Cobb, "Less well known than Dewey, but more penetrating in his reflections upon the power that calls us forward, is Henry Nelson Wieman. Wieman sees that man tends in each moment to absolutize the good he has achieved, and thus to obstruct the growth of new goods which at that point he cannot foresee or understand. Even his ideals, insofar as they are received from the past, can function to block rather than to foster growth.

"The process that bears man forward is the one in which men come to entertain new ideals rather than the abstraction and projection of already experienced values. This process is far less conscious, less intellectual, less voluntary than Dewey suggests. It works in us and among us already in infancy, for it is the process of human growth itself. It works through the creative interchange among persons in which each is transformed in ways which none can foresee or control. Awareness of this process as the 'source of human good' calls forth commitment to it and the willingness to subordinate all existent goods to it" (51–52).

Wieman's contribution to our understanding is a careful description of this process, but he does not elucidate the causes. Cobb affirms that this process is working out of the whole evolutionary growth process. Quoting the Cretan writer, Nikos Kazantzakis, he identifies the "cry upward" that will not let man rest in his present state any more than a lazy worm could rest in his home in the mud. "We're just fine here. We have peace and security. We're not budging" (53).

But man can't find his way out of trouble or despair without moving to some new ground or stance, and it is usually painful. "Whitehead saw that all growth requires the achievement of a novel concreteness. The introduction of novelty requires the confrontation of each situation by the realm of pure possibilities, the reality of which precedes man's experience. The achievement of concreteness requires that these possibilities be so ordered as to be relevant to the actual situation of each becoming entity. This ordering, too, is given for man and not projected by him" (54).

The Cry that lures us forward is to be understood as the claim of new, relevant possibilities throughout the domain of life. We are thus offered a vision of something beyond ourselves and our past that calls us forward in each moment into a yet unsettled future, luring us with new and richer possibilities for our being. That something is an ever-changing possibility that impinges upon us the relevant ideal for each new moment. It is the power that makes for novelty, creativity, and life. It is not coercive. It is effective.

Kazantzakis, more than Whitehead, sees how terrifying the call forward can be to us. Some of us must be dragged kicking and screaming into the twentieth century. Kazantzakis uses the term "Cry" to express how costly is the grace of God that calls us forward. It is, indeed, costly grace, to appropriate Bonhoeffer's term.

However, if people can be taught that their hope is in change, that change is not a threat, but a hope, then they can face the future with less fear, more equanimity, more openness and willingness to cooperate with God in bringing his Kingdom about. Cobb's view is that "That which calls us forward" has the unity, actuality, and worthiness of worship and commitment that makes it worthy of being called God (57).

Cobb disagrees with Dewey that the projection of an ideal makes the new possibility. He agrees with Whitehead that "only what is actual has agency" (58). And this actual agency must be individual. Christians think of God as an actual, individual agency that acts to create new good. Jesus was certainly this. This personalization certainly refers to some kind of identifiable force that thrusts us forward into new forms and patterns of behavior and relationship. One must be very careful and very honest about his preset state of insight when he thinks of God this way, but it loses some of its force. The world is not seen any longer as embodying an omnipotent sovereign's will but rather as responding ever anew to the possibility offered. That the response is imperfect does not imply the imperfection of what is offered. There is no world that does not reflect the influence of God's past agency, but there is also no world that is the product of that agency alone. The terrible reality of evil is neither denied nor attributed to God.

God understood in this way is not a repressive force, but a liberating one. The limits and burdens of the past are transcended by God, the Creative Process, who offer man fulfillment of his vital capacities for living and spending himself for the lives of others (64).

And we need not think of this "God who calls us beyond ourselves" to the more that is possible as an utterly different deity than the One whom we have known in our Christian experience. He may also be known as the Source of natural order, the Ground of Being, the Source of obligation, and the Holy One calling all to righteousness. It is simply the orientation to a repressive past and sanctifying that, in such a way [that] we are resistant to the claim of God for new possibilities that is negated.

"The God who calls us forward" does not function as a sanction for established rules and achieved goods, but calls us to go beyond them, whatever their merits may be. God does not hold us back from taking full responsibility for ourselves and our world, but rather calls us to precisely do that. God encourages us to become fully human.

In our time ultimate reality is an energy-event. An energy-event may be conceived as observed from without, or it may be conceived from within, as when we think of those events that constitute our own existence. If we think of God as an energy event from without, in an objective sense, we are far from the Christian God and in danger of idolatry. But if we think of God as an event from the inside as it feels to itself, as an occurrence of thinking, willing, feeling, and loving, then we are close to the heart of the Biblical faith. We are justified in thinking of God as a subject, like ourselves, rather than an electronic event in a nuclear oven.

But our own immediate experience cannot be a very close analogue for the experience of God because our experience is heavily dependent upon the contribution of our senses, whereas there is no reason to suppose that God experiences in that way. Human experience includes memory and thought, not only our awareness of our past and future, but also our conviction that there is a real world which exists quite independently of our experience of it, witnesses to the presence of nonsensory experience. Perhaps the best analogue for the experience of God is our experience of memory and our experience of vision as projection of possibility. The point is that it is, thereby, possible for us to imagine how

God might experience reality. We get away from the immediacy of sense experience and we transcend time and space.

Thinking of God in spatial terms requires that we say where he is. He can be either nowhere or everywhere. Nowhere is not satisfying to our conceptual apparatus. Everywhere is more satisfying. If we see reality in terms of events, this means he is in every event. There he is purposing, seeking to shape, responding. This means that God is no more at one place than at another, no more present in one time than in another. That does not deny the possibility and even the need for us to have a special time and place where we are aided in remembering and bringing to memory and perspective the way God has been present and probably will be present in the events of our lives.

Using the subjective stance of the self, thinking out into space and time, Cobb makes it clear how the events in the brain influence other events and are influenced by other events. Each has its unique autonomy and individuality, and yet they are related and responsive. Now, the spatial relation of God and the world is analogous. "God's standpoint is all-inclusive, and so, in a sense, we are parts of God. But we are not parts of God in the sense that God is simply the sum of the parts, or that the parts are lacking in independence and self-determination. God and the creatures interact as separate entities, while God includes the standpoints of all of them in his omnispatial standpoint. In this sense God is everywhere, as in Hartshorne's pan-en-theism, but he is not everything. The world does not exist outside God or apart from God, but the world is not God, or simply part of God. The character of the world is influenced by God, but it is not determined solely by God. The world, in its turn, contributes novelty and richness to the divine experience. "My Father is working still and I am working" (John 5:17).

Cobb does not conceive God as occupying another, supernatural sphere, not does he conceive of God as simply occupying the sphere of the earth. Like Hartshorne, he is a pan-en-theist. Pan-en-theism affirms, with pantheism, that God is not outside the world but that he pervades the world and is manifest in all its parts. Traditional theism is concerned that individual man have integrity within himself and not be subsumed in the Whole. This pan-en-theism accommodates.

This pan-en-theism is accomplished by the way God provides each occasion or event with an ideal for its self-actualization. Then, in relation to that ideal, each human energy-event actualizes himself. Whitehead put it this way: "In its initial phase every becoming occasion derives its initial aim from God. Every event is complex, but in each event God is present as novelty and the lure to richer and finer actualizations embodying that novelty. Thus God is the One Who Calls us beyond all that we have become to what we might be" (82).

Yet, evil needs to be reckoned with. It is easier to ignore the lure of God than to overcome the weight of that past; hence the appalling slowness of our progress toward full humanity and the ever-impending possibility that we turn away from it to some catastrophic end (82). But evil is seen as caused by finitude, stupidity, and false egoism rather than an external demonic force.

Cobb does not think that he can prove the existence of the Christian God, but he thinks he can show that the Christian can affirm God in rational faith that is philosophically responsible and that the recent attacks on belief in God are weakened.

Since God is participating in every event, all the events of our lives matter to God. God has a subjective aim in each of them. What happens really matters because it matters to God. It has some everlasting significance. It shapes the destiny of reality. It shapes God, in a sense—that is, what Whitehead calls the Consequent Nature of God. God must work with the event as it is shaped and man has some power to shape events, to negate or qualify the shape God would give an event. Spoken in Christian theological terms, God becomes a suffering God, a participant God, who enters into the finitude and suffering of man, with loving care and redemptive intent.

We can understand God's continuing work to be that of seeking ever higher and more inclusive values by which to enrich the lives of men. But there is always the accompaniment of ever greater evils. How does God endeavor to counteract this? God aims at strengthening the good in such a way that the balance of good over evil will be enlarged. We receive this ingression of God as the call to build structures of law that embody greater justice and by expressing mercy through more adequate structures both political and charitable. God also shares with us in the suffering that accompanies the existence God has given us. The hurt of God in the crucifixion of God's Son is the Christian symbol of God's risk-taking involvement with man. Not only man but also God is victim of man's age-long resistance to the call to love his neighbor as himself (97).

Since God is understood to be the Creator and re-creator of life, the individual cannot love God if he cannot love the creation and its possibilities. "He who hates the creation cannot love the creator. It is equally true that the possibility of affirming life and humanity depends on belief in God." The two are inextricably interrelated in reason and emotion.

This means that the goodness faith perceives in God is no mere function of the goodness seen in God's creation. The reality of God does not depend on man's thought about God. "The Christian apprehends God as embodying just that purity of goodness for which he searches the world and himself in vain. In worship we praise a divine perfection in which the hungry heart can come to rest, and an indestructible value whose incomparable superiority to all other values makes possible the contemplation even of man's extinction without complete despair. The Christian loves God finally not as an instrument of human good but for what God is in God's self, and that love can make possible the endurance of the terrors of history even when there seems to be no hope for man" (97).

I am reminded of the prayer of a little English girl reported in the newspapers of Detroit during the terrible German air raids over England in World War II. "And take good care of yourself, God, because if you die we have really had it."

John Cobb, *Christ in a Pluralistic Age*
Lecture notes, 1973

Christ is the central image of saving power in history, but its power is declining and threatening millions who have no vital image of saving power. Historically, Christ's power has been seen in people who give of themselves and of their substance to help those in need, who overcome temptation and evil, and who are forgiving of sin. This saving power transforms the world by making peace and overcoming evil, such as slavery. However, today Christ has been driven out of the world by profane consciousness, as in secularism and politics, and pluralism, which denies that there is one way to Truth and Goodness. Cobb's answer to that charge of pluralism says that Christ can be the best way without being the only way. Christ can transform daily work, bread, homelife, and politics into life in Christ and not as separated from God.

Christ is the personal image of God as Creative Transformation. I don't have to be exclusive about it. I can be open to others. Today spaceship earth is threatened. Christ calls me to live in a way that is best for all passengers on the spaceship. Christ must be seen as a reality, not a mystery or illusion. Christ is the Logos, creative wisdom power. Transformation is active in all areas of reality: self, relationships, social forms, eternal meaning.

The name of Jesus-Christ has to be cleansed of slavery, imperialism, torture and extortion, and many other evils done in his name. Christ must be open, responsive, forgiving, dialoguing with the other churches, religions, and culture. His name must be expressive of the one Logos-God.

There have been six basic Christologies:

1. Greek: liberation of man from finitude, death, and terror. The Apostle Paul said "The freedom wherein Christ has made us free" (Gal. 5:1).
2. Salvation from guilt by sacramental sacrifice of the God-man. (Jesus paid it all.)
3. Modern Protestantism: Synoptic Jesus represents personal and social ideal.
4. Recent Protestantism: The Kingdom is coming; the prophets and Jesus.
5. Luther: Contradicts it all! "Justification by faith."
6. Tillich: "The New Being," overcoming conflict and despair.

Today we are no longer existential in outlook. We are concerned about "spaceship earth," We are aware of two potential disasters that all of humanity faces: a nuclear war and extreme climate change.

Process theology offers an opening toward an answer in: personal devotional life, church, art, theology, and politics from the international to the local level.

Christ is the Logos, creative and transformative. Christ is personification, a teacher. Logos includes a sense of time, memory, association, creative imagination, prediction, creation of new forms. Logos equals Christ equals God. Christ is not only the name of Jesus or God; it is that immanent creative transformative power that is everywhere active, whether we recognize it or not. It is discoverable in nature, in history and in personal experience.

Jesus as Christ is a natural event, not supernatural. Jesus is different in degree rather than in kind from us. Life in Christ is both following his teachings and example and applying them to new situations. Jesus is a "field of force." Jesus as Logos is hope in a threatening world. We focus on realistic possibilities as Jesus did. Jesus and the City of God calls us to a new city of love.

The Kingdom of God is a vision of Hope. What is required for hope? Whitehead says three things are: (1) conviction of an open future, (2) social, not just personal, (3) a sense of being part of a wider process tending to produce real results that have been hoped for.

Jesus's teachings about the Kingdom of God gave vivid conviction about three possibilities: urgent decision, relevant action, and bringing in a new saving community. A hopeful outlook must defend against an emphasis on decay and death, entropy, chaos, conflict, and untrammeled powers. Both Jesus and Whitehead require inner purity of motive and outer social concern and cohesion.

Salvation is new life in Christ and the giving of mind and heart and energy to the perceived purposes of God, thus to be with God now and forever. We want to be remembered not only for our deeds but also as a whole person with feelings, intentions, and motives.

Chapter 50

CHARLES HARTSHORNE, EPILOGUE

Abstract and Concrete Approaches to Diety and the Divine Historicity

In answer to Bultmann's contention that we cannot attribute "historicity" to God, Hartshorne says that according to pan-en-theism, God is both external and historical, both transcendent and immanent, as it were. God is not transcendent in the sense of being totally other, but in the sense of being Unsurpassable except by God's self. God is participant in every concrete event. In fact, every concrete event of history shapes him in some way.

What is the nature of God? God is unborn and immortal, unsurpassable by another, and "one who is worshipped." Beginning-less and endless. In the sense of being without beginning or end, God is immutable.

But even the concrete life of deity has to be mutable. There are various kinds of mutability. Persons may increase or decrease. God can only increase. God can endlessly surpass God's self as well as all others. This means that in some sense God has past and future, but not in the deficient way that man has past and future, half-forgotten and poorly understood.

Hartshorne rejects as idolatry the identification of God with the Absolute, Infinite, Immutable, or Necessary. God is on both sides of such abstract contraries. He is finite and infinite, eternal and temporal, necessary and contingent, each in suitable and unique respects. The Greeks tended to worship the eternal or necessary as such, but we need not do so.

God does not need to be absolutely unsurpassable, but only unsurpassable by another. That God can surpass God's self is compatible with worshipfulness. Anselm saw that worship implies the absolute exclusion of rivalry between the worshipper and the worshipped. (If we could conceive a more superior being, we should have to worship that.) The result is the a priori logical exclusion of non-existence of God.

Even ordinary individuals do not have the determinate quality that can be defined, as they are capable of creative development. This is all the more true of God. God is growing too. God's creativity is inexhaustible, but this means growth. So God is always more than any person or object that can be pointed to. (As Tillich would say, God's the eternal subject, or you could say the eternal person or individual.) God as concrete is sensed in encounter, perceived as a participant in events. But God is not exhaustible by any concept or conscious perception of concretion.

How does all this prevent us from having some abstract concepts about God, correct so far as they go? It doesn't. Being ubiquitous, God can be encountered somehow in all experience. In God, we encounter not mere unsurpassability, but something infinitely richer than this abstraction. Bultmann, asked about difference between God of philosophy and God of religion, said: "The God of philosophy is anyone's God; the God of religion is your God and mine" (132).

This idea is consistent with Paul Weiss in *The God We Seek*. Each man must relate himself to God if he wants the full value of belief, and no concept can capture the concrete quality of this 'himself,' much less of the God of "himself." Since in the Pan-en-theist view, God is infinitely responsive to each creature in each event, God is far from being identical with God in General (an abstraction). God is "my" God. It is not even adequate to say God is the God of Abraham, Isaac, and Jacob, as Jews do. Hartshorne says this is just another way of calling attention to the errors of the Greek abstractions. The god of all creatures in general is inherent in all basic secular conceptions. Only intellectual inhibitions can keep this idea from being formulated.

Human beings form one another's *mitwelt* as they interact. Buber implies that they become identical or certainly overlap. Human beings do this in surpassable ways. Sometimes I can identify with you in depth, other times not. God always identifies with you in depth, "closer than breathing." We are finite beings. God is omnipresent in space. We act with a mixture of love, hate, and indifference. God acts persistently with unsurpassable love for all.

Surpassable modes of interacting are intelligible only if unsurpassable modes are intelligible. This already defines deity. Traditional metaphysics was too enamored of the supposed true idea of an absolute, immutable maximum to follow out the inherent logic of the idea of unsurpassable individual. It was held that while ordinary individuals interact, God acts only and does not interact. If God does not interact, this destroys all analogy between God and human creatures. It contradicts the very meaning of worship and related religious ideas.

This does not indicate a weakness in God. Just as man is greatly superior to animals because of his capacity to love, so is God greatly superior to man because of God's Unsurpassable capacity to love. Men have neither the responsiveness to, nor the power over others that God has. But metaphysicians for two millennia missed this and generalized about God being cause, we being effect; God the immutable, we the mutable, God the independent, we the dependent. These ideas made equally bad philosophy and theology.

The new ideas are much more complex than the old. There is no leap from time to eternity, from imperfect to completed perfect, from dependent to independent, from relative to completed absolute, from interacting individuals to impassable one ("not allowing passage over"). Hartshorne thinks that Heidegger hints at pan-en-theism when he says "not mere eternity, but infinite temporality may be the key to the idea of God" (*Being and Time*, 499). But Heidegger mistakenly limits religion to confession and denies the possibility of a natural theology.

It is only religion (concrete individuals and groups) that is non-theoretical and a sheer addition to any metaphysics. Abstract dealings with God should be more than that; they cannot be simply confessional. When I call God an "individual" or a "creature," it is with the understanding that God is cosmic in God's capacities. God interacts with all others. God is relevant to all contexts. In this sense God is absolutely universal. God is the only strictly universal individual. (This is not Hegel's concrete universal, because God as concrete is infinitely more than God in God's bare abstract individuality.)

"Being" is God as enjoying creatures. The creatures God does enjoy are the actual beings, along with the enjoyment itself. The creatures God might enjoy are what the creatures might become, as well as the becoming of new creatures. It is amazing how this slight revision of Anselm's ontological proof enables clarification of a viable conception of God. The transcendental snob or tyrant of traditional theology is replaced by the unsurpassably loving, interesting, presiding genius and companion of all existence.

Chapter 51

MY RETROSPECTIVE TWENTIETH-CENTURY THEOLOGY

1994

Paul wrote this essay especially for the benefit of his three sons so they might understand him better, but it is profound in the way it outlines his understanding of the Christian faith. He was an adherent of process theology and believed that God is always seeking to be in relationship with all people and all of God's creation.

Personal and Social Background

I assume that every theological position has a unique dimension. Hopefully, it includes eternal and profoundly true insights about reality, but it is always relative in the unique receptivity of the individual. That individuality is shaped by the scientific facts which were known as the individual was growing up and being educated. It is also shaped by the cultural biases and social contracts of his time and the nation in which he grew up as well as by the religious convictions of his parents and friends. Keeping these factors in mind, I will explain my background, assumptions, and biases.

I was born to a young couple, Madge and Louis Wassenich, in Houston, Texas, on September 20, 1911. My father was of German heritage, third-generation American. He and his people were Roman Catholic believers. My mother was of Protestant heritage, United Brethren (I believe but am not positive). At a crisis in her life, when I was seven years old, she became active in First Christian Church of Beaumont, Texas. I attended Sunday school there for two or three years and was baptized with a dozen other eleven- and twelve-year-olds. It was deeply moving and meaningful to me. I think in some sense the Church and related institutions, such as the YMCA, have been a substitute father for me.

In my youth in Beaumont, I found meaningful expression in Christian Endeavor (an ecumenical movement) and in the YMCA, which was also ecumenical, though essentially Protestant. Men in the YMCA who took an interest in me were responsible for me going to college by providing jobs for me. I earned my way through college and my first MA degree. Two ministers, Perry Gresham and Granville Walker, were responsible for me choosing the ministry instead of Y work as a vocation.

Assumptions about Truth: The Relation of Science and Religion

In early life, I was told to use my "common sense." In the sophistication of college and graduate school studies, trust in science as the highest level of "common sense" dominated my thought processes.

Two professors at TCU, H. L. Pickerill and Edwin A. Elliott, deepened my thought in this regard. Two courses in science, zoology and comparative anatomy, enriched that awareness. Pickerill gave me a personal assignment to read an article on evolution. That helped me think in a liberal vein about the relation of science and religion. He also sold me (25¢) a copy of *Science and the Modern World.* In a philosophy course at the University of Texas, I wrote a term paper on Herbert Spencer in which I was made aware that as science displaces religion or superstition in explaining "facts," God gets smaller and smaller.

So I began to realize that religions deal with the mysterious, the unknown, and sometimes the unknowable. My work in sociology and philosophy at the University of Texas (MA degree, 1936) prepared me for the advanced and tougher studies in the Divinity School at the University of Chicago. The "Chicago School of Thought" was anathema to many seminaries and divinity schools. It was as free as possible from dogmatic presuppositions. This was true of Dean Ames of the Disciples Divinity House, where I had a fine scholarship that made it possible for me to study full time for the first time in my life.

Dean Ames had been chairman of the Philosophy Department at the University of Chicago. Now retired, he was pastor of University Christian Church and Dean of the Disciples House. In one of his books, entitled *Religion*, he had said that "God is like Uncle Sam." One day at lunch he and I had a long argument about God in which I took the view of Henry Nelson Wieman, with whom I was studying, that God is not just a symbol, but the reality of creative goodness and developing new forms of goodness in culture. After half an hour of argument, he gave up, pulled out his watch, and said, "It's time to adjourn!" The other fellows, who had been following this argument with keen interest, laughed. Dean Ames was good-natured about it. At a party at his house after graduation and as I was to leave for my first pastorate, in Hicksville, Ohio, Ames said to me privately, "Paul, use your common sense in this country pastorate." I did.

Influential Persons

I will not take the time and space to explain in what way each of these persons was influential in shaping my life and thought, but I will name them because it might prove meaningful to some later reader. By the way, I am writing this statement of my theology for my three sons. It is not for use in churches. It has a quality of frankness and candor that I want them to catch because they have seldom heard me teach or preach. In fact, one of the regrets of my life is that I could not get them to join in candid discussions with me when they were in high school and college. I felt they never understood the old man. In this essay, I am reaching out to them. They will probably read it after I am gone.

The influential persons to whom I referred above are the following: Eddie Jones, Doak Proctor, Dr. Joseph Armistead, Hastings Harrison, Grover Good, C. G. Fairchild, Edwin Elliott, H. L. Pickerill, "Block" Smith, Perry Gresham, Granville Walker, F. L. Jewett, E. S. Ames, H. N. Wieman, Edgar J. Goodspeed, W.C. Bower, Charles Gilkey, and Harry Emerson Fosdick. I am also indebted to the "Chicago Point of View," as it was called in those days.

Of course, in their way, many of the lay persons taught me various things. I pastored the Community Church at Hollywood, Illinois, during the last two years I was in the Divinity School, 1937–39. Then I was in the pastorate of the Hicksville, Ohio, Christian Church during 1939–41. Next, during World War II, I was pastor of East Grand Boulevard Christian Church, Detroit, Michigan. It became Bethany Christian Church.

The impact of World War II was great. Under the influence of a debate between Reinhold Niebuhr and Charles Clayton Morrison in the *Christian Century*, I shifted from one of my basic tenets of faith, pacifism, to Niebuhr's unique "impossible possibility" position. When I preached the sermon sharing this shift with my wonderfully understanding congregation, they said I must mimeograph it and send it to our fifty-five persons in the military services, all over the world.

Two of the reactions were surprising. One man, who had gone into the army as a Red Cross orderly because he would not agree to kill anyone, said he had been counseled by his commander to carry a side arm because the Japanese where they were fighting did not recognize the noncombatant status of a Red Cross orderly. Several orderlies had been killed recently in the jungle where the combat lines were unclear. He did and prayed he would not have to shoot anyone.

The other letter came from a pilot who was flying the Burma "hump." He said he was sorry to see me change my mind because one of the things he said to himself when the going got tough out there was that he was fighting this war for my freedom to be a conscientious objector.

Drafted into College Teaching

In 1945, in the middle of a busy, significant, and happy ministry at East Grand Boulevard Christian Church, Detroit, a visitor appeared in my congregation. He was Dr. Robert Hopkins, Executive Secretary of the United Christian Missionary Society. After church and at lunch, he said he wanted me to accept, as Dr. Frank Jewett of the Texas Bible Chair at the University of Texas, Austin, had requested, the teaching position there. I turned him down at the time. But he came back, saying that Dr. Jewett and he, Dr. Hopkins, insisted. At that point, Ruth and I gave it very serious thought. We accepted with fear and trembling. Yet, over the thirty years of my teaching career, it appears that it was "meant to be" or a "call from God," as some would say.

Teaching and the studies associated with it deepened my thought in many profound ways. I had felt a "ceiling" in the ministry that required a surface-level treatment of topics that I wished to study more profoundly. After a year of refresher work at the University of Chicago Divinity School, I began teaching in the Texas Bible Chair in 1946. Though I chafed under the limitations of Bible studies, I continued to study theology. When Paul Tillich's first volume of his *Systematic Theology* appeared, I began to devour it. It was the first point of view beyond Wieman's that I found compelling. I managed to stimulate a number of students with theological discussions, some of whom later became PhD graduates of Chicago and professors in their own rights.

I was greatly stimulated by my 1954 trip to the Holy Lands in which I followed in the steps of St. Paul. I was also stimulated by teaching students and adults in summer conferences, leadership training schools, and Religious Emphasis Weeks in numerous universities.

When TCU called me in 1957 and Dr. Noel Keith, Chairman of the Religion Department, allowed me to teach Christian ethics and Current Trends in Christian Thought, I moved increasingly into theology, reading all the major theologians and teaching them to my senior-level course and my graduate seminars. Now, with this introduction to help you understand what "baggage" I come with in stating my theological position, let us begin.

I. Epistemology: How Do We Know?

In my junior year at TCU, I began to respond to sophisticated philosophical/theological thought. H. L. Pickerill, with whom I studied and for whom I worked as office secretary at Brite College of the Bible, made me think deeply and responsibly. I decided that any theological position, such as Fundamentalism, which had to deny scientific fact and contradict responsible scientific theory, such as evolution, the geologists' concept of the age of the planet and the solar system, the solar-centered universe instead of earth-centered, and the round earth instead of the Biblical flat earth theory or assumption, was ridiculous. I thought that by the 1970s or 1980s, fundamentalism and Biblical literalism would be dead! It was very difficult for me to see major trends of Christian thought becoming anti-scientific. I think such anti-scientific religious thought will ultimately be rejected by the majority of thoughtful people as ridiculous.

Later, at the University of Chicago, I heard Dr. Aubrey and Dr. Wieman ridicule a European theologian, Karl Barth, who said in public, "Faith takes reason by the throat and chokes the demon!" This I considered an absurd position. Barth was big in Europe, and some theologians at Yale and Union Seminary, New York, followed him, so I had to study his works. Gradually I came to appreciate some of his insights, but I could not accept his *Sola de* position. My position for the past sixty years has emphasized *faith and reason.*

My first "mature" position (at age twenty-five) was to become a partisan follower of Professor Henry Nelson Wieman. I still appreciate his work, although I accept some of the refinement of Charles Hartshorne and John Cobb and the enrichment of the Tillichian position. Wieman and Hartshorne were leaders of the Chicago School of Process Theology or Philosophy of Religion. Hartshorne considered his position to be metaphysics rather than theology. Wieman and later Cobb considered theirs as philosophical-theology. It was epistemologically basically a reasoned position based on scientific knowledge, but it reckoned with insights from the Biblical heritage. Wieman's most mature and basic book is entitled *The Source of Human Good.* I still appreciate his work sixty years later, though Cobb, Peters, Bernard Loomer, and other authoritative process theologians have ceased quoting him and tend to quote Whitehead and Hartshorne as basic authorities.

Wieman says that, by empirical reason, not by irrational faith, one can see in nature the Creative Process that he thinks is what the Bible and other theologians have called God through the ages. This idea is called Natural Theology. God or Creativity is:

- The emergence of new values,
- The integration of new values with old, established values,
- The expansion of the appreciable world, and
- The widening and deepening of Community.

For example, Hitler's movement was not of God, for though it fulfilled the first three of these steps, it failed to fulfill the fourth.

Wieman's work and Hartshorne's were grounded in the philosophy of an English mathematician, Alfred North Whitehead, particularly his Magnum Opus, *Process and Reality,* published in 1929. After he retired from teaching mathematics at Manchester University in England, Harvard University called him and encouraged him to write his philosophic point of view, which resulted in this book. Wieman and Hartshorne both studied with Whitehead. Since Whitehead found a concept of God to be a necessity in describing reality, let's briefly describe his concept of God.

Whitehead's thought is empirical. We experience table, chair, tree, dog, atom, etc. All of these are "actual events" or "actual occasions." We analyze reality in terms of events or actual occasions. These may be simple or complex. Every event can be analyzed from several different perspectives: physical, biological-chemical, psychological, sociological, mathematical, philosophical, theological. The last perspective is the most inclusive. All other knowledge contributes.

Every event is part of a series of past, present, and future. This present "conversation" with you boys is part of a series of past conversations and experiences we have had as parent and sons, and with Ralph Stone, Granville Walker, and others. It has your present attention and may affect the way you instruct or converse with sons, relatives, and friends in the future. In class I always used an illustration to show this dynamic process.

Each circle represents an actual occasion with a greater or lesser degree of objectivity or subjectivity. Beneath all this flux of change is Creativity, working in and through the reality of those events. God is active in each event, seeking to accomplish God's purpose. We have some freedom and power to cooperate with God's purpose, if we can understand it. We also have the power and freedom to block God's purposes and to be so abysmally ignorant we can't grasp the significance of the event. Obviously, God is not omnipotent.

It is the endless coming into dynamic being with infinite potential that is the basic process of reality. The essential wildness of creation is not God. It is the nature of reality. This is the stuff of reality on which God and persons work to bring about their purposes.

Whitehead's concept of God is a trinity. First, the primordial nature of God is almost like wild creativity, but it is not quite the same. Wild creativity makes no distinction between a jungle and a garden, between normal cell growth and cancerous cell growth, between millions of fish eggs and the destruction of them by an oil spill. This primordial nature of God is always struggling to inject the eternal forms (roundness, squareness, redness, greenness, truth, beauty, goodness, etc.) into actual occasions and, therefore, into a series of events, like a person's life or the life of a nation. We respond to these lures and pressures of God and other agents in an actual occasion with a "feeling awareness," which is a mixture of objective fact and subjective feeling and valuing.

The consequent nature of God is a catch-all that reckons with the fact of God remembering (how do ancient events still affect current events?). God takes into God's self the values achieved by persons, families, churches, nations, etc. God remembers the value. God learns from experience and injects this learning into new events. God did not get God's way with the Hebrew people but kept coming back and luring and pressuring them to new heights of value. Even in an evolutionary model, God, or whatever is over all and through all, must learn from experience.

God as subject-superject refers to the act or presupposition of faith that God enters as a subject with a purpose into every actual occasion or event—perhaps even an entire life or the life of a nation. Obviously, there is more significance in one event than another. This position is not pantheism. Everything or every event is not God. It is, as Hartshorne points out in *A Natural Theology for our Time*, pan-en-theism. That means that God is not the event, but God is active in all events.

But what about the Bible as a Way of Knowing?

The Bible is not a book of science. It is not objectively historical. It often conflicts with historical fact as recorded by other cultures. It often conflicts with common sense as well as with modern science (ax head floating—II Kings 6:1–7) and Jesus walking on the water (Matthew 14:24–27, Mark 6:48–51, John 6:19–21). Why are these accounts included in the Bible if they are not true? They are honorific stories that attempted to convince nonbelievers that Jesus was a supernatural figure in an age that was filled with supernatural figures. One of my Chicago professors, Dr. Case, Dean of the Divinity School, once said: "It was easier to meet a god than a man walking down the street of an ancient city." He was thinking of Athens, for example.

The birth stories of Jesus cause a problem for many persons who do not understand the role of myth in ancient religions. The Gospel of Mark has no birth story. Matthew emphasizes the royalty of Jesus, with wise and powerful men coming from other nations to worship him, and generations of relatives relating Jesus to King David. Luke, on the other hand, has him born in a stable, with humble shepherds coming to worship the child. John, the fourth gospel, has no birth story to parallel these but offers the "Logos doctrine" to explain Jesus's injection into the world by God. This theory of origin was more understandable and meaningful to Gentile Greeks. Most serious scholars today assume that Jesus was born to Mary and Joseph in Nazareth in a natural manner.

The conflict between Galatians 1:16–17 and Acts 9:23–26 is clear. Galatians has more authority because it was written by Paul himself. Obviously, Paul did not go to Jerusalem to get authority bestowed by Peter but went to the desert to think through his role in his newly converted life. After some time (we don't know how long), he went back to Damascus and then to Jerusalem to get the stamp of approval of Peter and the Twelve.

The concept of a three-tiered universe—heaven, earth, and hell—is absurd today as we find not only new knowledge of the solar system but also have men walking on the moon and men and women circling the globe in 99 minutes. If you think with any consistency at all, you can't picture God as in the Negro play, *Green Pastures.* The perennially burning hell as pictured in Dante's *Inferno* just can't function to scare people into doing the right thing and avoiding evil. This is part of the reason for the serious breakdown in social order. Jesus's teaching about "outer darkness, where there is weeping and wailing and gnashing of teeth" (Matthew 13:42, 50) loses its power for negative motivation too.

Nowadays, a contemporary scientific view of space indicates no 1500-square-mile satellite spinning around the earth, as expressed in Revelations 21:15–21. Describing heaven as a place so crowded with angels that medieval monks argued about how many angels could stand on the head of a pin is ridiculous and no longer relevant.

What are some of the enduring ideas of the Bible?

- The Ten Commandments as ethical guidelines.
- The ideas of the prophets about God's concern for justice, mercy, and peace. "Men shall beat their swords into plowshares, their spears into pruning hooks; nation shall not lift up sword against nation; neither shall they learn war anymore" (Isaiah 2:4).
- A sense of moral order in which sin or immorality tends to chaos and moral and mutual responsibility leads to creative community. I do not think the basic Jewish idea of a chosen people will wash anymore.
- Forgiveness of guilt and salvation (acceptance) by God and neighbor, which renews a right mind and relationship, is profoundly meaningful and necessary. However, it is handled today in the light of significant insights in psychology and psychiatry. Jesus taught forgiveness and even love of enemy in the Sermon on the Mount (Matthew 5:6–7), the Parable of the Good Samaritan (Luke 10:25–35), and the story of the Prodigal Son (Luke 25:11–32). The profound sense of love of God is communicated in many ways in the New Testament, as in I Corinthians 13 and in I John 4:7–12.

Thus, while we recognize that there are numerous passages in the Bible which we cannot accept as realistic and meaningful today, let us not "throw the baby out with the bath water."

In a broad perspective, the enduring values of the Bible are these:

- A profound sense that reality has some enduring significance which can be communicated well by speaking of God as Creator, Sustainer, and Redeemer of humankind.
- An understanding that the Bible at its high points presents a useful and essentially valid moral code that holds society together. Many of the social code ideas appear in other religions such as Buddhism, Hinduism, and Islam, which gives them an additional significance for mankind. Taboos against theft, lying, adultery, covetousness, as well as an expression of monotheistic worship and the sense of the holy (see Rudolf Otto, *The Idea of the Holy*) give stability and meaning to individual and social life.

II. The Concept of God

One of the first ideas that hit me in college, mostly through bull sessions and through an article handed to me by H. L. Pickerill, my professor in religious education and my boss in my junior year as I worked as secretary to the faculty of Brite College of the Bible, was the fact of evolution and the necessity to develop a theological position that would include evolution.

The second thing that hit me in college as I learned more about scripture was the invalidity of the miracle stories, both then and now. I was forced to think with the assumptions of science about natural law.

The third idea I had to struggle with I found in E. S. Ames's idea of religion. He said that God has always been a symbol, like Uncle Sam. He is not real, but symbolic. I had a tough exchange with him at a Disciples House luncheon in 1937. I took Wieman's position and defeated him in argument, causing him to adjourn the meeting. Wieman's position emphasized the reality of God as Creativity, which was and is always present in natural reality. God is a vital force, not just a social symbol.

The fourth idea I carried forward from my teen years, when I was very conscious of not having a father, was the Biblical idea of God as a loving, caring, guiding Father, which was very meaningful to me. Relatedly, some men in the Beaumont, Fort Worth, Austin, and State of Texas YMCA were important father figures to me. So I added to this personal, loving, caring concept of God Wieman's idea of God as Creativity. To the emergence of new values, the integration of new values with old values, the expansion of the appreciable world, and the widening and deepening of community, I added Transcendence.

The fifth idea came from Paul Tillich in my forties as he published the three volumes of his *Systematic Theology*. God is Ultimate Reality and Ultimate Being. God is not a being but Being itself. God is not something other than being, but *sein an sich*, as the Germans say, Being itself. You can see the emergent forms of being in the evolutionary picture as God at work in nature and history.

The sixth idea came from John Cobb, professor of theology at Claremont Theological School of California. He carried forward an idea I first heard from Bernard Loomer at Chicago, the lure and pressure of God. God lures us forward in new and better forms of being. As James Russell Lowell said in *The Present Crisis*, "New occasions teach new duties, time makes ancient good uncouth." There is the constant emergence of new values, which are usually linked in preceding values. Cobb spoke of "the One who calls us forward" in his book *God and the World*.

Seventh, in my thirties, I had no use for Karl Barth and his writings, but in my fifties and sixties I began to use some of his ideas. I could not and never did appreciate his statement that "Faith takes reason by the throat and chokes the demon." He himself came to regret that he said that, but he was emphasizing that even reasonable persons need to recognize their limitations and that God or Ultimate Reality is Transcendent! One evening at TCU some Brite faculty and Religion Department faculty met together with Dr. Albert Outler, a famous theologian at Perkins School of Theology at SMU. He was given the topic of God. He talked for about an hour and fifteen minutes about his own experiences with various concepts. At the end, he said, "Nevertheless, when all is said and done, I must in all honesty and candor say that all concepts of God fall short of the ultimate truth and reality. God is ultimately transcendent, ultimately a mystery. I agree, yet I do not belittle the efforts of great minds and spirits to describe what they feel or know to be true about God. Even so, humility in this realm becomes us all."

III. Persons, Sin, and Estrangement

Through the centuries, theologians have called this topic the doctrine of man. However, today we are conscious of how ridiculous we have been for not recognizing and acknowledging the equality of women. In fact, in my pastorates I found many women to be more clearly committed Christians than men. So today we speak of the doctrine of persons.

Contemporary theology of any significance does not say we are all sinners because of the original sin of Adam and Eve. Today the emphasis of all significant theologians is upon the egotism that we all show in some way. We tend to overreach as Reinhold Niebuhr would say. At base, in common-sense language, it is selfishness. In the twentieth century, we have been greatly helped in self-understanding by the studies known as psychology and sociology.

Psychology helps us to understand our psyches. Sociology helps us understand our socios, that is, our groups. Persons tend to overreach as persons and as groups. Nations overreach and cause wars that are increasingly devastating. The role of religion is to help persons and individuals to "love others as we love ourselves." And to love God above all!

The disciplines of economics and political science are also relevant to any adequate understanding of sin and estrangement, especially in today's world. Presidents and Congress war over these problems routinely. Is the US government to concern itself with the unemployed and the poor, the sick, the aged? Theology generally emphasizes the responsibility of the individual, but in both process thought and in Tillich's thought there is an awareness of the sociological impact on our understanding of responsibility one toward another.

Today churches have not accepted their responsibility to try to influence the government to care for the poor, the elderly, and the sick. Some churches have tried to do something themselves, but the problems are too large for the churches to finance the answer to these questions.

IV. Salvation

Salvation is not seen by contemporary liberal theologians as saving us from an eternal burning hell as in Dante or even one of the teachings of Jesus (see Luke 13:23–28). It is appreciated as the renewal of a person put back in touch with reality after a period of estrangement.

Salvation is seen as:

- A person finding a new orientation after being involved with drugs or other belittling and estranging activities.
- Returning to church after years of irresponsible life-style.

- Finding ultimate security among family and friends after a period of wandering and meaningless behavior.
- Relating again to God after a period of trying to live without any thought of God.
- Living in such a way as to be in touch with the Mind of God, eternal verities.
- Returning to consideration of what is ultimately true, good, and beautiful after living at a level of triviality.
- Discovering in a mature way that the Ten Commandments, the prophets, and the teachings of Jesus are profoundly relevant.

V. Christian Ethics

Christian ethics refers not to simple things like swearing, cheating on exams, cheating on your income tax, etc., though these things are lower-level ethical matters. Christian ethics are concerned, as in Richard Niebuhr's *Christ and Culture,* with issues of church and state, of economics that consider the welfare of all and not just one's own welfare, with basic generosity of spirit and giving. Christian ethics considers issues like the responsibility of business firms toward customers and employees, regarding a quality product at a fair price, fair wages and hours, and employment conditions for those who work for that business.

Christian ethics concerns the problems between the races, the nations, medical practices, educational opportunities, and the universal important issue of war and peace.

VI. The Church

Though I was christened in the Catholic church because my father was a Roman Catholic, I am a profoundly Protestant thinker. Protestantism is freer and more responsive to change and new ideas than Catholicism. The koinonia fellowship of Protestantism is basic to me. The fellowship of kindred minds and spirits in responding to the good and evil in the secular culture is important. Mutuality is basic.

Also, the ethical leadership of Christians as individuals belonging to work, political, and other groups in society is a Protestant idea. The church is not an institution of the state, where clergy is paid by the state as in many European countries. It is separate and a critic of the practices of the state. As Niebuhr says in *Christ and Culture,* it is not a Christ <u>of</u>

culture position. It is not a Christ against culture. It is a Christ in dialogue with culture position.

VII. Eschatology

I do not expect Christ to return in judgment, as the New Testament teaches, as both Jesus and Paul as well as Revelations say. The end of history as well as the end of an individual life, however, deserves some attention. Scientists currently believe the earth is approximately five billion years old. Human beings evolved in the past 100,000 years or less. It is thought that the sun may keep the earth alive for another billion or more years, although no one really knows. Nevertheless, it is important to think about your personal end and mine. We all die.

I am not certain that there is such a thing as eternal life for an individual, certainly not for our bodies. I am not sure what a soul is, except, as Tillich would say, the essence of our being. I like Whitehead's idea that God remembers, and what he remembers are the things we have done that are useful to God in accomplishing his purposes among human beings and in the total environment of earth.

Cultures rise and fall, and the concern of God is toward each one. God is relevant to every event, every actual occasion, as Whitehead says in his great book, *Process and Reality.*

The eschatological fact is that we human beings are capable of thinking about our own end, the end of cultures, the end of civilization, and the end of the whole earthly adventure. A cosmic accident, for example, could end it all. So live so as to please God, whatever the end.

Chapter 52

MY ESSENTIAL SELF: EXAMPLES OF MORAL COURAGE

January 8, 2001: I promised Ruth I would record a series of events in my life that I value as expressive of my essential self.

During my senior year at TCU, while working for the Y, I helped organize an older boys conference in Fort Worth. The International Relations Club at TCU was invited to give an evening program on Issues of War and Peace. As one of the four speakers, I made an impassioned plea for pacifism at the Christian answer to war. An extreme statement that I made about munitions workers and other profiteers of war got picked up by the *Star-Telegram* and aroused the Fort Worth Chapter of the American Legion, which said they were going to call in the FBI to investigate me for sedition. This debate went on in the newspapers and elsewhere for two weeks.

In 1940 in Detroit, before I arrived as minister at East Grand Boulevard Christian Church, a young man with one year of college spoke to the youth group advocating atheism. His wife taught Sunday School. After she got to know me, she said she'd like for her husband to meet me. She brought him to the door of the church when he came to get her and introduced us. Then she invited Ruth and me to supper so we could get better acquainted with her husband, Chuck Bare. After supper, as the ladies were washing dishes, Chuck and I had a chance to talk. We covered a gamut of topics: philosophy, economics, and theology. Later, Chuck suggested that we spend New Year's together; so we did at our apartment. About 3 a.m. he said, "I could do a better job of sponsoring your youth group than that lady you have doing it now." I said, "Yes, but the Elders wouldn't allow it because you are not a baptized church member." He said, "I think we can take care of that." The next Sunday he came forward and was baptized that night. He went to Europe during World War II and fought in the Battle of the Bulge. He came home, went to Transylvania University and Lexington Theological Seminary, and became a Disciples minister. He later had a significant book published.

In 1941, I gave my first Labor Day sermon at East Grand Boulevard Christian Church. My theme was that it was possible for management and labor to work together if they really trusted each other and management was fair in its dealings. I could see that Russ Koppin, CEO of a manufacturing plant and chair of the church board, was visibly uncomfortable during the sermon. We went out to lunch after the worship service to talk. Five years later, as I was leaving Detroit, Koppin spoke before the board of the church and said, "We will always remember Pastor Wassenich for what he has taught us about race relations." He said to me afterward, "I should have told them 'and for what he has taught us about relations between labor and management,' but I didn't have the guts." As I had continued to emphasize Christian, humane labor-management relations, Russ decided since he was a Christian, he'd better try out some of those practices. Then he admitted that the changes worked, and there was a much better work spirit at his company following those changes.

In Austin about 1947, I was voluntarily directing the Disciples Student Fellowship (DSF) during the second year of University Christian Church's life while I served as a professor in the Texas Bible Chair. I invited some Negroes from our Negro Disciple Church to attend a DSF meeting out on the patio between the residence and the Bible Chair building. Judge Beauchamp happened to come over and saw this group meeting. On Monday he called Pastor Sisterson and me to his office and said that if we were going to get support from the churches for the buildings of University Christian Church, we would have to quit having blacks in our services. Sisterson agreed to do so. I said I would not, could not.

During my last year in Austin, I welcomed a Negro to worship with us. Windy Savage collared me and said, "What the devil are you trying to do? Trying to destroy our developing church?" I said, "No, I'm trying to help it grow into a truly Christian Church."

Around 1959 or 1960, I joined two Brite Divinity students, one black and one white, in going to a hamburger stand to see if we would be served. The waitress was so flustered she screamed and called the police. We decided it would be best to retreat.

I spoke to Louis Saunders, Executive Director of the Fort Worth

Council of Churches, around 1962 to express my concern that the integration of the Fort Worth Public Schools could be a dangerous event if someone did not prepare the public to receive it peacefully. Louis formed a conference of City leaders that met at First National Bank. Among other things, we agreed that several articles in the newspaper (*Star-Telegram*) appealing for public cooperation were needed. Our group included an attorney whom I had led as a Hi-Y boy from Poly High many years ago. He told Y leaders that Paul Wassenich had opened his eyes on the race issue when he was a senior in high school. He told about the time that I had several of the Hi-Y boys join with a Negro Hi-Y group at the Negro Y. So, about thirty years later, he joined me and a Negro in having our picture printed on the front page of the *Star-Telegram* appealing for peaceful acceptance of public school integration. I'm sure there were many factors that made the integration of the Fort Worth schools peaceful, but I like to think our appeal helped.

About 1963, Joey Jeter, a TCU student, went to Mississippi to one of the Martin Luther King demonstrations where he was put in jail with about a dozen ministers of various denominations. In Chi Delta Mu, the kids were discussing that incident in a generally critical manner. I stood up and said, "I disagree with you. I really think we should all be with Joey in jail instead of being here badmouthing Joey while we're safe." There was a quiet response.

Around 1965, Dr. Moudy, then Chancellor, called me and asked who was behind the position of the AAUP chapter, of which I was President, to press for higher salaries and compare TCU's salary scales with other universities. I took responsibility for that, but it was actually a professor in chemistry and one in psychology who had been pushing for the salary increase.

Toward the end of that decade, as Noel Keith was retiring from TCU and as chairman of the Religion Department, he said in a faculty meeting that he hoped we would continue to use his textbook for Introduction to World Religion. I stood up and told him that I didn't think that was fair, that he should leave it to those of us who would be teaching the course to choose a text. No one else said anything, but that is what we did. A few years earlier, Dr. Moudy had called me and asked what I thought of the text. He had heard some criticism of it. I told him there were several errors in it and it was not the best text, but we could correct a few items in it and get along with it, since we had done that for several years. I added that I thought we really needed a new text now that Noel was leaving.

Dr. Moudy appointed me to lead the committee for the study of the total university at the time of TCU's centennial, 1973. Toward the end of our study, we had agreed that we would recommend that football be dismissed as it was costing too much money and faculty salaries needed to be raised. As we approached the Christmas Holidays, I appointed a subcommittee of administrators to study the TCU budget and see if we were going to be able to meet it. They came back without a significant report. I blew my top.

As a result, I had a personal conference with Dr. Moudy, the Vice Chancellor for Advanced Studies and Research, and the Chief Financial Officer. I recalled that I was asked to read the Princeton report when we started the study. I did and noted that Princeton was going in the red and had to make significant cuts. I was not willing to turn in a report from this study that did not make realistic recommendations and that we could not tell what was realistic if we did not know the real fiscal situation. Dr. Moudy replied that they held those figures, that information, close to their chests, but he assured us that TCU was not operating in the red and would not have to in the next fiscal year. So we had to be content with that assurance in finalizing our report.

Courtesy of TCU.

Appendix I

PASTORATES, SERMONS, AND SEMINARS

For some time, I have wanted to list, for any posterity that might be interested, the churches in which I preached or taught seminars. My first and very inadequate sermon was in the First Christian Church of Nederland, Texas, at age fifteen. The next one was at my home church, Washington Boulevard Christian Church, in Beaumont. During this period of my life, I often spoke at Hi-Y meetings and State Conventions in Beaumont, College Station, Temple, Waco, Austin, Lubbock, and Galveston.

While a student at TCU, I spoke at Hi-Y conferences in Lubbock, Fort Worth, and Galveston, at a camp at Glen Rose, and at the Waco Y camp on the Bosque River, the Y Camp at Camp Ross Sterling on Trinity Bay, and the Fort Worth Y Camp near Weatherford.

In 1933 I went to Cleburne Christian Church for a number of weekends to work with the youth there and teach a Sunday School Class. I took the boys on an all-night outing in rather cool weather. We huddled around the fire throughout the night.

After graduating from TCU in June 1934, I preached at the Children's Church at Cheley Camp while "Chief" preached at the Adult Service.

While in Austin, I spoke to the young people at Central Christian Church and Hyde Park Christian Church and preached at Hyde Park. Dean Colby Hall of TCU asked me to join four others in ordination at TCU in 1935. Dr. Jewett asked me to preach at the Bible Chair Chapel service the next Sunday at UT-Austin.

The minister at Taylor, Texas, came over and asked me to consider preaching twice a month at Elgin Christian Church, which I did, after talking with the leading elder, Mr. Abrahamson, while he milked his cows on a rainy afternoon. While in Elgin, I organized an interdenominational Youth Group that met once a month and spoke to them several times. Some of them were high school seniors, so I was asked to give the Baccalaureate sermon at the First Baptist Church. As I recorded in my autobiography, it was exciting because I had to cross a flooded creek to get there.

While at the University of Chicago Divinity School (1936–39), I preached every Sunday for two years (1937–39) at a Community Church in Hollywood, Illinois, west of Chicago.

In June 1939, Ruth and I moved to Hicksville, Ohio, where I became Pastor of First Christian Church. We were there twenty months. Of course, I preached there each Sunday. I also spoke to union Thanksgiving services at a small Lutheran Church. At one of these conferences in Wauseon, Ohio, I ran into my former TCU professor, H. L. Pickerill, now at the University of Michigan. He recommended me to the Elders at East Grand Boulevard Christian Church in Detroit, Michigan. They sent a committee to hear me in my Hicksville pulpit and then called me to be their minister.

Of course, I preached many sermons in that situation for four and one-half years. We had evening services as well as morning services. In addition, I spoke to Christian Endeavor conventions in Flint, Grand Rapids, and Detroit. I spoke to Disciples ministers in Toronto, Canada. Lloyd Channels (who was at Benton Harbor) and I joined to lead worship at the International Convention of Disciples held at Grand Rapids.

I spoke on the radio in Detroit, giving the Sunday morning sermon for shut-ins, sponsored by the Detroit Council of Churches, with which I worked and served on the board. I spoke a number of times during Lent to the employees of Goodwill Industries. I preached at two different Negro churches. I gave vesper addresses to young people at Crystal Lake, where we had our summer conferences. I preached Lenten series at the Christian Churches in Lansing, Petosky, and Benton Harbor. I spoke to Pickerill's students at the Guild House in Ann Arbor, Michigan.

As Detroit became a center for industry during World War II, I began going to the Chrysler plant at 6 a.m. on Sunday mornings to meet and speak to the men leaving after their twelve-hour shift and the ones waiting to start their shifts. Those men worked seven days a week during the war and were rarely able to attend church.

After being called by Robert Hopkins of the United Christian Missionary Society to teach at the Texas Bible Chair, University of Texas at

Austin, we spent a year at the University of Chicago while I took courses to refresh and sharpen my mind to teach. While there, I recall giving only two addresses. One was after worship to the folks at University Christian Church on the assigned topic of the atomic bomb, which had just been used against Japan. I said that in my opinion, it was impossible to stuff it back into the womb of history. Now that it had been born, nations would use it, much as they had used other weapons and that the future looked bleak, like Armageddon. It was not a popular speech.

When we arrived in Austin, I established University Christian Church at the suggestion of Frank Jewett and Chester Crow. However, John Barclay of Central Christian Church and Patrick Henry, the State Secretary, opposed this move. I preached every Sunday that first year without any pay from the church. (My salary came from Indianapolis for teaching in the Texas Bible Chair.) The next summer (1947) the leaders, particularly Judge Tom Beauchamp, decided I was too liberal for that pulpit, that I would alienate folks around the state who would otherwise send us money to help build the needed sanctuary; so, I was given a tennis racquet as my pay for about 50 sermons. (The main problem was that Judge Beauchamp objected to a meeting of the DSF that I had organized which had Negro speakers from our Negro Christian Church.)

Over subsequent years, I also spoke at University Presbyterian Church, Southside Christian Church, Hyde Park Christian Church, Christian Faith and Life Community, many sororities, retreats of Greeks, and Religious Emphasis Weeks at UT-Austin, SMU, Texas A&M, Texas State University, Texas Tech, South Texas at Kingsville, TCU, Tarleton State College, and Colorado State University. In addition, I spoke at DSF National Conferences in Wisconsin and Norman, Oklahoma. I spoke at youth conferences at First Christian Churches in San Antonio, San Angelo, and Houston, and in McAllen, Huntsville, Burnet, Luling, Kerrville, Mo Ranch and the camps in Athens and Lake Brownwood.

During 1950–53, I preached every other Sunday at Johnson City Christian Church where Lyndon Johnson was a member. However, I never saw him until I came back to preside at the funeral of Dr. Emmette Redford's mother after I moved to Fort Worth. I also performed a wedding in Johnson City Christian Church for Clarence and Betty Doss.

My friend Oliver Harrison was pastor of First Christian Church, Corpus Christi, during these years and for many years after. He invited me to come there over a period of years to preach and teach, particularly his men's group. The last occasion was at the HEB camp southwest of Kerrville.

The second year in Austin (1947), I arranged a trip for eight students and two adults to a work camp at the Disciples mission in Aguascalientes, Mexico. I was asked to preach in that church—in Spanish! I did it, but one man smiled all through the sermon. Afterwards, I asked what he was smiling about. He replied, "Some of your pronunciation." Well, I tried.

I was also asked to address the students of the Methodist Fellowship at Southwestern University in Georgetown, Texas. Stanley Jones and I were the two main speakers at an Ashram at the Methodist Camp near Kerrville. In addition, I was asked many times to teach and preach at University Christian Church, Austin.

After moving to Fort Worth in 1957, I preached or taught classes at the following Fort Worth churches: Arlington Heights Christian, Central Christian, Community Christian, First Congregational, Handley Meadowbrook Christian, Hurst Christian, Magnolia Christian, Memorial Christian, Richland Hills Christian, Ridglea Presbyterian, Rockwood Christian, and Westcliff Methodist. In addition, I also preached or taught at the following churches in other parts of North Texas: Midway Hills Christian Church and Central Christian Church in Dallas, East Dallas Christian Church, First Christian in Burleson, First Christian in Sherman, First Christian in Wichita Falls, and University Christian in Austin. There were probably more, but I couldn't recall them.

After I retired in 1976, I often taught several classes as a series in churches, sometimes on a busy weekend, sometimes staying six or eight weeks. Some of these places were: Alamo Heights Christian in San Antonio; Central Christian in Dallas and Greenville, East Dallas Christian; First Christian in Abilene, Arlington, Breckenridge, Center, Dennison, Graham, Irving, Levelland, Lufkin, McKinney, Mineral Wells, San Angelo, Stephenville, Temple, Texarkana, Tyler, and Wichita Falls. Other places included: First Congregational and First Presbyterian in Fort Worth, Jarvis Christian College Chapel; Lubbockview Christian; Meadowbrook Methodist in Fort Worth; Lakewood Christian, Midway Hills Christian, Northway Christian, Oak Cliff Christian, Oakmont Christian, and Rosemont Christian Churches, all in Dallas; Ridglea Presbyterian in Fort Worth; Southside Christian in Greenville; University Christian in

Austin; and University Christian in Fort Worth. In addition to preaching and teaching, I also conducted several ordinations and weddings.

Although I had retired in 1976, Jim Kelly, then the director of the Honors Program, asked me in 1985 to come back and teach the Values Colloquium. This was the last academic course I taught.

I had told Ruth that I would quit after I finished my series at Meadowbrook Methodist in October 1994. However, I began to feel better and, therefore, taught my last series at First Methodist Church in Fort Worth in 1995.

Appendix II

SELECTED PERSONS AND ORGANIZATIONS NAMED IN THIS BOOK

Adams, Henry (1834–1910), an American historian and a member of the Adams political family, descended from two US Presidents. His life's work involved analyzing and commenting on American life and thought.

Aesclepius, also Asclepius. The god of medicine in ancient times.

Ames, Edward Scribner (1870–1958). Dean of Disciples Divinity House of the University of Chicago from 1927 to 1945. He received his BD from Yale, 1892, and PhD in philosophy from the University of Chicago, 1895, awarded by professors John Dewey and James Tufts. Ames was a mentor and recruiter for Paul in the 1930s and 40s.

Anselm of Canterbury (1033/4–1109) was an Italian Benedictine monk, abbot, philosopher, and theologian of the Catholic Church.

Aquinas, Thomas (1225–1274) was a Dominican friar, philosopher, Catholic priest, and doctor of the church. He is an immensely influential philosopher, theologian, and jurist in the tradition of scholasticism. He was the foremost proponent of natural theology.

Augustine of Hippo (354–430) was a Roman African, early Christian theologian, and Neoplatonic philosopher from Numidia. His writings influenced the development of the Western Church and Western Christianity.

Barber, Stella Mae (1919–2018) and Quentin (1919–2017). Quentin was a dentist with an office near TCU, and Stella Mae worked in TCU administration. They were longtime members and leaders at South Hills Christian Church. To honor Paul and Ruth, they endowed a scholarship at TCU in 1983 known as the Paul and Ruth Wassenich Disciples Scholarship.

Barth, Karl (1886–1968). A Swiss theologian best known for his landmark *The Epistle to the Romans* and his five-volume theological summa *The Church Dogmatics.*

Beauchamp, Tom L. (1892–1964). Justice of the Texas Court of Criminal Appeals, 1939–1953, which is the final appeal court for criminal cases. While he was Assistant Attorney General, Judge Beauchamp was famous for his successful defense of the McDonald bequest to build an astronomical observatory for the University of Texas and for his support to create Big Bend National Park while serving on the Texas State Park board. A founding member of University Christian Church in Austin and a conservative in Disciples religious beliefs and politics, he often disagreed with Paul's more progressive theological, ethical, and philosophical positions. However, he respected Paul's reasoned and carefully developed arguments when they debated informally or in small groups after some controversial sermon. He acknowledged that Paul opened his mind to the possibilities that Black and lower-income criminal defendants were not always afforded justice in the criminal courts.

Bergson, Henri (1859–1941) was a French-Jewish philosopher who was influential in the tradition of continental philosophy, especially during the first half of the twentieth century.

Brightman, E.S. (1884–1953) was an American philosopher and Christian theologian in the Methodist denomination. He was associated with Boston University and Liberal Theology.

Brown, William Adams (1865–1938), a Presbyterian minister, an ecumenist, and Professor of Systematic Theology at Union Theological Seminary in New York City.

Bruner, Heinrich Emil (1889–1966). A Swiss reformed theologian, he is commonly associated with Karl Barth and neo-orthodoxy on the dialectical.

Buber, Martin (1878–1965), an Austrian philosopher best known for his philosophy of dialogue, a form of existentialism centered on the distinction between the "I-Thou" relationship and the "I-It" relationship.

Calvin, John (1509–1564) was a French theologian, pastor, and reformer in Geneva during the Protestant Reformation. He is associated with the founding of the Presbyterian denomination.

Cheley Colorado Camps, Estes Park, Colorado. Paul worked summers at Cheley Camps during and after college as counselor, wrangler, and camp director in the 1930s. After their marriage, Ruth also worked there. Paul's connections with the YMCA secured this position, as "Chief" Frank Cheley had developed his leadership skills in YMCA work.

Christian Endeavor or C.E. A nationwide and European non-denominational organization providing a structure for church youth to work together to know God in Jesus Christ. The Society was particularly strong in the late nineteenth and early twentieth centuries and then declined as denominational youth societies imitated and adapted the forms of Christian Endeavor. It enabled youth to express themselves while participating in useful tasks. In Texas it was influential among protestant youth in Paul's formative years.

Cobb, John (b. 1925). Professor of Theology at Claremont Theological School of California.

Colquitt, Betsy Feagan (1926–2009). TCU Professor of English and frequent Honors colloquia teacher, 1948–1991.

Colquitt, Landon (1919–1991). TCU Professor and chairman of the Department of Mathematics. 1948–1991.

Conner, William C. (1907–1992). Chairman of the TCU Board of Trustees and chairman of Alcon Labs in Fort Worth.

Cox, Harvey (b. 1929). Hollis Professor of Divinity at Harvard Divinity School until his retirement in 2005. Author of *The Reshaping of Religion in the 21st Century, Secular City, Religion in the City,* and *Liberation Theology and the Future of World Christianity.*

Echols, Hugh, and Ruth. Early and lifelong members of University Christian Church, Austin. Hugh was Assistant Superintendent of Austin Public Schools.

Elliott, Edwin A. (1891–1986). BA TCU 1923, MA, University of California 1925; PhD University of Texas 1930. TCU economics professor 1930–1934. First Regional Director of the National Labor Relations Board 1934–1961, South Central region.

Erasmus, Desiderius (1466–1536) was an important figure in classical scholarship. He was a Dutch philosopher and Christian humanist who is widely considered to have been the greatest scholar of the Northern Renaissance.

Flowers, Ron (1935-2021). Professor of Religion in the undergraduate department of TCU. He delivered the eulogy at Paul's funeral in 2005 and Ruth's in 2012.

Freud, Sigmund (1856–1939) was the founding father of psychoanalysis, a method for treating mental illness and a theory which explains human behavior.

Fromm, Erich (1900–1980) was a German Jew who fled the Nazi regime and settled in the US. He was a social psychologist, psychoanalyst, sociological humanistic philosopher, and democratic socialist.

Frondizi, Risieri (1910–1983). Brother of Arturo Frondizi, president of Argentina, 1958–62. Risieri Frondizi was Rector of the University of Buenos Aires. A university repression in 1966 led to the exile of 301 university professors, including R. Frondizi, who later taught at Yale, University of Pennsylvania, University of Texas at Austin, UCLA, and Baylor.

Frye, Bob (1939–2016). Professor of English and rhetoric at TCU from 1966 to his retirement. He taught colloquia in the Honors College and gave the Founders Medal to the Outstanding Student at the Honors Banquet.

Good, Grover. YMCA director for whom Paul worked in the 1930s.

Goodspeed, Edgar J. (1871–1962). American theologian and scholar of Greek and the New Testament at the University of Chicago. His collection of New Testament manuscripts was enriched by his searches; the collection is named in his honor. He is widely remembered for his translations of the Bible: *The New Testament: an American Translation* (1923), and *The Bible, An American Translation* (1935), the *Goodspeed Bible.*

Gresham, Perry E. (1907–1994). BA TCU 1931; BD TCU 1933; Minister of University Christian Church, Fort Worth 1933–1942, president of Bethany College, 1953–1972.

Gunther, Ralph (1914–2000). PhD, University of Rochester, 1948; TCU professor of music, 1948–1980. Ralph and wife, Lavonne, were close friends of Paul and Ruth.

Hall, William "Bill" (1914–2000) and Mary Lu (1916–2002). Bill received his BD at Yale Divinity School and was Brite Divinity School Professor of Missions 1956–1980. He was also director of Doctor of Ministries for the past five years. Mary Lu was a catalog librarian for TCU library 1968–1981 and worked with Ruth Wassenich. The four were close friends for decades.

Hammarskjöld, Dag (1905–1961). Swedish economist, Secretary General of the United Nations, recipient of the Nobel Peace Prize.

Hornack, Adolf (1851–1930). Recognized as one of the outstanding church historians of his day, he taught church history at the Universities of Leipzig, Giessen, Marburg, and Essen.

Harrison, Dean. Classmate at TCU with Paul.

Harrison, Hastings (1895–1985). Beaumont YMCA leader (1924–30), known for reducing the bitterness from the KKK uprising in the 1920s, which split Beaumont society.

Harrison, Oliver. Classmate of Paul at both TCU and Disciples House, University of Chicago. Minister of First Christian Church in Corpus Christi, TX, and on the Board of Trustees for TCU.

Hartshorne, Charles (1897–2000). American philosopher, theologian, and educator, known at the most influential proponent of "process theology," which considers God a participant in cosmic evolution.

Hegel, Georg Wilhelm Friedrich (1770–1831) was a German philosopher and is an important figure in German idealism. He achieved wide recognition in his day.

Hilgers, William Blank "Bill" (1924–2020). BA and Law degrees, University of Texas, Austin. Bill was a state tax attorney, CPA, and well-connected civic leader. He was president of the board of the Texas Bar Association. His family, the Blanks and Nordens of Lockhart, were key persons in "The Committee of Forty" which helped fund the building of the Texas Bible Chair and University Christian Church, Austin. Bill and his wife Sara, a librarian, were founding members of University Christian Church, Austin, and remained members ever since. They were close friends of Paul and Ruth.

Hordern, William (1920–2014), a Canadian, authored *A Layman's Guide to Protestant Theology* and *Living by Grace*, which emphasized a generous acceptance of other people just as God generously accepts and affirms us. He was president of Lutheran Theological Seminary Saskatoon.

Hume, David (1711–1776), a Scottish Enlightenment philosopher, historian, economist, and essayist, who is best known today for his highly influential system of philosophical empiricism, skepticism, and naturalism.

Isaachs, Clyde. Student at UT Austin. He lived in the Bible Chair building in the post-World War II period along with other students and the Wassenich family when there was a severe housing shortage.

Jewett, Dr. Frank L. (1874–1969). Founding minister and professor of the Texas Bible Chair at UT Austin 1905–1946. Dr. Jewett chose Paul to succeed him in this position and contacted Dean Ames at Chicago to recruit and train Paul for the position.

Jones, Eddie. Young YMCA leader in Beaumont, Texas.

Kant, Immanuel (1734–1804) was an influential German philosopher in the Age of Enlightenment. In his doctrine of transcendental idealism, he argued that space, time, and causation are mere sensibilities, things-in-themselves that exist, but their nature is unknowable.

Kierkegaard, Søren (1813–1855) was a Danish philosopher, theologian, poet, social critic, and religious author who is widely considered to be the first existentialist philosopher.

Koppin, Russell. Outstanding layman of East Grand Boulevard Christian Church, CEO of Koppin and Chrysler that made special refrigeration units for industry.

Lauderdale, Sam (d. 2001). A WWII veteran student who, with another veteran Frank Smith, renovated the dilapidated carriage house and servant quarters behind the Bible Chair in Austin. They lived there during their college years. Both became engineers. Sam was known as "Squeak" due to his continuous whistling, a nervous habit from two years posting on a remote island near New Guinea. Sam and his fiancée Mary Jane Horton, who later became his wife, cooked hundreds of fruit cakes in the Wassenich kitchen late at night to sell and finance their education. After graduation they created the famous Mary of Puddin Hill fruitcake business. All were active in the Disciples Student Fellowship at Austin.

Lehrmann, Paul (1906–1994). Presbyterian, civil libertarian. Taught at Princeton Theological Seminary, Harvard Divinity School, and Union Theological School. Author of *Christian Ethics in Context.*

Loomer, Bernard (1912–1985). PhD University of Chicago 1942. Professor and later dean, University of Chicago Divinity School. He was a leading proponent of Process Theology in which God, the world, people, and knowledge develop together in mysterious existence. This continuous exploration and advancement of understanding is ever changing. He decried theological certainty and delighted in the wonder of existence. His ideas followed Henry Nelson Wieman and Alfred North Whitehead, but he felt even they held concepts of "misplaced concreteness."

Lünger, Irvin (b. 1912). Pastor of University Christian Church in Chicago and then president of Transylvania College in Lexington, KY.

Luther, Martin (1483–1546) was a German professor of theology, composer, priest, monk, and a seminal figure in the Protestant Reformation.

Melacthon, Philip (1497–1560) was a German Lutheran reformer who collaborated with Martin Luther. He was the first systematic theologian of the Protestant Reformation and the intellectual leader of the Lutheran Reformation. He was also an influential designer of educational systems.

Moltmann, Jürgen (b. 1926) is a German Reformed theologian who is Professor Emeritus of Systematic Theology at the University of Tübingen.

Moudy, James C. (1916–2004). TCU Graduate, 1943, and BD 1949. PhD, Duke, 1953. Dean of the Graduate School, TCU, 1957; Vice Chancellor for Academic Affairs, 1962; and then Chancellor of TCU, 1965–79.

Niebuhr, Reinhold (1892–1971). Eden Theological Seminary, St. Louis, Mo. 1913, BD Yale 1915. As pastor of Bethel Evangelical and Reformed Church, Detroit, Michigan, from 1915 to 1928, he experienced the difficulties that modern industry created for labor and the urban areas in which it existed. He became a serious critic of capitalism and the politics of the time. From 1928 until 1960, he was professor of applied Christianity at Union Theological Seminary, New York City. He studied the persistent roots of evil, raising as problems the pride and hypocrisy of nations and classes and egoism. He saw these as manifestations of insecurity and defensiveness of human finiteness. Using Reformation-style theology, he strove to give hope and guidance to those working to improve society. In his *The Nature and Destiny of Man*, 1941–43, he expressed his outlook: "The saints are tempted to continue to see that grace may abound, while sinners toil and sweat to make human relations a little more tolerable and slightly more just." This perspective also led him to move Christianity and Judaism closer together.

Niebuhr, H. Richard (1894–1962). Eden Theological Seminary 1915, PhD Yale 1924, professor of theology and Christian ethics at Yale

1931–1962. His "Christ and Culture" (1951) sets out the transcendence of God over all history. Along with Karl Barth he accepts neo-orthodoxy in Christian belief. While God may be absolute and transcendent, humans are not. They are part of the evolution of the world. Thus human perception of God evolves. As an ethicist his concern was how humans relate to God, to each other, their communities, and the world.

Odum, Harold (1925-2004). Fort Worth businessman and Member of the Mayor's Human Relations Committee in Fort Worth in the 1960s.

Origen of Alexandria (184–253) was an early Christian scholar, ascetic, and theologian. He was one of the most influential figures in early Christian theology and has been described as "the greatest genius the early church ever produced."

Pannenberg, Wolfhart (1928–2014) was a German Lutheran theologian and is considered to be one of the most important theologians of the twentieth century with his magnum opus, the three-volume *Systematic Theology.*

Pickerill, Harry L. TCU religion professor 1925–33. He then served in the United Christian Missionary Society and the University of Michigan Foundation for twenty-three years. TCU conferred an honorary Doctor of Divinity degree upon him in 1973.

Rauschenbusch, Walter (1861–1918) was an American theologian and Baptist pastor who taught at the Rochester Theological Seminary and led the Social Gospel movement in the United States.

Ritschl, Albrecht (1822–1889) was a German Lutheran theologian who showed both the religious and ethical relevance of the Christian faith by synthesizing the teaching of the Scripture and the Protestant Reformation with some aspects of modern knowledge.

Sadler, M.E. (1896–1966). BD and PhD from Yale. President of TCU 1941–59 and chancellor of TCU 1959–65. During his long tenure, TCU grew in shape, size, and endowment. Listed among the major achievements during his time as the head of TCU is the start of the Honors Program.

Sansom, Charles and Charlie. Early members of University Christian Church, Austin. Charles was Assistant Superintendent of Austin Public Schools. They were close friends of Paul and Ruth.

Saunders, Louis. Executive Director of the Fort Worth Council of Churches (1957–64) and Greater Dallas Community of Churches

(1964–78). Member of Midway Hills Christian Church in Dallas. His wife, Jeanne, and Linda Wassenich worked together at the Visiting Nurse Association of Texas.

Schleiermacher, Friedrich (1788–1834) was a German theologian, philosopher, and biblical scholar known for his attempts to reconcile the criticisms of the Enlightenment with traditional Christianity. He is often called the "Father of Modern Liberal Theology." The neo-orthodox movement of the twentieth century, spearheaded by Karl Barth, was in many ways an attempt to challenge his influence.

Smith, "Block." Director of the Campus YMCA, Austin 1930s to 1950s.

Social Gospel Movement was a theological concept that viewed social problems as moral problems. While most active in the pre-WWI era, it gained strength after WWII and was an influence on the civil rights movement of the 1960s. In post WWII Austin, a group of ministers that included Paul and the following: Carlyle Marney, minister of First Baptist Church; "Block" Smith, Director of Campus YMCA; Blake Smith, minister of University Baptist Church; several Presbyterian and Methodist ministers and Catholic Newman Club priests were considered Social Gospel leaders in Austin, in the University of Texas, and even among some state government officials. Lyndon B. Johnson's leadership in looking at major social problems from a moral view was influenced by these preachers and this movement.

Socianism was a Christian doctrine named for Italians Lelio Sozzini and Fausto Sozzini (Latin for Sozzini is Socian) that was developed in Poland in the sixteenth and seventeenth centuries. The followers professed belief in God and adherence to Christian Scriptures but denied the divinity of Christ and, therefore, the Trinity.

Spencer, Herbert (1820–1903) was an English engineer who thought that evolution arose from the principle of conservation of energy, a theory that enjoyed great vogue in the late nineteenth and early twentieth centuries.

Teilhard de Chardin, Pierre (1881–1955) was a French idealist philosopher and Jesuit priest, trained as a paleontologist and geologist. He took part in the discovery of Peking Man and worked to understand evolution and faith. He is known for his theory that man is evolving, mentally and socially, toward a spiritual unity.

Tillich, Paul (1886–1965). PhD University of Breslau 1911, theology degree at Halle-Wittenberg 1912. German born and US theologian and philosopher whose discussions of God and faith drew traditional Christianity and modern culture together. Pressured by the Nazis and invited by Reinhold Niebuhr, he moved to Union Theological Seminary in 1933. In 1955 he took a position at Harvard Divinity School. He brought existential religious and moral thought to the general public through his works *The Courage to Be* (1952), and *Dynamics of Faith* (1957). For the diligent theological student, his *Systematic Theology* in three volumes represents his contribution to understanding. In its introduction Tillich states: "Theology formulates the questions implied in human existence, and theology formulates the answers implied in divine self-manifestation under the guidance of the questions implied in human existence. This is a circle which drives man to a point where question and answer are not separated." Paul was such a student.

UCMS, United Christian Missionary Society. This was the arm of the Christian Church (Disciples of Christ) that sponsored the missionaries. The Texas Bible Chair position was one of domestic missionary.

YMCA, Young Men's Christian Association, a movement to provide moral, social, and recreational services to urban youth in areas lacking social support. It was an important part of urban living in many early twentieth-century cities. Paul was active in Beaumont, Fort Worth, and Austin.

Walker, Granville T. (1908–1991) was minister of University Christian Church, Fort Worth, 1940–1973. TCU conferred an honorary Doctor of Divinity upon him in 1947. He was chair of the National Council of Churches. Granville and Paul grew up in Beaumont, Texas, and attended First Christian and Washington Boulevard Christian Churches together. They traveled together to TCU by train. Although they worked within blocks of each other in Fort Worth for decades, both were extremely busy and did little collaboration. However, after retirement, Granville, Paul, and their wives, Earline and Ruth, enjoyed monthly, leisurely meals at Pulido's Mexican Café for many years.

Walsh, Chad (1914–1991) was an Episcopalian priest, former English professor at Beloit College and author of poems and twenty books.

White, Conrad. A University of Texas student in the late 1940s and member of the Disciples Student Fellowship.

Whitehead, Alfred North (1861–1947). BA Trinity College, Cambridge 1884. He taught at University of London and Harvard. His main contributions were to Process Philosophy and Process Theology. He stated that reality is best understood as processes rather than material objects. Relationships of processes rather than views of reality constructed by bits of matter was closer to understanding the world. His important books include *Principia Mathematica, Process and Reality*, and *Science and the Modern World*. In education Whitehead advocated teaching transdisciplinary general principles laden with values that provide students with a foundation of wisdom and ability to make connections between areas of knowledge.

Wieman, Henry Nelson (1884–1975). PhD, Harvard 1917. He developed philosophic and theological views which brought together religion and rational and scientific thought. He taught theology at the University of Chicago from 1929 to 1949 and led the school to further develop Whitehead's thoughts.

Wiseman, Michael. TCU Honors Graduate '66. Tenured professor of economics at University of California-Berkeley and at University of Wisconsin in Madison; Research Professor of Public Policy, Public Administration, and Economics at George Washington University; consultant to US Department of Health and Human Services, Social Security, and other federal, state and nonprofit organizations.

ACKNOWLEDGMENTS

This book would never have happened if it had not been for the encouragement of Dr. Dan Williams, director of TCU Press, who read Paul's papers and thought there was enough material for a book, and TCU Press staff Kathy Walton and Molly Spain, who helped with editing. More fundamentally, it would not have happened if Paul's wife, Ruth S. Wassenich, had not organized his papers in such a logical way. She also saved tribute letters and newspaper clippings, all of which give a fuller, more complete picture of who Paul Wassenich was.

Some of the tribute letters were in our files. We appreciate Dr. Michael Wiseman's letter of memories of "Dr. P" and Tim Weaver's reflections. They were both Honors students, graduating in 1966 and 1972, respectively.

Mark added so much to the content based on his own memories of Paul's trip to the Holy Lands and his work on civil rights. Mark also found and annotated the pictures to accompany this story of Paul's life.